The Town That
Started the Civil War

The Town That
Started the Civil War

Nat Brandt

Syracuse University Press

Library of Congress Cataloging-in-Publication Data
Brandt, Nat.
    The town that started the Civil War / Nat Brandt. — 1st ed.
      p. cm.
    Includes bibliographical references.
    ISBN 0-8156-0243-X (alk. paper)
    1. Oberlin (Ohio)—History. 2. Wellington (Ohio)—History.
3. Underground railroad—Ohio. 4. Fugitive slaves—Ohio. 5. United
States—History—Civil War, 1861–1865—Causes. I. Title.
F499.O2B86 1990
977.1'23—dc20   89-26094
                CIP

Manufactured in the United States of America

BOMC offers recordings and compact discs, cassettes
and records. For information and catalog write to
BOMR, Camp Hill, PA 17012.

"Oberlin! wher Ablishnism runs rampant—wher a nigger is 100 per cent. better nor a white man—wher a mulatto is a objik uv pity on account uv hevin white blood! Oberlin! that stonest the Dimekratik prohphets, . . . Oberlin, that gives all the profits uv her college to the support uv the underground railroad— . . .

"Oberlin," continyood I, "that reskoos niggers, and sets at defiance the benificent laws for takin on em back to their kind and hevenly-minded masters! Oberlin!— . . .

". . . Oberlin commenst this war. Oberlin wuz the prime cause uv all the trubble."

Chapter v: Annihilates an Oberlinite, *The Struggles (Social, Financial and Political) of Petroleum V. Nasby*[1]

To my children

A journalist by profession, Nat Brandt has been a newswriter for CBS News, a reporter on a number of newspapers, an editor on the *New York Times*, managing editor of *American Heritage*, and editor-in-chief of *Publishers Weekly*. Since 1980, Mr. Brandt has been a free-lance writer, chiefly in the area of American history. He is the author of *The Man Who Tried to Burn New York*, which won the 1987 Douglas Southall Freeman History Award, and with John Sexton, *How Free Are We? What the Constitution Says We Can and Cannot Do.*

Contents

Illustrations

Preface

This is a story about courage—about physical courage and moral courage. About citizens of a small town, black and white, living and working side by side in unusual harmony. They were ordinary people—tradesmen, shopkeepers, students, teachers. Some were educated, some were not. Some had experienced slavery firsthand, some could only imagine what it was like. Yet, when a relative newcomer, an escaped slave, was trapped and spirited away, they left their shops, their homes, and their classrooms without hesitation, without debate, without regard to consequences, to rescue a man whom most of them did not even know.

This is also a story with contemporary parallels. The clash between the law of the land and an individual's conscience, between what a government decrees and what those in Oberlin believed to be "Higher Law," the law of God, continues into our own time. It is represented today by the Sanctuary movement, in which Protestant and Roman Catholic clergymen and lay workers are shielding Central American victims of oppression from deportation.

The title of the book is, of course, an exaggeration. But like any exaggeration, it bears a kernel of truth, indeed more than a kernel. Writing under the nom de plume Petroleum V. Nasby early in the second year of the Civil War, humorist David Ross Locke echoed a theory that became widely held, at least in the Western Reserve: "Oberlin commenst this war. Oberlin wuz the prime cause uv all the trubble." A simplistic view, the stuff of which local legend is made. However, what is known as the Oberlin-Wellington Rescue reflected in myriad ways the forces that were dividing the United States and leading to war, as well as issues such as states' rights and civil rights. Its uniqueness lies not only in the singular events of the Rescue, the trials and the martyrdom in a Cleveland prison, but also, and most especially, in the attention the Rescue received throughout the country, particularly in the North. It was, for want of a better word, the epitome of incidents regarding the Fugitive Slave Law of 1850, and it thrust the question of that law into the forefront of national politics—much to the dismay of Abraham Lincoln.

In addition, as a story, the Oberlin-Wellington Rescue seems unequaled in political chicanery, convoluted legal maneuvering, incredible audacity, and ironic twists. It has moments of intense religious fervor and personal passion as well as ones of low buffoonery. It is, in that sense, a very human story about a group of idiosyncratic individuals who were willing to go to jail for what they believed in and who, for the most part, left vivid recollections of their experiences. Only the man who was the subject of all the uproar, the escaped slave John Price, left no record.

Acknowledgments

This book could not have been written without the cooperation shown to me by William A. Moffett and his staff at the Oberlin College Library—Bill Ruth and Shirley Williams. I am especially indebted to Oberlin College Archivist Roland M. Baumann, whose continued support and encouragement were critical to the writing of this book. He always anticipated my needs and gladly gave of his time to a sometimes bewildered author. I will always be grateful for his concern, guidance, and patience. His assistants—Anne Pearson, Lisa Pruitt, and Liz Chiego—were especially kind to me. A special thanks would have gone, too, to Gertrude Jacob, volunteer researcher, who unfortunately died before the book was published. I am also indebted to Dina Schoonmaker, curator of special collections and preservation officer, and Emily Epstein, acting archivist, Special Collections. I was overwhelmed by the generous spirit and enthusiasm for my research expressed by all of those connected with the Oberlin College Archives and will always remember warmly my visits to Oberlin because of them. I have never stopped talking to friends about the unstinting assistance that was shown to me.

A number of other individuals in Oberlin were also very helpful, not the least of whom was Marlene Merrill, who both provided me with new avenues of research and was kind enough to vet the chapter on Oberlin's history. She also provided sage advice on the Epilogue.

A special word should also be said about James F. (Bill) Long, former manager of the Co-Op Book Store, whose idea to turn the Oberlin-Wellington Rescue into a television script first drew my attention to the story. His own play about the incident, *The Feast of Felons*, is often performed in Oberlin.

I am also thankful to Dorothy Inborden Miller of Washington, D.C., granddaughter of Wilson Bruce Evans and owner of the Evans home, 33 East Vine Street (Mill Street in 1858–59). Also to Michael Copeland of Topeka, Kansas, a descendant of the Copeland family, who steered me to the photograph of John A. Copeland, Jr., that appears in the book. Others who went out of their way to offer information and insights were Bob Thomas, who was especially helpful on the town's recent history, and Phil Tear, former editor of the *Oberlin Alumni Magazine.*

Albert Grimm, curator of the Spirit of '76 Museum in Wellington, was most cooperative in trying to solve some of the questions relating to that town, and William Bigglestone, former Oberlin College archivist, shared with me—from his retirement home in Arizona—his extensive knowledge about the town and the black citizens who lived in it.

I wish to thank also Dr. John J. Grabowski, curator of manuscripts, and Ann K. Sindelar of the Western Reserve Historical Society Library in Cleveland; Nancy Applebee, collections/education co-ordinator, Lorain County Historical Society, Elyria; Alan Patterson, who teaches in the Oberlin public school system; Mrs. William A. Kendall, librarian, Mason County Museum, Maysville, Kentucky; Mary Ronan of the National Archives in Washington, D.C., and Kenneth Shanks of the National Archives branch in Chicago.

I am grateful to Richard Dupuis of London, England, who graciously shared the research he compiled for a new, annotated edition of the memoirs of Charles Grandison Finney. Like our friends in the Oberlin College Archives, he took me into his office and opened his files for my perusal.

My dear friend Professor Bernard A. Weisberger kindly read and helped me to perfect the manuscript from a historian's vantage.

As has been true in all my career endeavors, I could not have written this book without the inspiration, support, and advice of my wife, Yanna.

New York City   NAT BRANDT
September 1989

Cast of Characters

The Fugitive Slave

John Price, property of John P. G. Bacon

His Captors

Anderson Jennings, Bacon's neighbor in Mason County, Kentucky
Richard P. Mitchell, former Bacon employee
Jacob K. Lowe, U.S. deputy marshal, Southern District of Ohio
Samuel Davis, Lowe's assistant, a jailer-cum-deputy sheriff

The Rescuers

James H. Bartlett, Oberlin cobbler
James Bartlett, his son, also a cobbler
Eli Boies, Wellington physician
Simeon Bushnell, Oberlin clerk and printer
John A. Copeland, Jr., Oberlin carpenter
Robert L. Cummings, Wellington resident
Matthew DeWolf, Wellington resident
Henry Evans, Oberlin cabinetmaker and undertaker
Wilson Bruce Evans, his brother, also cabinetmaker-undertaker
James M. Fitch, Oberlin printer and bookseller
Jeremiah Fox, fugitive slave working in Oberlin as a teamster
Thomas Gena, fugitive slave living in Oberlin
Matthew Gillet, Wellington farmer
Chauncey Goodyear, Penfield resident
John Hartwell, fugitive slave living in Oberlin
Lewis Hines, Wellington farmer
Charles H. Langston, schoolteacher, visiting in Oberlin
Franklin Lewis, Oberlin resident
William E. Lincoln, Oberlin student
Abner Loveland, Wellington farmer
Ansel W. Lyman, Oberlin student
John Mandeville, Wellington brickmaker
Henry D. Niles, Pittsfield lawyer

Henry E. Peck, Oberlin lawyer
William Sciples, Wellington resident
John H. Scott, Oberlin harness- and trunkmaker
William D. Scrimgeour, Oberlin student
Jacob R. Shipherd, Oberlin student
Walter Soules, Wellington farmer
Loring Wadsworth, Wellington farmer
Orindatus S. B. Wall, Oberlin shoemaker
David Watson, Oberlin farmer
John Watson, Oberlin grocer
William Watson, John Watson's son
Daniel Williams, Wellington farmer
Richard Winsor, Oberlin student

Unsung Heroes

John G. W. Cowles, Oberlin student
James H. Fairchild, Oberlin professor
James L. Patton, Oberlin student

The Betrayers

Seth Bartholomew, Oberlin tin peddler
Lewis D. Boynton, Russia Township farmer
Shakespeare Boynton, his son
Anson P. Dayton, U.S. deputy marshal, former Oberlin town clerk
Bela Farr, Oberlin laborer
Edward F. Munson, Oberlin postmaster
Chauncey Wack, Oberlin hotelkeeper
Malachi Warren, former Alabama planter living in Oberlin

The Trials

THE JUDGE
Hiram V. Willson

FOR THE PROSECUTION
George W. Belden   George Bliss

FOR THE DEFENSE
Franklin T. Backus   Albert G. Riddle
Seneca O. Griswold   Rufus P. Spalding

COURT OFFICER
Mathew Johnson, U.S. marshal, Northern Judicial District

CUYAHOGA COUNTY JAIL
David L. Wightman, sheriff   John B. Smith, jailer

CHIEF JUSTICE OF THE OHIO SUPREME COURT
Joseph R. Swan

ATTORNEY GENERAL OF THE UNITED STATES
Jeremiah S. Black

COUNSEL FOR JENNINGS AND MITCHELL
Richard H. Stanton, Mason County, former Kentucky congressman

RESCUER ALLIES
W. W. Boynton, Lorain County prosecutor
Roeliff Brinkerhoff, kin of Ohio Justice Jacob Brinkerhoff
Hermann E. Burr, sheriff, Lorain County
Charles H. Doolittle, judge, Court of Common Pleas, Elyria
Roswell G. Horr, clerk, Court of Common Pleas, Elyria

And sundry and various citizens of Oberlin and Wellington as well as other residents of Ohio and Mason County, Kentucky.

The Town That
Started the Civil War

Ohio Late 1850s

Oberlin had rail service, but it was between Cleveland and Toledo. To head south, the slave hunters who captured John Price had to go to Wellington to catch a train to Columbus, where they could get a hearing under the federal Fugitive Slave Law. The inset shows the relationship of Oberlin to communities in the area, Lake Erie, and Cleveland.

ONE

The Slave and the Student

*. . . the river was swollen and turbulent; great cakes of floating
ice were swinging heavily to and fro in the turbid waters. Owing to
the peculiar form of the shore on the Kentucky side, the land bending
far out in the water, the ice had been lodged and detained in great
quantities, and the narrow channel which swept round the bend
was full of ice, piled one cake over another, thus forming a temporary
barrier to the descending ice, which lodged, and formed a great,
undulating raft, filling up the whole river, and extending almost to
the Kentucky shore. . . .*

*A thousand lives seemed to be concentrated in that one mo-
ment to Eliza. Her room opened by a side door to the river. She
caught her child, and sprang down the steps towards it. The trader
caught a full glimpse of her, just as she was disappearing down the
bank; and throwing himself from his horse, and calling loudly on
Sam and Andy, he was after her like a hound after a deer. In that
dizzy moment her feet to her scarce seemed to touch the ground,
and a moment brought her to the water's edge. Right on behind they
came; and, nerved with strength such as God gives only to the desperate, with one wild cry and flying leap she vaulted sheer over the
turbid current by the shore, on to the raft of ice beyond. It was a
desperate leap,—impossible to anything but madness and despair.*

Chapter VII: The Mother's Struggle,
Uncle Tom's Cabin; or, Life Among the Lowly[2]

The Ohio River between Kentucky and Ohio was like a sieve.
For 160 miles, as the river wound its serpentine way between the
two states, any cove that could hide a boat or raft, any clump of
trees that bordered the southern bank, could be the launching site
for the escape of a slave. And on the opposite bank, there were
more than twenty Ohio towns that were starting points for an informal but vast network of routes that stretched northward through
Ohio, creating the largest branch in the North of what became
known as the Underground Railroad. Although most southern
Ohioans sympathized with their slaveholding neighbors across the
river—sometimes even hiring Kentucky slaves at harvest time—
there were compassionate individuals who were prepared to assist
runaways in their desperate flights. Some were Quakers and Pres-

byterians, but most were black themselves, free or freed or fugitive. A newspaper in Lexington, Kentucky, complained as early as 1838, "Already the value of slave property has depreciated twenty per-cent in all the counties bordering the Ohio River."[1] And a Unitarian minister wrote that if the state of Ohio did ever become "abolitionized," it would be because of fugitive slaves from Kentucky: "Their flight through the State is the best lecture—the pattering of their feet, that's the talk."[2]

One of the main routes of the Underground Railroad began in Brown County, Ohio. There, in the town of Ripley, overlooking the Ohio River, an unimposing brick-faced house stood on a steep hill. It was a beacon for fugitive slaves. Some one hundred rickety wooden steps led to it from the town below. The hill was known as Liberty Hill, and "the house on the hill" was the home of the Rev. John Rankin, a founder of the so-called New School Presbytery, a white man but a refugee himself from Kentucky, which he had had to abandon because of his antislavery sentiments. There were many blacks in the area, too, men and women who were willing to risk their own safety to shelter the frightened but determined runaways. Between 1830 and 1865, it was estimated, more than two thousand fugitive slaves passed through Ripley.[3]

Ripley was across the river and about eight miles downstream from Maysville, the seat of Mason County, Kentucky, the gateway to Lexington and the Bluegrass region. A picturesque port built on a bluff, Maysville had been a prosperous community since its founding in the late eighteenth century, when pioneers landed on its shore en route to settle the interior of Kentucky and points farther west. Its landing, on a point jutting out into the Ohio River at the mouth of Limestone Creek, proved an easily accessible distribution hub for goods and merchandise received in and shipped from the area. If Cincinnati, as it was said, faced south, Maysville faced north and east. Its townspeople were dependent on the trade that steamboats carried between the rolling hills of the meandering Ohio. It farmers grew grain and hemp but were especially known for the burley tobacco they cultivated. The town's success was reflected in the comfortable two- and three-story brick homes built on the hills above the river. In 1848, Kentucky acknowledged Maysville's preeminence by moving the seat of Mason County from Washington a few miles away to Maysville. Its city hall, a graceful, towered white structure with a Grecian-style portico that had been built three years earlier, was officially designated the county courthouse.

Although Kentucky was never one of the larger slaveholding

states, it had become after 1849 a major market for the purchase
and sale of slaves. In that year the Kentucky legislature repealed
a nonimportation act, thus allowing slaves from other states to be
brought into Kentucky to be sold within the state or to be shipped
for sale to other states. As a result, trafficking in black men,
women, and children developed into a major enterprise in Kentucky. Free blacks became a favorite target for slave hunters; they
were especially vulnerable because, as one local judge put it,
"Color in Kentucky in generally considered *prima facie* evidence
of slavery." In Lexington, the notorious Lewis C. Robards, already
the most unscrupulous "nigger trader" in that city, reportedly ran
a gang of "nigger thieves," kidnappers who roved along the Ohio
River in southern Ohio, searching for blacks—free or fugitive—to
bring back for sale in Kentucky. Lexington itself—the favorite resort of Bluegrass horse breeders and gamblers—achieved a reputation second only to New Orleans for the auctioning of "fancy
girls." By 1859 there were as many slave traders as mule traders
in Lexington, and firms such as Murphy & Ferguson could adver-
tise that it was "ready to buy 'good negroes of all descriptions.'"[4]

Although some thirty-five hundred slaves resided in Mason
County,[5] most white residents owned only a handful of them and,
as a result, did not consider themselves major slaveholders or traders. Yet much to the community's embarrassment, Maysville was
developing into a way station for the slave traffic. It began one
November day in 1849, shortly after the state's repeal of the nonimportation act, when the steamer *Herman* from Charleston drew
up to the town landing to disgorge its cargo—forty-four black men
and women. Two white traders led them through Maysville's
streets in handcuffs and chains.

The townspeople became increasingly outraged by the slave-
hunting gangs that subsequently sprouted up in the area, one of
which made its headquarters in town, selling its contraband to
dealers in central Kentucky. The gangs made no more distinction
between runaways and legally owned local slaves than they did
between free blacks and slaves. Two slave hunters even threatened
to burn down the town after police officers started to investigate
their kidnapping of a young mulatto girl from a home in southern
Ohio.

Although Maysville was strategically located for the slave-hunting gangs and kidnappers who could ferry across the Ohio River
and infest southern Ohio on their forays, it was not an ideal jumping-off spot for runaways trying to escape into Ohio. Despite its
closeness to Ripley, the river in the vicinity of Maysville was too

busy. Ferries and steamboats constantly plied back and forth and along the waterway, making secret crossings difficult, if not impossible. It was a different story, however, when the river froze over, as it did every few years. When it did, when the weather was so frigid that all movement on the bustling river came to a halt, slaveholders all along the southern bank grew alarmed at the opportunity for escape that the river provided.

The river froze over in the winter of 1855–56. Perhaps John Parks Glenn Bacon should have worried about the possibilities that the ice-choked Ohio presented, but he evidently had no reason to suspect that either or both of the two slaves he owned might bolt. Bacon, a native-born Kentuckian of gentlemanly airs, was twenty-nine years old. He had spent several years away at school before marrying and starting a farm in Mason County. His property was about a quarter of a mile inland from the Ohio River, near Beasleys Creek, about six miles from Maysville and only a couple of miles from the ferry opposite Ripley. In mid-January, Bacon took his family—his wife, Jacova, and two small children—to visit Jacova's father, who lived four miles away.[6] They planned to stay for several days. Before leaving his farm, Bacon took the precaution of locking his house. Otherwise unconcerned, he left behind, in their respective cabins, an Irish worker named Peter and the family's two slaves, "a tall, slim" woman named Dinah and her cousin John. The Irishman was a hired hand who shared "equal authority" with John—"Neither could control the other."[7] John had been born on the farm of Bacon's father, who had at one time owned as many as twenty-five slaves, among them both John's grandmother and his mother, Louisa. Bacon had inherited John and Dinah when the elder Bacon died in 1846. His mother, Elizabeth Bacon, still retained Louisa.

Dinah, who was about twenty-one or twenty-two years old, was of a "dark copper color," walked "very straight" with her head held "high," and evidently had a reputation for being sharp-tongued: she was "very quick spoken." John's description would be a subject of dispute later. He was somewhere between five feet four or five and five feet eight or ten, and he weighed anywhere between 140 and 170 pounds. At a time when the skin color of blacks was specifically delineated, he was described variously as either "copper colored" or "a decidedly black man." However, everyone who met him agreed that he was heavyset or stoutly built, with broad shoulders. In addition, he had one distinguishing mark over which there was no dispute—"a huge, shapeless foot," with an "enormous heel, and with the best of the muscle of his leg on the wrong side." The "large leg . . . turned back when he stood up."[8]

John and Dinah had obviously been waiting for the chance to escape. As soon as Bacon left, they took from the barn, without the Irishman's knowledge, two high-spirited horses that John was accustomed to riding and, by prior arrangement, rendezvoused with a slave friend from the farm of Richard E. Loyd in nearby Bracken County. The friend's name was Frank. He was twenty-six years old, six feet tall, and had "large pop eyes." Frank spoke "rather thick tongued."[9]

With Dinah seated behind one of the men on a horse, the three slaves quickly reached the frozen Ohio River. Either to the east or to the west, toward Maysville or toward Cincinnati, the river was about half a mile wide. The three crossed the slippery ice but could not at first find a spot on the other side to pull up from the riverbank. Their faces, hands, and feet began to freeze as they rode up and down the Ohio side all through the night, searching for a way to get onto the northern side. Finally, at daybreak, they came upon a road that cut up through a hill. They galloped up it and into Brown County, Ohio. They rode four or five miles into Ohio when they suddenly encountered an old man. Fortunately for them, he was a Quaker. The Quakers had banned their members from holding slaves as early as 1800. "Friends," he said, "thee must be nearly froze, thee had better stop here in my house and warm."[10]

John, Dinah, and Frank were so cold and stiff that they had to be helped down from the horses, which were then turned loose and started to gallop back to the river. Bacon would find them a week later. The three runaways stayed at the Quaker's house for two weeks, recovering from their ordeal. Once they were able to travel, they were sent on their way. At some point, Dinah left the two men to go on her own.

John and Frank continued their flight northward. Like so many runaways before them, they probably followed the North Star. Perhaps they had heard the advice of Frederick Douglass, himself an escaped slave, to steer by that star to a land where blacks were free, protected, wanted—Canada. They undoubtedly continued to travel at night—the favored time for fugitives. They might have had to hide out in stables, attics, cellars, or behind sham walls in the homes of friendly antislavers. They might have had their faces whitened with flour, or been dressed in woman's clothes to escape detection from pursuing slave hunters. And if hungry, they would have had to live off the land, sometimes stealing a chicken if necessary.

Sometime in February, when the weather was still freezing cold, John and Frank were guided to the home of a man named John Phiney, who lived near Mansfield in north-central Ohio, nearly 180 miles from where they had started out on the Ohio River. Their journey almost ended there. Phiney hid the fugitives in a small load of hay in back of a sleigh and started out for the home of Samuel Smith, another conductor on the Underground Railroad. But as Phiney turned from the main road, the sleigh tipped over and the hay fell out, toppling John and Frank into the snow. A prominent politician who was known throughout the state for his support of the Fugitive Slave Law happened to be walking by at the time and saw them. As Phiney crawled out from the overturned sleigh, the man said, "Why Phiney you are in a bad fix," and then, to Phiney's amazement, he helped to right the sleigh. "I don't think Brother Smith will need that hay tonight," the man said to Phiney. "Jump in every one of you and git, but, say, Phiney, for God's sake don't ever tell anybody that I helped you."

Smith put the two escaped slaves into the care of a brother, who in turn took them to the home of a man named Beabout. Beabout transported them to the home of a man who evidently lived on Lake Erie near Toledo, ordinarily a jumping-off point to Canada. But both the lake and the nearby Detroit River were so clogged with chunks of ice that they were impassable. Besides, slave hunters were said to be patrolling the banks of both, making any attempt to cross foolhardy. So John and Frank were taken instead to the next best place, an isolated college community several miles from the lake with a reputation as a sanctuary for blacks.

*

That March, after river traffic resumed, William Ellaby Lincoln, a pale but tall and impetuous twenty-four-year-old student from Oberlin College in Ohio, was on the upper deck of a Cincinnati steamboat as it headed upriver toward Maysville, when suddenly he heard "a confusion of curses" and the sounds of a scuffle coming from the deck below. "In with him," someone shouted. Rushing to the ladder leading to the lower deck, Lincoln saw "a crowd of excited cursing men" surrounding a Catholic priest. They were trying to shove the clergyman from the boat. The influx of foreigners of different religions—German and Irish immigrants in the main—had soured relations in the region, pitting Protestant against Catholic. Lincoln had no special liking for a "Romish priest," but without hesitating, he raced down the ladder. Before he reached the lower rungs, he jumped from the ladder, landing between the mob and the priest and crying out at the same time, "If you get this man, you go over me." One of the ruffians shouted back that Lincoln was "a Jesuit; in with them both." But Lincoln stood his ground. "No I am not," he said and, lying slightly—he was unlicensed—added, "I'm a Congregational minister; this man has as much right to his opinion as you to yours." As he was speaking, the priest lunged for the ladder and started up it. Lincoln quickly followed him. The troublemakers did not pursue them, but, nevertheless, once on the upper deck, the priest was worried. Would Lincoln accompany him to his cabin?—"or they will get me yet." Lincoln escorted the priest to his quarters and once there suggested that they offer a prayer of thanks. But the priest begged off, saying he had a violent headache and had to lie down. "I saw," Lincoln realized, "he wd. not pray with a Heretic." Still, when the steamboat docked at Maysville, the priest was grateful to have Lincoln at his side as they disembarked and strode up the earthen ramp that led up from the landing to Maysville's Sutton Street.[11]

Lincoln was an Englishman by birth, the son of a physician and the grandson of an army surgeon who had served at the Battle of Waterloo. During the past winter, he had become so ill with consumption that he had been "given up by the doctor to die." He had rallied, however, and now felt better but was still "too weak to study at college." The winds off Lake Erie, near Oberlin, were "hurtful to his lungs." So he decided to travel into what he believed would be the more beneficial climate of Kentucky and do what many Oberlin students customarily did with their vacation time, even if they were not yet ordained: go "into the South to preach & do what I could agst. slavery." He hoped, among other things, that he also could be a colporteur for the American Missionary Association, peddling devotional tracts. He was "determined," he said, that "if I had to die, to die preaching."[12]

Lincoln was a rabid abolitionist. A fellow student had urged him to "read a novel"—one that the *Village Item* of Oberlin said "bids fair to do more good than all the sermons ever preached upon the subject."[13] Lincoln did not even want to look at the book at first, "regarding it as lost time very largely." But at his friend's "earnest request," he relented and began reading *Uncle Tom's Cabin*:

"The interest was intense & when I reached the death of Uncle Tom, in tears I knelt & raising my hand, promised the Lord that I wd. do all I could to bring the horrible institution of Slavery to an end."

Lincoln vowed that he "would never cease struggling until the last slave was free."[14]

The next day, after reaching Maysville, Lincoln started out on foot for Cabin Creek, in neighboring Lewis County. There, only a few miles from Maysville, lived John G. Fee, a noted antislavery minister and educator, "the noblest, bravest & meekest man" Lincoln believed he would ever meet.

Lincoln was at Oberlin College when Fee came to speak there in 1855. The son of a slaveholder, Fee, who was about forty years old, had risked his life on more than one occasion to preach against slavery. He had been forced to abandon every church he started because of his abolitionist sentiments. Fee was in the midst of trying to get support to found what would become Berea College, which he hoped would "be to Kentucky what Oberlin is to Ohio, Anti-slavery, Anti-caste, Anti-secret societies, Anti-rum, Anti-sin."[15] He urged Lincoln to take his message against slavery into Breathitt County, about seventy-five miles from Maysville over rough roads and narrow pathways. Taking Fee's advice, Lincoln started out on foot. On his first day on the road, he was passing a cluster of broken-down houses surrounded by dogs, pigs, and cows, when he was startled by the voice of an old man, who cried out: "Is you the Abolition preacher[?]" When Lincoln replied in the affirmative, the old man shot back at him, "Did yer never read yer Bibul." Citing Genesis 9:25—the curse put on Canaan by Noah—the elder Kentuckian continued, "dont it say . . . a sarvent of sarvents shall he be to his brethren; aint we his brethren. This nigger wench & her brats, ant they mine didnt I buy her with my hard erned wages & isnt they all mine; & you want to steal them from me; you darn theef Reed yer Bibul you darned fool." Lincoln suggested that the words of the Bible had been fulfilled "long ago & that negros were not Canaanites &c," but the old man persisted, continuing to call him a thief and fool as Lincoln walked off into the forest.

Not far from where he had encountered the old man, Lincoln came upon a church whose minister had two families—"one of the parlor & one of the kitchen; one white, the other, black." The minister informed Lincoln that he intended to pay the college expenses of his white sons by selling one of his black children. The minister invited Lincoln to preach in his church. The young man did so, taking the opportunity to condemn what he regarded as the minister's "villainy." But the minister had his revenge: "A dog was lying near the wide fireplace, & he [the minister] winking to the boys, spat with wonderful skill, a mouthful of tobacco juice, into the dog's eye, & the scene of confusion as the dog howling rushed among the women, causing confusion & cries, disturbed my preaching & rejoiced his crowd. A revelation of the blinding influence of sin."

Lincoln resumed his journey toward Breathitt County, trekking over "hill and dale, rivulet & scenes of rolling wavings of green." Upon arriving at his destination, he met and stayed with a man who was an abolitionist but who was "careful not to expose himself too much" because of the "violent determination" of local slaveholders "to maintain even by mob violence their cruel & degrading system." That Sunday the two of them went to the local meetinghouse, where they heard a "colored preacher . . . whose sermon was a careful steering between the master & the slave." But first, at his host's request, Lincoln was asked to guess the race of the male parishioners as they entered the church. "I made 11 mistakes in 15 minutes," Lincoln acknowledged. Apparently, work outdoors in the sun and wind had tarnished the face and hands of the men. "One case, were I put on oath, I shd. still affirm to be colored," Lincoln said. "He had shot 2 men for affirming he was a colored man."

That afternoon, Lincoln himself was to preach to the congregation. As he approached the meetinghouse, he noticed a sheriff and two deputies, pistols drawn, outside, ordering slaves out of and away from the building. Lincoln's sermon was drawn from Jeremiah 18—"the law of national life & death . . . I applied the law to the U.S. affirming that unless the slaves were freed that God wd. pour out his fury upon the nation." As he spoke, Lincoln noticed that the attention of the congregation had been drawn to his side. "I turned & saw the sheriff & a deputy pointing 2 pistols at the pulpit & I said 'Ye seek to kill me, a man that hath told you the truth'. The effect was strange; yet scriptural. The men turned pale their pistols fell from their hands; & clattered upon the floor & they followed & lay prone upon the seats. I preached on & at the end, young slaveholders came & with tears pressed me to ride at a gallop out of the valley; as the sheriff & his 2 deputies had sworn they wd. kill me; & they offered to keep them back, so I could escape." Lincoln answered the friendly slaveholders "very foolishly," saying: "If I begin to escape by hurried flight, I shall have to keep it up; I shall walk my horse out of the valley."

Lincoln started on his way, turning out of the valley and back up the mountain to the house of his host, who had stayed at home out of fear of what might occur. As his horse ambled along, the sheriff and his two deputies "trotted up & engaged me to preach at their place, the following Lord's day. Parting, they rode toward a large rock, by a stream, & I turned & rode up the mountain. The next thing I sensed was 3 pistol shots; I turned my horse & rode toward the 3, who with level pistols, stood near the rock. I raised my hand, to expostulate with them, when 3 more shots came, one grazing the horse who turned very suddenly from the shots & threw me out of the saddle & fear of being dragged to death crossed my mind. While out of the saddle 3 more shots came, 2 just by my head & perhaps 1 foot off. Had I been in the saddle, I shd. have been killed, pierced by 3 balls. My horse took fright & carried me up the mountain with dangerous speed. I had saved myself from being thrown by catching the pommel of the saddle by my foot."

Back at his host's home, Lincoln recounted what had happened. "My escape made no great stir; for such experiences were not unknown to the brethren; some met death & martyrdom for the slave & God's truth."

✳

In a little more than two years, and several hundred miles away in northern Ohio, the lives of William Lincoln and the slave John would intersect in a fateful test of one of the most controversial pieces of legislation ever passed by Congress.

TWO

The Law

"... is it true that they have been passing a law forbidding people to give meat and drink to those poor colored folks that come along? ..."

"There has been a law passed forbidding people to help off the slave that come over from Kentucky, my dear; so much of that thing has been done by these reckless Abolitionists, that our brethren in Kentucky are very strongly excited, and it seems necessary, and no more than Christian and kind, that something should be done by our state to quiet the excitement. ..."

"Now, John, I don't know anything about politics, but I can read my Bible; and there I see that I must feed the hungry, clothe the naked, and comfort the desolate; and that Bible I mean to follow."

"But in cases where your doing so would involve a great public evil—"

"Obeying God never brings on public evils. I know it can't. It's always safest, all round, to do as he bids us."

Chapter IX: "In Which It Appears That a Senator Is But a Man"

The news on the front page of many American newspapers in the late 1850s was misleading: titillating details of the trial of Congressman Daniel Sickles, accused of murdering his wife's lover; sordid items about the polygamous Mormons in Utah; or the latest dispatches from abroad about war clouds gathering over Austria and France, Garibaldi's movements in northern Italy, civil war in Mexico. But turn the page and the story was different. Despite all the attention President James Buchanan paid to foreign policy, no matter how much he wanted to enlarge United States power and influence in Central and South America—purchase Cuba, protect the trade route across the isthmus of Nicaragua, intervene in Mexico—he could not avoid the sectional crisis that was dividing the nation. It seemed as though almost every week there was a new headline to aggravate the situation: a report about an escaped slave caught in a Northern city and forced to return to his owner, or an account about an illegal slave ship captured off the coast, sometimes its human cargo thrown overboard by the crew to avoid prosecution.

The nation Buchanan governed was in the midst of the Industrial Revolution. The year before he took office, the first train to cross the Mississippi spanned the river between Rock Island, Illinois, and Davenport, Iowa. During his administration, the transatlantic cable, linking North America to Ireland, was laid, and the first commercially productive oil well was drilled near Titusville, Pennsylvania. The country was vibrant, alive with new ideas about science and technology and government. Yet despite all this progress and excitement, the United States—at a time when slavery had been abolished throughout almost all of the rest of the civilized world—was still half-slave, half-free. There was, however, a spirit of change in the air; increasing numbers of Americans each year opposed the institution. But the growing opposition to slavery only seemed to stiffen the resolve of Southern slaveholders; they campaigned aggressively for the extension of slavery within the United States, and many of them also wanted to repeal the ban on the importation of slaves from abroad. Weak, inept, naive, Buchanan thought that the sectional clash could be resolved legally. He believed that Supreme Court decisions such as in the *Dred Scott* case delineated congressional powers over territories that were prospective new states. When Buchanan supported proslavers in Kansas—"Bleeding Kansas," as it was called even before he became president—he unleashed hostilities in the North that he was unable to control. Buchanan wanted to be an empire builder, but he was incapable of halting the division of his own country.

The issue of slavery had become tinder dry. For the best part of the nineteenth century the nation had been torn: by battles over the admission of new states to the Union—should they be free or slave?—by the Kansas-Nebraska Act, which in effect repealed the Missouri Compromise of 1820 and permitted the extension of slavery; by divisions over the *Dred Scott* decision that legalized slavery in all territories and denied blacks any rights under the Constitution; by tragic incidents and stories of brutality told by former slaves or free blacks such as Solomon Northup who were shanghaied into slavery; by recurring reports of slave ships landing half-starved Africans in Southern ports. Kindling the resentments that resulted were disputes between states and the federal government over the jurisdiction of cases involving runaway slaves and by the animosities in both the North and the South regarding enforcement of the Fugitive Slave Law of 1850.

Perhaps no law enacted by Congress in the nineteenth century stirred up passions as did the Fugitive Slave Law. It was a law that almost begged to be disobeyed. It was a law based solely on property rights—the rights of the slaveowner. It totally disregarded individual rights. Alleged fugitives were denied the benefit of a trial or even the chance to testify in their own behalf. Ordinary citizens could be called upon—ordered, in fact—to participate in the capture of a runaway no matter what they thought about the institution of slavery. The law was a sop to the South, but, ironically, in practice it pleased Southerners no more than it did Northerners.

The law was one of the eight components of the Compromise of 1850, that crazy quilt of measures intended to keep the warring factions of the nation united. Its opponents argued that the law—and especially its failure to allow trial by jury—did not protect the liberty of free blacks living in the North. But Southerners believed that trials would only prove another impediment to the recovery of their property. Even with such a favorable law, many of them did not think Congress had gone far enough to correct the lack of enforcement and inadequacies of the law it was meant to put teeth into: the Fugitive Slave Law of 1793. That act had been prompted by a controversy between Virginia and Pennsylvania over the extradition of three Southerners who had kidnapped a free black and sold him into slavery. Its basis was the so-called slave clause of the Constitution—clause 3, Section 2, of Article IV—which, without mentioning the word *slavery*, nevertheless upheld the practice by providing:

> "No person held to Service or Labour in one State, under the Laws, thereof, escaping into another, shall, in Consequence of any Law or Regulation therein, be discharged from such Service or Labour, but shall be delivered up on Claim of the Party to whom such Service or Labour may be due."[1]

Southern slaveholders were never happy with the 1793 law or with the way it was enforced. Their unhappiness was intensified by an 1842 United States Supreme Court decision in another Pennsylvania case in which the Court struck down a state law that barred forcibly seizing a slave and removing him from the state. But the Court, in holding that the execution of the slave clause was exclusively a federal power, said that states were therefore not obliged to enforce the 1793 law; that was strictly a federal function. The decision provided a ready excuse for Northern states to enact laws that prohibited state authorities from helping to recover and return fugitive slaves.

Six years later a concerted effort was made to stiffen the 1793 act. The stimulus for the change came from the Kentucky legis-

lature, which had received a petition from the citizens of two
counties complaining about the way the agent for several slaveholders had been treated when he tried to reclaim some fugitive
slaves in Michigan. The Kentucky lawmakers forwarded the petition to Congress with the demand that a more encompassing law
be enacted.

The Fugitive Slave Law that was finally passed was a paradox.
It was, for one thing, a law sought by a section of the country that
considered slavery a matter of states' rights yet yielded to the federal government the exclusive authority to enforce those rights.
It was a law that, of all the varied segments of the Compromise
of 1850, had stimulated the least debate in Congress yet would
prompt the most extensive controversy. It was, in addition, a law
intended to secure the institution of slavery in Southern states but
in fact served to extend slavery into free states, where slave hunters—armed with the slightest proof—could range freely in their
search for runaways. The law's provisions, if nothing else, had an
unforeseen result. It drove many Northerners who had stayed on
the sidelines straight into the antislavery camp.

One of the provisions of the law called for the appointment of
federal commissioners to decide, solely on the evidence presented
by a slaveowner or the owner's agent, whether the alleged fugitive
was really the owner's property. That evidence could be an eyewitness identification of the alleged runaway, or it could take the
form of an affidavit taken out and certified in the owner's home
state identifying the missing slave. The alleged fugitive could not
utter a word in defense. Should the commissioner decide in the
alleged fugitive's favor—that is, free him or her—he was entitled
to a fee of $5. But should he decide in favor of the slaveowner, the
commissioner received $10—presumably for the extra paperwork
such a decision necessitated. Needless to say, Northerners believed that the higher fee for deciding in a slaveowner's favor precluded a just decision.

One feature of the law especially rankled antislavers. It specified
that "all good citizens" were "commanded to aid and assist in the
prompt and efficient execution" of the law, no matter what their
personal views. The commissioners were empowered to appoint
federal marshals to execute warrants for the seizure of alleged fugitives, and the marshals in turn were authorized to command the
assistance of ordinary bystanders—what was called *posse comi-
tatus*—to help them. In addition, to forestall the possibility that a
federal marshal would not execute a warrant, the law provided that
he was to be fined $1,000 if he refused to do so, and if a fugitive

escaped from his custody, "whether with or without the assent of such Marshal or his Deputy," the marshal was liable to pay the full value of the fugitive to the slaveowner. Anyone trying to obstruct the marshal, or harboring or hiding the fugitive, or helping in the fugitive's escape would be fined up to $1,000 and imprisoned up to six months. And if such assistance resulted in a successful escape, the person had to pay the slaveowner $1,000 for each fugitive that was lost.[2]

The legislation was signed into law by President Millard Fillmore on September 18, 1850, and almost immediately triggered a series of incidents that drew a storm of protest from both sides. For, ironically, the law stimulated the flight of slaves, especially those on the border states of Kentucky, Virginia, Maryland, and Missouri. Following the North Star, they poured across the borders between slave and free states, many of them headed for Canada, where there was no danger from the new law. Sympathetic whites and blacks—both free blacks and those who were themselves runaways—sped them on their way through the loosely defined system known as the Underground Railroad. Although never formally organized, the system was effective in passing fugitives from one household to another. The runaways crossed into Canada from upper New York and Vermont, from cities such as Cleveland, Buffalo, and Detroit, and from small lake ports such as Sandusky. They walked north into the Maritime Provinces or landed in open boats at one of the scores of easily reached ports along the Great Lakes.

England refused to extradite the fugitives from Canada, saying that its government could not "with respect to the British possessions where slavery is not admitted, depart from the principle recognized by the British courts that every man is free who reaches British ground."[3] Moreover, Canadian authorities, eager to settle their vast hinterlands, welcomed the fugitives, offered them land, even granted them citizenship—which they were denied in the United States—on the same terms as other immigrants. Blacks could vote, a right that free blacks enjoyed in only five Northern states—Massachusetts, Maine, New Hampshire, Rhode Island, and Vermont. Those fugitives who chose urban life over rural were able to find work in the building trades or in other crafts and as hotel and railroad workers. There are no accurate or reliable figures to document the number of slaves who escaped from Southern states, nor any idea of exactly how many fled to Canada, but, according to conservative estimates, at least twenty thousand black men and women crossed into British North America—

mostly in the area around Ontario known as Canada West—in the decade between 1850 and 1860. By 1861, some sixty thousand blacks were believed to be living in the provinces,[4] and in some communities they had been elected to local offices, had served on juries (which free blacks could do only in Massachusetts), were school directors and road commissioners. And that estimate does not take into account the number of runaways who never made it to Canada but settled in Northern towns and cities.

Southerners who considered the fugitives chattel translated those figures into dollars. A healthy black male adult, for example, was worth about $1,000 at that time; one who was skilled, such as a blacksmith, brought several hundred dollars more. A Virginia senator put the annual loss to his state at $100,000. The yearly loss in Kentucky, according to a Louisville newspaper, was $30,000. A Maryland senator said his state lost $80,000 worth of slaves each year. A South Carolinian reckoned that all the Southern states lost $200,000 in slaves annually.[5] The governor of Mississippi estimated that slaves worth in excess of $30 million were lost by all the Southern states between 1810 and passage of the Fugitive Slave Law of 1850.[6] A Georgia congressman complained to the House of Representatives that "predatory bands are kept up by private and public subscriptions among the Abolitionists" and border states were each year losing "thousands and millions of dollars' worth of property by this system of larceny that has been carried on for years."[7] The more than two thousand members of the Underground Railroad in Ohio—which shared not only a 160-mile border with Kentucky but also some 225 miles with Virginia—were believed responsible for assisting between forty and fifty thousand slaves to escape by 1861, at a cost to their owners of $30 million.[8]

Estimates of the economic loss in runaway slaves may have varied or been overblown, but to Southerners the escapes threatened their survival. Ever since the importation of natives from Africa was outlawed in 1808, slaves had become a precious commodity. Even though an estimated total of nearly fifty thousand black men and women were illegally brought into the country in the next fifty years, the thirst for more slaves was unquenched. "Everywhere in the South we hear the cry, 'More Slaves!'" the *Mississippi Democrat* declared. "Without an increase of slave labor the South cannot progress." As a result, there was widespread support in the South not only for compelling Northern states to abide by the Fugitive Slave Law but also for repealing the ban on importing slaves. A Georgian named Col. Gaulden, the *Savannah News* reported, declared that "African slavery is morally and legally right; that it has been a blessing to both races; that on the score of religion, morality and interest, it is the duty of the Southern people to import as many blacks direct from Africa as convenient."[9]

Almost from the day that the Fugitive Slave Law was signed into law, abuses occurred—free blacks shanghaied into slavery by gangs of slave traders, runaways captured but then rescued. The seizures riled Northerners, and the rescues enraged Southerners. Even the relatively few who were able to escape from states in the Deep South aroused Southern resentment. "Negroes do escape from Mississippi frequently," declared Senator Jefferson Davis in the midst of debate on the Compromise of 1850, "and the boats constantly passing by our long line of frontier furnish great facility to get into Ohio; and when they do escape it is with great difficulty that they are restored. We, though less than the border states, are seriously concerned in this question . . . those like myself, who live on that great highway of the West—the Mississippi River—[and] are most exposed have a present and increasing interest in this matter."[10]

However, what exasperated Southerners even more were statutes called personal liberty laws enacted by a number of Northern states, including Ohio. They were designed specifically to counter the Fugitive Slave Law. Many of the statutes, clearly aimed at protecting both free and fugitive blacks, established the right to a jury trial and the privilege of seeking a writ of habeas corpus. The function of the writ was to bring the alleged fugitive before a state court or judge in order to free him or her from unlawful restraint.

One of the first incidents to provoke Southern resentment was the arrest in Boston in mid-February 1851 of Frederic Wilkins, a fugitive slave from Virginia, who was working in a coffee house under the name of Shadrach. A group of men entered the courtroom where he was being confined and bore him away. When last heard from, Shadrach was in Montreal.

That fall, in Syracuse, three deputy marshals and a local police officer seized William Henry, a runaway who was known as Jerry, while he was alone and working in a cooper shop. The news of his capture spread rapidly through the city. All the church bells in Syracuse except those of the Episcopal church rang the alarm. Upon hearing of Jerry's capture, a convention of the Liberty party that was in progress quickly adjourned, and its members, together with a local vigilance committee and other abolitionists, crowded into the office of the federal commissioner who would decide Jerry's fate. Suddenly a number of them surrounded Jerry and rushed him through the door. As it was slammed shut, a powerful man threw Jerry bodily down the stairs of the courthouse to the sidewalk. Jerry ran down the block but was overtaken and brought to the offices of the police justice, where his legs were shackled and a guard placed over him. Meanwhile, the crowd grew, and some began to throw stones at the windows of the building. And that evening, rescuers armed with clubs, axes, rods of iron, and a battering ram assaulted it. In the melee that ensued, a marshal fired at one of the assailants, wounding him, then jumped from a window, breaking his arm. Jerry was spirited away, sheltered at first in a local home, where the shackles were removed, then put aboard a British boat and taken across Lake Erie to Kingston, Ontario. He lived and worked there until he died of tuberculosis two years later.

Less than a month after the Jerry Rescue, in what became known as the Christiana Riot, the first serious defiance of the Fugitive Slave Law resulting in bloodshed occurred in southern Pennsylvania. A Marylander arrived in Christiana looking for four escaped slaves. He, his son, and four cohorts went to the home of William Parker, himself a runaway, who was suspected of harboring the Marylander's slaves. Blacks in the area were already incensed by the seizure of a fugitive six months earlier by a slavehunting band known as the Gag Gang. When the Marylanders appeared, Parker's wife blew a large dinner horn, summoning twenty-four blacks to the scene, and soon gunfire broke out. The slave master was slain and his son was badly wounded.

Among the states that passed personal liberty laws was Wisconsin, which had become involved in a dispute with the federal government over the indictment of a rescuer of an escaped slave. The case began in March 1854 with the arrest in Racine of Joshua Glover, who was claimed as the slave of a St. Louis man. Glover was taken to Milwaukee and lodged in the county jail pending a hearing. Within hours of his seizure, a group of citizens from Racine reached Milwaukee by steamboat, rushed the jail, and set Glover free. He returned to Racine and from there escaped into Canada. One of the men subsequently indicted for his rescue was convicted, fined $1,000, and sentenced to serve one month in prison. The Wisconsin Supreme Court, however, granted him a writ of habeas corpus, on the ground that the charges against him did not indicate an offense over which federal courts had jurisdiction. A complicated legal struggle ensued until the case finally reached the United States Supreme Court in 1858. Its decision, a unanimous one, was written by Chief Justice Roger B. Taney, who was also the author of the majority opinion in the *Dred Scott* case. Taney affirmed the supremacy of the national government over individual states, and, in passing, upheld the constitutionality of the Fugitive Slave Law. Saying it was "unnecessary" to comment on the issue, Taney nonetheless declared that "it is proper to say that, in the judgment of this court, the act of Congress commonly called the fugitive slave law is, in all its provisions, fully authorized by the Constitution of the United States."[11]

Both the rescue of Joshua Glover in Milwaukee and an even more dramatic event two months afterward in 1854, the so-called rendition of Anthony Burns, occurred while the Kansas-Nebraska Act was pending in Congress. The measure stirred deep resentments in Northern states. It was designed to repeal the Missouri Compromise of 1820 prohibiting slavery north of 36° 30′ latitude. The demonstrations and, in particular, the severe reaction that the Burns case prompted, were in part symbolic protests against the act.

An escaped slave, Burns was arrested in Boston late in May by three slave hunters from Virginia. Two days later antislavery activists tried to storm the courthouse where he was being held. The attack was repulsed, but a guard was shot and mortally wounded. As a result, federal and state troops were summoned, and they and local police set up a cordon around the building. Although nine hundred antislave proponents subsequently showed up outside the courthouse for Burns's hearing, further violence was averted. No sooner had a federal commissioner decided in favor of Burns's master, however, than many shopkeepers displayed black crepe in their windows and a huge coffin was strung over State Street. "Our worst fears are realized," a black teenager wrote. "A cloud seems hanging over me, over all our persecuted race, which nothing can dispel."[12]

Several days later, as anywhere from twenty to fifty thousand Bostonians watched in disgust from the sidewalks and from windows of buildings along streets that were hung with slogans and emblems of shame, Burns was taken to the harbor to be returned to Virginia. A regiment of Massachusetts militia lined every street and lane that Burns was to take. Preceded by a mounted company of Massachusetts troops, surrounded by federal soldiers with their sabers drawn, and followed by the federal troops with an artillery piece in tow, Burns left the courthouse and walked down Court Street. The procession made its way from Court to State Street and thence to Commerce Street, detouring around Long Wharf, whose proprietors had refused to allow the marchers to pass along it. All along the way, hisses and groans greeted the marching units. Burns was put on a steamboat that took him down the harbor to a waiting United States revenue cutter for the trip back to Virginia.

The sorry spectacle of Burns's return to slavery under an escort of federal and state troops became a turning point for many Northerners who had straddled the fence on the issue of slavery. Clergymen who had remained silent on the issue because defiance of the Fugitive Slave Law meant defiance of the Constitution as well could now feel they could be "Christians, without being traitors."[13] Burns's fate catapulted Frederick Douglass from the nonviolent approach espoused by the otherwise militant abolitionist William Lloyd Garrison. Slave hunters, Douglass said in discussing the proposition "Is it Right and Wise to Kill a Kidnapper?" had forfeited their right to live, and blacks should not have any scruples about dealing with them with force. It was time, he insisted, to abandon the stereotype of the black as patient, passive, and meek. "This reproach must be wiped out, and nothing short of resistance on the part of colored men, can wipe it out. Every Slave-hunter who meets a bloody death in his infernal business, is an argument in favor of the manhood of our race."[14] Although the *Richmond Enquirer* was gratified by the return of Burns to his owner, it nevertheless pointedly commented that "a few more such victories and the South is undone."[15]

The manner in which Anthony Burns had been returned to Virginia stunned the North, but a further shock was in store. The very same month that the slave John escaped from John Bacon's farm in Mason County—January 1856—a slave woman named Margaret Garner also took advantage of the frozen-over Ohio River to escape from Boone County, Kentucky. She crossed it into Cincinnati with her husband, his parents, and their four children. When overtaken by pursuers, she started to murder her children "rather than see them again reduced to slavery." Margaret had already slain a daughter and was in the process of killing another child when she was stopped. In a macabre twist to the tragedy, state and federal authorities got into a dispute over which had jurisdiction in her case: the state wanted to try her on murder charges; the federal government wanted to pursue fugitive charges. In the end, Margaret Garner and her family were returned to slavery. She and an infant child were then sold and were being taken to a new master when the steamboat they were on collided with another boat and the child drowned. "The mother," said the *Louisville Courier*, "exhibited no other feeling than joy at the loss of her child."[16]

Shadrach, Jerry, Joshua Glover, Anthony Burns, Margaret Garner—their real-life travails were among the few hundred recorded
court cases involving fugitive slaves that occurred between 1850
and 1861, each of which aroused the sympathies of Northerners.[17]
None, however, had the impact, or elicited the emotional response, that was engendered by a piece of fiction—Harriet Beecher
Stowe's *Uncle Tom's Cabin; or, Life Among the Lowly*. The novel
was based on true stories, harrowing accounts Mrs. Stowe heard
from escaped slaves while living in Cincinnati as well as tales told
by friends who were slaveholders. Mrs. Stowe lived across the
Ohio River from Kentucky in Cincinnati for eighteen years, her
own home a refuge for fugitives. She had witnessed a slave auction
while visiting a Mason County, Kentucky, family.[18] After returning to her native New England in 1850, she began writing the story
as a serial for a Washington-based paper, drawing upon her experiences in Ohio. Uncle Tom was really Sam Pete, who was so
terribly beaten that he could never afterward lift his hands to his
head to wash or dress himself. (But rather than servile, Pete was
aggressive; he escaped to Canada and, later, going by the name of
Josiah Henson, labored as a minister among fellow blacks who
found asylum in Canada.) The Aunt Chloe of the book was his
wife, Charlotte. Simon Legree was evidently based on the overseer
of a plantation in Maryland, Bryce Lytton. Eva St. Clair was in
actuality Susan St. Clair, who lived on a plantation in Davis
County, Kentucky, though her character was a composite of several Southern girls. Simeon and Rachel Halliday were modeled on
the well-known Quaker abolitionist Levi Coffin and his wife,
Catherine, whose home in Newport, Indiana, where three escape
routes converged, was called the "Grand Central Station of the
Underground Railroad."[19] George Shelby was in reality Amos Riley, Jr., George Harris was Lewis Clark, and so it went with the
other characters in the story. Published in book form, the novel
was astonishingly popular. Three thousand copies were sold
within twenty-four hours, ten thousand within a week, three
hundred thousand within the first year. Among its most avid readers were mothers, who, although they could not vote in the America of the nineteenth century, nevertheless exercised a potent
political influence on their sons, many of whom were soon to cast
their first ballots. Stowe, who lost an infant child during a cholera
epidemic in 1849, later explained that "it was at his dying bed and
at his grave that I learned what a poor slave a mother may feel
when her child is torn away from her."[20]

Like nothing else before it, *Uncle Tom's Cabin* aroused the nation to the evils of slavery and made people aware of its painful personal and social implications. It was, of course, coincidence that John Bacon's slave John escaped from the very same area and under similar conditions depicted as Eliza's flight in the book. John was illiterate and could not have read the book, and it seems most unlikely that his master would have read it to him. But it was no coincidence that John's fate would contribute, as did *Uncle Tom's Cabin*, to a new political awareness in the North. Of all the fugitive slave cases, none would have the reverberations that his would. It occurred in the fall of 1858, while John was living in Oberlin, Ohio, and going by the name of John Price.

THREE

"Nigger" Town

It was the first time that ever George had sat down on equal terms at any white man's table; and he sat down, at first, with some constraint and awkwardness; but they all exhaled and went off like fog, in the genial morning rays of this simple, overflowing kindness.

This, indeed, was a home,—home,—a word that George had never yet known a meaning for; and a belief in God, and trust in his providence, began to encircle his heart, as, with a golden cloud of protection and confidence, dark, misanthropic, pining, atheistic doubts, and fierce despair, melted away before the light of a living Gospel, breathed in living faces, preached by a thousand unconscious acts of love and good-will, which, like the cup of cold water given in the name of a disciple, shall never lose their reward.

Chapter XIII: "The Quaker Settlement"

On September 8, 1858, William Lincoln celebrated his twenty-seventh birthday, a not extraordinary age for an Oberlin student, though, because of his illness and then stints of teaching in Kentucky and Indiana, he was still only a freshman. From his cramped room, Number 77, in the southeast corner of the fourth floor of Tappan Hall, he could see across the college campus to where the Historic Elm stood. Lincoln's room was on the top floor of Tappan Hall, the men's dormitory and the tallest building in Oberlin. The campus—which also served as the village green and was officially called Tappan Square—already had a number of good-sized trees, including red oaks and white swamp oaks. They were the result of what was becoming almost an annual tradition, Arbor Day, which had been instituted in the mid-1840s. In their zealousness to tame the wilderness—to erect cabins, begin a school, sow food crops—the first settlers had leveled the dense forest, stripping the square so bare that only two trees, one of them the elm, remained in "Stumpville." But now a string of white oaks and scotch pine led diagonally across the campus from Tappan Hall to the elm, and plans were afoot to plant about two hundred trees, mostly spruce, in the early spring of 1859.

Tappan Hall was completed two years after Oberlin Collegiate Institute, as it was first called, opened in 1834. It was an outwardly

Tappan Hall, the men's dormitory at Oberlin College, right. At left is the College Chapel. The photograph was taken about 1860. Courtesy of Oberlin College Archives

imposing wooden building topped by a cupola, but its construction had been rushed; it creaked in the cruel winds of winter, and its ninety dormitory rooms were small and uncomfortable. South of the building stood the College Chapel, built in 1854 to accommodate the increasing number of students the school—by then renamed Oberlin College—was attracting. South of it, across College Street, were two college buildings. One was Colonial Hall, built in the autumn of 1833 largely through the largess of the community's first settlers and the site of their Sunday worship services. Four recitation rooms now occupied the space of the old chapel. The other college building was Ladies Hall, completed in 1836 and first called Boarding Hall because for a while it also housed male students on the third floor. Nearby, on the corner of College and South Main, was the school's oldest building, Oberlin Hall, built in 1833, but it was now privately owned and housed mercantile shops. An unimposing Music Hall and an ivy-covered brick chemical laboratory, diagonally across from each other on Professor Street, parallel to South Main, completed the school buildings. Although its student population had quadrupled in twenty years, and Oberlin was now the largest school in Ohio, no new dormitories had been put up during that time, and nearly half of the young men and women who matriculated had to board in private homes.

Dispersed in and about the campus, on aptly named Professor Street, for one, were the homes of teachers and other town residents. Like the New England villages from which most of them came, their houses were painted white and had tidy little gardens adorned with flowers, shrubs, and vines. Picket fences abounded. Even Tappan Square was girded by one, erected originally to keep out the stray pigs, chickens, and cows that used to roam the dusty streets; a hedge of osage orange helped to mask the privies.

The quiet of the campus was punctuated by the school bell, which tolled for the changing of classes and to call students to prayer. The students were a sober lot—not grim, not incapable of laughter—but they exhibited a religious fervor, determination, and industriousness that was unusual. Part of that may have been because of their maturity; the average age of a college graduate was about twenty-five, and many of those in the Theological Department were in their late twenties. By and large the sons and daughters of farmers, the greater number of them residents of Ohio, the students were preparing to go out and save the world as preachers, teachers, and missionaries.

The school's atmosphere pervaded the town itself. The business life of the community was quiet, too. There were no saloons or billiard parlors, no distractions whatsoever—no gaming, no gambling; even smoking in public was illegal. The town's chief hotel, the Palmer House, across from the Historic Elm, was owned by the school and leased under rigid rules to "keep it on strictly temperance principles, neither keeping for sale nor selling anything that can or will intoxicate, including under this, ale, strong drink, hard cider, tobacco and cigars." A visitor who put up at the hotel said he "found no swearing, no drinking or smoking, no noise and confusion."[1] Most shopkeepers and artisans were religious, too. Businesses might stay open until 8 o'clock in the evening, even later on Saturdays when farmers came to town to shop, but the stores closed at 6 on Thursday evenings so everyone could attend prayer meetings. And riding in a carriage on a Sunday was taboo.

What was remarkable about Oberlin, however—what set it off from other look-alike villages in the Western Reserve settled by New Englanders like themselves—were the black residents. You could not only see black men and women in the classrooms of the college, sitting next to white students, but you could see black youngsters in the public school as well—a marked contrast to public schools elsewhere in Ohio, which were separate but hardly equal. You could find black families in First Church, praying next to white parishioners. You could shop in one of their stores on South Main. You could hire a black man as a lawyer. You could find their names on voter registration lists at a time when black men did not enjoy the franchise in Ohio. And you could stroll through Westwood Cemetery and see the gravestones of both black men and women beside those of whites. At a time when blacks were not welcome or encouraged or respected virtually anywhere else in the United States, Oberlin was—in spite of some shortcomings of its own—an integrated community. Its black residents, and many of its whites as well, did not observe the Fourth of July: that would have been a "cruel mockery" because the Declaration of Independence was intended only for whites; instead, antislavery meetings were held that day.[2] Oberlin blacks celebrated August 1, the day in 1834 on which the British ended slavery on the island of Jamaica, where many missionaries from Oberlin had gone. Other than the relatively few Episcopalians who lived in Oberlin, no residents observed Christmas either; that day was like any other day. Instead, Thanksgiving and Washington's birthday— which bracketed the school's long winter vacation—were the times for celebration. "Oberlin," as one of its founders, John Jay Shipherd, put it, "is peculiar. Oberlin is peculiar in that which is good."[3]

Piety was Oberlin's unspoken motto. William Lincoln "was struck with wonder, at the manifest presence of God, everywhere," when he first arrived in Oberlin.[4] One Sabbath day, after teaching Sunday school a few miles outside of town, he was walking back to the college campus when he thought he heard the humming of bees. It was the same sound he had heard three Sundays earlier, when, coming home from the school, he had seen a swarm of bees on the trees near Tappan Hall. But this time Lincoln could not see any bees. He looked around for them but still could not find them. Then he noticed that because it was a hot day, the windows of the all the students' rooms were open. Listening "with more keen attention," Lincoln discovered the sound was "the hum of the voices of the students" preparing for the evening prayer meeting.[5]

Prayer. That one act of devotion symbolized all that Oberlin College stood for. For Oberlin—the school and the colony—had been founded in 1833 both as a community devoted to virtue and religious piety and as an institution that would send its students into the frontier settlements of what was then the new West to civilize and Christianize the inhabitants. By the late 1850s, it would have earned a reputation—partly undeserved and frequently exaggerated—for self-righteousness and heresy in religion and radicalism in education and racial attitudes.

Oberlin was John Shipherd's idea. He was a Presbyterian minister from New York State, who—like so many other reformers in early nineteenth-century America—had a dream: to establish a utopian community in the Mississippi Valley that would be a model for the rough-and-tumble villages and towns springing up and, at the same time, train young adults to spread the gospel throughout the area. In 1832, Shipherd, then only thirty years old, was preaching in Elyria, in northeastern Ohio, in the heart of the area that was still popularly called the Western Reserve. It had also been known as the Connecticut Western Reserve, or New Connecticut. It constituted nearly 4 million acres of land that King Charles II of England granted to the Connecticut colony in 1662— a huge swath of territory that extended from Providence Plantation to the Pacific between the forty-first and forty-second parallels, though excluding New York and Pennsylvania. Settlement began modestly with passage of the Northwest Ordinance of 1787 and accelerated after Ohio was admitted to the Union in 1803. Meanwhile, in 1795, Connecticut sold off to speculators most of the Western Reserve; only a vast tract known as "Sufferers' Lands," or "Firelands," was put aside for victims of British raids into the heart of Connecticut during the American Revolution. Once the War of 1812 was over and with it the last threat of depredations by Erie Indians, the Reserve began to attract families from New York, Pennsylvania, Massachusetts, Vermont, New Hampshire, and Rhode Island as well as Connecticut. It was these settlers who stamped the region with its New England flavor—village greens surrounded by white-painted churches and homes and towns with names such as Amherst, Deerfield, Greenwich, Hartford, Litchfield, New London, Norwalk, Southington, Windsor. A seeming anomaly was Russia Township, some six miles south of Lake Erie in the west-central portion of Lorain County; how it got its name is unknown.

Shipherd shared his dream with a childhood classmate, Philo T. Stewart, a thirty-four-year-old former missionary to the Choctaw Indians in Mississippi. They were able to obtain five hundred acres of land in Russia Township and purchased an additional six thousand acres adjoining it for resale to provide the funds needed to establish their school. The land they chose was an isolated virgin forest on a flat, clay plain—purposely insulated from the vices and temptations of cities and large towns, accessible but difficult to reach, set apart in such a way that Oberlin could, by its location alone, be considered unusual. As Professor James H. Fairchild, who had been one of the school's first students, later put it, "If the place had been attractive to manufacturers and large establishments had sprung up with many workmen, the tone of society would have been changed, and saloons and similar nuisances would have multiplied upon us. . . . The intractable soil and the impassable roads have had something to do in securing privileges. They brought hardship and expense to the early colonists . . . but there is a moral discipline in outward conditions which must not be overlooked."[6]

Through the forest, from the north, ran a rough road, which was really more a path and could not sustain carriages. It stretched from the mouth of the Black River on Lake Erie to Wellington, less than nine miles to the south. It was at the side of the road where the founders knelt to give thanks to God beneath an elm tree that became the center of the community. The tree itself, the Historic Elm, was ever afterward venerated.

Shipherd and Stewart called their utopia Oberlin in honor of the self-sacrificing spirit and achievements of John Frederick Oberlin, a German pastor who had labored among the French and German populations of a valley on the borders of Alsace and Lorraine in the late eighteenth and early nineteenth centuries. In keeping with their lofty goals, colonists—at least in the first years anyway—had to sign a covenant that reflected the reformers' dim view of the state of the world. It began somberly: "Lamenting the degeneracy of the Church and the deplorable condition of our perishing world, and ardently desirous of bringing both under the entire influence of the blessed gospel of peace; and viewing with peculiar interest the influence which the valley of the Mississippi must exert over our nation and the nations of the earth." The covenant not only committed the colonists to an austere and pure life but also pledged them to offer all their surpluses beyond "necessary personal or family expenses" for use in paying for the spreading of the gospel. They were required to "eat only plain and wholesome food" and to give up "all bad habits, and especially the smoking and chewing of tobacco, unless it is necessary as a medicine." Liquor was forbidden, as were "all strong and unnecessary drinks, even tea and coffee, as far as practicable." Even clothes and furniture came under the strictures. There was a prohibition against "all the world's expensive and unwholesome fashions of dress, particularly tight dressing and ornamental attire," and the colonists had to "observe plainness and durability in the construction of our houses, furniture, carriages." Their sons and daughters were to be educated "thoroughly" and trained "in body, intellect and heart for the service of the Lord." And each signer of the covenant promised to "strive to maintain deep-toned and elevated personal piety, to 'provoke each other to love and good works,' to live together in all things as brethren, and to glorify God in our bodies and spirits which are His."[7]

The clearing of the forest began in the spring of 1833, and the first log cabin, a rough-hewn, windowless, one-room affair, was soon erected along the newly widened north-south road, across from the elm tree under which Shipherd and Stewart had knelt in prayer. That road became Main Street, and a parallel road became Professor Street. Two roads bisected them, Lorain Street and College Street. The colony that grew around the rectangular campus that was thus formed followed with little variation the same deliberate north-south, east-west pattern as other streets were laid out.

There was much to remind the settlers of home, the variety of trees, for one thing—whitewood, ash, black walnut, chestnut, hickory. The striking contrasts in seasons were familiar, too, though there were no barriers to block the wintry blasts coming off Lake Erie to the north. But for those accustomed to the hills and valleys of New York and New England, the boring flatness of the land—the almost total lack of even the slightest elevation—must have surprised them. Yet what they talked unceasingly about was how muddy the ground became after a rain. "Mud—mud—mud," a visitor once complained. "I had no idea of mud from New England roads."[8]

Soon ten acres had been cleared and six of them given over to planting. By the second week of June ten families were settled, and they were enjoying regular religious services and a Sabbath school. And that December—amid the sound of "great trees falling ... fires blazing, & new houses going up in all directions"[9] (the houses originally painted a long-lasting red as an economy measure)—the Oberlin Collegiate Institute opened. Its first forty-four students were from New York, Pennsylvania, Massachusetts, Michigan, Vermont, New Hampshire, and Ohio, but none from the colony itself. Many of them had walked the entire distance from their homes to attend the school. Classes met in Oberlin

Hall—then called Preparatory Hall—which was also the boarding hall and in which both the Shipherd and Stewart families initially lived as well.

From the outset, the school was innovative in several ways. For one thing, it admitted not only men but also women, the intent being to train the latter to teach and work alongside their future husbands in spreading the gospel. The women had a special curriculum, but they were permitted to take a number of college-level classes, and in 1837 they were allowed to matriculate in the school's college course. The three women who graduated from the course in 1841 were the first women in America to receive baccalaureate degrees.[10] However, having young females in the institution raised eyebrows in the outside world and prompted anxieties within the colony itself. Strict rules were adopted to prevent even the semblance of sexual license. The most important was a provision against a student of one sex visiting the room of a student of the opposite sex; violators faced expulsion. Female students— who alone were required to provide character references to be admitted—had to be in their rooms at 7:30 in the evening, 8 o'clock in the summer. As an added precaution against unseemly fraternization, in 1852 a lock was put on the door leading to the cupola atop Tappan Hall, the all-male dormitory, and female students were not permitted to take in the view from it without special permission. Moreover, though family life was fostered, early liaisons were not; couples who married before commencement were denied graduation. Nevertheless, both male and female students sat in the same classes and took meals together.

Educators were critical of Oberlin's curriculum at first, especially its deemphasis of Latin and Greek in favor of Hebrew, English literature, and other less conventional subjects. In time, however, Hebrew was dropped and the number of courses in Latin and Greek reached the level required by other colleges. The classics were stressed in the first year, mathematics in the second, science in the third, and philosophy in the fourth. Every college student had to attend a weekly Bible class, and rhetoric and oratory exercises were emphasized.

Oberlin Collegiate Institute began as a manual labor school. Tuition was low: $10 to $14 a year at first, later $18 in the collegiate department, at a time when Harvard was charging $72, Princeton and Yale $40, Union $57, and even the so-called poor man's college, Dartmouth, $27.[11] At first, students were required to devote four hours of each day to work in support of the school. Male students tended the farm that was laid out, milked the few cows that were purchased, helped in the sawmill that was put up or assisted in the craft shops that supplied necessary items. Female students did housekeeping chores in the dormitory and kitchen. Even though the school later adopted as its motto "Learning and Labor," the idea of combining an academic education with manual labor proved inefficient and unproductive, and the plan was gradually abandoned. For one thing, it cost more to raise food through student labor than to buy it from neighboring farmers. In addition, the soil, if treated properly, might grow small grains and be good for grazing, but some agricultural savvy was essential to working it. Mulberry trees were planted during a silkworm mania in 1836, but not one cocoon appeared. The school finally leased out its lands to farmers with the proviso that they hire students to help work them. For a while tuition was free for college students, and it was always free for theological ones. To make ends meet, a few upperclassmen could earn money as tutors in the Preparatory Department, but more especially a three-month-long winter vacation enabled nearly half the student body to earn the money necessary to pay tuition and board by working in communities outside Oberlin as teachers or substitute preachers. Moreover, the truly needy were never denied admission.

John G. W. Cowles, the youngest of three sons of Professor Henry Cowles, remembered the rigidity and discipline of growing up in Oberlin in the school's first years. "The law of our household was first religion; second, work; and third study," he wrote, continuing:

The thirty acres of woodland, pasture, meadow, corn fields and orchards on the edge of the village, with garden near the house, were the field of thrifty husbandry and sturdy labor, from the youngest who could pull weeds or pick up chips, to the older and stronger who could hold the plow and swing the scythe or cradle each in his turn. We had our own athletics and plenty of them. The "field day" was every day, for certain hours: in winter with the axe in the wood—or wood yard—and in springtime, summer and autumn with the impliments of seeding, cultivating or harvesting in their seasons.

With us law meant not only submission and obedience, but regularity and order, system and method, both in religion, work and study. Breakfast at ten minutes past six each morning, summer and winter, Sundays included; dinner at ten minutes past twelve, and supper at six; bed at nine and up at five, was the time schedule of our express train running under full head of steam from the primer to the college graduation. . . . The college bell, heard throughout the village, was the signal for sleeping and for waking, for prayers before breakfast and at the evening hour, for study, for recitations, and for work, and for return from work in the woods or fields, to get ready for the next duties. One must always be "on time."[12]

And one must always pray. Every recitation at the school opened with prayer, or at least a hymn. Some classes had a weekly prayer meeting, and all students came together for a prayer meeting on Monday nights. In addition, students were expected to attend Sabbath services, both morning and afternoon sessions, which could be so tiring that it was not unusual to see hundreds of them on their feet during the services to keep awake.[13] "I know of no place where the Bible is more highly prized, or more generally studied, in Bible classes, and Sabbath schools," wrote James Fairchild's brother Edward, also an alumnus and later principal of the Preparatory Department. "There are not less than forty prayer meetings in a week continually."[14] William Lincoln said that "every influence was made to induce such prayers."[15]

Oberlin Collegiate Institute began as a preparatory school, but it soon became evident that it would have to add a college course, a theological course, and a female course. However, financial difficulties, which would plague the school on and off for the next fifteen years, arose, and the immediate problem became one of survival. The resolution of that problem would provide Oberlin with yet another innovation, one that not only gave the school and the community their distinctive character but would also have repercussions in the decades ahead.

As students at Oberlin Collegiate Institute were completing their first year in 1834, some two hundred miles away at the Lane Theological Seminary in Cincinnati, a Connecticut-born student by the name of Theodore Weld was finishing preparations for a series of eighteen evening meetings devoted to a discussion of slavery. Weld opened the first four meetings—actually lectures—with a plea for immediate emancipation, after which eyewitnesses, some of them sons of slaveholders, took the rostrum to detail the horrors of the institution. Weld hoped to launch a nationwide antislavery crusade to persuade slaveholders of the moral reasons for liberating their slaves voluntarily. After half the scheduled meetings were held, a vote was taken, with all but a handful in the audience for immediate emancipation. The rest of the meetings were given over to a debate about the colonization movement, then a favored idea of many Northerners, who believed that returning blacks to Africa or settling them on some island in the Caribbean would solve the problems they represented. At the conclusion of the discussions, the seminary students formed an antislavery society, pledging to approach "the minds of slave holders

[with] the truth, in the spirit of the Gospel"—but "not instigating slaves to rebellion," or "advocating an interposition of force on the part of the free states," or seeking "congressional interference with the constitutional powers of the States." And true to their vow, several students immediately set out to lecture for the cause while others began schools and a library "elevating the colored people in Cincinnati."[16]

The students' action aroused Lane's Board of Trustees, most of whose members were conservative local men whose business interests, like those of many other Cincinnati merchants, rested in large measure in the South. Cincinnati was especially sensitive to the race question. It had a large black community in a section called Bucktown, which was the site of riots five years earlier, spurred in good part because blacks and immigrants, mostly Irish, were in competition for jobs along the city's busy riverfront. The blacks harbored runaway slaves, many of whom escaped from steamers that pulled up to the city's wharves to unload their cargoes. During the summer of 1834, while the school's president, Lyman Beecher—Harriet Beecher Stowe's father—as well as several members of the faculty, including her husband, Calvin E. Stowe—were away, a special subcommittee of the trustees' executive committee adopted a resolution barring the establishment of any association or society not directly connected with school activities and banning the discussion of any subject that would detract from studying, especially topics that were a "matter of public interest and popular excitement."[17] At the same time, a professor who sympathized with the students, John Morgan, was fired. When in the fall the full Board of Trustees ratified the subcommittee's action, thirty-nine students immediately presented their resignations and began their own school a few miles away.

Shipherd, meanwhile, was searching for benefactors. Not only did Oberlin need funds to put up more buildings and purchase equipment, but it also needed a president and more teachers. Shipherd headed for Cincinnati. En route he met the new president of the Oberlin Board of Trustees, John Keep, an early advocate of female education. Keep encouraged Shipherd to contact the Lane Rebels, as they were called, and when Shipherd did, he discovered that they were willing to come to Oberlin if certain conditions were met: if one of the seminary's trustees, the outspoken abolitionist and black sympathizer Asa Mahan was named Oberlin's president; if John Morgan was hired for the faculty; if freedom of speech was guaranteed; if blacks were admitted to Oberlin; and if the outstanding nineteenth-century revivalist Charles Grandison

Finney was hired to teach theology. Finney was the darling of the Tappan brothers, wealthy New York merchants and abolitionists, who had been backers of the Lane Theological Seminary and were already donating to Oberlin. They were committed to supporting the Lane Rebels. Elated, Shipherd agreed to the terms.

Back in Oberlin, much to Shipherd's amazement, news of the agreement raised an outcry of protest. Although only one black resided in all of Lorain County that fall of 1834, and no black had ever sought admission to the school, both the colonists and the students were afraid that the school would be deluged with hundreds of blacks. It was one thing, many thought, to be in favor of granting blacks legal protections and to be against slavery—slavery was a sin—but quite another to think that blacks were equal to whites in intelligence, physical stamina, and ambition, or that they should share political and social equality with whites.

Such a belief in black inferiority was not unusual among some sympathetic Northern abolitionists. They may have railed against the plight of slaves in the South, but they referred to blacks—as did Abraham Lincoln—as "niggers," and they accented stereotypical mental and physical characteristics—blacks' meekness and servility, their comical and minstrel-like traits. No less a spokesperson for their plight than Harriet Beecher Stowe would refer to blacks as members of "a race hitherto ignored by the associations of polite and refined society; an exotic race, whose ancestors, born beneath a tropic sun, brought with them, and perpetuated to their descendants, a character so essentially unlike the hard and dominant Angle-Saxon race."[18]

Before the close of 1834, a straw poll of sorts was taken among the students about admitting "persons of color."[19] The vote was thirty-two to twenty-one against doing so. Feelings became so heated on the subject that the trustees, scheduled to meet on the first day of 1835, moved their meeting from Oberlin to Elyria. The acrimonious meeting failed to settle the question. The trustees said they were not prepared to decide on the issue of admitting blacks. They wanted more time and more information, and they made it clear that they did not wish to be different from other schools. In the meantime, however, Arthur Tappan subscribed $10,000, and his brother Lewis and others said they would pay eight professors $600 yearly if Finney were appointed professor of theology.

Exhausted by his revivalist activities, Finney had already considered giving up his preaching in New York City and had long thought about starting a religious school, but he had terms of his own. For one thing, he wanted to be able to spend three or four months each winter away from Oberlin, preaching in New York or other cities. In addition, he wanted the management of the school taken out of the hands of the trustees. Finney was no saint on the issue of racial equality; he was against slavery, which was an "unblushing wrong," but acknowledged having a "constitutional" dislike of blacks, though that did not "necessarily deprive any man of any positive right."[20] Yet Finney wanted the faculty to handle the school's management, "inclusive of the reception of students," which meant that he favored the admission of blacks. Shipherd, who had gone to New York City to enlist Finney, wrote back to Oberlin, urging the trustees to reconsider. He had no intention, he said, "to hang out an abolition flag, or fill up [the school] with filthy stupid negroes."[21] Shipherd pointed out, however, that other schools had admitted black males—Princeton Theological Seminary, Western Reserve College, even Lane. White students, he explained, would not be compelled to be with blacks, and the fear that had been raised about "amalgamation"—intermarriage—was, he said, without foundation. If academic freedom were not allowed—if the trustees would not guarantee open discussions and allow the faculty to control the school's affairs—Shipherd said he would resign.

Faced with that ultimatum, the trustees called a special meeting at Shipherd's home on February 9, 1835. It, too, was a bitter session. The trustees adjourned until the next morning when, again, a heated discussion took place. As the trustees argued, Esther Shipherd, busy with housework, anxiously passed by the open door of the parlor where they were meeting. Seeing her, John Keep came out to tell her that the board seemed hopelessly divided and he feared it would reject Finney's provisos. Quickly, Mrs. Shipherd gathered the other wives from the community and began to pray. And when the board was deadlocked four to four, Keep, who once had started a free school for blacks in Massachusetts, cast the deciding vote: the faculty would manage internal school affairs, students would be free to discuss any subject and to form associations, and qualified males and females were to be admitted "irrespective of color."[22]

Together with Mahan and Morgan came most of the Lane Rebels, as well as Weld, who delivered twenty lectures in his "surpassing eloquence and power."[23] Soon an additional fifteen students arrived from Western Reserve College in Hudson, where their antislavery inclinations had also been stifled. Less than five months after the decision was made to admit blacks, the Oberlin Anti-

Slavery Society was organized, and that fall the Oberlin church voted that because "Slavery is a Sin," no slaveholder could preach, serve, or "commune" in it."[24] Within a matter of two short years, Oberlin was "abolitionized," every man and woman in the school committed, in varying degrees, to seeking the emancipation of all slaves. And soon students were carrying the message throughout Ohio and into other states, including the South, or teaching in schools especially established for blacks.

A financial agent for the school had warned that "as soon as your *darkies* begin to come in in any considerable numbers, unless they are completely separated, . . . the white will begin to leave— and at length your Institute will change colour. Why not have a black Institution, Dyed in the wool—and let Oberlin be?" But the fear that the school would be flooded with blacks was never re-alized. Black students never made up more than 5 percent of the student population before 1861. By the spring of 1859, there were only 32 blacks in a student body that totaled about 1,200, and of the nearly 8,000 students—in the Preparatory, College, Ladies, and Theological departments—who attended at some time between 1835 and 1861, only 245 were black.[25] In all, 100 blacks, only half of whom had been born free, attended the college before 1865. Those in the Preparatory Department included the children of some well-known black leaders, among them Rosetta Douglass, the daughter of Frederick Douglass, and Mary and Emily Edmond-son, who were supported at Oberlin by Harriet Beecher Stowe; Emily had escaped from the slave ship *Pearl* but been recaptured and her freedom subsequently was purchased by abolitionists. Al-though relatively few in number, many of the blacks became no-table. Oberlin's most distinguished black student and resident— John Mercer Langston, lawyer, later diplomat, university presi-dent, and congressman—was one of them. Oberlin College blacks would later make up one-third of the faculty of Wilberforce Uni-versity during the first thirty years of that black institution.[26]

The admission of black students did not disrupt the school in any way. No course was altered to accommodate their previous educational experience, and, despite fears, there were no serious incidents. One female student wrote back to her worried parents that "we dont have to kiss the Niggars nor to speak to them with-out we are a mind to. . . . I have not kissed a Niggar yet nor ant a going to nor hant seen any one else."[27] A male student wrote, "Almost every fifth one at the table is a darky, and the best ap-pearing chap I have seen here is black."[28] According to Professor

Henry Cowles, "The white and colored students associate together in this college very much as they choose."[29]

Despite the low proportion of black students, Oberlin soon earned a reputation, as an African Methodist Episcopal clergyman put it in 1844, of being the only place in the United States where a black might get an inexpensive education and, "at the same time, be respected as a man." And while other schools might have had no stated policy about black students—Amherst had graduated a black male in 1826 and Bowdoin had graduated two that same year—such schools "encouraged a prejudice," an abolitionist remarked, "which created an atmosphere in which a colored student could not live."[30]

Interestingly, Finney, whose ultimatum caused the profound change in Oberlin's policy, within a few years tried to put a damper on antislavery fervor. Spreading the gospel, he said, was more important. The end of political and social ills such as slavery would automatically follow if the converted lived as they believed. To Finney, conversion was the first priority.

Finney's rigid views led the school into a storm of a different kind that also enhanced the community's notoriety for what, to the world at large, appeared to be unsavory radicalism. In his mid-forties, a striking six feet two with piercing eyes, Finney was a spellbinding preacher. Whirling his long arms, he railed at congregations, castigating unbelievers, humbling sinners. It was said that no one who heard his sermon "The Wages of Sin" ever forgot it. One seminary graduate, the self-styled "pioneer preacher" Sherlock Bristol, recalled that at Oberlin "one breathed the atmosphere of nearly a perpetual revival."[31]

Most students were afraid of Finney, but he had a sense of humor—caustic at times, to be sure—and was not above what other students and faculty considered the informality and cheerfulness that pervaded the school. People greeted each other as "Brother" or "Sister," and titles such as "Father" were extended to revered elders such as John Keep. William Lincoln recalled that a friend of his, "a student of keen mind," Arabella Phillips of Orangeville, New York, was "somewhat contemptuous" of all the prayer exercises. "She reckoned that she had to pray 21 times in a day." One day, when Finney met her on the campus, "he looking at her said 'Good morning, Daughter of the Devil' She extending her hand said 'I'm glad to see you, Father'. He in tears at the witty answer plead with her to give her heart to God, & I think made a deep impression. I think he succeeded."[32]

Finney was a proponent of "perfectionism." He believed that sinners could repent—that it was, indeed, a duty to do so immediately—and that salvation was possible for everyone, not just an elite few. Akin in spirit to the Oberlin community he joined, Finney considered liquor, tea, coffee, and tobacco abominations in the eyes of God, promoted strict dietary reforms, and denounced idle social gatherings and parties as "'a grand device of the devil,' taking people away from time better spent at prayer meetings. Parties were wasteful of time and money, leading to 'excess in eating and drinking,' vain conversation, and 'nameless fooleries.'"[33]

Finney was an ordained Presbyterian, as were Oberlin's founders as well as five of its first professors, and the school's trustees all belonged to churches connected with presbyteries. But Finney's views were considered so heretical that a schism resulted. Conservative Presbyterians were shocked by his extremist theological philosophy, liberal Presbyterians by the fanaticism of the long, vigorous harangues he indulged in. Many persons were also critical of Finney's perfectionism and revivalist excesses, and, in spite of his admonitions, were especially put off by the thrust of politics into the pulpit by Oberlin's young, traveling ministers-to-be. The Huron Presbytery, for one, declared in 1841 that it was "inexpedient for the churches to employ ministers known to entertain Oberlin sentiments."[34] Students who hoped to become missionaries found their careers blocked. As a result, Oberlin became a prime mover in the establishment of an association of Congregational churches in the Western Reserve.

Although Finney succeeded Mahan as president of Oberlin in 1851, he devoted most of his energies to preaching in First Church and at his revivals away from Oberlin, teaching so little that a "theolog" student could not count on studying under him for more than one semester in a year. Perhaps because of his regular absences, the school continued to be a center for antislavery agitation, and the fervor welled over into the town itself.

For nearly a quarter-century until 1861, a constant stream of runaway slaves passed through Oberlin. One of the first incidents on record occurred in the spring of 1837, when a former student brought four fugitives into town in a wagon en route to Canada. Four years later, slave hunters caught an escaped black couple in Oberlin, but students and townspeople dogged the captors to Elyria, where the two blacks were able to escape from jail. Although harboring and helping the runaways were standard practice, Oberlin leaders did not countenance openly inciting slaves to bolt their masters. Nevertheless, three students did go into the South to persuade and lead slaves away; one of them, Calvin Fairbanks, who claimed to have guided forty-seven slaves to freedom, served more than sixteen years in Kentucky prisons, where he was severely whipped and beaten by jailkeepers. Students who went out from the school to lecture and preach against slavery were frequently ridiculed and chased, often had objects thrown at them, sometimes were beaten.

The school was also the focus of attacks because of its antislavery stance. By 1843, it had survived four attempts in seven years by Democrat-controlled state legislatures to repeal its charter. Critics charged that the school was using its funds "in aiding slaves to escape from their masters." In response to a state senate inquiry, a disgruntled former student wrote, "The managers, professors, and other teachers, have emphatically used their influence to inculcate the doctrines of abolitionism in the minds of those under their charge, and to promote the general cause of the abolitionist. From the president down to the tutor, they preach it in the desks, inculcate it in their prayers, talk it in their recitation rooms, support it in common confab, and attend public deliberations for its promulgation."[35] In the same vein, the *Pennsylvanian* of Philadelphia would later charge,

With arithmetic is taught the computation of the number of slaves and their value per head; with geography, territorial lines and those localities of slave territory supposed to be favorable to emancipation; with history, the chronicles of the peculiar institution; and with ethics and philosophy, the "higher law," and resistance to Federal enactments. Hence the graduates of Oberlin are Masters of Art in abolitionism, and with the acquirement of their degrees, are prepared to go a degree or two further, if occasion requires. . . . So long as Oberlin flourishes, and educates 1,250 students per annum, male and female, abolitionsts [sic] will continue to multiply.[36]

The third attempt to repeal the school's charter, in 1842, was provoked in part by a petition from irate citizens of Richland County in central Ohio. A letter accompanying the petition charged that "treasonable abolitionist factionalists have established many routes throughout this State along which they convey runaway, or decoyed away slaves to Canada. . . . All these negro thoroughfares point toward Oberlin."[37] In fact, six well-established routes of the Underground Railroad ran through Oberlin—three from the communities immediately to the south, one from Norwalk to the west, and two running north to nearby ports on Lake Erie.[38] As many as three thousand escaped slaves were said to have found a haven, at least temporarily, in Oberlin,[39] and the *Oberlin*

Evangelist acknowledged in 1856 that the community was "second only to Canada as an asylum for the hunted fugitive."[40]

Feeling his work was completed, Shipherd had left in 1844 to found a similar school in Olivet, Michigan, where he died shortly afterward. Oberlin's other cofounder, Stewart, who with his wife was in charge of the dining room in the Boarding Hall, had left in 1836 under a storm of protest. Students complained of inept management and particularly about the plain diet the Stewarts espoused—bread with water, bread with salt, bread with milk, bread with gruel, and bread with a gravy made from flour and water mixed with "pot liquor." Ironically, Stewart subsequently became a successful businessman.

The school was renamed Oberlin College in 1850, two years after the town was incorporated. By 1855, its population was slightly over twenty-one hundred, exclusive of students and a growing but transient population of fugitive slaves. Many of the latter purposely lived northeast of town in what was being called New Oberlin. It was near an inaccessible swampland called West Marsh, where "Great quantities of unusually large Grapes [cranberries] grow."[41] The town's growth and success were represented by the many new avenues that had been laid out since the village was founded in 1833—Water Street, which ran parallel to Main on the east; a short Pleasant Street one block from the center of town; and streets called Mill, Morgan, South, and Mechanics in the southern part of town, where the tracks of the Cleveland and Toledo Railroad, first laid in 1852, ran. New gable-roofed wood-frame homes now graced the streets, indicating a trend away from the austerity of the earlier period.

Downtown, the main shopping and business district had spread from Main Street north of College Street, across from Tappan Square, to Main south of College, where mercantile establishments could be built on both the east and west sides of Main. Some of the streets even had wooden sidewalks; they were a major improvement in muddy weather, though slippery when wet. There were, among others listed in an 1859 directory, two bookstores, three dry-goods stores, seven groceries, three stores that sold boots and shoes, two butcher shops, two drugstores, a marble dealer, two stove and tinware shops, two hotels, and two jewelry stores, as well as harnessmakers, cabinetmakers, blacksmiths, builders and joiners, stone and brick masons, three lawyers, four physicians, a dentist, a barber, four "merchant tailors," three milliners, and a "Daguerrean Artist."[42] Many of the store proprietors and artisans listed in the directory were black men.

The physical center of town was the intersection of Main and College streets; on its northwest corner stood the Historic Elm, the cornerstone, as it were, of Tappan Square. Spiritually and socially, however, the center was one block north, at the intersection of Main and Lorain streets, where, on the northwest corner, First Church had been built. Finney had wanted its design to mirror that of the Tabernacle that was built for him on Worth Street, east of Broadway, in New York City. That idea had to be modified, but the Oberlin structure was nevertheless an imposing orange-brick edifice. Inside, a graceful, curved balcony swept around the walls, encircling the pulpit, behind which was a powerful, resounding organ and a choir loft for 150 singers. The feeling of intimacy that was created was, however, deceptive. First Church could hold eighteen hundred people, provided some sat on chairs along the walls and aisles or on the steps of the gallery. When completed in 1845, it was the largest building west of the Allegheny Mountains, and the size of its congregation was rivaled only by that of the Plymouth Church in Brooklyn, New York, the congregation of Harriet Beecher Stowe's brother Henry Ward Beecher. Finney was First Church's pastor for thirty-seven years.

In the fall of 1858, seven years after he became president of the college, Finney prepared for a trip to England that would take him away from Oberlin for two years. The college could now boast an enrollment of 736 "Gentlemen" and 513 "Ladies" in all its departments, a grand total of 1,249 students.[43] And their influence was enormous. As many as 500 would set out from Oberlin during the unusually long winter vacation to teach in Ohio schools or work as substitute preachers. Wherever a graduate settled, it was said, a way station on the Underground Railroad could be found. Oberlin alumni were now serving as ministers in the West or as missionaries to the Ojibwa Indians in what later would be Minnesota, among blacks in Jamaica, and at the Mendi Mission in West Africa. Nine out of ten of the missionaries sent out by the American Missionary Association were former Oberlin students.[44] And what did they preach? "Those who looked to the Scriptures" to resolve the slavery question, James Fairchild wrote, would discover "the fugitive slave law of the Mosaic institutions, 'Thou shalt not deliver unto his master the servant which is escaped from his master unto thee; he shall dwell with thee, even among you, in that place which he shall choose, in one of thy gates where it liketh him best; thou shalt not oppress him.'"[45]

The attitude Fairchild expressed and the persistent antislavery efforts of Oberlin students and graduates made Oberlin the constant butt of taunts from outsiders. When a student gave a lift in his buggy to a sick black girl on an innocent jaunt into the countryside, the ever-critical *Cleveland Plain Dealer* was quick to headline the item "Marriage Extraordinary"—and forty newspapers across the country were as quick to reprint the latest "Oberlinism."[46] Not many miles away, it was said, a road sign showing a fleeing black slave was erected as a marker pointing to Oberlin. Other guideposts to the town were splattered with mud or used for target practice. A tavern on the way to Elyria had for a time a sign showing a black being pursued by a tiger. Newspapers in the South were quick to reprint critical news about the town or the college, as Kentucky's *Louisville Courier* did in reprinting for its readers the latest "Oberlin Joke":

> So embittered is Oberlinism to anything Southern, that at one time the faculty and students resolved to use no product of slave labor; of course they cut cotton and eschewed tobacco altogether. An ardent young student, deeply imbued with the anti-slavery sentiment, happened to think one night after retiring to bed that he was between a pair of cotton sheets; out he jumped, took a blanket and slept on the floor until morning. It was rather a hard bed, but it was better to rest but little and turn over often, than to snooze all night in the sweat of the slave. Upon waking in the morning he found that the carpet on which he slept was *half cotton!* He probably took to the bed after that.—*Cleveland Plaindealer.*[47]

When, later, the associate editor of the *Plain Dealer*, the wit Charles Farrar Browne, paid a lecture visit to Oberlin, he reported, writing under the pseudonym Artemus Ward:

> Oberlin is whare the celebrated college is. In fact, Oberlin *is* the college, everything else in that air vicinity resolvin around excloosivly for the benefit of that institution. It is a very good college, too, & a great many wurthy yung men go there annooally to git intelleck into 'em. But its my onbiassed 'pinion that they go it rather too strong on Ethiopians at Oberlin. . . . on rainy dase white peple can't find the way threw the streets without the gas is lit, there bein such a numerosity of cullerd pussons in the town. . . .
>
>   Oberlin is a grate plase. The College opens with a prayer and then the New York Tribune is read. A kolleckshun is then taken up to buy overkoats with red horn buttons onto them for the indignant cullered people of Kanady. I have to contribit librally two the glowrius work, as they kawl it hear. I'm kompelled by the Fackulty to reserve front seets in my show for the cullered peple. At the Boardin House the cullered peple sit at the first table. What they leeve is maid into hash for the white peple. As I don't like the idee of eatin my vittles with Ethiopians, I sit at the seckind table, and the kon-

sequence is I've devowred so much hash that my inards is in a hily mixt up condishun.[48]

"The schools our students taught," said Edward Fairchild, "were called 'nigger' schools, the churches where they preached were 'nigger' churches; the preachers themselves were 'nigger' men. Oberlin was a 'nigger' town."[49]

Oberlin had certainly become a haven for blacks, free and fugitive. To ensure that it would remain one, its "colored citizens" gathered together in 1849 and drew up a series of resolutions, one of which promoted "the doctrine of urging the slave to leave immediately with his hoe on his shoulder, for a land of liberty," and another of which alerted "all colored persons and their friends, to keep a sharp look-out for men-thieves and their abettors, and to warn them that no person claimed as a slave shall be taken from our midst without trouble."[50]

In the decade following the passage of the Fugitive Slave Law in 1850, the black population of Ohio increased 45 percent, but in two counties alone—Cuyahoga (Cleveland) and Lorain—the increase was more than 100 percent. Of the 549 in Lorain County, a large percentage was settled around Oberlin—about 420 in Oberlin itself, 80 on the outskirts in Russia Township, but only 47 in all the rest of the county.[51] For example, although a number of whites were connected with the Underground Railroad in Wellington, less than nine miles south, that town did not have a single black registered among its 1,149 residents in the 1860 census.

Nearly nineteen months before the census was taken, on the first day of January 1859, John Watson, a black who ran a grocery and confectionery store on South Main, counted the black population of Oberlin, finding 344 in all, including 28 fugitives and some 50 children who had been born in freedom.[53] When the federal census was taken in July 1860, 2,114 "free inhabitants" were registered in Oberlin, 416 of whom, or nearly 20 percent of the town's reported population, were black men, women, and children.[54] The greatest number were from North Carolina, half of them free or emancipated blacks.[55] The men worked chiefly as laborers and farm workers, though there were also a number of barbers, teamsters, shoemakers, carpenters, painters, and masons. The women worked as maids, cooks, and dressmakers. Many black males had established themselves as shopkeepers and merchants, and one—John Mercer Langston—claimed that he was the first black man ever nominated and elected to public office in the United States when he was voted clerk of neighboring Brownhelm

Township in 1855. He served as clerk of Russia Township for two years from 1857 and later was on Oberlin's Board of Education.

But Langston and the other successful blacks were a minority within a minority. There were innumerable fugitive slaves living in Oberlin. Though John Watson counted less than one hundred adult fugitives and their children in 1859, Langston believed that the majority of "colored persons" living in the community after 1844 were runaways. Whatever their number, most of the refugee blacks were illiterate, poorly housed and clothed, and socially inept. Although Oberlin's public school was integrated, relatively few black youngsters attended, apparently because they felt ill at ease. A so-called Liberty School was maintained in a "conspicuous part of the town"[56] to teach fugitive adults and children until it burned down in the fall of 1860.[59] Integrated housing was virtually nonexistent, though Langston, for one, lived next door to whites on fashionable East College Street, and he and other black as well as white residents took in black students as boarders. Otherwise, however, blacks lived mainly in "Little Africa," just east of the campus, or in the southeast section of town, near the train depot.

Moreover, as abolitionist as most white citizens of Oberlin were and as committed as they were to accepting blacks into their community, the nineteenth-century belief that whites were superior persisted. One observer divided the blacks of Oberlin into three classes: "A considerable portion" who were "intelligent, industrious, well-to-do, thoroughly respectable and in every way good citizens"; a second class, a "few" of whom were superior as blacksmiths and builders but the "larger number" of whom, though "good-natured and well-meaning and harmless," were only "semi-industrious and seriously lacking in forethought, ambition, and energy, content therefore to live from hand to mouth"; and, finally, an "overlarge fraction composed of the shiftless and worthless, shading off into the vicious and criminal" to whom work was "an intolerable evil" and who were "given to drink, petty thieving, and related offences."[58]

Though the college and the town had grown side by side, they were also growing slightly apart, and the solidarity exhibited over the issue of slavery by the school's faculty and student body did not exist within the residential community. Oberlin was no longer just a college town. There were active businesses that did not rely solely, if at all, on the school or its faculty and students to survive—a planing mill, a sash, door, and blind factory, a gunsmith, two flour mills, a sawmill, a carriage maker, and two restaurants. Still, a visitor in the mid-1850s observed that the atmosphere seemed to be "one of constraint" and wondered whether "the soul had *free play*, whether there were amusements enough to recreate and unbend the mind."[59] Most residents, to be sure, were anti-slavery and had progressed from being Whigs to members of the Liberty party, the Free Soil party, and, after the election of 1848, the newly formed Republican party. Oberlin's heavily Republican vote held the balance in the county, and a school trustee, Norton S. Townshend, was one of two lawmakers who held the balance of power in the state legislature and was instrumental in the repeal of the state's notorious Black Laws and the election of Salmon P. Chase to the United States Senate in 1849. As the *Plain Dealer* declared in 1859: "A man can no more go to Congress from this Reserve without Oberlin, than he can to heaven in a sling."[60]

However, the town had its opposition faction, too, Democrats in the main, many of them—such as Postmaster Edward F. Munson and United States Deputy Marshal Anson P. Dayton—attached to Christ Church, an Episcopal parish that had been established in Oberlin in 1855. The church was on South Main Street, across from the homes of some black residents, in a part of town where almost all its parishioners lived or worked. It was established to counteract the "wild ultraisms," "indecent dogmatism," "politico-religious teaching," and "disgusting puerilities" of Finney and the First Church Congregationalists.[61] As it was, the Episcopal church in the United States was by and large for the status quo. It had affiliates both north and south of the Mason-Dixon Line so its leaders were uncomfortable with the idea of opposing the Fugitive Slave Law. Even those against slavery did not see it as the sin that the Oberlin Congregationalists did. An evil, yes, but no reason to flout authority and undermine the very foundations of American democracy, which would provoke anarchy and greater evil.

The Episcopal view was diametrically opposite that of the prevailing opinion in Oberlin. The majority of people thought that the Fugitive Slave Law was contrary to the higher law of God. They believed that the law, in demanding that citizens participate in the capture of a runaway slave, required one person to sin against another, in direct violation of God's precepts. Accordingly, the act must be disobeyed. On the other hand, the abolitionists were not anarchists; they did not want it to appear that any citizen could decide to ignore any law without repercussions. They agreed that anyone who violated the Fugitive Slave Law should accept the legal consequences. Indeed, although Oberlin was considered radical on the subject, its leaders were decidedly on the side of preserving law and order. They had early on rejected the extremism of William Lloyd Garrison, who took the occasion of a Fourth of July celebration in Massachusetts to burn the Constitution in public, declaring, "So perish all compromises with tyranny!"[62] Despite the opposition he met in Oberlin, Garrison nevertheless conceded that "Oberlin has done much for the relief of the flying fugitives from the Southern prison-house, multitudes of whom have found it a refuge from their pursuers, and been fed, clad, sheltered, comforted, and kindly assisted on their way out of this horrible land to Canada."[63]

The division between Republicans and Democrats, between those advocating the end of slavery and supporters of President James Buchanan, who wanted to keep the Union together at all costs, was indicative of Ohio's own split personality. The state's northern tier, settled in large part by Yankees of Puritan heritage from New England and New York, was predominantly antislavery and increasingly Republican. In the four years between 1834 and 1838, when Oberlin was becoming firmly committed to the abolitionist cause, the number of antislavery societies in the Western Reserve increased from a dozen to more than three hundred. The election of 1855, in which Salmon P. Chase was elected governor, assured the permanence of the Republican party in Ohio. Quakers migrated from Pennsylvania to settle in parts of eastern and central Ohio, where they also formed the nucleus of an antislavery movement.

In contrast, Ohio's southern tier was sympathetic to Southern interests. Most of its pioneers were Virginians; others had come from Kentucky, Tennessee, Maryland, and North Carolina, and their accents could be heard there. Abolition to them was synonymous with slave rebellions and black equality, and many of their politicians insisted that abolition would lead to dissolution of the Union. In addition, from the time of its admission to the Union shortly after the turn of the century, Ohioans had worried that their state would become overwhelmed with blacks. Although Ohio's constitution, based on provisions of the Northwest Ordinance, prohibited slavery, the state militia was restricted to whites, and as early as 1804 the first of a series of racially restrictive Black Laws was enacted; it provided that no black or mulatto could settle in the state without a certificate of freedom. A stiffer law in 1807 required blacks to post a $500 bond in order to settle and forbade blacks from testifying against whites in court. An act of 1831 disqualified them from jury duty, and an act of 1838 provided public schooling only for white children. Even though the

Black Laws were repealed in 1849, the relationship between the races throughout most of Ohio was precarious, and blacks never achieved full equality in the antebellum period. Professor James Monroe of Oberlin made valiant attempts to rectify the inequalities when he served in the Ohio legislature. During his very first session and with Republicans in power in 1856, he was able to have a personal liberty law enacted in reaction to the Fugitive Slave Law. The loophole it provided enabled an alleged runaway slave to apply for a writ of habeas corpus, thus freeing the suspected fugitive and preventing him or her from being immediately returned to the South. But when Democrats returned to control two years later, they repealed the law.

Monroe and John Mercer Langston were of like minds on the subject of black rights. They joined forces to fight for voting rights for black males throughout the state. Enfranchisement, Langston believed, was essential—"a source of very great power" that could be used to "stab the demon of slavery."[64] But their efforts were unsuccessful. Conservative Republicans in southern Ohio were leery of giving blacks such power and, at the same time, were eager to displace "radicals" such as Monroe who had taken over the party's control. They even talked of uniting with moderate Southern Democrats who supported Stephen A. Douglas. For their part, Ohio Democrats feared that granting blacks the vote would unleash a potent and hostile political force. Even though the Democrats won control of both houses of the legislature in the state election of 1857, Salmon P. Chase was reelected governor. But the gubernatorial vote was close, so close in fact that Democrats charged that it was the votes cast illegally by blacks in Oberlin and other abolitionist enclaves in northern and central Ohio that provided Chase with his narrow victory.

What Republican abolitionists and proponents of black rights needed was a rallying point. It came, from Oberlin, so unexpectedly that even Monroe himself did not appreciate the impact it would have, although he was there, in town, when it happened.

FOUR

The Man-Stealers

"He's a shocking creature, isn't he,—this trader? so unfeeling! It's dreadful, really!" . . .

But who, sir, makes the trader? Who is most to blame? The enlightened, cultivated intelligent man, who supports the system of which the trader is the inevitable result, or the poor trader himself? You make the public sentiment that calls for his trade, that debauches and depraves him, till he feels no shame in it; and in what are you better than he?

Are you educated and he ignorant, you high and he low, you refined and he coarse, you talented and he simple? . . .

In concluding these little incidents of lawful trade, we must beg the world not to think that American legislators are entirely destitute of humanity. . . .

Who does not know how our great men are outdoing themselves, in declaiming against the foreign slave-trade? . . . Trading negroes from Africa, dear reader, is so horrid! It is not to be thought of! But trading them from Kentucky,—that's quite another thing!

Chapter xii: "Select Incident of Lawful Trade"

Oberlin was tense in the late summer of 1858. Slave hunters had made three attempts to seize black families in the community. Each had been foiled. Oberlin abolitionists liked to boast that not one slave had ever been returned to bondage from their town, yet there had never been "an instance of bloodshed or personal harm."[1] Nevertheless, the mood of Oberlin's blacks was especially wary. They were keeping watch on any strangers who arrived in town. Many of them had guns or other weapons at the ready.

If John Price was aware of the danger, he did not indicate it to anyone. Perhaps he was distracted because he felt so ill. He had lost weight and was considerably bloated. He was down on his luck, too; residents were being paid out of the town's pauper funds to take him in. The allotments had started in March.[2] He was now boarding north of East Lorain Street, outside of the town proper, with a black farmer. His friend Frank apparently lived nearby. John attended a Sunday school taught by an Oberlin student. Whenever he could, he worked in the fields around Oberlin, earning a dollar a day by helping with the harvest. That August he was able to find

50

eleven days of work, at a dollar a day, in a field belonging to Norris Wood, a livery stable keeper. In spite of the work, he must have felt homesick because he confided to Wood that he was planning to return home to Kentucky.[3]

*

A mile or so from where John boarded, an alert ten-year-old boy from Warren, Ohio, named William Cochran was spending several weeks at the home of his Aunt Elizabeth, the wife of Stephen W. Cole. It was a visit he would never forget.

One day he walked down South Main Street past a disreputable hotel near the train depot known variously as the Railroad House, the Russia House, or, simply, Wack's Hotel. Its proprietor, Chauncey Wack, was the town character. He smoked cigars, drank ale, and liked to dance. Wack had been born some forty-odd years earlier in Bennington, Vermont, a state whose constitution, adopted in 1777, prohibited slavery, yet he was decidedly antiblack. He was also a Democrat and Southern sympathizer. His establishment attracted transients who did not feel comfortable in the college-owned Palmer House in the center of town.

As William and a cousin passed by Wack's, William noticed several "rough looking" men sitting on the hotel porch. His cousin told them they were slave hunters—"the most depraved of human beings—worse than thieves, burglars or murderers." Young Cochran decided to give Wack's "a wide berth after that."[4] His aunt and uncle, he had figured out, were helping fugitive slaves. They would prepare baskets of food and take them out into the countryside, telling the youngster that the contents were for "the rabbits." But once, when William accompanied them to retrieve the baskets, he noticed that the rabbits had "folded their napkins."[5]

William often accompanied his uncle on visits to a nearby smithy run by a black, Augustus Chambers. Once they went to have a horse shod, another time to have a wagon tire reset. The boy did not understand the reason for a third visit until the blacksmith suddenly exploded with rage, slamming his hammer down on the anvil and then throwing it into a corner. "So they tried to steal that mammy and her children right under your noses!" His eyes "flashed fire."

Speaking in hushed tones, Cochran's uncle explained what had happened. Sometime about August 20, slave hunters tried to seize a black woman and her children. Her screams had been heard as far away as the college, a mile from where she lived.[6] The slave catchers were accompanied by the man who was anathema to most Oberlin residents, Anson P. Dayton. Dayton, who had been appointed a United States deputy marshal on the recommendation of Oberlin's Democratic postmaster, Edward F. Munson, seemed to harbor grudges. He was one of Oberlin's first two residents to practice law in the town; the other was John Mercer Langston. Dayton had been town clerk; Langston had replaced him in that post. Light-skinned or not, the son of a Revolutionary War officer notwithstanding, Langston was a black. Dayton had no truck with blacks.

Young Cochran's uncle went on to explain that, although their first attempt to seize the woman failed, the slave hunters determined to make another effort. They chose the very moment during the bright moonlit evening of Monday, August 23, that the president of Western Reserve College, H. L. Hitchcock, was delivering an address to Oberlin College's literary societies during the school's commencement week exercises. This time, fire bells rang out in alarm. Residents, students, and commencement visitors rushed to where the fire engines were kept and raced with them to the woman's home to chase off the intruders.

The uncle had come to the smithy to warn Chambers that the slave hunters were on the prowl in the vicinity.

"Well! how long are you going to let these man-stealers lie around Oberlin?" Chambers paced back and forth, his voice rising, his arms swinging wildly.

The uncle tried to calm him down. He suggested that Chambers go into hiding in nearby West Marsh, the swamp northeast of Oberlin that extended almost all the way to Elyria. Many blacks, it was believed, hid in the swamp, and Chambers was reportedly in close touch with them. "No, Sir! *I stay right here.* And if any one of those men darkens my door, he is a dead man."

As young Cochran watched, the blacksmith showed his uncle the hammer and iron bar he kept ready and the sharpened poker that rested amid the burning coals of the forge. They then followed him into a lean-to in back. A double-barreled shotgun "loaded with buck" hung over the door. A pistol and knives hung near his bed. "But, Chambers!" the uncle protested, "you wouldn't kill a man, would you?"

"Kill a *man?* No. But kill a *man-stealer?* Yes! Quicker'n a dog. As God is my judge, the man who tries to take my life will lose his *own.*"

"But we all know you are a freeman and have your *papers,*" the uncle said.

"Any white man who wants to make a few hundred dollars can swear away my rights," Chambers replied. As a free black, he knew he could not expect justice. He had "no rights that a white man was bound to respect." It was all too easy for kidnappers to falsify a claim under the Fugitive Slave Law. "These man-stealers are just lying around Oberlin until they can spot a likely negro, get his description down pat—size, marks and all—then get some fellow down South to claim him and give him his affidavy and then they will sail in and take him. An average negro in good condition is worth $1,000. On account of my blacksmithing, I s'pose I would be worth $2,000 on a big plantation."

Cochran's uncle promised that he and others would testify in his behalf, but to Chambers the answer to that was obvious.

"Think they are going to have me tried here? They will take me way off somewheres you-uns can't come and more'n likely they won't try me at all. They'll slip me over the Ohio river if they can and say nothing to nobody. If they do dry to prove up it will be in the back office of some Commissioner appointed by a Democratic judge, with no one present, but the men who get me, who say their say, and I am not allowed to say anything." The blacksmith was sure no commissioner could be trusted to give him a fair hearing. "When you pick up a negro worth $1,000 or $2,000, there is *money to divide among all concerned.* There is *nothing coming* to anybody if you set him free."

The blacksmith's words made a lasting impression on young Cochran. So did one of the speeches he heard during the Oberlin College commencement week. During the exercises, held in First Church, other students in addition to the graduates gave orations, delivered essays, and performed musical programs. The college did not keep a record of students' grades, did not rank them, and did not confer honors—there was no valedictorian, no salutatorian, no *cum laudes*—but students were encouraged to give prepared recitations and recitals. One who did was a dour-faced, fiery twenty-nine-year-old Scotsman named William Douglas Scrimgeour. The industrious Scrimgeour, who was completing his junior year, was an editor of the *Students' Monthly*, a member of the Phi Delta debating society, and a tutor in the Preparatory Department. He attracted young Cochran's attention by using "plain Anglo-Saxon language and some striking similes" that "brought down the house." Scrimgeour's topic was slavery:

"The day for soft speeches is past. The time for action has come. You'd as well try to knock down this meeting house with a *pancake* as to destroy slavery by a string of resolutions."

*

Black residents had reason to be edgy not long after commence-ment week was over. There was a bustle of activity at Wack's Hotel because of a new stranger in town, a stranger who was un-doubtedly a Southerner. The stranger was trying to keep to himself and out of the public's eye, but it was clear from the moment Anson Dayton went to the hotel to meet with him that he could only be a slave hunter. The blacks decided to keep watch on the hotel.

The unusual comings and goings started one day shortly after graduation ceremonies were held for college seniors and theolo-gians on August 25; the school's fall term began the same day. The stranger who entered Wack's Hotel that day was dark-com-plexioned and so tall—six feet four—that it was impossible not to notice him. He was well-proportioned, too, except for his short neck, which prompted one person to call him "a buffalo bull" of a man.[7] Though only in his early forties, the stranger had gray hair and sported a bushy beard, also gray. He spoke with a heavy, un schooled Kentucky accent. His name was Anderson Jennings. He was a neighbor of John Bacon from Mason County. A farmer and livery stable owner, Jennings owned thirteen slaves.[8] He happened to be in Oberlin because he was looking for an escaped black named Henry, the property of his late uncle James, whose estate he administered. Hidden in his pockets, the Kentuckian carried two revolvers and two pairs of handcuffs.[9]

It was natural that Jennings would seek out Anson Dayton for help in finding Henry. As town clerk, Dayton knew which blacks Oberlin was caring for out of its pauper fund—and they were most likely to be runaway slaves. As Dayton described them, the Ken-tuckian recognized John Price. Jennings had seen John as many as ten to fifteen times on Bacon's farm, the last time about a year before the slave fled. "His marster," Bacon, was building a new house, and Jennings remembered watching John haul a load of sand for it. Jennings immediately sat down and wrote a letter to Bacon, urging him to send him the authority to act in his behalf and capture John.[10] Jennings also knew Dinah, who had fled with John. It was possible that she and Frank, from Richard Loyd's farm, were in Oberlin, too.

Jennings asked Dayton whether he would handle the arrest of the slaves. The deputy marshal agreed only to join in the search for Henry.[11] Jennings had heard that his uncle's slave might have fled to Elyria, the seat of Lorain County, about nine miles northeast of Oberlin. Before they left for Elyria, the Kentuckian was introduced to another Southern sympathizer, a man in his mid-sixties with an unsavory reputation: Malachi Warren. To the consternation of Oberlin's prudish citizens, Warren lived out of wedlock with a slave he had purchased when he was a planter in Alabama. Five of their six children lived with them. The sixth, a daughter named Mary, feared that her father would sell her into slavery and had run off and now was married and living in Wisconsin. She had wanted to go to Oberlin College, but the school said she could not attend as long as she lived at home and her parents "sustain the relation to each other they do at present."[12] Jennings apparently established an instant rapport with Warren and soon had reason to rely on his advice.

Sometime in that last week of August, Jennings and Dayton went to Elyria. They didn't find Henry, but they did learn that he had gone on to Painesville, a well-known embarkation port for fugitive slaves on Lake Erie east of Cleveland. Their arrival there, however, almost touched off violence. Jennings found Painesville "a worse place than Oberlin." He had never seen "so many niggers and abolitionists in any one place in my life." As suspicious of strangers as the residents of Oberlin were, the citizens of Painesville seemed even more so. They quickly spread the word that two strangers were in town asking the whereabouts of a particular black. Jennings and Dayton were soon surrounded on the street by fifty to sixty armed men and given twenty minutes to leave town. Fearing for their lives, the two men quickly fled, boarding the next train out of town. "Might as well try to hunt the *devil* there as to hunt a nigger," Jennings grumbled. "Glad to get away as fast as" they could, the two men returned to Oberlin.[13]

In Kentucky, meanwhile, Bacon had received Jennings's letter and had gotten in touch with Richard Loyd. Frank was one of five slaves whom Loyd owned.[14] He also contacted Richard P. Mitchell, a farmer who had once worked for him, knew John, and had, in fact, tried unsuccessfully to pursue the runaway slave in Ohio. Mitchell had red hair and whiskers. Like Jennings he was tall, had a dark complexion, and spoke with a heavy accent, though he wasn't given to saying much. "Never talk to men about my business unless I know who I am talking to" is the way he put it.[15] Mitchell, who had worked alongside John on Bacon's farm, recalled last seeing the slave just before his escape, either on Christmas Day of 1855 or New Year's Day of 1856, he wasn't sure. A former constable who had tracked fugitive slaves into Ohio before, Mitchell had twice searched for John; on one of those occasions, about a month or so after John's escape in 1856, he traveled nearly fifty miles into Fayette County, Ohio, in pursuit of him.

On Saturday, September 4, Bacon, Loyd, and Mitchell went together to the office of the Mason County clerk in the courthouse in Maysville. There Bacon and Loyd swore out a power of attorney. The clerk, Robert A. Cochran, a bachelor lawyer who boarded at the nearby home of a wholesale grocer,[16] was not there so his deputy drew up the document by hand. It appointed Jennings as the representative of Bacon and Loyd "to capture and return to our service and possession in Kentucky, three negroes now at large in the State of Ohio." Loyd signed first, followed by Bacon. The attestation was made out in Cochran's name, but because the clerk had not yet shown up, the deputy signed Cochran's name. He evidently was used to doing so. Under Cochran's name, the deputy signed his own name. No sooner had he done so and Bacon and Loyd were out the doorway and heading down the steps than Cochran appeared. He asked what was going on. Bacon handed him the power of attorney, which he read. Cochran said he wanted something added to it. He went into his office and handed the paper back to his deputy and had him insert, "The said parties are personally known to me, and the said acknowledgment is according to law."[17] Cochran then returned the paper to the two slaveowners, though, strangely, for some reason he still had not signed it himself.

Once outside the clerk's office, Bacon turned the power of attorney over to Mitchell, instructing him to hand the paper in turn to Jennings and then to assist him in capturing the runaway slaves. He gave $50 for expenses to Mitchell, who expected also that he would get $1 a day "for his time."[18] In addition, Bacon told Mitchell to contact Anson Dayton when he reached Oberlin. Mitchell set out for Ohio immediately.

Power of attorney in hand, Mitchell took a steamboat from Maysville to Cincinnati and from there a train north via Columbus, probably to Wellington, some eight or nine miles from Oberlin. There was no north-south railroad that served Oberlin. Meanwhile, Jennings had made a quick trip to Sandusky to see if he could find his uncle's slave Henry. When he didn't, he started back to Kentucky. Unaware of what the other was doing, Jennings and Mitchell evidently crossed paths on steamboats on the Ohio River, Mitchell on his way to Oberlin with the power of attorney, Jennings returning to Mason County to get the document from Bacon.

Sometime either on Sunday, September 5, or the next day, Monday, September 6, Jennings met with Bacon and discovered what had happened. Jennings urged Bacon to go after John himself, but Bacon said he could not. After thinking about it for a while and realizing he had made Bacon go to a lot of trouble to swear out the power of attorney, Jennings offered to return to Oberlin to capture John. Bacon then informed Jennings that he had no intention of keeping John—a troublesome slave might run away again. It was better to sell him. He offered Jennings $500 if he could bring John back, and Jennings went away believing that he would get $500 from Loyd for returning with Frank as well. No mention was made of Dinah—Jennings must have discovered that she was no longer with John and Frank.

Mitchell, meanwhile, holed up at Wack's Hotel, hoping for Jennings to show up. He kept to himself and avoided appearing in public. He was inside the hotel and looking out a window when all of a sudden John walked by on the street outside.[19] Mitchell instantly recognized him, but he made no attempt to speak to him. There was no point in scaring him off. He sent a message to Dayton and on Tuesday, September 7, conferred with him at the hotel in an attempt to find out where John lived and to persuade Dayton to handle the matter. But Dayton was still shaken by his experience with the armed mob in Painesville. He had also recently taken part with a deputy marshal from Columbus, Jacob K. Lowe, and the two other Kentucky slave catchers in a midnight attempt to seize the Wagoner family. Wagoner, shotgun in hand and shouting loudly to arouse the neighborhood, had driven off the marauders.[20] It was the third attempt to seize blacks in Oberlin in the past month; the town was "filled with alarming rumors."[21] Dayton had no desire to help in the capture of Bacon's and Loyd's slaves. He refused to cooperate, even though, by law, he was subject to a fine for not carrying out his official duties.

Meanwhile, Jennings had started back to Oberlin on Monday, September 6—the same day, coincidentally, that two Oberlin professors, James Monroe and Henry Everard Peck, were helping to spirit to freedom five fugitive slaves coming from nearby Medina.[22] Jennings reached Wack's Hotel between nine and ten o'clock at night on Wednesday, September 8, to find Mitchell on the hotel veranda. As he turned over the power of attorney to him, Mitchell explained that Dayton would not assist in the seizure of the slaves. Who else was there to ask? The obvious answer was to go to Cleveland, the headquarters of the Northern District of Ohio, to enlist the services of a federal marshal there. Oberlin was in that federal judicial district, and Cleveland was only thirty-five miles away, an easy hour's train ride. On the other hand, its proximity might prove a handicap because it was likely that friends of John would hasten there to see that he received a fair hearing before a commissioner. Moreover, Cleveland had a large antislavery faction and a considerable black community. So Jennings opted to go instead to Columbus, the seat of the Southern District, more than a hundred miles away, a trip that entailed traveling to Wellington for a train connection south. He was acquainted with Jacob Lowe, who had participated in the aborted effort to seize the Wagoner family. Perhaps Lowe would accept the assignment.

Jennings also decided to ask Malachi Warren's advice on how best to capture John and Frank. Trying to keep a low profile in town, unaware that the hotel was being watched by blacks,[23] Jennings on the next day, Thursday, September 9, sent a message to Warren, asking to meet with him in his room at Wack's Hotel. Perhaps Warren became aware of the surveillance of the blacks when he arrived at Wack's. The one-time Alabama planter warned Jennings that it would be unwise to seize John and Frank at night— the Kentuckian "Might get shot and never know who done it."[24] It was better to capture the two fugitive slaves in broad daylight, but the seizure should definitely not take place in Oberlin. The best thing would be to lure the two black men to some spot out of town where nobody could witness their capture. Jennings asked Warren whether he knew of any man he could trust to help in the arrest. Yes, he did, Warren answered: Lewis D. Boynton, a farmer in his late fifties—and yet another Democrat—who lived about two and a half miles northeast of Oberlin in Russia Township.

Jennings made a mental note of the name. First, he had to find Lowe. He left Oberlin early the next morning, Friday, September 10, and, on reaching Columbus, was able to track down the deputy marshal at the city fairground. Lowe knew Oberlin; he had visited it on two previous occasions in search of fugitives. He agreed to help the Kentuckian. Jennings said he realized they would need "all the help they could get" so Lowe suggested they ask Samuel Davis, a Columbus jailer and Franklin County deputy sheriff, to join them. Expecting that Bacon would be good for the money, Jennings promised Lowe that he and Davis would not only be paid for any expenses they incurred in getting to Oberlin but also would share $100 if they caught "any of the niggers," an offer Lowe later claimed to have refused. Lowe, who figured that his services were worth $2 a day, advised Jennings that he would need a warrant to seize the fugitives so the two men went to the federal offices in Columbus to procure one. The man who processed the warrant, Sterne Crittenden, was an acting commissioner and had never issued such a warrant before. Instead of an official seal, he put a "scroll" on it. An affidavit accompanying the warrant described John Price as "one negro slave John, a fugitive and person escaped from service by him owed to John G. Bacon." The warrant specifically called for federal marshals to bring John's "body" forthwith before a United States commissioner "within and for the Southern District of Ohio" for a hearing.[25] After obtaining the warrant, Jennings and Lowe found Davis, who agreed to assist in the slaves' capture.

That evening, the three men—Jennings, Lowe, and Davis—returned to Oberlin. They arrived about dusk at Wack's Hotel, where Mitchell was waiting for them. The next day, Saturday, September 11, Lowe and Davis conferred with Malachi Warren to get a better feel of the situation in Oberlin, and then about three o'clock in the afternoon Jennings and Lowe set out for Lewis Boynton's farm.

Boynton was out when they arrived and not due back until late. Jennings explained to his wife, Azula, that he and Lowe were interested in purchasing some cows. She urged the two men to stay the night so that they could talk to her husband the first thing the next morning. She would feed them supper. The two men agreed to stay. They retired before Boynton arrived home. When his wife told him about the two strangers—that they were interested in buying cows, and that, from their conversation, one seemed to be from Columbus—the farmer was not fooled. People didn't come from Columbus to buy cows in Russia Township. He knew something else was up.

While Jennings and Lowe were at the Boynton farm that Saturday night, two strange but apparently unrelated events occurred. Malachi Warren's barn burned down, and John's friend Frank was knifed in a brawl with some black men.

It was at breakfast the next morning, Sunday, September 12, after milking, that the "General"—an honorary title Boynton had earned while serving with the state militia—met the "two gentlemen." As they were eating, the farmer's youngest son, William Shakespeare Boynton—better known as Shakespeare Boynton, or just plain "Shake," a shrewd, sassy youngster of thirteen—came in and asked his father if he could go to Oberlin early the next day. Jennings thought the boy "looked so smart" that even though he considered himself a pious man and ordinarily "don't often do business on Sunday," he decided to sound out Shakespeare about participating in the plot to capture John and Frank. He followed the boy out of the house, catching up with him at the gate. Jennings offered the youth $10 to get John to come with him in a cart and $10 more if he could also lure Frank into the vehicle. All he had to do was transport them away from prying eyes. Lowe and the two other men would handle the rest. The boy said he would try. Apparently he knew where John and Frank were staying or Jennings had found out, possibly from Dayton. The two fugitive slaves were actually living not far from the Boynton farm. Jennings told Shakespeare to report to him the next morning at Wack's Hotel when he got into town. Then the Kentuckian realized that he had better check with Boynton and see if the "old man" approved.[26]

Jennings and Lowe followed Boynton to the creek where the farmer had gone after breakfast to water his cattle. Lowe told Boynton what they were up to and asked if he minded if his son was a party to their plan. The farmer offered no objection. Shakespeare, he said, was able to arrange his own affairs, and Jennings and the boy "could fix it up" between them.[27]

Jennings and Lowe stayed at the Boyntons till it began to get dark. By the time they got back to Wack's Hotel, their plan had been all worked out. The next morning would be a busy one—and dangerous.

✳

That evening, just about the time that Jennings and Lowe were returning to the hotel, John went to see Norris Wood. Wood still owed him $6, the balance due for the eleven days' work in August when he had helped with the harvesting. Wood paid him the money. John repeated what he had told Wood before: He was "going home."[28] He then shook hands and left.

FIVE

Ambush

Mr. Haley and Tom jogged onward in their wagon, each, for a time, absorbed in his own reflections. . . .

As, for example, Mr. Haley: he thought first of Tom's length, and breadth, and height, and what he would sell for, if he was kept fat and in good case till he got him into market. He . . . then thought of himself, and how humane he was, that whereas other men chained their "niggers" hand and foot both, he only put fetters on the feet. . . .

As to Tom, he was thinking over some words of an unfashionable old book, which kept running through his head again and again, as follows: "We have here no continuing city, but we seek one to come; wherefore God himself is not ashamed to be called our God; for he hath prepared us for a city." These words of an ancient volume, got up principally by "ignorant and unlearned men," have, through all time, kept up, somehow, a strange sort of power over the minds of poor, simple fellows, like Tom. They stir up the soul from its depths, and rouse, as with trumpet call, courage, energy, and enthusiasm, where before was only the blackness of despair.

Chapter XII: "Select Incident of Lawful Trade"

Monday, September 13, 1858, began as a pleasant, quiet, late summer day in Oberlin. There was a hint of autumn in the air; the night before was cold enough to warrant the use of fireplaces. The sun rose at 5:37 and would not set until 6:16, twelve hours and thirty-nine minutes later.[1] Most people—residents as well as students, who were accustomed to awakening before dawn and having breakfast at 6:00 A.M.—were up and about when the school bell tolled for the first classes, freshmen rhetorical exercises, at eight o'clock.

There were some unusual stirrings, but nothing appeared out of the ordinary. Because only recitations were held on Mondays at the college and no classes were scheduled whatsoever for theological students, Monday was ordinarily a "holiday" for the Rev. James H. Fairchild, professor of mathematics and natural philosophy, so he was taking his wife and six children on a visit to friends in a neighboring community.[2] Traffic on the road to Wellington was uncommonly busy. Lewis Boynton was on his way early in the day to attend a Democratic convention in Ashland; he was a delegate to it. Anson Dayton was planning to go to Ashland, too, with a local laborer named Bela Farr. Dayton's tacit rival, John Mercer Langston, left his home on East College Street to attend to business in the next county; today, incidentally, was the fourth anniversary of the black man's admission to the Ohio bar. Only Seth Bartholomew, a tinware peddler, who now considered himself in "show business," seemed aware of anything unusual; as he passed Wack's Hotel en route to Pittsfield, halfway to Wellington, to post some signs for a "panorama," he saw a stranger outside, a man so tall and burly that he made a mental note of him.[3]

Perhaps the first traveler on the road to Wellington that morning was Jacob Lowe. He left so early, before anybody else was up, that he did not bother to wash until he reached Wadsworth's Hotel in Wellington.[4] The deputy marshal had gone there to borrow a carriage from the hotelkeeper. Lowe did not explain why he wanted the conveyance—a covered, two-seated, double vehicle drawn by two horses—but he promised to return it later in the day.

✳

The tall stranger Bartholomew spotted outside Wack's Hotel—Jennings—was waiting for Shakespeare Boynton to appear. Sometime after 10:00 A.M. the boy drove up in a horse and buggy. He told Jennings that he had gone to where John and Frank were staying and asked John to come to his father's farm to dig potatoes. But John was concerned for Frank; his friend had been badly cut in the brawl Saturday night and needed attention. John said that he had to stay to take care of him. However, John knew a black man in New Oberlin who might be interested in harvesting the potatoes, and he said that he would help Shakespeare find the man. As planned, the boy told John he had to go by the blacksmith's first, to attend to his horse. Instead, he went to Wack's Hotel to report to Jennings.

The Kentuckian expressed disappointment that he would not be able to catch both fugitives at once. He told Shakespeare to pick up John and seek out the man John had recommended for digging the potatoes. Meanwhile, Lowe had returned from Wellington with the carriage. Its team of horses had been fed and was ready to go. As soon as Shakespeare headed back to get John, Lowe, Mitchell, and Davis got into the carriage and, with Lowe driving, headed up the same road that Shakespeare was taking. It was about eleven o'clock when they left Wack's. Jennings, who stayed behind at the hotel, kept the power of attorney. Lowe was in possession of the federal warrant. He was unarmed, but his assistant Davis had a revolver, and Mitchell carried both a revolver and a dirk.[5]

Shakespeare returned to get John, and the two of them set out to find the black man John had recommended. They were barely outside of Oberlin when they met him in the road. The man declined the offer to go to the Boynton farm; he already had a job. The quick-witted Shakespeare turned to John. "Well, John," the teenager said, "you've been cooped up there so long, the fresh air must feel good to you; and you may as well have a good ride while you're about it. I'll bring you back again." With that, Shakespeare started for the road that led to his father's farm. John raised no objection. He and Shakespeare chatted amiably as the horse leisurely pulled the buggy along, Shakespeare purposely keeping the animal at a "slow walk."[6] As they talked, John took a penknife from his pocket and began to pick his teeth with it.

Shakespeare and John reached the Oberlin corporate line, a mile and a half or so from the center of town, about noon.[7] The dirt road they were traveling on was broad, its shoulders lined with tall old trees that sheltered it from the sun. Glancing over his shoulder, Shakespeare spotted the carriage with Lowe, Mitchell, and Davis drawing close, its horse "trotting."[8] Unsuspecting, John was still cleaning his teeth with the penknife when suddenly the carriage pulled up on the right side of the buggy. Davis, who was sitting next to Lowe on the front seat, jumped down into the road and reached over and grabbed hold of John even before Shakespeare brought his horse to a halt. Mitchell quickly stepped from the carriage and ordered John to get into it. He told John to drop the penknife he had in his hand. John objected, but Mitchell moved his hand toward his inside pocket, starting to reach for his gun. Frightened, John dropped his knife. Lowe now ordered Davis and Mitchell to "bring him along." John did not resist. "I'll go with you," he said, stepping down from the buggy. Davis and Mitchell held onto John's clothing until he was seated in the back of the carriage. Mitchell got in beside him.

Meanwhile, Shakespeare Boynton turned his horse and buggy around and started to drive off to report back to Jennings in Oberlin. Lowe then turned his carriage around and headed back down the road, too.

John had pretended not to know Mitchell when they first confronted each other, but now they shook hands and talked about Kentucky. John laughed; he said he had immediately recognized Mitchell. He asked where he was being taken. "To Elyria." Elyria, the county seat, was a friendly, Republican-dominated, antislavery community. "All right," John said.

Lowe turned the carriage eastward when they reached the extension of Lorain Street that ran into the road to Elyria.[9] But as soon as they reached the road to Elyria a little more than a mile farther on, instead of turning left—northward—to Elyria, Lowe turned right, to the south. When John saw that they were headed in the wrong direction, he asked again where he was being taken. Lowe then told him the truth, that he had a warrant for his arrest. He showed it to John, but it was obvious that the black man could not read, so Lowe read it to him. Lowe informed John that he was taking him "back to his master." They were now on what was called the diagonal road between Elyria and Columbus to the south. The road bypassed the heart of Oberlin but intersected the road to Wellington.[10] A train was due at 5:13 P.M. at Wellington, on a regularly scheduled Cleveland-to-Columbus run. The diagonal road they were traveling was slightly longer than the main road from Oberlin to Wellington, but it was infrequently used; it wound by a few isolated farms, dipping under, then rising over small hills along much of the way. Lowe figured that he could skirt Oberlin without being seen, wait for the 5:13 train at Wadsworth's Hotel in Wellington, and be safely in Columbus that night. It was only a matter of a day or so before John would be back in Kentucky.

*

Meanwhile, back in Oberlin, Shakespeare Boynton drove up to Wack's Hotel to tell Jennings what had happened. Pleased at the result, Jennings decided to give Shakespeare the full $20 he had promised for the capture of both John and Frank. After the teenager left, Jennings returned inside the hotel and, without any reason to rush, ate dinner, got his bags, and paid the hotel bill. He hired Wack's buggy and with "a boy"[11] whom Wack sent along to bring it back, Jennings set out for Wellington. He left Oberlin sometime about 1:00 P.M., going at such a leisurely pace that it took him an hour and a half to travel the distance, less than nine miles.

*

The diagonal road that the carriage carrying John was following intersected the main road to Wellington just south of Pittsfield, a little more than halfway between Oberlin and Wellington. There was a small cemetery about fifty yards south of the corner where the two roads met.[12] As the carriage rounded a sharp bend in the diagonal road just before the intersection, it was spotted by two young men who were passing the cemetery on their way home to Oberlin. The two young men knew each other but were not friends. One was Ansel W. Lyman, the son of an Oberlin farmer, a tall, bearded twenty-two-year-old student of English at Oberlin College. The other was Seth Bartholomew, returning home after posting the signs for his panorama show. Bartholomew had a reputation for being a liar and ne'er-do-well. Some ten years earlier, when he was about thirteen or fourteen years old, he took some money and "something else" from his employer. He had paid back the money and liked to explain, "I once stole half a cheese to keep from starving, and was put through for it."[13]

Up to now, John had passively resigned himself to his fate. He was being held by three men, had no weapon, and no chance for escape. But when he saw Lyman and Bartholomew, he saw his chance, and he suddenly made a bid for freedom. As the carriage turned onto the road to Wellington and passed by the two young men going in the opposite direction, John cried out for help.[14]

Neither Lyman nor Bartholomew budged. They didn't even acknowledge John's pleas. Bartholomew wouldn't have, anyway. He didn't like the black man. John, he thought, was "a *poor louzy pup.*"[15]

Lyman, however, was considered a fearless man. Perhaps the better part of valor led him to realize that he had no chance against the three white men with John Price, all of whom might be armed. The carriage with John still in it continued on its way, uninterrupted.

✳

That morning, Wellington was crowded with people. Farmers had come from miles around, drawn to the community by the billowing black smoke of a fire that had begun in a harness shop on the west side of Main Street opposite the dusty Public Square. A number of adjoining stores had burned down. Their ruins were still smoldering.

Many of the townspeople and farmers who had assembled to help put out the fire, or just to watch, were standing about, apparently waiting in the square for a trial scheduled to begin that afternoon in the local court at the Town Hall, a lawsuit over an assault case. They were idly talking and chatting as the carriage carrying John hove into view and pulled up in the Public Square.

Fronting on the square and set back from the east side of Main Street were Wadsworth's Hotel and, a few doors down, the Town Hall. Known also as the Wadsworth Tavern, the hotel, which was a short block and a half from the railroad station, had been erected about 1834 on the corner where Main crossed Mechanics Street. A rambling wooden building with some pretensions toward architectural elegance, it was a favorite stopping place for traveling salesmen and had a sample room where they could display their goods. The main entrance was three steps up off Main Street. A porch supported by white columns extended along the hotel's front. Above it, off second-floor rooms, was a similarly supported balcony with a low wood railing, also painted white. The peaked roof that rose from the center of the brick structure contained, among other rooms, an attic with a fan window. The windows of the rest of the hotel were tall and double-hung with painted shutters bracketing them. The hotel was actually three stories high. The building was on a rise in the ground and had a lower floor in back, where the kitchen, barroom, and dining room were located; a sloping pathway by the hotel's north side led to their entranceway and to several outbuildings—a feed barn where guests could leave their horses for the night, an icehouse, a woodshed, and a chicken coop. A garden in the rear supplied vegetables for the hotel's dining room.[16]

Lowe, Davis, and Mitchell entered the hotel with John. Lowe arranged for a room on the second floor, off the balcony, planning to wait there for the arrival of the 5:13 train to Columbus, but the three white men were so hungry that they soon went down to the barroom to eat, taking John with them. It was crowded, but no one paid them any attention. Lowe and the others were purposely behaving as though John was a traveling companion. It was, the Kentuckian Mitchell remarked, "the *first* time I ever eat with a nigger though."[17]

✳

Bartholomew and Lyman had continued on toward Oberlin, and a couple of miles farther on the road they encountered Wack's buggy with a man and a boy in it headed for Wellington at a leisurely pace. Bartholomew recognized the driver. It was the stranger, Jennings, whom he had seen that morning outside the hotel.

As the two young men approached Oberlin, Bartholomew suggested that neither he nor Lyman say anything to anyone about

John and the men in the carriage until the next day. He "wished," he said, that "they would take him off."[18] But "Anse" Lyman was a militant abolitionist.[19] He had served as a lieutenant in John Brown's army during the bloody warfare in Kansas two years earlier. He had no intention of keeping silent.

SIX

To the Rescue

In order to appreciate the sufferings of the negroes sold south, it must be remembered that all the instinctive affections of that race are peculiarly strong. Their local attachments are very abiding. They are not naturally daring and enterprising, but home-loving and affectionate. Add to this all the terrors with which ignorance invests the unknown, and add to this, again, that selling to the south is set before the negro from childhood as the last severity of punishment. The threat that terrifies more than whipping or torture of any kind is the threat of being sent down river. We have ourselves heard this feeling expressed by them, and seen the unaffected horror with which they will sit in their gossiping hours, and tell frightful stories of that "down river," which to them is

> *"That undiscovered country, from whose bourn*
> *No traveller returns."*

Chapter x: "The Property Is Carried Off"

Chauncey Wack was upset. A $10 bill that Anderson Jennings had paid his bill with looked counterfeit. Wack, however, was uncertain. There was no bank in Oberlin so he went to a dry-goods store on North Main to get the opinion of some "money judges."[1] Everyone he saw agreed that the bill did not look genuine, so Wack decided to follow Jennings to Wellington to try to get his money.

As Wack walked out of the store, there seemed to be some sort of disturbance off in the distance, in the middle of town. He caught up with three men whom he knew who were walking toward the center of town—Seth Bartholomew, Norris Wood, for whom John Price had worked in August, and master carpenter Marshal T. Gaston. Like Wack, they were all Democrats. Bartholomew had just put away his horse, and, although he had promised himself not to say a word, he told Gaston, a onetime neighbor on Mill Street, about what happened on the road to Wellington. Wood, who happened by on his way back to his livery stable after dinner, joined them and was also informed. Then Wack hailed the trio and was filled in, too. They all agreed to keep the news quiet, but as they approached the center of town, Bartholomew spotted Ansel Lyman talking and gesturing. The secret was obviously out.

Rescuer freeborn John A. Copeland, Jr., who later participated in John
Brown's attack on Harpers Ferry. Courtesy of Kansas State Historical Society

Lyman had "immediately aroused the people"[2] once he returned
to Oberlin, and now the streets, South Main in particular, were
becoming thronged with people. John Watson, who had been born
a slave in Virginia, burst out of his grocery and confectionery shop,

Rescuer freeborn Wilson Bruce Evans, Oberlin cabinetmaker, in later
life. Courtesy of Dorothy Inborden Miller

jumped into a wagon with another black man already in it, and,
flailing the reins, sped off down Main Street toward Wellington.

Excitement now engulfed the town. Clusters of people milled
around the front of three stores—Watson's shop; a harness and

trunk store owned by John H. Scott, who was also black; and a flour and feed establishment three rods away from Watson's run by Oberlin's mayor, A. N. Beecher. Outside one of them, a circle of men, black and white, surrounded Lyman, who was talking animatedly. Men were rushing up to join the circle, others breaking away and running toward livery stables.

At that point, Charles T. Marks, a butcher and also a Democrat, drew up with a horse and buggy beside where Bartholomew and his friends stood. Norris Wood hoisted himself into the buggy with Marks. Both men wondered what was going on in Wellington. Now that he thought about it, Wood recalled having seen a tall Southerner—Jennings, though he didn't know his name then—when he passed Wack's Hotel that morning.[3] Marks was about to drive off when Wack asked to hitch a ride with them. As they started out, about 1:00 P.M., the hotelkeeper noticed six black men inside a grocery store on the east side of North Main. They were loading guns "rapidly, others handing them paper for wadding." Wack thought he recognized one of the blacks: a runaway slave named Jeremiah (Jerry) Fox, who worked in Oberlin as a teamster.[4]

Not many people in town knew John Price, and fewer still were aware that he was a fugitive, but the fact he had been captured was enough to rouse virtually everyone who was against slavery. The news spread quickly: A black man had been seized in Oberlin by Southerners! The kidnappers were headed to Wellington!

Left by his friends, Bartholomew joined three men whose abolitionist ideas he did not share at all: Professor Henry E. Peck, lawyer Ralph Plumb, and bookstore proprietor James M. Fitch. Although uninvited, Bartholomew approached them as they were standing in the road at the corner of Main and College streets. One of the three suggested that they had better check whether John Price was indeed gone from where he lived. But Bartholomew said they "needn't be to that trouble" because he had seen John on the road to Wellington. The three men then walked toward Fitch's store nearby on East College Street, Bartholomew in their wake, tagging after them, he said, "for the purpose of telling them more."[5] As they reached the store, Fitch's clerk and brother-in-law, Simeon Bushnell, accosted them on the doorsill. Bushnell was short and "not physically strong," but he was feisty and easily aroused on the subject of slavery.[6] Was it true what he had just heard? Bushnell asked. Had a black man been kidnapped?

Several persons were in the bookstore when Bushnell and Peck entered it "greatly excited." Adelia A. Field, an Oberlin graduate who was the principal of a seminary in Tennessee, was visiting

Rescuer James M. Fitch, Sunday school superintendent. Courtesy of New York Public Library

her mother in nearby Rochester and had driven in a buggy with her to Fitch's store to buy some books.[7] She overheard Bushnell and Peck talking with Fitch about rescuing John. Adelia and her mother immediately went out, got into their buggy, and joined the now veritable crush of people heading for Wellington.

A man who was in the bookstore at the same time remembered

Rescuer Professor Henry E. Peck. Courtesy of Oberlin College Archives

that a "gentleman"—evidently Bushnell—"came rushing in, pale with excitement, and cried out, 'They have carried off one of our men in *broad daylight*, and are an hour on their way already!'

"'*They can't have him*!' we all screamed together and rushed into the street." Although a number of people raced to the several

Rescuer Ralph Plumb, Oberlin lawyer, in later life. Courtesy of New York
Public Library

livery stables in town to get horses, nearly all of them had already
been taken. Instead, many people "chartered" farmers' wagons,
private carriages, "and every hack in town." Within fifteen minutes, the man said, "the square was alive with students and citizens armed with weapons of death."[8]

Some of those who could not get a vehicle requisitioned one.
Several persons approached a wagon and inquired whose it was.
When its owner said, "What's up?" he was told, "Why, a man has
been kidnapped and we want to go after him," and, saying so, they
commandeered the vehicle and left for Wellington.[9]

Artemas Halbert, a seventeen-year-old housepainter, heard that "Southerners had kidnapped the negro, contrary to all law" while he was standing in front of Watson's store, where Lyman was repeating his story. He saw Bushnell talking with Orindatus S. B. Wall, a black shoemaker and store proprietor, about getting a horse to go to Wellington. Wall said they shouldn't go without a gun. Bushnell replied that he knew where he could get one. Halbert, who had a gun himself, hung around the store for some time before leaving for Wellington.[10] Others already on their way included the Bartletts, father and son. James H. Bartlett was an English-born cobbler who worked for a shoemaker named Royce; his son and namesake was a cobbler, too.

Lysander S. Butler did a sensible thing. Butler, who was reading law with Ralph Plumb and his brother Samuel, simply hopped aboard the regularly scheduled stagecoach to Wellington.

Although his store on South Main had become a rallying point, John Scott was unaware of what was happening. He was at First Church attending a prayer meeting. Suddenly, Lewis Sheridan Leary appeared. Scott, who was from North Carolina, had once been bound as an apprentice to Leary's father, a freeborn harnessmaker. Now young Leary worked for Scott as a harnessmaker. "Shurd" was "all excited."[11] He told Scott about John Price's capture. "We'll get him," Scott said. He went across the street and borrowed a "swift mare" from the widow of Oliver P. Ryder, who had operated a livery stable.[12] "If necessary," Mrs. Ryder told Scott, "spare not the life of my beast, but rescue the boy."[13] Scott was able to obtain a buggy, then returned to his store on South Main, where he quickly retrieved three rifles.

Scott was about to drive off with another black man, Andrew Jackson Chesnutt, when Richard Winsor rushed up to them. Minutes before, Winsor, a junior in Oberlin College's Preparatory Department and John Price's teacher in the Sunday school on East College Street, heard the commotion in the center of town and told a friend, "I must see what the matter is." When he learned that John had been seized, Winsor raced about, trying to find room in a vehicle. The English-born young man—he was four days shy of his twenty-third birthday—had a horrific memory of what being a slave meant: Nearly four years earlier, he was in Boston and witnessed the rendition of Anthony Burns. "State Street," to him, "became a Roman altar."[14]

Spotting Scott and Chesnutt, Winsor jumped into the buggy, saying, "I go with you." He reached for the three rifles Scott had brought along, and as he held them in an outstretched hand, the

Rescuer former slave John H. Scott and his wife, Cecilia, with two of their children. Courtesy of Oberlin College Archives

Rescuer William D. Scrimgeour, Oberlin student. Courtesy of Oberlin College Archives

buggy took off through the crowded street. Winsor doffed his hat with his other hand and, waving both the rifles and the hat, shouted, "I am going to rescue John Price."[15] He was greeted with answering cheers as Scott goaded the mare on. The buggy was soon passing the other vehicles.

Rescuer Jacob R. Shipherd, Oberlin student. Courtesy of Oberlin College Archives

The news of John's capture spread rapidly among Oberlin's black residents, and they rushed to join the exodus. Henry and Wilson Bruce Evans, brothers who were married to Lewis Sheridan Leary's sisters—and were so light-skinned they could be taken for whites—left their cabinetmaking store on South Main Street. Henry, who was armed with a small rifle, didn't think John was "wuth shucks,"[16] but he was enraged at the seizure of the black man. Leary was on the way, too.[17] The Evanses' nephew John A. Copeland, Jr., a carpenter and a special friend to runaway slaves, was rushing to Wellington, as were three escaped slaves who made their home in Oberlin—Thomas Gena, John Hartwell, and Jerry Fox. So, too, was Orindatus S. B. Wall; the husky shoe merchant, whose sister Caroline was married to John Mercer Langston, left in a buggy with "Sim" Bushnell.[18] Charles H. Langston, who was visiting at his brother John Mercer's home, also went, a pistol tucked inside his coat. John Watson's troublesome son William followed his father. David Watson—no relation—a farmer, former Oberlin preparatory student, and onetime partner of Orindatus Wall in a boot shop on East College Street, was on his way as well.

The campus was now astir, too. William Lincoln was in his room on the top floor of Tappan Hall when he heard "sharp, shrill cries" and "trampling" from the wooden walks below, but he ignored the noise.[19] The Englishman was about to return to work on a lesson he was preparing when there was a "hurried tap" at his door. Lincoln opened it. In the hallway were some young students, one of whom was brandishing a rifle that the dormitory manager[20] had sent with the "request" that Lincoln "go & rescue a slave, who had been kidnapped." The request made Lincoln feel "up slump." He asked the students to wait outside his room for a moment. Closing the door on them, he took his Bible and knelt by the bed.

Lincoln was a troubled young man. Perhaps because of his earlier bout with consumption, he was subject to fits of doubt and depression. The past two years since his first trip to Kentucky had been difficult ones. In debt, he lived on the edge of poverty, and, in spite of his experience as an itinerant preacher and teacher, he was uncertain about what to do with his life. He vacillated between wanting to teach, wanting to preach, and wanting to become a missionary in Africa. The young Englishman had come to Oberlin because of Charles Finney, whom he heard preach in London many years before. Lincoln became a devoted disciple of Finney's, promoted the revivalist's meetings in London, and then followed Finney back to Oberlin. But disciple and master were now at loggerheads, and Lincoln felt "publicly disgraced." Lincoln was sure that he had incurred Finney's displeasure because he embarrassed him by pointing out in class some minor mistake Finney had made in a theology book. The other students in the class had laughed at Lincoln. Finney dismissed the incident, saying "Pshaw," but the revivalist threatened nevertheless to write the American Mission-

Rescuer Richard Winsor, Oberlin student. Courtesy of Oberlin College Archives

ary Association—to say, Lincoln was certain, that he "knew very very little of theology," that he could "not be relied on" and was "not the man" to take on an assignment in a neighboring state if

the association "could get anybody else." Lincoln needed some
sign to restore his self-confidence. The previous fall, when his
handwriting became almost illegible, his letters incoherent at
times, and he seemed on the verge of a nervous breakdown, the
Oberlin faculty refused to ordain him or to participate in his or-
dination. Their rejection inspired him to "be the first scholar in
my class," but Lincoln sometimes complained, "Oh my head tonight. It is swimming God preserve my health."

Kneeling by his bed, Lincoln asked for God's guidance. What
should he do? After all, he was a pacifist, a "non-resistant," as he
put it. The answer came quickly: "If it were your own brother,
what would you do? The answer: Rescue him or die in the attempt.
Is not this poor negro your brother? Yes, Lord."

Lincoln went back to the door, opened it, took the rifle, and ran
down the stairs and across the campus to the Historic Elm on the
corner of Main and College streets. He jostled his way to a light
wagon drawn by two horses that was surrounded by armed men,
both white and black. Lincoln grabbed a seat in the wagon and,
with eight others who crowded onto it, "off we started on the
gallop." Lincoln was convinced that John's rescue was in his
hands, that "in some way, I know not how, that leadership was
quietly given to me." And he meant to exercise it.

Lincoln seemed to be the only student who hesitated about racing to John Price's rescue. A nephew of Oberlin's cofounder,
twenty-two-year-old Jacob R. Shipherd, a seminary preparatory
student although already an ordained Congregational minister,
was one of the many young men who rushed to Wellington. Another was Edward G. Sackett, a junior prep. Ione Munger remembered being in Professor James Monroe's rhetorical class, which
fourth-year students of the Young Ladies' Course shared with college seniors, when first one male student, then another, then yet
another left the classroom, "till finally all including the Professor
had gone." The women followed to see what was the "occasion of
such a stampede." Off in the distance, toward the town's business
section, they saw "wagons filled with men, who were armed with
muskets and fire-arms of all sorts and kinds," many of which
looked so rusty and old that they "would probably have injured
the man at the firing end of the gun, as much as the one at the
other end."[21]

John G. W. Cowles, now a senior in the Theological Department,
was at home, on the northwest corner of Professor and Lorain
streets, when after dinner, about 2:00 P.M., two student friends of
his—the hot-blooded Scotsman William D. Scrimgeour and a fel-

Unsung hero John G. W. Cowles, Oberlin student. Courtesy of Oberlin College Archives

low senior, James L. Patton—appeared at his room "in haste" with the news that "a boy had been kidnapped."[22] They asked Cowles to get his horse and go in pursuit. It took Cowles five minutes to harness the horse and, once done, he was off. There was still a crowd in front of Watson's store on South Main Street as he swept

Unsung hero Professor James H. Fairchild. Courtesy of Oberlin College Archives

by. Scrimgeour and Patton, meanwhile, set out to find other means of transportation.

About that time, G. Frederick Wright, a frail twenty-year-old college senior who weighed only 120 pounds, "was snugly en-

Unsung hero James L. Patton, Oberlin student. Courtesy of Oberlin College Archives

sconced" with two others in a buggy. They were just passing the tiny brick Episcopal church on South Main when Patton ran up and stopped the buggy. "Fred," the robust Patton[23] said to Wright, "what are you going to Wellington for? You are too small to do

anything." Patton told Wright to "get out and let me get in."
Wright did, and Patton took his place.[24]

Not everyone could find room in a cart, wagon, buggy, or carriage. Some people had to walk. One was A. B. Nettleton, a nine-
teen-year-old student, who "carried a big stick to Wellington."[25]
Another Oberlin student, Edward C. Kinney, who first heard the
news of the kidnapping as he was on his way to recitation class,
also started out on foot.

It seemed as though every male in Oberlin, white and black, was
racing to Wellington, all but a handful—some Democrats went
out of curiosity—intent on saving John Price. There were, however, some men who did not go: Professor James Monroe for one,
and three men who would become conspicuous by their absence—
Henry Peck, Ralph Plumb, and James Fitch.

*

The road from Oberlin to Wellington is almost flat and nearly
arrow-straight except for a few gentle curves just south of Oberlin
and farther on where the West Branch of the Black River crosses
it near Wellington. It cuts through land so perfect for grazing that
the area would within a decade be called the "Cheese Empire of
the nation."[26] Except for the small community of Pittsfield, equi-
distant from Oberlin and Wellington, the road in the late 1850s
ran through a sparsely settled area, with only a farm here or there
along its edges. Ordinarily, it was a moderately trafficked road, but
now it must have seemed as though all of Oberlin was on it. And
so many people were egging on their horses and driving so swiftly
that mishaps were bound to happen.

The wagon carrying William Lincoln lost an iron tire from a
front wheel about a mile below Oberlin. Everyone got out and
began pulling the wagon along by hand until they came into the
yard of a farm. They found a wagon almost identical to their own
there, but it was owned by a Democrat who didn't want to loan
it "to save a d——d nigger." Though offered "full remuneration"
for it, the farmer remained adamant: "Let the nigger be taken. It's
the law." Afraid to waste more time haggling, Lincoln and his
companions took the wagon despite the farmer's objections, leaving theirs in its stead and promising "to make all square" eventually. Their two horses were quickly hitched to the good wagon
and within a matter of minutes they resumed their chase, kicking
up "dust galore in our wake."[27]

The passengers in another wagon, which lost a wheel a few miles farther along, were able to fix it themselves within ten minutes and "pressed on hard." Passing through Pittsfield, they "hallooed" to a group of men standing outside a store, urging them to join in the pursuit, but one of them replied, "We're all Democrats here!" The wagon continued on and was within two miles of Wellington when a young man came "driving furiously" in the opposite direction. He urged the wagon "to push on with all possible haste, as the rascals were already overtaken and surrounded."[28]

John Cowles, who was on horseback and able to pass several overloaded wagons and carts, met a horseman coming from Wellington with the same urgent message. The horseman continued on to Oberlin: More men were needed in Wellington.

SEVEN

The Rescue

Marks had got from his pocket a greasy pocket-book, and taking a long paper from thence, he sat down, and fixing his keen black eyes on it, began mumbling over its contents: "Barnes,—Shelby county,—boy Jim, three hundred dollars for him, dead or alive.

"Edwards,—Dick and Lucy,—man and wife, six hundred dollars; wench Polly and two children,—six hundred for her or her head. . . ."

"I suppose you've got good dogs," said Haley.

". . . Dogs is no 'count in these yer up states where these critturs gets carried; of course, ye can't get on their track. They only does down in plantations, where niggers, when they runs, has to do their own running, and don't get no help."

. . . If any of our refined and Christian readers object to the society into which this scene introduces them, let us beg them to begin and conquer their prejudices in time. The catching business, we beg to remind them, is rising to the dignity of a lawful and patriotic profession. . . . The trader and catcher may yet be among our aristocracy.

Chapter VIII: "Eliza's Escape"

Deputy Marshal Lowe jumped up from the dinner table to see what the matter was. Someone was making a ruckus in the Public Square. Leaving the table where he and the others were eating, Lowe looked out the door of the hotel's barroom and saw John Watson shouting and gesturing. Lowe didn't know who Watson was and couldn't quite make out what he was saying, but he saw that Watson and another black man in his wagon had guns.[1]

Edgy and suspicious, Lowe returned to the table. Within minutes, the hotelkeeper's wife, Alma Wadsworth, approached. She said that the hallway "was pretty full of people that seemed to be excited."[2] She offered to lead Lowe and his companions to their second-floor room by a back stairway. Mitchell and Davis left immediately with John, while Lowe stayed behind in the barroom, on the lookout for Jennings.

Watson had reached Wellington in less than forty-five minutes, pulling up in the Public Square sometime about 2:00 P.M. Without wasting any time, he ran into the Town Hall to get a warrant to block John's captors.

Watson had driven past Jennings on the road to Wellington without realizing who the Kentuckian was. Jennings, who had no reason to hurry, did not reach the town until about thirty minutes
later. Unaware of any problem, Jennings tarried several minutes
in the Public Square, talking to a man, before he entered the hotel.
But as soon as Lowe filled him in on the situation, Jennings rushed
upstairs to the second-floor room where John was being held. For
the first time since stopping off in Oberlin nearly a week ago,
Jennings saw John. They recognized each other immediately. John
called Jennings by his name. The two men—the fugitive slave and
the Kentuckian—shook hands.

Outside, more and more wagons, carts, and buggies were arriving
in the Public Square, their drivers reining in their horses in front
of the hotel. Out of the vehicles spilled a growing number of angry
whites and blacks. They swelled the crowd of townspeople and
farmers who were already in the square because of the fire that
morning. Wagons and carts were now arriving as well on side roads
from nearby communities—Rochester, Huntington, Spencer, Sullivan, Litchfield. "The leaves of the forest seemed to carry the
news," said an eyewitness.[3]

By the time one wagon reached Wellington, the Public Square
was so crowded that those aboard it had to alight "a little outside,
and forming in order marched up with arms in sight." The crowd
greeted the newcomers with "great cheering," as they did everyone
else who arrived.[4]

"Hundreds of ladies," another eyewitness said, "crowded the
sidewalks, the stores, all adjacent windows, and the nearest roofs."[5]
One of the youngest was ten-year-old Mary Tripp, who was playing
in a third-floor storage room in her father's buggy factory across
from Wadsworth's Hotel when she heard "a great commotion."[6]
Looking down into the Public Square, she saw a large crowd gathering and a man she mistakenly took to be a federal marshal brandishing two revolvers.

As Adelia A. Field drove up in the buggy with her mother, a
woman burst into the street. "What are we coming to?" she cried
out. "A fire in the morning and war at night."[7]

✳

The events of the next few hours occurred so swiftly one after
another, that no one remembered with any certainty what happened when. The Public Square was filled with a leaderless mob.
A group of black men was gathered in one part of the square, a

group of white men in another, a group of both whites and blacks in yet another part. The few Oberlin Democrats who went to Wellington out of curiosity—Norris Wood and Charles Marks, in particular—mingled with the group of white men. Rumors swept across the square, passed from one group to another. Everywhere, men were milling about, calling out to friends, waving weapons, waiting for someone to tell them what to do. In the confusion, a few persons were trying to calm the excited crowd, but they were outnumbered and outshouted by others who wanted to storm the hotel. It became increasingly clear that many in the crowd did not know that John Price was an escaped slave and that there was a power of attorney and a federal warrant outstanding for his capture. As the afternoon progressed, it was uncertain who saw either or both documents or to whom they were read.[8]

In truth, the angry rescuers did not care if John was free or slave. They simply determined that he not be taken away. By well past 3:00 P.M., anywhere from two hundred to five hundred men surrounded Wadsworth's Hotel—the estimate varies from eyewitness to eyewitness. There was a growing tension in the air, spurred in large part by a rumor that spread quickly through the crowd: The federal law enforcement officers had wired for troops. The Cleveland Grays, a state militia unit that ordinarily drilled on Mondays, was reportedly on its way, due on the 5:13 train. Everyone seemed to shout at once: *"Bring him out!" "Bring out the man!" "Out with him!" "Out!" "Out!" "Out!"*[9] A confrontation seemed unavoidable.

✳

Inside the hotel, the first of a series of peculiar and sometimes bewildering incidents occurred. Despite the attempt of John's captors to seal themselves off, many persons were able to get into the room where he was held, some apparently by feigning support for the slave hunters, others by offering to work out a settlement between the two sides. The first to gain entry was Jacob Wheeler, a farmer and the Democratic postmaster of Rochester, who had, considering all the turmoil, a ludicrous request.

Wheeler, who had come to town that morning to watch the fire, heard that two of the persons holding John in the hotel were from Kentucky. It just so happened that Wheeler had a stepbrother living in that state. Wheeler went up to the innkeeper, Oliver Wadsworth, and asked him to pass along a message to them. Wheeler wondered if the Kentuckians knew his stepbrother.

Wadsworth had by this time closed off the hotel and stationed
employees and friends at its entrances and on the stairways. As a
precaution, Jennings had moved John to an attic room on the topmost landing that was reached by a crude eight-step wooden staircase that looked like a ladder. The room was the only one in the
attic that had a window, the small fan-shaped one that could be
seen from the Public Square. Wadsworth went up and spoke to
Jennings and Mitchell and soon Wheeler was summoned to the
attic room. Mitchell, indeed, did know his stepbrother, but he was
amazed that Wheeler and the stepbrother "had the same father."
Their "Complexions ain't much alike," he noted.[10] When Wheeler
learned that Mitchell knew his relative, he sent word back outside
the hotel for his brothers John, Edward, and Conrad to join him in
the attic room to hear the family news. Incredibly, Wheeler intended to hold an informal family get-together despite the tumult
outside in the Public Square.

＊

John Watson showed up at the Town Hall to get a warrant for
the arrest of John's captors just as the proceedings in that afternoon's lawsuit were ending. He vouched that John Price was a
"freeman."[11] Although he had no idea who John's captors were,
Watson was able to obtain a warrant charging them with kidnapping. Fictitious names were used in the document to identify
them. Joseph H. Dickson, a former Lorain County district attorney
who happened to be in the courtroom, drew up the affidavit upon
which the warrant was made out. Justice of the Peace Isaac Bennett
issued the warrant and handed it to Wellington's constable, Barnabas Meacham, to serve.

＊

While he was waiting for his brothers to appear in the attic room,
Wheeler asked Lowe if he could speak to John. The deputy marshal
had no objection so the farmer "catechized" the fugitive slave. He
asked John whether Bacon had ever abused him, and John's hesitation in responding led Wheeler to understand that "he was
abused sometimes." Had Bacon "ever used him worse than some
white folks punish their children[?]" John said he "didn't know as
he did." John told Wheeler he was willing to go "anywhere" with
Mitchell. Why Mitchell? he was asked. John said he "knew" that
if he went with Mitchell he "would get to see his massa John and
his old mistress." Didn't he want to see his mother, too? one of

the Kentuckians asked. Yes, he did, John said, but, surprisingly, he added that he "would *much rather see his old mistress!*"[12]

Suddenly there was a knock on the door. Constable Meacham appeared with John Watson. The constable told Lowe that he had a warrant and began to read it to him, but Lowe interrupted him. The constable, he said, had no authority to arrest him or any of the others, and with that, Lowe showed Meacham his federal warrant. The deputy marshal warned the constable that he would be legally and financially liable if John "was lost."[13] Confused by the turn of events, Meacham went back to the town hall to seek the advice of Justice of the Peace Bennett. During the interchange, Jennings reclined on the bed in the room, following the conversation but not saying anything or identifying himself.

Within a short while, several other persons were able to get upstairs to the attic room. They were all from Wellington and had apparently convinced innkeeper Wadsworth that they were trying to help him. Among them were William Sciples, Walter Soules, John Mandeville, and a man who wore his hair unusually long, Chapin S. Fay. Invoking the Fugitive Slave Law, Lowe asked everyone in the room to assist him in carrying out his duties. Sciples, who had been in the courtroom when Watson took out the warrant, complied, running errands for the deputy marshal. Fay went downstairs to help guard the stairway. Soules went downstairs, too, but he left the hotel without any intention of helping the federal agents. Mandeville, who was drunk, took matters into his own hands. He began to shout taunts to the crowd from the tiny window of the attic room, hollering that "they was d——d cowards and fools." Jennings thought Mandeville was "purty reckless." Everyone told Mandeville to "hush," but nobody seemed able to control him.[14]

While this commotion was going on, Wheeler spoke to John once more, then went over to Lowe and suggested to the deputy marshal that John be allowed to talk to the crowd outside from the second-floor balcony. Wheeler assured Lowe that John would indicate his willingness to return to Kentucky. The slave had told him that "he s'posed accordin' to the laws of the country, he was obleeged to go back."[15]

It was evident by now that the Kentuckians as well as the federal marshals wanted to prevent violence. They were badly outnumbered. Lowe had indeed wired for aid from Cleveland, evidently sending the urgent appeal by messenger to the telegraph office at the passenger depot. But there was no guarantee that troops or law enforcement personnel would be on the 5:13 train. Several of the

Scene of the Rescue, Wadsworth's Hotel, after being renamed the
American House. John Price spoke to the excited crowd in the Public
Square from the balcony over the front door. He was rescued from an
attic room whose fantail window can be seen directly above the
balcony. Courtesy of Spirit of '76 Museum, Wellington

men agreed with Wheeler that John should talk to the crowd. It
might calm them down.

Jennings, Mitchell, and Lowe led John down to the second floor.
Lowe's assistant, Samuel Davis, brought up the rear, though he
seemed more and more reluctant to take part. Jennings went out
the hallway door that led to the balcony above the entrance to the
hotel. The Public Square was bristling with guns.

The Kentuckian tried to placate the crowd. "I want no controversy with the people of Ohio," he began. "This boy is mine by
the laws of Kentucky and of the United States."

"You dry up," someone in the crowd shouted back, "there are
no slaves in Ohio and never will be north of the Ohio river."

"The boy is willing to go to Kentucky," Jennings insisted.

"Let him come out and speak for himself."[16]

Jennings turned and got John. The Kentuckian said that anyone
could ask the slave whatever they wanted. Did John want to go
back to Kentucky? a man asked. Docile, and undoubtedly afraid
to anger his captors, John answered that he "supposed" he would
have to return, that "they had got the papers for him." Several

Side view of Wadsworth's Hotel showing the side alley to the lower floor of the building, where the barroom, dining room, and kitchen were situated. Courtesy of Oberlin College Archives

other men spoke up. Was he a slave? John said he was. He was "going home"; his master "had sent for him."[17]

"I s'pose I've got to go back to Kentucky," he added.

"If you want to go to Kentucky you can go," said Walter Soules, who had left the attic room to join the crowd, "if you do not want to go all hell can't get you there. Had you not rather go to Canada?"[18]

Before John could answer, John Copeland of Oberlin raised a gun and told John to jump while he shot "the damned old rascal," Jennings.[19] Hastily, the Kentuckian drew back, pulling John from the balcony with Davis's help and retreating inside the hotel as shouts of "Jump!"—"Jump down!"—"Jump off!" rang through the air.

Together with Mitchell and Lowe, they all raced back upstairs to the attic room. The crowd, it seemed, was in no mood for compromise.

✳

As John was pulled from the balcony, Charles S. Griffin, a noted antislavery lecturer from Medina, drove up to the Public Square in a carriage. Seeing two Wellington citizens whom he knew, he stopped and inquired what was the matter. When told, he asked, "Why don't you get that slave away from his master?" The two men said they were afraid of running afoul of the Fugitive Slave Law.

"Pay no attention to the laws," said Griffin.

Encouraged by Griffin's offhand manner about the fugitive law, one of the men hailed a youngster and gave him ten cents to fetch a ladder that would reach the attic window of the hotel. When the youth returned with it, Griffin himself climbed to the topmost rung and called out to John to come down and go to Canada. He warned John's captors, "Don't you stir."[20]

✳

Constable Meacham was now elbowing his way through the dense mass of people churning outside the hotel. He was searching for Bennett but could not find him. Worried that he might get into difficulty with the federal government, Meacham was uncertain what to do next. Several persons in the crowd, including John Mercer Langston's brother Charles, told him it was his duty to serve the warrant against the kidnappers, but Meacham hesitated.

Meanwhile, John Watson was able to get onto the hotel balcony.

He hoped to quiet the crowd. He told them "to wait," that "as soon as they could have the men arrested, it would all be right."[21]

Unable to find Justice of the Peace Bennett, Constable Meacham returned inside the hotel and approached Lowe with an idea to resolve the dilemma. Would Lowe go with him to the Town Hall to straighten out the matter? Lowe didn't want to leave the hotel but said he would see Bennett if he came to the hotel. Meacham hurried out to look for him again, and this time he found him. The constable and the justice of the peace went up to the attic room to meet Lowe. The deputy marshal promised that he would take his papers to the town hall for everyone in authority to study if Bennett could get the crowd outside to "fall back."[22] Otherwise, he had no intention of bucking the hostile crowd.

Bennett now went down to the second floor and out onto the balcony. He called to the crowd to give him a minute to speak, but before he could say another word, a black man shouted, "Bring down the man. We'll have the man." At the same time, the man pointed a gun at Bennett. Bennett was carrying a pistol himself, but he didn't have time to take it out. Instead, he was wrestling with a ladder that Oberlin Democrats Charles Marks and Norris Wood had thrown up against the side of the building "to see the fun." Wood may have been tipsy. He had been to a local saloon, ostensibly to buy some cigars.[23] Wood started up the ladder. Bennett at last drew his pistol, pointed it down at Wood, and cocked it. Marks quickly pulled his friend back.

Unable to quiet the crowd, Bennett left the hotel, though first Lowe showed him the federal warrant and the power of attorney. Outside, the justice of the peace encountered Charles Langston and told him that he had been shown papers. He hadn't read them, he said, but as far as he knew they seemed legal, though he noticed one of them lacked a seal.

Langston could now be seen everywhere in the square and beside the hotel—by the entrance, in the side alley, on a platform south of the building. He was moving from one group of men to another, trying to calm them down, to keep their excitement in check, hoping to prevent violence. Langston knew all too well how easily an unruly mob can turn violent. Ten years earlier, while repeal of Ohio's Black Laws was being debated, the schoolteacher went to deliver a lecture in the tiny village of Marseilles in north-central Ohio. A group of young white ruffians broke up the lecture and forced Langston and a companion who sold subscriptions to Frederick Douglass's *North Star* to hole up in the local hotel. Shouting "Burn them alive—kill the niggers," the ruffians started a bonfire outside the hotel and argued whether to lynch the two black men or sell them in the South. Langston and his friend were able to steal away at dawn while guards around the hotel slept.[24]

Determined to prevent the situation in Wellington from getting out of hand, Langston believed that the best course was to follow legal measures. The constable, Meacham, should serve the warrant; he was obligated to do so. Oberlin student James Patton, who was also trying to pacify the crowd, agreed, but said that if Meacham refused to serve the warrant maybe someone should ride to Elyria, ten miles away, to get a writ of habeas corpus. Langston said he would go if he could get a horse and buggy. Oberlin law student Lysander Butler went up to Norris Wood and asked to borrow his, but Wood pointed out that he had come in Charles Marks's buggy. Butler then asked Marks, but the Oberlin butcher turned him down.

*

Meacham, the harried constable, was, meanwhile, being pressured as well by some Wellington residents to serve the kidnapping papers on John's captors. Three of them who had helped put out the fire that morning—Matthew DeWolf, Abner Loveland, and Loring Wadsworth—urged him to execute the warrant. As confused as ever, Meacham ran into Joseph Dickson, who had helped to draw up the warrant, and asked for his help. Dickson went into a drugstore next door to the hotel and got a form for an indemnification bond. If the constable were to do his duty and be sued, the signers of the bond were pledged to underwrite the damages. Dickson, however, said that he would not sign the bond himself, nor would he recommend that others do so. In fact, he advised Meacham not to serve the warrant at all. DeWolf circulated the indemnity bond but could only get a few people to sign it.

Still trying to resolve matters, Meacham persuaded Dickson to speak to John's captors. As they were allowed into the hotel, Oberlin student Richard Winsor and his school tutor, William Scrimgeour, approached the constable and asked to join him. Meacham agreed to take Scrimgeour along but refused to let Winsor go because he was carrying a rifle. Stuck outside but determined to get into the hotel, Winsor brashly informed the men guarding the front door that he had authority to enter. When Winsor was told that he couldn't bring a weapon in with him, he handed over the rifle. As the guards broke it over a brick wall, Winsor made his way upstairs to the garret.

Once upstairs in the attic room, Scrimgeour and Winsor stood by quietly, assessing the situation. First, Lowe showed Dickson the federal warrant. Dickson sat down on the bed to read it. He pointed out to Lowe that it lacked a seal, but the deputy marshal replied that it was not customary for a warrant to have one. Although he was a former prosecuting attorney, Dickson acknowledged that he was not acquainted with such papers, and then he did a strange thing. He turned abruptly to Jennings, whom he thought was John's owner, and asked him what he "would take for the negro." The Kentuckian said $1,400. Jennings's compatriot, Mitchell, then said Jennings had "better take twelve hundred dollars if he could get it." As abruptly as Dickson made the offer, he dropped it. Nothing further was said about buying John, and neither of the Kentuckians indicated that they had the authority to sell John or showed Dickson any power of attorney. Lowe suggested that the two Kentuckians hire Dickson to represent them in any litigation that might follow as the result of John's seizure, but Dickson squelched the idea. He left, returning outside by the back door to the "promiscuous crowd."[25]

Scrimgeour and Winsor, who had picked up and read the federal warrant while Dickson was talking to Lowe and the Kentuckians, stayed in the room. They hadn't said a word.

✳

Old Matthew Gillet had a simple solution. Gillet, a white-haired Wellington farmer in his early seventies who was fondly called "Father" Gillet, went up to Oliver Wadsworth in the hotel backyard and urged the innkeeper to open the building and let the crowd rescue John. But Wadsworth—"a faithful Buchaneer"[26]—didn't like the idea of having his hotel "ransacked by a mob." Gillet then suggested that a committee of perhaps ten or twenty men be allowed in to confer with John's captors "peaceably, and see what could be done in a proper manner." Wadsworth had no objection.[27]

✳

Looking out the attic window, trying to assess the crowd's state of mind, Lowe spotted Charles Langston in front of the hotel. The deputy marshal knew him from Columbus; Langston was, in Lowe's words, "a reasonable man."[28] Lowe asked John Watson to bring Langston to the attic room.

When Langston appeared, Lowe explained to him about the papers the captors held and offered to have a committee accompany him to Columbus for a hearing before a federal commissioner. After reading the federal warrant, Langston said he was satisfied that John was being held legally. He said that he would go down to the crowd and present Lowe's offer, though he expressed doubts whether the crowd would agree to it.

Before leaving the room, Langston said either "*We* will have him any how" or "*They* will have him any how"—a choice of pronouns that would be disputed later.

✳

Running one of his errands, William Sciples found Justice of the Peace William Howk and asked him to come to the hotel. Howk had been in the courtroom at Isaac Bennett's request, sitting with his fellow justice of the peace during the lawsuit earlier in the day, when John Watson came in to get the kidnapping warrant. Although he was suffering from a bad cold and could barely speak, Howk went with Sciples to the attic room. It was now late afternoon and the sunlight that filtered through the hotel windows was dimming. Lowe took Howk aside at the head of the stairway to show him a paper. But Howk could barely make it out; besides, he had forgotten to bring his eyeglasses from the courtroom. He made out the word "Columbus" on the paper, but he could not tell whether it was handwritten or printed. He handed the paper back to Lowe, who then offered, as he had to Langston, "If a half dozen or so of your men will go with me to Columbus, and this thing isn't a straightforward thing, I'll let the boy come back." Howk, however, didn't want to get involved. He said that he "wanted nothing of the boy"[29] and returned downstairs. As he left the hotel, he bumped into Bennett, who told him that he had read the papers and they seemed legal. But Howk didn't bother to tell anyone what Bennett said. His throat hurt too much to talk.

✳

The crowd in front of the hotel was growing increasingly restless as the time for the arrival of the 5:13 train from Cleveland drew close. It was obvious that they would have to act soon if they were going to storm the hotel and rescue John Price. But no one seemed in control or tried to issue any orders.

Just then, William Lincoln arrived in the Public Square. Despite the breakdown of his wagon and the time it took to exchange it for another, Lincoln had reached Wellington in only three-quarters of an hour.[30] He quickly learned that everyone was worried that troops were aboard the 5:13 train. Eager for action and ready to assume leadership, Lincoln was all for rushing the hotel. But someone told him that an Oberlin student named James Patton was making still one more attempt to get John Price "by a palaver."

Patton's efforts threw Lincoln's plan "out of gear."[31] Though ordinarily rash and impatient, he decided he had better wait to see what would happen.

*

Patton had gone to the hotel's back door and asked Wadsworth if he could see the marshal. The innkeeper refused at first, but Patton pressured him and he relented. Patton was led up to the garret. Outside the attic room, Wadsworth knocked on the door, and Lowe, who also knew Patton from Columbus, came out. Taking Patton by the arm, Lowe led the young student into a little room next door and informed him that he had sent for aid from Cleveland. He showed Patton the federal warrant, which Patton glanced at but did not read thoroughly; he evidently took Lowe's word that the document was valid. Lowe asked Patton to tell the crowd outside that he was legally empowered to arrest John and "must" take him to Columbus. Then the deputy marshal repeated his earlier proposition: let the crowd choose a committee to accompany him there to see that John "had a fair trial." Lowe even offered to read the warrant to the crowd if Patton would accompany him outside; he was "afraid" to go alone. Patton agreed to do so.

Before they went downstairs, Patton confronted Jennings. Because the door had no handle or bolt, the Kentuckian was standing by it, holding onto a rope that kept the door pulled shut. Did *"the boy"* belong to him? Patton asked. Jennings replied that he did so Patton assumed that Jennings was John Bacon.[32]

As Jennings relaxed his hold on the rope so that Patton and Lowe could leave, two unidentified men, one of whom wore spectacles, appeared and asked to enter. For some reason, Jennings allowed them in. One of the two strangers must have brandished what looked like a legal document. The two men took hold of John and started to lead him to the door. All of a sudden aroused, Jennings asked what they were doing. They said they were leaving. "Not with that nigger," the Kentuckian said. He turned the two men around and pushed them out the door, telling them that "papers or no papers they could not take the nigger out o' that room."[33]

*

With Constable Meacham along for added protection, Patton and Lowe made their way downstairs, left the hotel by the back door, and walked into the square by circling the south side of the building. There, the two men mounted the steps of the neighboring drugstore, where they could see over the heads of the restive horde of people.

The appearance of Patton and the deputy marshal drew a small throng of men, but most of the people in the square did not notice them. Lowe tried to draw the attention of the crowd by reading the warrant, but his voice was so soft that he could hardly be heard. Patton took the paper from him and began reading it to the crowd, but even though he spoke loudly he was drowned out by the noise and excitement in the square. Most people could not hear him. Besides, spoke up the antislavery lecturer Charles Griffin, it was immaterial whether anyone heard what was read. "The crowd," Griffin declared, "care nothing for papers; they will have the nigger anyhow."[34]

Just then, cries rang out. Looking toward the hotel, Patton and Lowe saw a rush of men pressing against the front door. Obviously angered that "advantage had been taken of his absence," Lowe caught Patton by the arm, and the two men quickly retraced their steps around the back of the hotel.[35] Griffin, who Patton took to be a friend of Lowe's, joined them.

The three men got into the hotel by the back door and made their way up the stairway to the second floor without any difficulty but found some men gathered by the ladder to the attic. It had gotten so dark inside the hotel that Lowe "couldn't tell a white man from a black."[36] The three men pressed ahead, crowding into the attic room.

*

Chauncey Wack was relieved. The $10 bill Jennings had given him that morning turned out to be genuine. Satisfied, Wack decided to stay in Wellington to watch the goings-on at the hotel, moving about the Public Square all afternoon much as Charles Langston was doing. He had seen John Price make his little speech on the balcony, had watched Justice of the Peace Bennett trying to quiet the crowd, had heard James Patton read the federal warrant. Hungry, Wack went to the back door of the hotel and tried to get into the kitchen, but the women inside would not let him in. Wack worked himself "nearest to the nigger crowd" and over-heard John Copeland and Jerry Fox "say they did not care for papers, they'd have him any how." Others chimed in in the same vein. Wack decided to wait to see what would happen when the 5:13 train came in, though he "expected there would be some shootin' going on" and he "didn't want to die just then."[37]

✳

Everyone in the Public Square grew still as the train from Cleve-land pulled into Wellington. Would there be troops aboard? Would there be bloodshed? So far, nothing serious had occurred, but the men with guns were getting itchy. The sun was lowering in the sky. Dusk was a matter of only an hour or so away. If anything was going to be done to rescue John Price, it had better be done before dark.

Word came back swiftly from the passenger depot a little more than a block away: No troops had disembarked from the train.

✳

As the 5:13 drew into the station, Lowe and Langston were meeting again, this time in the little room adjoining the attic room where John was being held. They were sitting on the bed.

Langston was not optimistic about working out a compromise. He had gone out onto the hotel balcony to explain to the crowd about the papers the captors held, but "the crowd were very much excited, many of them averse to longer delay and bent upon a rescue at all hazards." Because Lowe was "an old acquaintance and friend," Langston "was anxious to extricate him from the dan-gerous position he occupied." He advised Lowe to tell Jennings "to give the boy up."[38]

Again, to Lowe's surprise, Langston, rising from the bed to de-part, repeated—as Lowe remembered it—that "we will have him any how."[39] Lowe didn't ask for an explanation, but he was dis-appointed by his friend's attitude.

✳

William Lincoln had no intention of waiting any longer. A new rumor was going around: that troops would arrive either on the next train, at 8:00 P.M., or on a special train. He sensed that the time for action had come. Everyone was nervous, anxious to do something.[40] It was obvious that they were waiting to be told what to do.

John Cowles had heard several persons say they wanted "some one to take the lead."[41] He went up to Lincoln in the square and said, "If anything is done to save the man, you will have to do it." Convinced that Cowles's words "threw the leadership into my hands again,"[42] Lincoln told Cowles, "Get me one dozen men."[43]

Cowles swiftly circulated through the crowd, calling for volunteers, but despite all the threats and posturing that men made that day, only five of them pushed their way to Lincoln's side. Ansel Lyman, who had roused Oberlin to John's seizure, and fellow Oberlin student Edward G. Sackett responded to the call, as did law student Lysander Butler. The two others were black men. Lincoln exchanged weapons with one of the black men, Lincoln handing him his rifle in return for a revolver.

Despite the disappointing response, Lincoln led the men to the front door of the hotel and was about to force it open when farmer Jacob Wheeler, who had earlier "catechized" John, beckoned to him and urged him not to try to rescue the slave. Lincoln, Wheeler said, "ought to have better sense than to crowd them colored men up where they might be dangerous." The passageway inside the hotel, the farmer continued, "was narrow." It would be difficult to get up it, and "if one gun was fired, more would be fired." Lincoln shrugged off Wheeler's warning. He was, he said, "a child of God and had as lief die in a good cause as live." If Lincoln "got in the way," Wheeler responded, "God would let a bullet go through him just as quick as through one of those black fellows."[44]

But Lincoln was determined. "Are you ready?" he called out to his men.[45]

"Yes!" came the answer.

"Then in with you!"

The six men rushed forward, grappling with the men guarding the hotel's front entrance. For three minutes they fought hand to hand—"heavy breathing, struggles, guns hurled here & there, men on the floor"—until Lincoln pointed his revolver at the head of one of the guards and warned, "Quit, or Ill [sic] blow your brains out."

As the man retreated "pretty tired & humbled" into a side room, Lincoln and his men bolted up the staircase. "Forward! Forward!" he called so loudly that he could be heard across the Public Square.[46]

Lincoln and his men raced up the stairs. Suddenly they confronted two young women, who were descending the staircase "weeping & trembling." Lincoln paused briefly to try to calm their fears, telling them that they were in no danger.

Once on the garret floor, Lincoln approached the door to the attic room where John Price was held. He could not wrest it open. "Shall I smash the door?" asked Sackett, raising the heavy rifle he carried. "No," answered Lincoln. He looked around the hallway. The light was now so dim that he could not get his bearings at first, but he realized that his voice could be heard through the thin wood partition that separated the hallway from the attic room. Lincoln knew that John's captors were better armed than he and his men. He had five shots in his pistol, but they had "50 shots to my 9. The 50 were in experienced hands; my 9 in inexperienced hands, save the John Brown man [Lyman]; who had however only 1 shot."[47] So Lincoln decided on a ruse. He knew that John's captors had no idea how many men were assembled in the hallway, spoiling to break in. He would call out to his men not to give any quarter, making it sound as if they were prepared to die in the attempt to rescue John. Just as he was about to do so, the black man who had traded weapons with him dislodged some bricks from an outside wall, letting some light into the hallway and disclosing, Lincoln was sure, that there were only six men in his raiding party.

Lincoln was upset. His "bluff was shattered." He berated the man for not following his orders, but the black retorted, "If I have got to be killed I want to die in the light."

"Providentially," as Lincoln later realized, the man's disobedience forced him to come up with what he believed was a better plan. But just as Lincoln began to work it out in his mind, his eye caught the sight of a pistol inches from his head, aimed through a hole high in the wall near the door where a stovepipe once ran. The hole had been papered over but now was exposed.[48] Lincoln warned his men, and keeping out of range of the pistol, he called on Sackett and one of the black men to follow him down to the floor below. There, in a guestroom directly under the attic room, he ordered them to pile bedding, furniture, and straw taken from the mattresses into a heap on the floor.

✳

Meanwhile, a group of blacks, led by John Scott, had launched their own independent assault on the back door. The Evans brothers, John Copeland, and Jerry Fox were with Scott. Like William Lincoln, Scott believed the time for action was at hand, now that the 5:13 train had come and gone. With Charles Langston following in their wake, the blacks broke through the door.

Innkeeper Wadsworth, Chapin Fay, and Constable Meacham were stationed there when the door burst in. Farmer Jacob Wheeler was nearby; he had been able to get back inside the hotel by way of the back door while Lincoln and his men were assaulting the front door. Wheeler was now convinced that *"lower orders,"* some of them "a little intoxicated" and making *"pooty hash* expressions,"[49] had taken over the crowd. At Wadsworth's request, he was guarding the foot of the back stairs, together with William Sciples and N. H. Reynolds, a local shoemaker. Reynolds made no secret of being "troubled with cowardice."[50] Wheeler, however, threw off his coat, ready to fight, as soon as he heard the commotion.

One of Scott's men was overexcited, "so crazy mad that he said, 'The first Democrat who keeps us from going up stairs I will shoot.' " And he did, pointing at one of the white men and firing. Just as he did, though, Scott and some others knocked the barrel of the gun up. The bullet went into the ceiling. Worried that another incident like that "would have ruined our calculations," Scott ordered one of his men to guard the trigger happy black so he wouldn't cause any further harm.[51]

The black men pressed ahead, shouting and arguing, some threatening to shoot. They pushed Fay to the ground, and one of them tried to strike him with a rifle, but Wheeler rushed to his aid and snatched it away in time. He threw it into the street through a dining room window. Not content with that, Wheeler rushed into the street, picked up the weapon, threw it against the wall of the hotel, breaking it, picked it up again, and tossed it away from the building.

Wilson Bruce Evans, meanwhile, continued to struggle with Fay. Scott came up and threw both of them to the floor, clearing the path up the staircase while Evans held onto Fay's long hair.

*

The two assault groups led by Lincoln and Scott converged in the hallway outside the attic room where John was being held. Lincoln and his men had gotten up the narrow staircase first, and he seems to have assumed command of both groups. With Scott were John Copeland and Henry Evans.[52] One of them apparently went up to Lincoln and passed along the latest rumor, that the Cleveland militia was on its way on another train. Knowing the "slaveholders" could hear him through the stovepipe hole, Lincoln went over to it and said loudly, "I have made arrangements for

that. I have a large pile of straw & furniture & bedding all ready
& the moment the train comes in sight, I shall set fire to the mass
wh. is directly under this attic; I shall defend the staircase below
& the officers must look out for themselves."

✳

Inside the attic room, there were anywhere from eight to twelve
men with John Price. The men were separated in several groups.
The Kentuckians, who had their weapons drawn, were by the door.
Jennings was holding tightly onto the rope that held it.

Oberlin student Richard Winsor was with John Price, his Sunday
school pupil, near the door, close enough to hear the sound of
voices in the hallway. At one side of the room, Deputy Marshal
Lowe was huddled with Oberlin student James Patton and Charles
Griffin. Lowe's shrinking assistant, Samuel Davis, hung back in
the shadows.

Patton and Griffin were urging Lowe to release John. "You had
better let the boy go than to lose your life," Griffin said.⁵³ But
Lowe wouldn't consider the idea. He said he knew he was responsible for John's rendition under the Fugitive Slave Law.

Winsor recognized the voices of students he knew in the passageway outside. He started to take John to the other end of the
room, but the two Kentuckians told him to leave the black man
alone. They were distracted, however, by the goings-on in the hallway, and when they turned away, Winsor motioned John aside and
asked him whether he wanted to return to Oberlin.

John, who had been submissive up to now, must have felt the
tide at last turning in his favor. Obviously heartened by the rescue
efforts in his behalf, he said he wanted to go to Oberlin. Winsor
knelt down near a closet and, by the wan light of the setting sun
coming through the fan window, he was able to write a note on a
slip of paper without attracting the Kentuckians' attention. "Put
a string 'round the latch of the door," it said, "and pull hard and
the door will open."⁵⁴

Winsor put the note up the sleeve of his coat and went to the
stovepipe hole in the wall, which was near the door. Hearing Lincoln's voice on the other side, he said, "Lincoln, give me your
hand." Lincoln reached inside the hole. As he did, Winsor let the
note slip out of his sleeve and into Lincoln's hand.

Lincoln read the note and then called through the stovepipe
hole, "If you don't open this door, I will stave my gun through and
shoot you."⁵⁵ With that, he shoved his pistol into the hole. Jen-

nings, who had heard him, looked into the hole just as Lincoln poked his gun through. It struck Jennings on the head, knocking his hat off and stunning him so that he fell down.

As he stumbled, Jennings relaxed his grip on the rope that held the door. Lincoln and Sackett were able to pull the door open enough with a sudden jerk to thrust some weapons inside, keeping the door from being closed. Then, with a great heave, they forced the door completely open. Jennings and Mitchell stood their ground in the doorway. The two tall Kentuckians shouted at Lincoln, and he shouted back. Just then, the fan window at the far end of the room shattered as the top of a ladder struck it.

Winsor saw his chance. He grabbed John and, with his back to him, put John's arms around his waist and told him to keep his head close to his back and between his shoulders. Winsor stood beside the arguing Kentuckians and, making it seem as if he was trying to listen in on the "warm debate," he pushed his head and shoulders forward little by little until he was able to make a sudden lurch and spring through the door, his "prize"—John Price— at his back.[56] As he did so, Lincoln, about to force his way into the room, sensed "in the dimness, something like a shadow" passing by him.

Winsor raced down the rough ladder and the stairwell below. Behind him, John was being passed down over the shoulders of the men who filled the stairwell.

A great shout went up as Winsor burst from the hotel door followed by some men carrying John. The buggy John Scott had driven to Oberlin was backed up to the hotel entrance. Simeon Bushnell held the reins. John was tossed bodily into it. Winsor then jumped into the buggy.

✳

Nearly four hours after John Watson first reached Wellington, Edward Kinney finally arrived. Kinney, who had started out on foot, managed to hitch a ride in a wagon with a fellow student. It was sunset when they reached the northeast corner of the Public Square. To his amazement, Kinney recognized Bushnell and Winsor with John Price in a buggy approaching them. Bushnell was trying to rein in the horse, which was "on the jump." Winsor was swinging a gun in the air, yelling "all right!" and "All is well."[57] The buggy started off at a gallop northward to Oberlin, shouts of triumph on everyone's lips. With each cheer, hats were tossed into the air.[58]

＊

In the hotel, meanwhile, Lincoln ordered his men back down
the stairs. He brought up the rear, keeping watch that the Kentuckians and the federal marshals didn't follow, at the same time
warning his men to guard him from any interference below.

John's captors had no intention of following. They were more
concerned about their own safety. Patton and Lowe appeared at
the broken fan window. Calling down to the crowd, Patton asked
whether it would be safe, now that John had been saved, for the
deputy marshal to come out. "Yes," someone shouted back. "They
will be safe now, if they are never to come again; but if they come
again, no one will be accountable for their lives a moment!" The
statements drew cries of "Aye! Aye! Aye!" from the crowd surrounding the speaker.

Then Jennings appeared at the window. He said he had come to
"execute the laws," an eyewitness related, "but we had been too
much for him!" A man sprung up on a box in the square and begged
Jennings to carry him back to Kentucky—"That no one need come
here to carry off our citizens, for they would find us too much for
'em every time! We believe in State Sovereignty, and the moment
a slave touches Ohio soil he is free, and all the South combined
cannot carry him back, if we say No!"[59]

Jennings, like Lowe, asked for safe-conduct and was assured he
would have it.

＊

John Mercer Langston returned to Oberlin at sunset to discover
"neither life nor stir in or about the village." He quickly ascer-
tained what had occurred and set out for Wellington, hoping to
arrive "in time to play some humble part" in the rescue. He drove
off in the lingering twilight and was about four and a half miles
down the road when he saw a buggy speeding toward him from
Wellington. In it were Bushnell, Winsor, and John Price, who was
"under the intensest excitement." Bushnell, who was "proud of
his triumph," urged Langston to return with them to Oberlin.
"John is safe; here he is; I have him. Come back!" he said. But
Langston decided to press on to Wellington "to meet the multitude, now victorious, and return with them."[60] Within a moment
or so, he came upon both his brother Charles and Orindatus Wall.

*

Bushnell drove up to James Fitch's home, situated on the east side of Professor Street, in the south end of Oberlin. He entered by the back door with John. His sister Jane was "excited and anxious for news" and "demanded" that he tell her at once what had happened. But Bushnell threw her a look of caution, which, "in those days, was all that was required."[61]

John was placed in one of the "secret rooms" of Fitch's house while Bushnell conferred with his brother-in-law. The bookstore proprietor was a known conductor on the Underground Railroad. It would be safer to find somewhere else to hide him. But who in Oberlin would not be suspect?

*

Shortly after Professor James Fairchild returned home with his family that evening from their day's outing, there was a knock at his door. Fairchild's house was on the west side of Professor Street, about two blocks north of Fitch's home. Standing on his doorstep were James Fitch and Professor James Monroe.[62] Until that moment, Fairchild "had never seen or heard" of John Price. Fitch and Monroe told him about the fugitive slave's rescue. They were quick to point out that they themselves were well known for harboring escaped slaves and their homes were bound to be watched by any federal lawmen searching for John. Fairchild, however, "would never be suspected of doing such a thing as breaking one of the Laws of the United States."[63] Fairchild was the logical person to hide him. Would he take John Price into his home?

By Oberlin standards, Fairchild was considered conservative and law-abiding. He had never harbored a fugitive slave before. But though Fairchild was not as militant as other professors at the college, he was a strong opponent of slavery. His wife, Mary, was a native of Jamestown, New York, and had grown up in Minden, Louisiana, where her father had moved because of his health. When her father died, Mary asked that as her share of his estate she be given one of his slaves, whom the Fairchilds promptly emancipated. The onetime slave, a forty-three-year-old woman who was named Mary Kellogg after her mistress, lived with the Fairchilds as their servant.[64]

Without a moment's hesitation, Fairchild agreed to hide John. The slave was brought in and led to a back room on the second floor.

The hideaway, Professor James H. Fairchild's home on Professor Street, where John Price was secreted. Courtesy of Oberlin College Archives

Mary Fairchild had in the meantime gathered their six children together in a front room and "cautiously locked the door."[65] She apparently did not want them to be put in the position of being witnesses to anything incriminating. But they could hear the sound of footsteps hurrying up the staircase.[66]

With "hushed voice," Mary Fairchild told the youngsters about John's capture, his rescue, and his concealment in their home. She warned them not to say a word because if they did their father would be arrested and jailed. "You must never tell any one in the world that John is here," Mary added. "And so long as you live, perhaps it will never be safe to betray the fact that we have sheltered in our house a runaway slave."[67]

For several days, until John left for Canada, the children saw their father carrying food upstairs. "They were so frightened," one of them later recalled, "they said nothing."[68] How easy it was to be a "transgressor," Fairchild thought.[69]

*

The trek back to Oberlin was a march of triumph, joyous and noisy. John Mercer Langston found everyone he encountered "shouting, singing, rejoicing."[70] Farmers and their families spilled out of their homes along the way to watch the parade. Above, a tiny sliver of moon stood low in the westerly sky and a reddish tail, the barest trace of a comet, blinked in the northeast,[71] though no one seemed to notice either.

John Scott was walking. The last he had seen of his buggy was the "dust" of it "in the distance," as Bushnell drove off with John and Winsor. Uncomplaining, Scott walked halfway home before he could get a lift.[72]

The entire town of Oberlin seemed to be out as the rescuers marched up Main Street. Soon, two groups formed spontaneously, one by the Historic Elm, the other a block away beside First Church. Bushnell was at one, Winsor at the other. They were telling the townspeople and students who hadn't gone to Wellington what had happened.

At one of the rallies, John Mercer Langston spoke. Then there were cries of "Charlie! Charlie! Charlie!" until his brother Charles got up to speak.[73] Oberlin student Jacob R. Shipherd led the gathered people in "three terrific groans" for the federal government and "three glorious cheers for Liberty."[74]

"Gentlemen," one speaker declared, "we know not what may hereafter be attempted. But we want to know who can be relied on. So many of you as will here solemnly pledge yourselves to rally on the instant of an alarm, armed and ready to pursue and rescue, says 'Aye.'"

"Aye! Aye! Aye!" responded his listeners. Then Shipherd moved for three groans for Anson Dayton, the despised deputy marshal who everybody was sure had betrayed John Price.[75] He had already "wisely" left Oberlin.[76]

William Lincoln, now a hero, spoke, describing John's rescue. He impetuously started to identify by name those who had rescued John, but James Fairchild's brother Edward cautioned him against naming names.

The celebration went on until a late hour. Oberlin went to bed that night in a jubilant mood. There was much to be thankful for. Another black man had been saved, no blood had been shed, the detested Buchanan administration had been outwitted. But Edward Fairchild had warned with good cause. Oberlin's Democratic postmaster, Edward Munson, had been seen moving among his fellow townspeople while the speeches were going on. He was taking notes.

EIGHT

"From Snowy White to Sooty"

*In Tom's hurried exchange, he had not forgotten to transfer his
cherished Bible to his pocket. It was well he did so; for Mr. Legree,
having refitted Tom's handcuffs, proceeded deliberately to investigate the contents of his pockets. He drew out a silk handkerchief,
and put it into his own pocket. Several little trifles, which Tom had
treasured, chiefly because they had amused Eva, he looked upon
with a contemptuous grunt, and tossed them over his shoulder into
the river.*

*Tom's Methodist hymn-book, which, in his hurry, he had forgot-
ten, he now held up and turned over.*

*"Humph! pious, to be sure. So, what's yer name,—you belong to
the church, eh?"*

"Yes, Mas'r," said Tom, firmly.

*"Well, I'll soon have that out of you. I have none o' yer bawling,
praying, singing niggers on my place; so remember. Now, mind yourself," he said, with a stamp and a fierce glance of his gray eye,
directed at Tom, "I'm your church now! You understand,—you've
got to be as I say."*

Chapter xxxi: "The Middle Passage"

Oberlin, it seemed, was content to resume normal activities and
accept the praise of neighbors. Typical was the comment of the
weekly *Lorain County Eagle* of Elyria:

"We have heard of many foolish things in this world, but to
think of carrying off a fugitive from Lorain County seems to us to
cap the climax in the line of folly."[1]

Foolish? The Buchanan administration in Washington did not
think it was foolish for a slaveowner in Kentucky to invoke the
Fugitive Slave Law to recover his property. It had no intention of
letting the community's rescue of John Price become a precedent
in Ohio or in any other Northern state. The violators of the law
must be punished.

The citizens of Oberlin seemed oblivious at first to the repercussions that John's rescue would have outside the Western Reserve, though there is no doubt that they realized the law had been
broken. Simeon Bushnell told a companion while walking on Professor Street a few nights later that if rescuing John "is a crime, I

suppose I am guilty."[2] However, there is no indication that anyone imagined that the Rescue might become a national *cause célèbre* or that anyone believed, or even cared, that the Buchanan administration would retaliate.

On the day after the Rescue, Tuesday, September 14, two students returned to Wellington to retrieve a weapon they had left there. But Deputy Marshal Jacob Lowe was in the town, and when he found out what the students were up to, he chased them through the streets.[3] Why had Lowe stayed in Wellington? Why hadn't he returned to his office in Columbus?

A few days later, Mathew Johnson, the federal marshal attached to the Northern Judicial District in Cleveland, visited Oberlin, ostensibly to allay the hostility that many there felt toward his deputy, Anson Dayton. The town blamed Dayton for John Price's capture, and Dayton was worried that he might be assaulted. Johnson "consulted with a number of leading citizens" and, with "smooth and honeyed words," assured them that he disapproved of Dayton's conduct. His deputy marshal, he continued, didn't even have any business going with Jennings to Painesville to search for the slave Henry. If any warrants were to be served in the future, Johnson said, he would not only come himself to serve them but would also give ample notice of his arrival to "enable the fugitive to escape." Dayton, Johnson added, was distasteful to him: "I didn't like his looks, but appointed him because he was so well recommended by Postmaster Munson."[4] Furthermore, he told everyone that he would ask Dayton to resign.

Johnson, however, was lying. The truth seems to be that Dayton decided to resign because he was frightened by the threats being made against him. He had recently been beaten in public by James Smith, an escaped slave who worked in Oberlin as a stonecutter. Smith had learned that Dayton had written to his owner in North Carolina, offering to arrest Smith if he was sent a power of attorney. Smith confronted Dayton on the street and chased him into the Palmer House, where he struck the deputy with a hickory cane.[5] It was also common knowledge that Dayton had been involved in the attempt to abduct the Wagoner family. A song was making the rounds, "in the style of Mother Goose":

> Who sought this place when purse was low,
> And he had nowhere else to go,
> And strove his legal wit to show?
> > Our Marshal

. . . .

Who was the first to shake with fright,
When out a "little late" one night,
To see a figure robed in white?
                    Our Marshal.
Who was the first to break and run,
Though strongly armed and four to one,
From Wagner [sic] with his lockless gun?
                    Our Marshal.

. . . .

Who, bearing his revolvers twain,
Fled from a boy but with a cane,
And bawled for help with might and main?
                    Our Marshal.

. . . .

Who fled from Painesville on the car,
Because he had no taste for war,
Or more especially for tar?
                    Our Marshal.
Long live Old Buck in power and might,
To *punish* wrong and *guard* the right,
And longer live the Gallant Knight,
                    Our Marshal.
When Liberty shall need a friend,
And threat'ning ruin shall impend,
May Government to rescue send,
                    Our Marshal.[6]

The town was taking its own vengeance. People to whom Dayton owed money began legal action to recover their loans. Five recovery suits were entered, and on December 1 all were granted in Oberlin's town court: a $5 balance due to Mayor A. N. Beecher on a loan of $54 plus interest; $3.88 for flour and meal owed to Beecher and his feed store partner; $29.50 due on a promissory note; $70.78 due on a similar note; and $6 due for six hundred feet of siding Dayton had purchased—in all, for that time, a hefty $115.16.[7]

Johnson's duplicity regarding Dayton was exposed when a letter he sent to Dayton was discovered and published. "You must not resign," Johnson wrote. "I am not disposed to be driven by the violators of the laws and Constitution of the United States, to discharge a deputy for doing his duty, nor do I wish such a deputy to resign. You need fear no violence. It is all bravado—an effort to scare you into a resignation."[8]

Another example of Johnson's duplicity occurred that very same

September day that he visited with Oberlin's leading citizens. He also paid an important secret call on some other Oberlin residents, all Democrats, among them Dayton's friend Bela Farr, Chauncey Wack, and Dayton's fellow Christ Church parishioner Postmaster Edward Munson. A week before the month was out, the anti-Oberlin *Cleveland Plain Dealer* made it quite clear just what had been discussed. The newspaper divulged that those involved in John Price's rescue "are to be immediately prosecuted."[9] Even so, no one guessed that Farr, Wack, and Munson were in any way connected with the investigation. They all believed that Dayton was the betrayer.

Politics was the keynote in the coming months of legal maneuvering and litigation. When United States District Judge Hiram V. Willson summoned a federal grand jury to hear evidence in the case, every juror on the panel was a Democrat even though the Western Reserve was overwhelmingly Republican. Moreover, one of the grand jurors who was chosen was, astonishingly, a party to John's capture and surely biased: Lewis Boynton, the father of Shakespeare Boynton. The selection of an all-Democratic jury and the seating of Boynton on it were but the first of a series of flagrantly biased tactics that the federal government would employ in the ensuing months.

In charging the grand jury, Willson left no doubt where he stood. The judge was a large, obese, gray-haired man who looked older than his fifty years.[10] A native of New York State, he had once participated in an attempt to seize an escaped slave in Buffalo.

There are some people, Willson said, who oppose the Fugitive Slave Law "from a *declared* sense of conscientious duty. There is, in fact, a sentiment prevalent in the community which arrogates to human conduct a standard of right above, and independent of, human laws; and it makes the CONSCIENCE of each individual in society the TEST of his own ACCOUNTABILITY to the laws of the land.

"While those who cherish this dogma claim and enjoy the protection of the law for their own lives and property, they are unwilling that the law should be operative for the protection of the constitutional rights of others."

The judge was clearly prejudiced against Oberlin. The dogma its leaders espoused, he said, "is a sentiment semi-religious in its development, and is almost invariably characterized by intolerance and bigotry. The LEADERS of those who acknowledge its obligations and advocate its sanctity are like the subtle prelates of the dark ages. They are versed in all they consider useful and sanctified learning—trained in certain schools in New England to manage words, they are equally successful in the social circle to manage hearts; seldom superstitious themselves, yet skilled in practising upon the superstition and credulity of others."[11]

The grand jury began to hear witnesses in the second week of November. It then adjourned for about two weeks while further witnesses were sought. Its indictments and warrants were drawn up, the true bills filed, and arrest warrants finally issued on Monday, December 6. Interestingly, there was no mention in the indictments of Deputy Marshal Lowe or the federal warrant that he and Jennings procured in Columbus. The indictments, couched in repetitious legalese, were verbose:

> The Grand Jurors of the United States of America, empanelled, sworn and charged to inquire of crimes and offences within and for the body of the Northern District of Ohio, upon their oath, present and find, that heretofore, to wit . . . a certain negro slave called John, a person held to service and labor in the State of Kentucky, one of the United States, the said John being the property of one John G. Bacon, of the said State of Kentucky, the person to whom such service and labor were then due, and the said negro slave called John, to wit, on the day and year last aforesaid, so being held to service and labor as aforesaid, and said service and labor being due as aforesaid, did escape into another of the United States, to wit, into the State of Ohio from the said State of Kentucky:—that afterwards . . . one Anderson Jennings, the agent and attorney of the said John G. Bacon . . . did pursue and reclaim the said negro slave called John . . . [that] together with divers, to wit, two hundred other persons, to the jurors aforesaid unknown, heretofore . . . with force and arms, unlawfully, knowingly, and willingly, did rescue the said negro slave called John, then and there being pursued and reclaimed, seized and arrested, and in the custody and control aforesaid, he, the said negro slave called John, being then and there a fugitive from, and held to service and labor as aforesaid . . . to the great damage of the said John G. Bacon; contrary to the form of the Act of Congress in such case made and provided, and against the peace and dignity of the United States.[12]

In all, thirty-seven persons, "From snowy white to sooty,"[13] were indicted—three for aiding and abetting in the rescue of John Price, the rest for their part in the rescue itself. Twenty-three of the Rescuers—as they became known popularly—were from Oberlin, but two others—a man from nearby Penfield and Charles Langston, who had once lived in Oberlin and attended the college—were identified with them, so it became customary to say that twenty-five of the indicted were from Oberlin. In similar fashion, eleven of those indicted in the Rescue (it, too, became capitalized) were from Wellington, but a Pittsfield man was identified with them, making the Wellington group number twelve. Of the twenty-five Rescuers from Oberlin, nearly half—twelve—were black men. Of those twelve blacks, three were fugitive slaves like John Price, six were emancipated slaves, and three were freeborn. Four other Rescuers were Oberlin students and one an Oberlin professor. One of the Oberlin Rescuers was born in Scotland and three others in England—a connection that would prove helpful in raising funds abroad for their defense. The Oberlin Rescuers included a bookseller-printer, a clerk-printer, a carpenter, two cabinetmakers, a lawyer, a harnessmaker, a shoemaker, a book and shoe merchant, and two cobblers. Six of the Wellington Rescuers were farmers; among the others were a physician and a lawyer.

There seemed to be no rhyme nor reason why some individuals connected with the Rescue were indicted and some were not. In some cases, it might have been a matter of identification or lack of identification. A large number of black men went to Wellington to rescue John Price, but it is likely that the government's witnesses did not know the names of all of them, especially if they were fugitive slaves. The problem with identifying those who participated was evident in the number of names that were boggled in the indictments. It also became evident that several persons were indicted for purely political reasons.

As the case against the thirty-seven unfolded, it became increasingly clear that the Buchanan administration was interested in only one thing: punishing Oberlin. The community was a defiant hotbed of abolitionism, and its citizens had continually resisted complying with the federal law. It was about time, many of Oberlin's enemies thought, that its self-righteous citizens were taught a lesson.

The indicted were:

The Oberlin Rescuers

JAMES H. BARTLETT: Cobbler, a native of England, forty-seven years old, father of six children. Resides on north side of Lorain Street, east of Pleasant. Works for Samuel Royce, shoemaker. A thin-faced man of average height.

JAMES BARTLETT: Son of James H. Bartlett and known as James, Jr. Also a cobbler.

SIMEON BUSHNELL: Clerk and printer, employee of James M. Fitch, his brother-in-law. Born in Rome, New York. Twenty-nine years old, married, father of an infant child. Family boards on the south side of College Street east of Main, near Fitch's book-store. Wears beard but no moustache. A short man with black hair, black eyes, known as "an unpretentious workman" and "humble artisan"[14] who is "poor in world's goods."[15] Known member of Underground Railroad.[16] Nephew of the Rev. Horace Bushnell of Cincinnati, an antislavery missionary.

JOHN A. COPELAND, JR.: Carpenter. Freeborn black, twenty-four years old, not married, a "good-looking, bright, mulatto" with "bushy head and near straight hair." Wears mustache.[17] Had briefly attended Oberlin College. Active member of the Oberlin Anti-Slavery Society.[18] Son of John Anthony Copeland, who was born a slave in 1808 near Raleigh, North Carolina, and emancipated when seven years old upon the death of his master. His mother, the former Delilah Evans,[19] sister of Rescuers Henry and Wilson Bruce Evans, was born free in 1809 and lived in Hillsboro, North Caro-lina. Because of persecution Copeland's parents experienced as free blacks, they migrated from North Carolina in 1843, when John, Jr., was about ten years old, going first to Cincinnati and then starting for Indiana but advised by an Oberlin graduate to settle in Oberlin, where they would be safe from kidnappers. Family home is on the southeast corner of Professor and Morgan streets, next door to Fitch's home. John, Jr., can "always be found" at meetings in the "Liberty School-house," where, hearing the stories told by runaway slaves, he signifies "often by the deep scowl of his coun-tenance, the moist condition of his eyes and the quivering of his lips, how deeply he was moved by the recital of wrong and outrage, and how glad he would be to see the institution under which such abuse was tolerated, overthrown and destroyed."[20]

HENRY EVANS: Cabinetmaker and undertaker. Freeborn black, forty-two years old, native of North Carolina. So light-skinned as to be "nearly white."[21] Hair light, also, and clean-shaven. Family traces ancestry to General Nathanael Greene of revolutionary war fame, "a direct ancestor."[22] Father of eight children. Wife, former Henrietta Leary, is sister of brother Wilson Bruce's wife and Lewis Sheridan Leary,[23] was born in 1827 in Fayetteville, North Caro-lina. Couple married about 1844 and moved with brother Wilson Bruce's family to Oberlin in 1854, where the brothers established a shop on East Mill Street. Two years later they purchased from Oberlin College Walton Hall, a two-story frame building on South Main that had served as a men's dormitory. They moved it to Mill Street, where it became their shop and store.

WILSON BRUCE EVANS: Like brother, a cabinetmaker and under-taker, born free in North Carolina, also very light-skinned, with hazel eyes and dark hair. Sports short beard but no mustache. Thirty-three years old. Married the same year he moved north to Oberlin, 1854. Father of three children. Wife, former Sarah Leary, is sister of his brother Henry's wife and Lewis Sheridan Leary. After two years in Oberlin, he built in 1856 hip-roofed brick house on Mill Street, between South Main and Water streets, five doors away from where Postmaster Edward Munson lives and a block from Seth Bartholomew's home.[24]

JAMES M. FITCH: Bookseller and printer, also superintendent of Oberlin Sunday school. Native of Lima, Livingston County, New York. Forty-three years old, father of five children. Son Albert, thirteen, and daughter Louisa, fourteen, students at Oberlin College. Wife, Jane, the sister of Simeon Bushnell. Wears beard but no mustache. Has high forehead and is distinguished looking. Though sometimes addressed as Reverend,[25] he is not a minister and always regretted not having become one, though he served for three years as a missionary in Jamaica and preaches regularly at the Sunday school. Illness when a teenager caused amnesia and later made studying difficult. One night four years later, when about eighteen, he "first shed tears of repentance" during inspirational religious experience while alone in a garden.[26] Attempted three times to establish a newspaper in Oberlin without success. Considered "as true as steel,"[27] but also a "wire bundle of nerves" whose "easily besetting sin was impatience and irritability." Quick to judge, "his sense of wrong so intensely hot, that he not only saw injustice sooner than others, but he saw it at times when it did not exist."[28] Known member of Underground Railroad. Home, on Professor Street, between South and Morgan, has two rooms especially built to hide runaway slaves.[29]

JEREMIAH FOX: Fugitive slave, known as Jerry. Mulatto, described as having black hair, eyes, and complexion. A teamster. Born in Flemingsburg, Kentucky, less than twenty miles from Maysville. Worked as a mason in building of College Chapel on Tappan Square in 1855. Lives with white woman, Elisabeth (Lizzie) Sullivan, a native of Ireland, and their two children. Has "Cheerful" personality.[30]

THOMAS GENA: Fugitive slave.

CHAUNCEY GOODYEAR: Resident of Penfield.

JOHN HARTWELL: Fugitive slave.

CHARLES H. LANGSTON: A schoolteacher. About forty years old.[31] A mulatto who, "like so many of her [Virginia's] scions of her best families, has an admixture of African blood."[32] Has devoted life to fighting against slavery. Currently recording secretary of Ohio State Anti-Slavery Society, headquartered in Cleveland. Previously a resident of Columbus, where he was not only active in anti-slavery affairs but also a proponent of educating blacks. Was president of the state black convention held there in 1849. Also a temperance advocate, was appointed western agent for the Sons of Temperance in 1848. Hair full and somewhat curly. Wears full beard. Twelve years older than brother John Mercer Langston. They and an older brother, Gideon, were children of Captain Ralph Quarles of Louisa Court House, Virginia, who served in the Revolutionary War under Lafayette. Mother, Lucy Langston, was a slave, part black, part Indian. Like John Mercer, considers himself a black man. The brothers were emancipated under terms of Quarles's will when he died in 1834. In the fall of 1835, Charles and Gideon enrolled in the Preparatory Department at Oberlin, becoming the first blacks to register at the school, and, in March of the following year, were baptized and received into membership of First Church. Gideon subsequently settled in Cincinnati, while Charles reregistered at Oberlin in 1841 and continued studies until the spring of 1843. While a student, taught at a black school in Chillicothe. Was instrumental in convincing John Mercer to continue college studies in Oberlin rather than attend a trade school. Related, through John Mercer's marriage to Caroline Wall, to Rescuer Orindatus S. B. Wall. Known as a firebrand and orator. Described by John Mercer as being "not large nor apparently firm of body; but well endowed intellectually. His disposition and temper though ordinarily well controlled, were not naturally of the easy and even sort. In his constitution, he was impetuous and aggressive; and under discipline and opposition, he was always restive," but "his knowledge and power in an emergency never failed him."[33]

FRANKLIN LEWIS: Oberlin resident.

WILLIAM E. LINCOLN: Oberlin College freshman. Rooms in Tappan Hall. Twenty-seven years old. Born September 8, 1831, in London. Entered Oberlin Preparatory Department in 1853–54 academic year. Missed 1854–55 and 1856–57 years. Tall, clean-shaven, good-looking, but subject to mood swings.

ANSEL W. LYMAN: Student in Preparatory Department. Twenty-two years old. Born May 6, 1836, in Brecksville, Ohio, son of Darius and Mary Lyman. Father now a farmer in Oberlin with land in south section of town. Ansel the oldest of four children. Tall, well-built. Wears beard but no mustache. Served as lieutenant in Kansas Free State Army in 1856, when the largest of several Oberlin contingents went to fight proslavers in Kansas. "Did not quail" before enemy forces.[34] A member of the Oberlin Fire Department. Called "Anse."

HENRY E. PECK: Oberlin professor of sacred rhetoric and adjunct professor of mental and moral philosophy. Thirty-seven years old. Born in Rochester, New York, July 20, 1821, the son of a Connecticut-born printer-publisher-bookstore proprietor. Married, the father of four children. Resides on north side of East College Street, across from the home of John Mercer Langston and down the street from the homes of Rescuers Orindatus S. B. Wall and Ralph Plumb. Wears beard but no mustache; has large wart on upper lip. Graduated Oberlin College in 1841, its Theological Seminary in 1845. Ordained that same year in Rochester and preached there until he joined Oberlin faculty in 1851. Active in local politics and in 1855 under consideration for the Republican nomination to the U.S. House of Representatives. He declined the offer after consulting with the college faculty, which advised him that his candidacy might not be good policy for the school. (Professor James Monroe, who assumed that the faculty would not object, accepted the nomination and was elected.) Advocated raising funds to buy rifles in support of the Kansas wars. One of the leading faculty members of the Theological Department, known as a "radical and something of an eccentric" and "not always in perfect agreement with the more conservative members of the faculty." Considered a "thorough abolitionist,"[35] active in helping runaway slaves flee to Canada. Also described as "quiet, unobtrusive and retiring" but "a bold, fearless and accomplished champion of freedom."[36] Monroe believes he is "one of the brightest and most estimable men that Oberlin has produced," intellectually "clear, clean-cut, instructive, magnetic, witty, incisive, logical, and analogical," and morally "'a Friend of Man,' sympathetic, helpful, watchful for the good of others, incited to action by a heart of love."[37]

RALPH PLUMB: Lawyer, in practice with his brother Samuel on South Main Street. Forty-two years old. Born March 29, 1816, in Busti, Chautauqua county, New York. Married, the father of three children. Resides on the northeast corner of East College and Water streets. Former state legislator. Brother Samuel, four years his senior, was in 1836 secretary of the antislavery society in Trumbull County, Ohio, and later served in Ohio legislature. Ralph Plumb was one of eight vice-presidents of the Kansas Emigrant Aid Association of Northern Ohio in 1854. He was elected to legislature from Hartford, Ohio, in 1855. The Plumb brothers came to Oberlin in 1857 and quickly established themselves as among the community's leading citizens and among its most successful financially. Cherubic-faced, bearded, described as a "genial and affable gentleman and a very entertaining conversationalist . . . a man whose strong individuality is the strength of integrity, virtue and deep human sympathy."[38]

JOHN H. SCOTT: Harness- and trunkmaker. Emancipated slave, the son of William Scott, a black, and Sarah Chance Scott, a Scots-woman. A mulatto but dark-skinned, described both as "copper-colored"[39] and "tinged with African blood."[40] Full-faced, tall man. Wears beard but no mustache. Thirty-one years old. Born in 1827 in Fayetteville, North Carolina. Married, the father of three children. Wife, Cecilia, born in 1829 in Fayetteville, is the daughter of free blacks and attended private school. Her first husband, John Willis, died in 1847. The couple married in 1849 and came to Oberlin in 1856, where Scott set up shop in the old Walton Hall, which the Evans brothers had purchased and moved to Mill Street. Lives across from Wilson Bruce Evans on Mill Street. Described as a "man of intelligence."[41]

WILLIAM D. SCRIMGEOUR: Oberlin College senior, also tutor in Preparatory Department. Twenty-nine years old. Born July 3, 1829, in Arbroath on the east coast of Scotland north of the Firth of Tay. Rooms in Tappan Hall, two doors down from Rescuer William Lincoln. Entered Oberlin as a freshman in 1856. Described as "a man of fine intellect and great industry"[42] and "one of the most extraordinary" students the school has ever seen: "His thirst for knowledge" is "unbounded." Has as well "a passion for teaching."[43] Also called "a hard worker," whose 'grim determination is shown in his countenance." He evidently carries "a heavy load." Friends have warned him, "You'll wear yourself out!" To which he has replied that it is "better to *wear* out than *rust* out!"[44]

JACOB R. SHIPHERD: Student in seminary preparatory course. Ordained as a Congregational minister in Sandbank, New York, in 1857. Twenty-two years old. Born Walton, New York, June 12, 1836. Nephew of cofounder of Oberlin. Boards on the east side of Professor Street, north of Lorain. Entered Oberlin in 1857. Genial-looking, sports beard but no mustache.[45]

ORINDATUS S. B. WALL: Shoemaker. Emancipated slave, about thirty-five years old. Born in 1823, a mulatto, the son of Stephen Wall, a wealthy planter who lived near Rockingham, North Carolina, and a slave woman named Priscilla, or Prissy Ely, sister of one of Stephen Wall's two other slave "wives." Stephen Wall, who had served in North Carolina Senate in early 1820s, emancipated Orindatus and two other children by Priscilla before his death in 1845, sending them to a Quaker settlement in Harveysburg, Ohio.

He also bequeathed to them property in Ohio. All but one child came to Oberlin, and all his daughters and all his sons but Orindatus entered the Preparatory Department. In October 1854, sister Caroline, then a senior in the Literary Department, married John Mercer Langston. He and John Mercer swapped properties in 1856, Wall giving John Mercer a new two-story frame house on East College Street in return for a farm in Brownhelm Township. In the same month that Caroline married Langston, Orindatus married Amanda A. Thomas, a mulatto born in Virginia who was then living in town. Has two children, expecting a third. He first opened a boot- and shoemaking business on East College Street in partnership with Rescuer David Watson. Current store is down from the Palmer House, on the north side of East College between Main and Pleasant streets. Resides two blocks away on East College, between the homes of Rescuers Henry Peck and Ralph Plumb. A heavyset, robust-looking man, well established in the community, having served at one time temporarily as a village marshal.[46]

DAVID WATSON: Farmer. Twenty-three years old. Mulatto, born in Charleston, South Carolina, with "no trace of African blood apparent."[47] Married, father of one child. Wife, Marie, also a mulatto, born in Louisiana. Clean-shaven, youthful-looking. Attended Preparatory Department, 1853–57, at which time he was listed as a resident of Washington, D.C. At one time, partner with Rescuer Orindatus Wall in a boot- and shoemaking shop. Only previous trouble with the law: fined $1 on August 28, 1857, for smoking a cigar in the street and on the sidewalks of Oberlin.[48]

JOHN WATSON: Grocer. About forty years old. He and wife, Margaret, two years his junior, both mulatto and born slaves in Virginia. Has two children. Heavyset, sports mutton chops. Before settling in Oberlin, the Watsons lived in Louisiana. Came to Oberlin "in order to gain some education and for the purpose of 'making a man of himself.'"[49] Learned how to read and write when in his thirties. At first worked as a drayer, but when his horse died he could not afford to purchase another. Began confectionery store on the southeast corner of Main and College streets in a lean-to built out into the street that had been a peanut stand. In 1852 built own store in center section of building called the Commercial Block, on west side of South Main between College and Mill streets. Operates grocery, restaurant, and ice cream parlor there. Resides on north side of Lorain Street, in the block east of First Church. Described as a "man of great energy."[50]

WILLIAM WATSON: Shop clerk. Son of John Watson. About nineteen years old. Mulatto, born in Louisiana. Attended Oberlin,

1854–57. Previous trouble with the law: October 2, 1857, fined $2.50 after pleading guilty to charge of riot; fined $5 on February 8, 1858, after pleading guilty to charge of "attempting to disturb the peace and dignity."[51]

RICHARD WINSOR: Junior in Preparatory Department. Twenty-three years old. Born September 17, 1835, in Gosport, England. Entered Oberlin in 1857. Clean-shaven, intelligent-looking, a little above average in height.

The Wellington Rescuers

ELI BOIES: Physician. About fifty-eight years old. Known member of Underground Railroad.

ROBERT L. CUMMINGS: Resident.

MATTHEW DeWOLF: Resident. About sixty-six years old. Known member of Underground Railroad.

MATTHEW GILLET: Farmer. Seventy-four years old. Native of Connecticut. Owned sixty-three-acre farm abutting the railroad tracks in the northeast section of Wellington. Called "Father" Gillet, "a remarkable patriarch."[52] Known member of Underground Railroad.

LEWIS HINES: Farmer. About twenty-seven years old. Born in Ohio. Has infant son.

ABNER LOVELAND: Farmer. Sixty-two years old. Born November 5, 1796, in Berkshire County, Massachusetts. Owns two parcels of farmland, of 75 and almost 120 acres, respectively, on both sides of Main Street, south of the center of Wellington. Known member of Underground Railroad.

JOHN MANDEVILLE: Brickmaker. About fifty years old. Born in New York state. Father of six children. Known member of Underground Railroad.

HENRY D. NILES: Pittsfield lawyer. About thirty-one years old. Born in Ohio. Father of three children, aged one to eight. Apparently a widower. Mother, Sophia Niles, abut fifty-nine, a native of Massachusetts, lives with him, as does sister, Delia, about sixteen.[53]

WILLIAM SCIPLES: Resident. Known member of Underground Railroad.

WALTER SOULES: Farmer. About twenty-nine years old. Born in Massachusetts. Father of five children. Known member of Underground Railroad.

LORING WADSWORTH: Farmer. Fifty-eight years old.[54] Born in Massachusetts. Two children, aged twenty-seven and twenty-nine, living at home. Daughter Olive attended Oberlin in 1840s. First came to Wellington in 1821, when there were only four or five houses in the community, and lived in log cabin his father built. Operates 288-acre Meadowbrook Farm in southeast section of Wellington. A gruff-looking, clean-shaven man. Active in local politics. Known member of Underground Railroad.

DANIEL WILLIAMS: Farmer. Owns 157-acre farm north of Wellington and back off the road to Oberlin, bisected by Black River.

Eight of the twelve indicted from Wellington seemed to have been singled out because they were conductors on the Underground Railroad; five of them happened to be fifty-eight years old or older. However, there seems, on the surface, no reason why Sciples was indicted; he had responded when Deputy Marshal Lowe invoked the Fugitive Slave Law and called on him for help. In contrast, Soules did not help Lowe, and Mandeville—according to Sciples—"was in liquor" and did not know "much" about what happened.[55] Gillet, of course, had urged innkeeper Oliver Wadsworth to open the hotel so that John Price could be rescued, and DeWolf had circulated the indemnification bond for Constable Meacham.

Not one Democrat was indicted, "not even," the *Cleveland Morning Leader* was quick to point out, Norris Wood of Oberlin, who had gone around boasting that "he was the foremost to mount" a ladder. "Why is this?" the *Leader* asked. "Why this discrimination? No man who has read the charge of Judge Willson, heard of the conduct of Marshal Johnson, and knows the circumstances under which Lewis D. Boynton was selected and served upon the Grand Jury, will be at a loss for an answer."[56]

In the case of the Oberlin Rescuers, the reason for the indictments was all too clear: They were Republicans, they were abolitionists, they were antiadministration. Of the twenty-five indicted, the three leading men, all outstanding citizens who represented Oberlin's philosophy and attitudes—Fitch, Peck, and Plumb—had not even gone to Wellington at all. Nor was the federal government aware of Fitch's role afterwards in taking John Price to James Fairchild's home; that secret was not revealed until many years later. Fitch, Peck, and Plumb were indicted for aiding and abetting the Rescue, for urging others to take action. They were the government's special targets; the federal grand jury had purposely taken a recess to find witnesses to testify against them.[57]

One difficulty the government did not foresee, one that would affect the course of its prosecution in the case of two Rescuers resulted from the misspelling or misidentification of several of the indicted. Jacob R. Shipherd was identified in the indictment as *James R. Shepard*, though everyone, including Shipherd himself, knew who was meant; Shipherd received the Shepard warrant from Johnson and went to Cleveland to be arraigned. Similarly, William D. Scrimgeour was named as *Wm. D. Scrimeger* or sometimes in court papers as *Scrimmager*, Richard Winsor was called *Robert Windsor*, and Orindatus S. B. Wall was indicted as *Oliver S. B. Wall*.

On Tuesday, December 7, a day after the federal grand jury released the indictments, Marshal Johnson and an assistant went to Oberlin armed with a "huge packet of warrants."[58] Evidently realizing that he would not be dealing with ordinary criminals, Johnson went first to Peck's home on East College Street and was shown into the professor's study. He informed Peck of the purpose of his visit, produced the warrants, and asked that Peck introduce him to those who were Oberlin residents so that he could then continue on to Wellington to serve the remaining warrants. Without protest, Peck escorted him through town. In all, they found fifteen of the Rescuers. Others were either not at home or at their businesses, or, in the case of William Lincoln and Richard Winsor, away from town altogether because of the school's long winter vacation, which had begun on November 14. Lincoln, who always needed money, was teaching in a school in Dublin, outside Columbus.

Johnson told those he and Peck found that they "would oblige him" if they would take the morning train the next day to Cleveland, where he would meet them at the depot. From there they could proceed to court for the arraignment. Ralph Plumb asked to be excused because of business engagements, but he promised to appear in Cleveland as soon as he could, and the marshal accepted his word. The rest agreed to follow Johnson's instructions, and so the marshal was able to leave town and go on to Wellington. It had all been handled in gentlemanly fashion. The marshal, in fact, told the *Leader* that he was treated "with the utmost courtesy and good feeling."[59] In Wellington, however, Johnson could not find anyone to assist him and was able to serve only a few of the warrants. Those persons he served gave only qualified promises that they would appear voluntarily in Cleveland.

At 10:42 the next morning, to the "shouts and huzzas" of a large crowd that accompanied them to the train station, the Oberlin contingent left for Cleveland. Several persons went with them, including Mayor Beecher, to see that they were "comfortably quar-

tered or safely returned." As expected, Marshal Johnson was waiting for them when the train arrived in Cleveland. He directed them
to omnibuses headed for the Forest City Hotel. The hotel, which
was also known as the Bennet House, was on the corner of Superior
Street and Cleveland's Public Square, a short block's walk from
the courthouse. The Rescuers were told to "take good care of
themselves" until 2:00 P.M., when the arraignment would take
place.[60] They dined at the hotel and then met there with their
counsel.

By this time, the Rescuers had selected three Cleveland lawyers
who had volunteered to defend them. Indeed, they had had a choice
of lawyers because nearly every member of the Cleveland bar offered his services. Two of the three men who were selected were
outstanding attorneys. The leader of the defense team was sixty-
year-old Rufus Pain Spalding, a former Speaker of the Ohio House
of Representatives and onetime associate judge on the state supreme court; although he considered himself a Democrat, he dif-
fered with the party over the slavery issue and was a friend and
supporter of Ohio's Republican governor, Salmon P. Chase. Spalding was being assisted by Albert Gallatin Riddle, another friend of
Chase's and a bitter foe of slavery; although only forty-two years
old, he had served as prosecuting attorney at different times of
both Geauga and Cuyahoga counties and been elected to the Ohio
House at age thirty-two. The third member of the team was the
relatively inexperienced Seneca O. Griswold, who was about to
celebrate his thirty-fifth birthday. Perhaps he was chosen because
he was an Oberlin graduate. There were snide comments that the
attorneys offered to serve "free of charge"[61] in order to better their
own political fortunes.[62]

Soon after two o'clock, the Oberlin Rescuers, accompanied by
their lawyers, proceeded to the courtroom. Johnson read off the
names of those to whom he had served warrants, and Spalding,
speaking for the defendants, entered a plea of not guilty on behalf
of all of them. At the same time, pleas of abatement were entered
on behalf of Shipherd, Wall, and Scrimgeour because of the misnomers in their indictments. Then Spalding stunned the government's prosecutor. Although none of the Wellington Rescuers had
showed up and nearly half of the Oberlin Rescuers had not appeared as yet either, Spalding requested that the trials start immediately.

The federal district attorney, George W. Belden of Canton, was
taken by surprise. A man in his late forties, Belden was something
of a political throwback for his times. He had at one time de-

nounced the Fugitive Slave Law but now was an ardent Democrat and advocate of strict enforcement of the act. He was bitterly opposed from the start to any wavering of legal procedure or any leniency toward the Rescuers, an attitude that prompted his critics to brand him an "Imbecile" and "a man of small intellect," who "glories in his own infamy. A tyrant by nature."[63] Spiteful, easily frustrated, Belden was under pressure from Washington to prosecute the case fully. However, three of his chief witnesses—John Bacon, Anderson Jennings, and Richard Mitchell, all of whom had testified before the grand jury in November—were now back in Kentucky.

Belden begged the court for a two-week continuance to enable him to send to Kentucky for his witnesses. Spalding quickly countered that "citizens of Ohio might think two weeks some time to lie in jail for the convenience of citizens of Kentucky." The presiding judge offered to free the defendants on bail, but Spalding said he doubted that all of them could furnish it. Would it be required? Belden insisted that it would, and the judge said he would set bail at a "very moderate" $500 each. But Griswold rose to say that only some of the defendants could afford bail "in any amount." Spalding then requested time to consult with the Rescuers.

After huddling with them a short while outside the courtroom, Spalding returned and told the judge that the Rescuers did not intend to give any bail, that "the accused were ready for, and demanded immediate trial. The United States had summoned them to appear for trial, and it was the business of the United States to be ready to proceed with the trial without any delay." If there was going to be a delay, Spalding added, the Rescuers were willing to be set free on their own recognizances and would promise to appear when called "but would do nothing farther."[64]

Despite Belden's opposition, the judge agreed that individual recognizances would suffice. But because the court's customary winter recess was approaching, the trial date was scheduled for three months hence, during the next court term, on the second Tuesday in March 1859. In the meantime, the Rescuers were free on their own recognizances, and similar recognizances would be issued as other Rescuers appeared in court to enter their pleas.

The sympathetic *Cleveland Morning Leader* considered the decision a victory for the Rescuers. The newspaper noted that among the defendants "were negroes, who, by the Dred Scott decision, are not citizens of the United States, cannot bring suit in the Federal Court, but who yet were permitted to depart upon their own recognizances. What will Mr. Buchanan say to such an interpretation of that decision? And what will he say to such execution of his pet niggercatching law?"[65]

Before the week was out, others who had been served warrants appeared in Cleveland and entered into personal recognizances. Bushnell showed up the next day, Wednesday, December 8. As promised, Ralph Plumb appeared on Thursday, as did three Wellington Rescuers—Mandeville, DeWolf, and Loveland. All the other Wellington Rescuers but Cummings entered pleas on Friday, December 10; Cummings did not appear in Cleveland until the next spring. Although Charles Langston had reportedly warned federal authorities "to make their peace with God before they lay hands on him,"[66] he appeared voluntarily on Christmas Eve.

Of all the thirty-seven Rescuers who were indicted, seven would never be apprehended. The three of them who were runaway slaves—Jerry Fox, Thomas Gena, and John Hartwell—had good reason not to appear publicly in court. The *Louisville (Kentucky) Daily Courier* carried a report from Cleveland that said they would "probably 'cut for Canada.'"[67] The other four who were never arrested were the younger Bartlett, John Copeland, Chauncey Goodyear, and Franklin Lewis. Copeland, it was rumored, had escorted John Price to Canada.[68]

Because of the college's winter vacation, there were two Oberlin students whom Marshal Johnson had been unable to serve: William Lincoln and Richard Winsor. Winsor would appear voluntarily in Cleveland to enter his plea sometime around the first of March, after the school's spring term began; he would also at that time have the misspelling of his name in the indictment corrected. Lincoln would be arraigned before then, under circumstances that would raise a hue and cry throughout the Western Reserve.

*

Dayton's worst fears were realized the night after the indictments were handed down. A shot had already been fired into his house, which was on the east side of Pleasant Street. Now, in the evening of December 7, a group of black men met in secret and then went to the deputy's home armed with clubs. Dayton's wife, Maria, answered the door. The blacks did not believe her when she said that he was not at home and said they wanted to see for themselves. Believing she could not prevent them, she allowed the black men to search the house. The incident disturbed Dayton so much that he decided to leave Oberlin.[69]

The *Plain Dealer* saw the intrusion in Dayton's home as another violation of the law by Oberlin residents. "If the white people of Oberlin do not restrain these negroes from such lawless acts," it warned, "there will be worse trouble than that arising from rescuing fugitives." But as its rival, the *Leader*, observed, "the citizens of Oberlin have great cause of provocation towards Deputy Marshal Dayton." The "official war on Oberlin," it said, had started with the appointment of Mathew Johnson, who "found a ready and willing tool" in Dayton. The *Leader* said that "the man-stealing propensity" of Dayton had already forced several blacks to flee Oberlin for Canada. Was it so strange therefore that both whites and blacks found him "obnoxious"? "Their forbearance is the greater marvel."[70]

NINE

Legal Maneuvers, Politics as Usual

"What makes you sad, and seems dreadful, Eva?"

"O, things that are done, and done all the time. I feel sad for our poor people; they love me dearly, and they are all good and kind to me. I wish, papa, they were all free.*"*

"Why, Eva, child, don't you think they are well enough off now?"

"O, but papa, if anything should happen to you, what would become of them? . . . What horrid things people do, and can do!" and Eva shuddered.

"My dear child, you are too sensitive. I'm sorry I ever let you hear such stories."

"O, that's what troubles me, papa. You want me to live so happy, and never to have any pain,—never suffer anything—not even hear a sad story, when other poor creatures have nothing but pain and sorrow, all their lives;—it seems selfish. I ought to know such things, I ought to feel about them! Such things always sunk into my heart; they went down deep; I've thought and thought about them. Papa, isn't there any way to have all slaves made free?"

Chapter XXIV: "Foreshadowings

The New Year—1859—began in an unseasonably mild fashion, an almost three-week spell of above normal temperatures. During the balmy spell, in the middle of December, Charles Grandison Finney went to New York and embarked with his wife on his scheduled two-year revivalist mission to England. He left Oberlin apparently without saying so much as a word about John Price's rescue; he left no special instructions, no words of advice, support, or consolation, even though one of his professors and four students were among those indicted in the affair that was now unofficially called the Oberlin-Wellington Rescue.

Both sides in the Rescue case were girding for the upcoming trials. Marshal Mathew Johnson began drawing up a list of prospective jurors. Meanwhile, the exclusion of Republicans from the federal grand jury that issued the indictments had taught the Rescuers a valuable lesson. They resolved not to be outwitted again. On January 4, the same day Johnson was told to prepare a juror list, the Oberlin Rescuers asked their Wellington counterparts to a conference to discuss their common defense. And, to demonstrate their confidence in the righteousness of their cause, they also asked the Wellingtonians to join them and a group of supporters at a special banquet to be held at 2:00 P.M. on Tuesday, January 11, at the Palmer House, a gathering, the *Oberlin Students' Monthly* pointed out, that was intended to effect "an organization for defence and offence."[1]

That day the temperature turned winter cold and there was snow on the ground, but as a correspondent reported in the *Cleveland Herald*, the mood was jubilant: "The day shone out rosy and glad, the south wind tickled us under the chin, multitudes of sleigh bells laughed outright at our meditated solemnities, acquaintances giggled at every corner and 'only wished they'd been indicted too'(!)."[2]

"The Felon's Feast," as the celebration was quickly dubbed, lasted more than four hours, replete with all the "fixin's."[3] While the Oberlin String Band played, sixty-four persons sat down to the meal, among them twenty-six of the Rescuers and nine of their wives—Mrs. James Bartlett, Henry Evans's wife, Henrietta, Jane Fitch, Esther Peck, Marrilla Plumb, Cecilia Scott, Amanda Wall, David Watson's wife, Marie, and John Watson's wife, Margaret. None of the Rescuers, the *Oberlin Evangelist* reported, "looked abashed; all carried themselves as if they felt that their case was well made with conscience and the Higher Law, however it might stand with human enactments and human tribunals! Nor did the guests . . . manifest the least compunction at consorting with the alleged criminals about them!"[4] The participants, the *Cleveland Morning Leader* observed, included "venerable gray-headed men, some of the early settlers of Lorain county—men who had felled the forest and built the humble log-cabins, school-houses, and churches of the wilderness—noble men, good men, and true men—men of Puritan and Covenanter stock, of Revolutionary blood, of spotless reputation—indicted criminals! and for what? for violation of the Bible injunction, 'Whatsoever ye would that others should do unto you, do ye even so unto them.'"[5]

The "sumptuous repast" was followed by a "feast of reason and flow of soul."[6] Speeches were given, toasts made, letters of support read—some high-spirited, some jocular, but all sanguine. The Rev. John Keep—"Father" Keep, the "Patriarch of Oberlin," for twenty-four years a member of its Board of Trustees, the man who had cast the deciding vote for the admission of black men and women into the college—opened the festivities with a prayer.

The first of a series of toasts—indubitably nonalcoholic—was for *The Inalienable Rights of Man*. Speaking to the topic, George

G. Washburn, editor of the *Lorain Independent Democrat*, criticized the Fugitive Slave Law, saying, "Making war as it does upon all that is manly in man, we will hate it while we live, and bequeathe our hatred to those who come after us when we die." Henry Peck said, "We mean to make patriotism a part of our religion," but "we hold that the commonwealth can prosper only when she is loyal to God."

Roswell G. Horr, clerk of the Court of Common Pleas in Elyria, drew laughter and applause when he said that the fugitive law "sometimes sunk men below the depths of manhood, and they became a *Dayton!*" Rescuer Ralph Plumb said he had searched his "past life" to try to discover what his crime was. "I find many things for which I ought to be condemned, but surely the wrong things of my life were not included in what I did on the 13th of September, 1858." His sins on that day, he continued, "were sins of omission, and not of commission. I did not go to Wellington, but I confess to you all (don't tell any of the witnesses what I say), that my whole being was stirred when the news came suddenly upon us that a man had been stolen from our midst at mid-day, and when the noble band of rescuers wended their way towards Wellington, my heart went up in prayer to Almighty God for the success of their enterprise."

Fellow Rescuer James Fitch won some chuckles when he said he had been indicted "for no cause, unless for his 'poor prayers' in behalf of the oppressed." And, in the same light vein, Mayor Beecher hailed the Rescuers as "Men of true grit. . . . May we never fall into worse company; and should the bloodhounds of Slavery again visit our county, may they find a *Wall Plumb* before them, *De Wolf* after them, and get well *Peck*-ed in the bargain." To which Henry Peck gleefully responded, "When those slaveholders come again, may we have a Beecher for *mare* to give them a trot!"

A number of letters were read, among them a note of support from George A. Benedict, editor of the *Cleveland Herald*, who said that "the spirit which dictates the festival, and which gave rise to it, meets my heartiest sympathy." John M. Vincent, former prosecuting attorney of Lorain County, wrote that the Rescuers' position "is a proud one. To be charged with the crime (?) of loving Liberty too well, enrolls your names with that immortal band of *Patriots* who gave us the 'Declaration of Independence,' and the foundation of a free government." Another Elyria attorney, Stevenson Burke, wrote,

> If there is any doctrine or creed to which I give my full and unqual-
> ified consent, it is the doctrine of political equality and individual

freedom; the right of man, black or white, native or foreigner, to carve out, under God, his own destiny, and choose his own rulers. . . . It is said that 'whom the gods would destroy they first make mad,' and that symptoms of madness have recently appeared in high places, cannot be denied. What may be determined on, therefore, by the ruling madmen, I know not. Nor can I tell what farther sacrifices it may yet become necessary for the lovers of freedom to make, to render our own beloved and beautiful Ohio, in deed and in truth the land of the free and the home of the brave—to deliver our people from the demoralizing spectacle of slave-catching and slave-hunting in our midst—to render it safe for the humanely disposed among us to feed the hungry, clothe the naked, or relieve the distressed, without fear of Government spies, or running the risk of fines, forfeitures, and prison bars and bolts.

It was John Mercer Langston who, portentously, raised the specter of war. Langston was among the first to recognize the possible impact of the Rescue case on public opinion. John Price had been saved less than a month and a half after an all-black state convention was held in Cincinnati at which Langston's brother Charles presided. Its major accomplishment was the founding of the Ohio State Anti-Slavery Society, whose goals were the abolition of slavery and the securing of black rights by, as its constitution cryptically put it, "political and moral means, so far as may be." Charles was set up with an office in Cleveland, where he served as executive secretary. John Mercer, who was elected president of the society and also become one of its traveling fund-raising agents, realized that the Rescue provided him with a unique opportunity to combine his role as the society's spokesman with that of advocate for the repeal of the Fugitive Slave Law. But more than anything else, John Mercer saw the campaign ahead as a struggle to attack and topple the proslavery Buchanan administration: "The Democratic party must be destroyed" became his motto. Langston's itinerary of speaking engagements was already being filled with rallies for the Rescuers, at which he fulminated against Washington and passionately urged his listeners to "trample under foot the Fugitive Slave Law as they did lately in Wellington."[7]

John Mercer had requested to speak at the Felon's Feast in his brother Charles's absence. He began by asking, "What is the work of the American citizen of to-day to accomplish?

"It is this. He is to reinstate the Declaration of Independence, and to reinstate the Constitution of the United States. American slavery has stricken down the first; the Fugitive Slave Law the latter.

"Shall we meet this duty?" Langston continued. "To do it, we must make sacrifices—go to prison, or, if necessary, go out on the battle-field to meet the Slave Oligarchy."

A similarly ominous note was struck when Ralph Plumb read a letter from an old neighbor of his in Ashtabula County, John Brown, Jr., "son of the famous 'Ossawatomie' Capt. John Brown." In it, young Brown declared, "Step by step the Slave power is driving us on to take one or the other horn of the dilemma, either to be *false* to *Humanity* or *traitors* to the *Government*. If we 'would ordain and establish Justice,' and maintain our Constitution not only in its essential spirit but its letter, strange to say we are *forced* into the *attitude of resistance to the Government*. I am glad the work of Judicial 'crushing out' is progressing not only out of Kansas but in Ohio—on the Western Reserve, the New England of the West."

There were several other speeches and toasts, the dinner finally concluding with the appointment of a committee to arrange for the Rescuers' defense and "to attend to *certain other items* not yet made public, but which some time may be, to the inconsolable astonishment of a few individuals, and their friends, if they have any." The "inconsolable astonishment" alluded to was a legal ploy, suggested by defense attorney Albert Gallatin Riddle, that was already the subject of discussions in Elyria by three Lorain County officials—Roswell Horr, Probate Judge James S. Carpenter, and the county's new prosecuting attorney. The last was a twenty-four-year-old man with a name that would have been familiar to John Price's captors: Washington Wallace Boynton, son of "General" Lewis Boynton and older brother of Shakespeare Boynton. Unlike his father, however, W. W. Boynton, as he was known, was an antislavery advocate. The three men had an idea: if the federal judge could summon a grand jury, why couldn't they do the same?

*

If the Rescuers glowed with self-satisfaction that January day, they were furious when, three days later, William Lincoln was brusquely arrested. Unaware that there was a warrant out for his arrest, the Oberlin student was teaching a class in Dublin, twelve miles northwest of Columbus, when two men with pistols in their hands barged into the schoolhouse. One was a local constable, the other Jacob Lowe's assistant in the seizure of John Price, Samuel Davis, who was both deputy sheriff of Franklin County and the county jailer. Davis asked Lincoln what his name was, and when Lincoln gave it, Davis said he was "the very fellow he was after."[8]

Without any further explanation, Davis took out a pair of hand-cuffs and, while Lincoln's young pupils watched in horror, fastened Lincoln's wrists. Davis told the schoolchildren that their teacher was "a bad man," but a teenage girl "cried thru her tears 'There is more goodness in his little finger than in your whole carcase.'"[9] Lincoln protested about being manacled, saying, "We never resisted Law." "Stop," he said, "I shall make no resistance; I shall of course go with you; you need not put these things upon me."[10] But Davis ignored him. Lincoln, who had been wearing a gown and slippers, was allowed to exchange them for an overcoat and boots. As Davis and the constable hurried him out the door, Lincoln called back to his crying pupils, "Come next Monday to school. I shall be here again by that time." The two men "thrust" him into a carriage,[11] and, after dismissing the constable, the deputy sheriff started for Columbus.

Davis, whose experience in Wellington had been "the worst scrap he had ever got into,"[12] cursed abolitionists all the way, making it clear to Lincoln "what he would like to do" with all the Rescuers. It was only after Lincoln insisted upon knowing under what authority he had been arrested that Davis showed him a "capias" issued in Cleveland.[13]

Davis and his prisoner had to cross the flooded Scioto River to reach Columbus. Lincoln's wrists were painfully sore from wearing the handcuffs, and he feared that the carriage might turn over as it plunged through the swollen river. He again asked that the handcuffs be removed, and again Davis refused.

Lincoln had been arrested about 1:30 P.M. By the time Davis drove into the capital, it was dark. As they rode by the State House, Davis, still cursing, said, "You d—— fanatical fool you, do you think the N.[North] & the S.[South] are such fools, as to cut each other's throats, over the d——d nigger." Lincoln responded that "God wd. smite N. & S. unless the slaves were freed." And then a bizarre thing happened. As Lincoln rebuked Davis for "his swearing & sin," the deputy sheriff "burst out sobbing as his tears fell & said 'By God, had I known who you were, I would not have arrested you, not for $1000.'" Hoping to take advantage of Davis's change of heart, Lincoln asked him to drive him first to see some friends he knew so that he could seek legal assistance, but Davis apparently felt pressured to continue on to the county jail. Lowe was waiting for him there. At the jail, Lincoln asked Lowe to let him contact friends but was turned down by him, too. Only later was Lincoln allowed to write a letter, but by then the local post office was closed and Lowe planned to take him on a 4:00 A.M. train to Cleveland before it reopened.

By now Lincoln's wrists were "severely galled."[14] Despite his pleadings to have the handcuffs removed, he was told that "his crime was not trifling enough to allow of favors." Before he was put into a cell, he asked once more that the manacles be removed and was refused. However, once he was safely inside the cell, Davis finally took pity and removed them. Lincoln had not eaten since noon. He was told that supper had been ordered for him. While waiting for it, he tried to lie down, but the straw pallet provided for him in the cell was full of rats and he had to drive them out before he could sit down on it to rest. He stuffed his nostrils with a handkerchief to keep out the stench. There were about forty inmates in the prison, and one of them called out from an adjoining cell, "What the devil are you in here for?" "For doing God's will," Lincoln answered. "And what may be doing God's will?" "Rescuing a slave from the U.S. marshals." "Boys," the man shouted to the other inmates, "let's give him 3 cheers."

The cheers were heartening, but Lincoln was also taunted by several men who came by the cell expressly to harass him. One of them was Anson Dayton, who had recently been rewarded with the position of clerk of the Ohio House by the ruling Democrats.[15]

The long-awaited supper never arrived. Lincoln finally managed to fall asleep, but he was abruptly awakened in the middle of the night and taken by Lowe to the train depot. There he finally got a cup of coffee and a piece of pie. It was the only food he would have for twenty-eight hours.

At four o'clock on the afternoon of Saturday, January 15, Lincoln—in a coat and vest he had to borrow for the court appearance[16]—was brought before Judge Hiram Willson, entered his plea, and was released on his own recognizance. He left the courthouse dazed, with only twenty cents in his pocket. He needed $1.10 for the train fare to Oberlin. Lincoln prevailed upon Lowe for help. The deputy marshal relented, giving him a dollar. When Lincoln reached Oberlin, he was welcomed with food and given the money to return to Dublin.

The circumstances of Lincoln's arrest produced a wave of indignation—and, for abolitionist forces, a moral and political victory. Both Republicans and Democrats in Dublin turned out for a public meeting, embarrassed by Davis's behavior because he had lived in the community before becoming the county jailer. They adopted not only a resolution condemning "the illegal, cowardly and insulting use of official authority" but also other resolutions applauding Lincoln's involvement in John Price's rescue and pledging resistance to the Fugitive Slave Law, "which compels us against the dictates of conscience and humanity, to assist in sending back a fellow citizen to slavery."[17]

Lincoln's arrest caught the attention of the public outside of Ohio, as well. Henry Peck, who had taken Lincoln into his home in the winter of 1855–56 when he was invalided with consumption,[18] wrote an account of the arrest for the *Columbus State Journal*. It was reprinted in William Lloyd Garrison's Boston newspaper, the *Liberator*. "Now, if *manacles* and *imprisonment in a jail* are not singular treatment for a man who is on his way to be discharged on his own recognizances, and whom the attending officer had reason to suppose would be so discharged," declared the Oberlin professor, "then I am altogether mistaken." Peck warned that "the fire which this outrage has kindled in Lorain will not go out till an effort has been made to teach these arbitrary and insolent officials that freemen know what their rights are."[19]

❋

Both sides in the case were now squaring off for what was going to be a legal confrontation with no quarter given. The Rescuers were counting at least in part on public sympathy to win their case. Meetings of groups such as the Langstons' Ohio State Anti-Slavery Society were held in the College Chapel in an effort to drum up support. Before returning to Dublin, Lincoln appeared before "an extraordinary meeting" held in the same chapel to describe his arrest.[20] English-born Hamilton Hill, the school's treasurer, wrote to the British Anti-Slavery Society, describing John Price's rescue and pointing out that "prominent in this humane transaction were three Englishmen and a Scotchman." Hill noted that each of the Rescuers faced not only imprisonment but also a fine of up to $1,000. "Any sums" that could be raised for their defense, he said, should be sent by a letter of credit to the cashier of the Lorain Bank in Elyria. His appeal was published in the society's *Anti-Slavery Reporter*.[21] Meanwhile, Professor James Monroe began compiling a list of contributors, accepting donations from individuals who pledged "to pay the sum annually annexed to our names to the 'Liberation Fund.'" Fifty-three persons donated sums ranging from $1 to $10.[22]

Clearly, however, public opinion and support, no matter how welcome, would not be enough. The Rescuers planned to coun-

terattack on the legal front, too. The "astonishment" promised at
the Felon's Feast was revealed on Tuesday, February 15, when the
Lorain County Grand Jury returned true bills against Anderson
Jennings, Richard Mitchell, Jacob Lowe, and Samuel Davis. Warrants were issued for their arrest. They were charged with kidnapping under a state statute that Rescuer Ralph Plumb had helped
to introduce in the Ohio legislature in 1857. It made the arrest,
imprisonment, kidnapping, or decoying out of Ohio of any free
black or mulatto or any alleged fugitive an indictable misde-
meanor. The indictment referred to John Price as a "free Black
person."[23] In charging the county grand jury, Judge James Carpenter declared that the "gist of the offence" was the taking of a black
out of Ohio "before he is proved to be a fugitive slave":

"The Constitution of Ohio inhibits slavery, and regards all persons as free except criminals. . . . Who, then, is presumed to be
free? Everybody. Every man, woman and child in Ohio, of whatever birth, descent, parentage, complexion, or comformation, is
presumed in law to be free." And free, Carpenter continued, meant
that the "instant" that "the slave . . . crosses our boundary, he is
baptized in the air of freedom; and that baptism is irrevocable."

Carpenter said his position was upheld both by the Ohio Constitution and that of the United States. "Our Bill of Rights," he
said, "begins 'Sec. 1. All men are by nature free and independent.'
. . . Does any caviller pretend that the words, 'all men' . . . were
meant to exclude blacks and mulattoes?" As for kidnappers, he
concluded: "He who handles the edge tools must run the risk of
cutting his own flesh."[24]

✳

Belden was busy, too. The case was time-consuming and complicated by the number of individuals indicted. On February 26,
Belden wrote to Washington, requesting United States Attorney
General Jeremiah S. Black for assistance. Black was a firm believer
in following the strict letter of the law. He had been chief justice
of the Pennsylvania Supreme Court, "an able, well-read" man, but
stubborn, temperamental, easily prejudiced, "humorless," and,
perhaps the result of a religious experience in the 1830s, "self-
righteous." He was, it was said, a strong foe, "not pro-Southern as
such, but he ardently disliked any kind of radicalism."[25] Oberlin
symbolized radicalism on the issue of slavery, and the man Black
was responsible to, President James Buchanan, was totally insen-
sitive on that issue. Northerners might applaud Buchanan's op-

position to repeal of the ban on the importation of slaves but would be shocked by his rationale. In rejecting the idea of repeal, Buchanan, in his Third Annual Message to Congress that year, declared:

> Of the evils to the master, the one most to be dreaded would be the introduction of wild, heathen, and ignorant barbarians among the sober, orderly, and quiet slaves whose ancestors have been on the soil for several generations. This might tend to barbarize, demoralize, and exasperate the whole mass, and produce most deplorable consequences.
>
> The effect upon the existing slave would, if possible, be still more deplorable. At present, he is treated with kindness and humanity. He is well fed, well clothed, and not overworked. His condition is incomparably better than that of the coolies which modern nations of high civilization have employed as a substitute for African slaves. Both the philanthropy and the self-interest of the master have combined to produce this humane result.[26]

Black had every intention of pursuing the case against the Rescuers to the fullest extent of the law. On March 10 he wrote back to Belden, authorizing him to hire an assistant counsel.[27]

As March 8, the date the Rescuers' case was to start, approached, Belden found he was not prepared to proceed. He was still waiting to hear from Black and was occupied with requesting subpoenas for, among others, John Bacon, Jennings, Mitchell, Mason County Clerk Robert Cochran, Deputy Marshal Lowe, and Deputy Sheriff Samuel Davis, as well as scores of Oberlin and Wellington residents who had witnessed the events surrounding John Price's rescue. Belden asked for and was granted a postponement until Tuesday, April 5. So instead of the trials starting on March 8, he and Spalding met that day to discuss arrangements and to select a jury. They agreed that the first Rescuer to be tried would be Simeon Bushnell. The trials of the others would follow in the order in which their names appeared on the court docket. There was never any explanation given as to why the Rescuers were not tried as a group, though it is probable that Belden wanted to separate the Oberlin defendants from the Wellington ones. Bushnell may have been chosen to be tried first because so many people had seen him driving off from Wellington in a buggy with John.

Next, Belden and Spalding selected the jurors. In picking a struck jury, each attorney had the right to strike off—that is, challenge preemptorily—twelve of the forty names Marshal Johnson had presented. The court clerk would later draw from the remaining

names the twelve men who would hear the case. Although Johnson included individuals from as far away as Williams and Henry
counties in northwest Ohio, not one of the forty persons on the
list was from Lorain County.[28] Moreover, of those forty persons,
thirty were Democrats and only ten were Republicans,[29] an im-
balance that enabled Belden to easily strike all the Republicans
and get an all-Democrat jury. Like the federal grand jury that had
indicted the Rescuers, the trial jury was completely one-sided. To
add further insult to the proceedings, one of the jurors finally chosen was an officer of the court, a federal deputy marshal from
Harrison County, though Spalding was unaware of it at the time.

However much of a triumph that may have seemed, the federal
district attorney hardly had time to savor it. He had a worrisome
problem on his hands. Lorain County law enforcement officers
were now on the lookout for Jennings, Mitchell, Lowe, and Davis,
planning to arrest them on the kidnapping warrants once they
reached Cleveland. Belden requested federal warrants to make certain that Jennings and Mitchell appeared as witnesses. He informed Judge Hiram Willson that he had learned that "efforts are
being made by certain ill-advised persons to prevent" their appearance.[30] Belden was sure that federal warrants superseded state
warrants. On Monday, April 4, the day before Bushnell's trial was
to begin, Mathew Johnson and Anson Dayton intercepted the two
Kentuckians on their way to Cleveland at a train stop outside the
city and took them into custody on the basis of the federal warrant
that Belden had secured.[31]

That same day, another burden fell on Belden. Democratic Congressman Samuel S. Cox, the influential owner and editor of the
Columbia Statesman, had written Secretary of the Interior Jacob
Thompson, requesting that the federal government pay for hiring
an attorney to defend two of his constituents, Lowe and Davis,
against the kidnapping charges. The two men, he said, were "vig-
ilant and courageous" and had acted "regardless of all consequences." However, they were "not well off," and, in Cox's
judgment, "the government owes them a defence." The administration, however, was not prepared to shoulder the cost of a Columbus lawyer. Instead, Thompson instructed Belden to take "all
necessary professional steps to defend" them and, while he was at
it, Jennings and Mitchell as well.[32]

The legal ploy by Lorain County officials snared only one of
John's captors. While en route from Columbus for the trial in
Cleveland, Lowe was arrested in Grafton on April 4 by a deputy

sheriff and lodged in the Lorain County Jail. However, Mayor P. W. Sampsell released him on $1,000 bail on the understanding that he would return to Elyria to stand trial, and the deputy marshal proceeded on his way once more to Cleveland.

*

There was, at the same time, both joyous and sobering news for the Rescuers. In a clear-cut measure of support for Simeon Bushnell, the bookstore clerk was elected town clerk of Russia Township in the annual election on April 4, the day before his trial was to start. However, it was now certain that William Scrimgeour was too ill to appear in Cleveland for the trials. Scrimgeour had taken to his bed on Tuesday, March 22, bleeding from his lungs "very badly."[33]

TEN

The Case Against the White Clerk

"Father, what if thee should get found out again?" said Simeon second, as he buttered his cake.

"I should pay my fine," said Simeon, quietly. . . .

"But isn't it a shame to make such laws?"

"Thee mustn't speak evil of thy rulers, Simeon," said his father, gravely. "The Lord only gives us our worldly goods that we may do justice and mercy; if our rulers require a price of us for it, we must deliver it up."

"Well, I hate those old slaveholders!" said the boy, who felt as unchristian as became any modern reformer.

"I am surprised at thee, son," said Simeon; "thy mother never taught thee so. I would do even the same for the slaveholder as for the slave, if the Lord brought him to my door in affliction."

Chapter XIII: "The Quaker Settlement"

The County Court House in which the trials were to be held was a splendid, recently completed Renaissance building that was so new that Marshal Mathew Johnson was still hurrying about, trying to get the federal offices inside it ready. The structure, of dressed stone, was three stories high with arched windows and quoins at the corners and stood across from the northwest side of Cleveland's Public Square, next to the First Presbyterian (Old Stone) Church and around the corner from the Cuyahoga County Jail. A short flight of steps from the sidewalk led to the ground-floor offices of, on the left, the county auditor and probate judge and, on the right, those of the recorder and treasurer. The second floor contained a courtroom and sheriff's office on the left and, on the right, a second courtroom, where the Rescuer trials would be held, a judge's chambers, and the office of the court clerk. On the top floor were two jury rooms and the offices of the Board of School Examiners. The building cost a then substantial $152,500.

Johnson, who was responsible for furnishing the federal courtroom and chambers on the second floor, pleaded with Secretary of the Interior Jacob Thompson for more funds. Congress had appropriated $7,100 for "fencing, grading, paving and furnishing" the building as well as a new post office and customs house on the

Scene of the trials, the newly built Cuyahoga County Courthouse.
Collection of the author

east side of the square, but Johnson had already spent $4,650 of that amount and needed $7,593 more to complete the work. He had brought over all the furniture from the old courthouse, on the southwest corner of the Public Square, but he hadn't been able to salvage "the old matting which covered the Court Rooms, and the old stoves which were burnt out." Moreover, Johnson expected "a large expenditure by the government" because of the trials of the Rescuers, which were about to start. "At least one hundred witnesses," he estimated, would be subpoenaed. He said that the cost of subpoenaing them, plus the per diem ("45 days at $2 per day each") and travel allowance for the jury, as well as usual court expenses, would total nearly $11,000—and he had only $2,465.50 in cash on hand. Johnson asked Thompson to "please" send the difference—$8,243.50.[1]

Johnson seriously underestimated the number of subpoenas that would be required. Twenty-nine persons would testify as prosecution witnesses for Simeon Bushnell's trial alone, and subpoenas would be issued for thirty others, some of whom were paid to travel to Cleveland but were not called upon to testify.[2] The defense had, of course, to shoulder the cost of serving its own subpoenas.

*

Though Tuesday, April 5, was a cold, nasty day—it snowed in the morning—the courtroom was packed. Friends, wives, and other relatives of the Rescuers were in the audience, many of the women patiently knitting. There were reporters from numerous newspapers and periodicals, including the *Worcester* (Massachusetts) *Spy*, the *Pittsburgh Commercial Journal*, and the *Law Monthly* of Cleveland, as well as correspondents from all the major newspapers in the Western Reserve. Typical of the current journalistic practice, their reports were being picked up and carried verbatim in newspapers throughout the country. In Kentucky, for example, both the *Louisville Daily Courier* and the *Tri-Weekly Maysville Eagle* carried accounts that first appeared in the *Cleveland Plain Dealer*. The *New-York Times* also relied on the *Plain Dealer* for coverage, while the *Daily National Intelligencer* in Washington carried reports culled from the *Daily Cleveland Herald*. (The *Herald*, which thought "no criminal court ever had a more respectable class of prisoners in the criminal docks," called the Rescuer trials "disgraceful to our country."[3]) William Lincoln reported on the trial for the abolitionist *Free South* of Newport, Kentucky, even though he was one of those indicted. Perhaps the most unusual reporter, however, was the *New York Tribune*'s man, "pallid" and "worn-looking" John H. Kagi, one of John Brown's chief aides, a veteran of the Kansas troubles, who "had more the appearance of a divinity student than a warrior."[4] Kagi, a twenty-three-year-old native Ohioan, was in Cleveland not only to cover the trial but also to raise funds for and to recruit members to take part in a scheme of Brown's.

The defense table was crowded. The defendant, Bushnell, was flanked by Rescuers Henry Peck and Ralph Plumb and now four defense attorneys: Spalding, Riddle, Griswold, and a new counselor, forty-four-year-old Franklin T. Backus of Cleveland. A former prosecuting attorney of Cuyahoga County who had served in both houses of the Ohio legislature, Backus was ordinarily a political rival of Riddle's. His appearance indicated the unanimity that the Rescuers' cause was attracting. The defense team had an invisible member: Governor Salmon P. Chase. The "Attorney General of Fugitive Slaves" was providing behind-the-scenes advice.[5]

Besides the three Rescuers seated at the defense table, seventeen other Rescuers were in the courtroom, among them, although a new school term had begun, Oberlin students William Lincoln, Ansel Lyman, Jacob Shipherd, and Richard Winsor. Even though their counsel had told them that their recognizances were automatically continued until they surrendered them, the Rescuers were apparently unsure whether they would be asked to renew the recognizances or be taken into custody. Therefore, they made it a point to appear in court each day. Six Wellington Rescuers had been excused from court by Belden for the time being, presumably because they had pressing business.

Belden had added a new member to his prosecution team, as well: George Bliss, a former state judge and Democratic congressman. During the last presidential election, Bliss had made a campaign speech in Oberlin, the first one ever, it was claimed, by a Democrat in that "Babylon of Abolitionism."[6]

At another table, Robert A. Cochran, the clerk of the Mason County Court in Kentucky, who was a prosecution witness, was allowed as a matter of courtesy to sit with the clerk of the federal court, Frederick G. Green. Green, a native of Maryland who had moved to Ohio in 1833, was a former congressman and advocate of the extension of slavery who voted in 1854 for repeal of the Missouri Compromise.

The government's case was simple: Bushnell violated the Fugitive Slave Law when he participated in the rescue of the slave John, who was the chattel of John Bacon. All Belden had to prove was that John was in fact Bacon's property, that he had been lawfully seized under a certified power of attorney, and that Bushnell had had a hand in the slave's subsequent escape from arrest. Belden planned to ignore, as much as possible, reference to the federal warrant that Bacon's agent, Anderson Jennings, and Deputy Marshal Jacob Lowe had procured in Columbus; he obviously realized it was a questionable document because it was issued in Columbus rather than Cleveland. He had no intention of even entering it into evidence. In fact, although he had subpoenaed both Lowe and his assistant, Samuel Davis, as witnesses, Belden would not call upon either man to testify.

Bushnell's defense, on the other hand, was complicated. First of all, there was the question of John Price's identity. Was he really the slave owned by John Bacon who had escaped from Kentucky in 1856? Did their descriptions match? And what about the power of attorney and federal warrant? Were they properly drawn up? Hadn't the Mason County clerk's name been forged on the power of attorney? Wasn't the federal warrant the document used as the basis for John Price's seizure? And if it was used, wasn't it invalid because it had been issued in the Southern District of Ohio rather than in the Northern District? Who knew about the two documents anyway? Who had read them? Who was in charge of the prisoner? In other words, even if John Price *was* Bacon's property, was he properly arrested? And even if the seizure was legal, did Bushnell, for one, know that John Price had been properly arrested? Then, too, there was the question of the legality of the federal act: Didn't the Ohio Constitution have precedence over the United States Constitution? Weren't states' rights paramount?

More than an individual was on trial. The defense attorneys were well aware that they were playing to the press and the spectators in the courtroom in an unabashed effort to rouse public sympathy against slavery, the Fugitive Slave Law, and the Buchanan administration. District Attorney Belden would complain that because of defense tactics he "did not know whether to address the court, the jury, or the audience."[7] The defense counsel would be accused of "killing two birds with one stone each. . . . defending the Rescuers and running for Congress at the same time."[8] Regardless of whether the defense lawyers hoped to further their own political careers, there seems to be no doubt that, faced with a Democratic judge, jury, and prosecutors, they did not expect an impartial trial or even contemplate a verdict of acquittal. So their appeal was broadened to make political hay of the slavery issue for the benefit of the Republican party.

The trial itself, which would last ten days, started slowly. Court convened at 10:00 A.M. on April 5, and it was evident from the outset that Judge Willson was averse to defense attempts to secure a fair hearing. Green, the court clerk, drew the names of twelve jurors from the sixteen Democrats still on the list. Spalding went through the formality of asking each one whether he had made up his mind about Bushnell's guilt or innocence—all answered in the negative—and Belden then requested Green to call out the names of the prosecution witnesses. The district attorney was surprised when twenty-nine did not respond, and he asked for an adjournment until the afternoon. Spalding was amenable, but he recommended that the jurors be sworn first, as "a matter of common prudence," so that they would not discuss the case outside the courtroom "with the community at large."[9] Belden, however, thought an admonishment from Willson was all that was necessary, and the judge readily concurred.

When the court reconvened at two o'clock, thirteen prosecution witnesses were still missing, but Belden was ready to proceed with the ones on hand. Before he was able to call his first one, however, Riddle entered a motion to quash the indictment. The motion was basically a statement of the arguments that the defense would stress throughout the trial—that the Fugitive Slave Law was unconstitutional, that the federal grand jury had been illegally impaneled, that Bushnell's indictment was defective because it was based on a warrant issued and returnable in the Southern Judicial District, that John Price was not legally a slave, and that Bushnell had no idea John had been legally seized. As might be expected, the judge deferred ruling on the motion and ordered the trial to begin. As the witnesses were then led to an empty jury room to wait their being called to testify, the judge told them not to return to the courtroom while testimony was being given unless they were summoned to testify themselves—an order that Chauncey Wack, for one, chose to ignore.[10]

At last, after some further routine court procedure, the first of the government's witnesses was called: John P. G. Bacon. Surprisingly, the slave master was treated with respect by the defense and the supporters of the Rescuers. They would make fun of Jennings and Mitchell, jeer at their accents, and interrupt their testimony with laughter; alluding to a character in *Uncle Tom's Cabin*, the *Herald* referred to Jennings as a "nigger catcher the perfect antitype of Haley."[11] But no one ever mocked Bacon, whose demeanor and manners were impeccable.

Belden handled the questioning for the prosecution, Backus the cross-examination for the defense. Bacon, of course, could not testify to Bushnell's implication in the Rescue. He was in court to describe John as well as to detail the events of the slave's escape from the Bacon farm, the power of attorney that was issued, and his recruiting of Jennings and Mitchell to bring John back. John, he insisted, was his property; he was not, Bacon said, a slave trader in the "business of capturing niggers."[12]

The power of attorney was introduced into evidence. It described John as "about five feet six or eight inches high, heavy set, copper colored, and will weigh about 140 or 50 pounds."[13] Robert Cochran was called to explain how his deputy had drawn up the power of attorney and signed it for him while he was absent from the Mason County Courthouse.

Cochran was followed on the stand by Anderson Jennings. The tall, rough-looking Kentuckian, who spoke in a coarse drawl that often prompted spectators in the courtroom to snigger or laugh scornfully, could not single out Bushnell among the hundreds who besieged the hotel. He could identify "only one man in that crowd, and he is a yaller man they call Watson. I see him sitting yonder."[14] Yes, Jennings repeated under cross-examination by Backus, he was certain of John's identity: "We have different names for different colored niggers at the South. Some we call black, some yellow, and some copper-colored. Yellow is part white and part black blood, usually about half-and-half. Copper color is between black and slight mulatto. Black is black—pure African. Some would call John copper color, but I should call him black." Jennings said he had never seen but one mulatto who looked more than half white until he went to Oberlin. There were "some of these real white ones" there.[15]

Seth Bartholomew, the young tinware peddler-cum-showman, provided damaging testimony because he implicated not only Bushnell but the three Rescuers who never went to Wellington at all—James Fitch, Henry Peck, and Ralph Plumb. Bartholomew testified to seeing Bushnell outside Fitch's bookstore and to overhearing his conversation with the three men. Bartholomew couldn't remember which one, but one of the three men then told Bushnell "to go out and get 'em ready, and they would come round and tell him." Bartholomew wasn't certain what the words meant, but Bushnell went off to join the growing crowd in the street. Several minutes later, Bartholomew heard Bushnell telling someone without a gun—a student, Bartholomew guessed—to get out of a buggy because "he had no business in there." Then, about ten minutes after that, he saw Bushnell in a buggy with "Oliver" S. B. Wall and another man; Wall had a gun.[16]

Bartholomew was the first of six prosecution witnesses who placed Bushnell in either Oberlin or Wellington on the day of the rescue of John Price. They and other witnesses detailed the events of that day in both towns and sometimes incriminated men who had not been indicted. Young Oberlin housepainter Artemas Halbert, who saw Bushnell outside Wadsworth's Hotel just before John's rescue, said Lewis Sheridan Leary took part in the Rescue; Leary had not been indicted. Halbert placed seven Rescuers in Wellington—the Evans brothers, William Lincoln, Ansel Lyman, John Scott, Orindatus Wall, and Richard Winsor.

The questioning and cross-examination dragged along so slowly that by the morning of the third day of the trial, Thursday, April 7, only six witnesses had testified. The first witness that day offered a revelation about John that was hooted down by the spectators. Jacob Wheeler, the Rochester postmaster and farmer who "catechized" John in the hotel, said the slave told him that "he had started to go back to Kentucky once; got as far as Columbus, and the folks from Oberlin overtook him and brought him back!" The courtroom echoed with laughter at the obvious ridiculousness of Wheeler's statement.[17]

Richard P. Mitchell, who followed Wheeler in the witness box, spoke with the same twang that Jennings did and drew contemptible laughter, too. He said he had known John "since he was a small child." He knew his mother, Louisa, too—in fact, he had seen her just last Friday evening in Kentucky. "I should call John a dark copper color, not a jet black," he said. "Full face, good-looking." Mitchell recounted his role in seizing John and what he witnessed during John's rescue in Wellington, though he was uncertain about the time sequence: "We Southerners call it evening after 12 o'clock at noon."[18]

One of the half-dozen witnesses who identified Bushnell was David Wadsworth, the brother of innkeeper Oliver Wadsworth. He said that he talked to the Oberlin clerk outside the hotel when "he was on foot."[19] Later he saw him drive off with John.

Bushnell was also identified by Oberlin student Edward C. Kinney, who had seen Bushnell and Wall leave Oberlin together for Wellington. In what could only be described as an understatement, Kinney said he noticed "nothing in their manner peculiar, except that I think Wall had a gun, which was nothing peculiar for that day." Kinney had also seen Bushnell and Winsor start back to Oberlin with John. He knew John was a slave: John had told him. But, Kinney said, there was "apprehension" that day in Oberlin that "fugitives *and free colored persons* would be taken away. . . . especially after the Wagoner affair." Kinney, who recalled hearing "the cry of murder" on the night the second attempt was made to seize a black woman and her children, said, "It was supposed and said that *Southerners* had carried off John because Southerners are the men that usually carry off people!"[20] Under cross-examination, Backus got Kinney to acknowledge that although he knew John was a slave, neither he nor anyone else realized that Bacon was John's owner, that Jennings had a power of attorney, or that Lowe had a warrant for John's arrest.

When Chauncey Wack, the prosecution's sixteenth witness, was called to the stand on Friday, April 8, an argument broke out immediately. The defense asked permission to introduce evidence that Wack had remained in court despite Judge Willson's admonition to the witnesses at the start of the trial. But Willson denied the petition and allowed Wack to be sworn in.[21]

Wack had much to tell—the comings and goings at his hotel,

what he saw when he went up into the center of Oberlin to check on the $10 bill Jennings had given him, as well as the events in Wellington he observed and heard. Despite all he had witnessed, however, Wack could not implicate Bushnell; surprisingly, he said that he never saw him at all that day.

By that Friday afternoon, after nineteen witnesses had testified, Belden announced that he was ready to rest his case. Without a respite in the proceedings, Riddle, taking over from Backus, opened the defense. In all, he would call eighteen witnesses. Bushnell, however, would not be one of them; he never appeared in his own defense.

The first witnesses Riddle summoned were the Boyntons, father and son. The lawyer's purpose in calling them was twofold: to underscore the deceitfulness of the ambush and seizure of John Price and to raise questions about Jennings's credibility. Both Boyntons seemed unimpressed by the seriousness of the proceedings. The father, Lewis D. Boynton, said that he supposed he would not be "driven out of the Court House if I say I went as delegate to a Democratic convention" on the day of John Price's seizure and rescue. "Not out of *this* Court House," said Riddle sarcastically, as the spectators broke into laughter.[22] Riddle tried to get Boynton to describe his talks with Jennings on the Sunday before the Rescue, but Belden objected to the question as immaterial. Even though Jennings had already given his version of the conversation, Willson sustained the objection.

The reporter for the *Herald* found Boynton "loud and boisterous."[23] His son Shakespeare was downright flippant. "Am thirteen years old," he said, identifying himself. "*Expect* I am a son of last witness, but it's hard telling now-a-days!" Shakespeare went into some detail about the capture of John on the lonely road outside Oberlin. He was "sorry," he said, that he hadn't gotten John's friend Frank, too. The $20 Jennings paid him, he assured the courtroom, was "good money."[24]

Shakespeare's testimony ended the fourth day of the trial. When court resumed at 9:00 A.M. Saturday, three of the four Rescuers who would testify in Bushnell's behalf followed one another to the stand. Their appearance was designed to impeach the testimony of Seth Bartholomew. Henry Peck testified first, emphatically denying that he met Bushnell on the steps of Fitch's bookstore, "either alone or with Plumb or Fitch," though he remembered that Bartholomew "came up at my back, with the evident manner of an *eave-dropper* [sic]."[25]

Peck also offered a description of John Price that was at odds

with the one in Bacon's power of attorney. Peck had often seen
John at the farm where he boarded, which was adjacent to a farm
Peck owned north of Lorain Street. John, the Oberlin professor
said, was a "decidedly black man," who was five feet five inches
tall but maybe shorter and when healthy weighed at least 165
pounds. But John was down to 135 pounds when Peck last saw
him: "He was evidently sick most of the time, and apparently sick
in a way a man ought not to be."[26]

The next Rescuer to testify, Ralph Plumb, corroborated Peck's
refutation of Bartholomew's testimony. "No such conversation
took place," he said. And Bushnell was neither outside the store
nor in it: "I should have seen him if he was, for the store doors
are glass."[27]

James Fitch was just as certain as Plumb, but on cross-examination by Belden, he wavered. "A few words," he admitted, "may
have been passed on the steps," but Bushnell had already left the
bookstore.[28]

Another instance of Judge Willson's attitude toward the defense
occurred when court opened the following Monday morning, April
11. Over the weekend, Riddle was alerted to the fact that one of
the jurors was a deputy marshal. He called Willson's attention to
the matter when the trial resumed. The judge took note of the fact,
but he said that he did not see any need to do anything about it.
It was a decision that even the biased *Cleveland Plain Dealer*
called "an unfortunate affair." Willson, it said, should have "the
good sense to see that an *officer of Court* was very much out of
his place sitting as a Juror."[29]

Forced to proceed, Riddle turned to the question of the federal
warrant. His next witness was Oberlin student James L. Patton,
who had been in the attic room in Wadsworth's Hotel and had
been told by Jennings that John belonged to him. Patton said that
he never saw any paper other than the federal warrant, which he
later read aloud outside the hotel with Lowe.

Lysander Butler, who was studying law with the Plumbs, said
that the only paper Patton had read outside the hotel was the
federal warrant. He was standing behind Patton at the time, looking over his shoulder, and, being a law student, was particularly
interested in its wording. He also knew John Price "well." He was
no taller than himself, about five feet five, "and probably not so
high as myself." As for Seth Bartholomew, whom Butler said he
had known "intimately" for ten years, "His reputation for truth
and veracity is not as good as that of men in general. If he had any

prejudices or personal interests in a suit, I should very much dislike to believe him under oath."[30]

Riddle wound up his defense Monday afternoon, calling his last nine witnesses. All of them were from Oberlin, and all but two were called for the express purpose of challenging Bartholomew's credibility. Three of them also knew John Price and described him differently than did Bacon's power of attorney. Typical was John J. Cox, a builder, who had lived twenty years in Oberlin and knew John "well." His height, Cox said, "was up to my ear, five feet four or five inches." Cox, who was in his early fifties, said he had "worked and scuffled with him an hundred times or more" and was "pretty sure he would not in health weigh more than one hundred and forty pounds." John was "very black, so black he shone." Cox had also known Seth Bartholomew "from his cradle." He was "notoriously bad."[31]

To confuse the question of John's description further, Philo Weed, co-owner of a stove, tin, and hollowware store, believed John Price to be five feet seven or eight, which he considered "rather short." Bartholomew, who had been an apprentice of his, had, he said, a poor reputation. Brewster Pelton, a merchant and college trustee, agreed about Bartholomew, and David Brokaw, a goldsmith and former mayor of Oberlin, who followed Pelton, concurred. Carpenter Clark Elliott said he had known Bartholomew for thirteen years and would not believe him "under oath." Mayor A. N. Beecher had known him twelve years and said it would "depend entirely" on the circumstances whether he would believe Bartholomew. Dr. H. A. Bunce, who ran a pharmacy, also doubted Bartholomew's "truth and veracity."[32]

Riddle's final witness was called to provide yet another description of John Price, but there was a moment's hesitation before he was sworn in. Rescuer Orindatus S. B. Wall was decidedly black—and blacks had no constitutional rights as a result of the *Dred Scott* decision. But Judge Willson decided to let him testify.

Wall said he knew John Price "very well." Wall was aware of "the colors by which people of color were classified. There were black, blacker, blackest. Then copper color, which," the shoe merchant continued, "is about the color of hemlock tanned sole leather. Then there are dark, lighter, and light mulatto." John Price was "a decidedly black man."[33]

With that the defense rested. Concerned by the attack against Bartholomew, Belden requested an adjournment until the next day so he could summon nine new government witnesses and recall six of his previous ones. All fifteen of Belden's rebuttal witnesses appeared briefly during that Tuesday morning, April 11, the seventh day of the trial. Almost all were Democrats, among them Norris Wood, Charles Marks, and Chauncey Wack.

It was 10:30 by the time the last of the prosecution witnesses stood down. Judge Willson adjourned the court until two o'clock that afternoon before closing arguments by both the prosecution and the defense would be presented. He rejected Riddle's request that the defense be allowed to make three closing statements. Instead, each side would be allowed only two. Even though those by Belden and Bliss would be relatively short by comparison with the arguments of Riddle and Spalding, all together the closing arguments would take up the best part of the next three days.

✳

That afternoon the courtroom was so crowded with men, women, and children that it was impossible to find a seat. Marshal Mathew Johnson had taken the precaution of reserving all the seats on the east side of the courtroom for women. They were quickly taken, as were all the rest of the seats in the courtroom, so Johnson had the door to the adjoining judge's chambers opened and chairs placed in it. "Every available spot was occupied by spectators," the reporter for the *Herald* observed, "and nothing save the admirable ventilation and the lofty ceiling, rendered the air of the room tolerable."[34]

Belden's assistant, George Bliss, offered the first, and the briefer, of the prosecution's closing statements. John Price was clearly a slave, he said: "Bacon swears he was his slave, and knew John's mother, and the maternity establishes the status as a slave or free man." Mitchell and Jennings also knew him as a slave: "This evidence is not contradicted." And the evidence, Bliss contended, "does not show" that John's description in the power of attorney was incorrect. In addition, he said, the "language" the Rescuers employed indicated that they knew John was a fugitive.

Bliss clarified the reason the prosecution had not offered into evidence the federal warrant for John's arrest. He pointed out that Bushnell's indictment "does not allege that he [John] was rescued from a warrant, but was rescued from Jennings acting under a power of attorney, assisted by other persons."

Bliss was especially critical of the Rescuers: "When these Oberlin men went down to Wellington, they proclaimed that they did so under the Higher Law, for they knew they were outraging the law of the land." But John's rescue was no laughing matter. "At Oberlin," Bliss said in conclusion, "this is thought to be a good joke. People around Oberlin think so little of their government and the statutes of the Federal Government, when they interfere with their sympathies with negro women and men, that they consider their violation a good joke."[35]

Bliss had spoken for two and a half hours. Riddle, who succeeded him with the first of the defense arguments that Tuesday afternoon, began a lengthy oration that took the rest of the afternoon and almost all of the next day to complete. Surprisingly, he did not dispel any doubts about Bushnell's complicity, saying that "the defendant and his associates" knew "John was a slave" but nonetheless "put forth their strong hands, and, wrenching John from the grasp of his captors, consigned him to the boundless realm of freedom!" Instead, Riddle chose to attack the government's case on technicalities and, beyond that, to turn the Rescue into an attack on slavery and the Fugitive Slave Law. Disregarding the indictment's failure to mention the federal warrant, he called into question the validity of both it and the power of attorney, expounding at length on the fallacies of each, how they were used, and how those who used them had done so wrongly. He compared the statements of the prosecution's chief witnesses, claiming that they contradicted one another. But his main thrust was emotional. "I am perfectly frank to declare," he said, *"that I am a votary of that Higher Law!"*

"This boy John, so poor that he had no father to give him a name, and so abased that he could never be called a man, and in mature years could only graduate an uncle—was held to service to John G. Bacon, in Kentucky. Held how? by what contract? under what obligations, and for what benefit conferred on him? Because he was a slave, is replied. Because he was that thing which all the laws of God declare cannot exist. How came he a slave? What great crime had he committed[?]" he asked. "The malignant genius of his race doomed him at birth—he was born a slave! He belonged not to the God who made him, the father who begot him, or the mother who bore him! but to John G. Bacon, of Mason county, Kentucky. He was a slave because his mother was a slave, and she because her mother was a slave. And *her* mother was ravished away from her demolished cabin, murdered husband, and slaughtered children, in the wilds of Africa, and did not perish in the horrors of the middle passage."

"And this John," Riddle continued, "thus held, and under this obligation, with the wrongs of generations burning in his veins—

with his face towards the North star, and, as if polarized, fled—fled in the night—frightened, as captives flee; over the snow-whitened earth, under the stars, and, at his approach, *the Ohio river congealed, that he might flee.*"[36]

"I have nothing to do with enticing slaves away, nor sympathy with those who do," Riddle declared, as the spectators burst out in applause, "but if a fugitive comes to me in his flight from slavery, and is in need of food and clothing and protection and means of further flight,—if he needs any or all the gentle charities which a Christian man may render to any human being under any circumstances, so help me the great God in my extremest need, he shall have them all!"[37]

The outburst in the audience annoyed Belden, who had already been bothered by the sniggers and laughter provoked by the drawl in which the Kentuckians Anderson Jennings and Richard Mitchell spoke. He hoped, Belden said, that if the "disturbances were repeated, the disturbers would be taken into custody." If so, Spalding retorted, such an order "might include members of the bar."

"*What, sir!* do you mean that you sanction such manifestations?" Belden shot back.

"I do, sir," answered Spalding.

"Well, sir," the district attorney said, "you will doubtless have an opportunity to leave with the rest then."[38]

Riddle, who had begun speaking late Tuesday afternoon, did not finish until the late afternoon of the next day, Wednesday, April 13. As he wound up his argument, he repeated his emotional appeal. He knew, he said, that the Fugitive Slave Law "is here held as law. That the decision of this Court is to add another scale to that great scab, that deforms and debauches American jurisprudence. . . . But it shall never be recognized and accepted by our people as law—never! never!!"[39]

Spalding now rose to follow his defense associate, speaking at equal length well into the afternoon of Thursday, April 14. His argument rested in the main on the intent of the Founding Fathers when they drew up the United States Constitution. Even Judge Willson, he pointed out, had in 1850 signed a petition calling the Fugitive Slave Law unconstitutional. "No article" of the Constitution, he added, "would have authorized" its passage. In logic reminiscent of arguments that Southern extremists were making about states' rights, Spalding said that Congress had no authority to enact the law. "There is scarcely any thing more of State sovereignty left us than the name," he declared. The decisions of the United States Supreme Court, Spalding continued, "have now come to pronounce upon and affect to regulate the private conduct of free citizens of the States with reference even to the discharge of high moral duties." Such a matter, he added, "belongs exclusively to State legislatures and State courts."

Like Riddle, Spalding attacked the testimony of the prosecution witnesses and then leveled an appeal of his own at the spectators. "Is it not important," he asked rhetorically, "that we ask whether the time will not soon be upon us when *our* own children shall have the manacles now brought from Kentucky for African slaves, encircling their fair limbs? But we are told that there is no danger of mistaking Saxon children for African slaves." Spalding pointed at a young boy in the audience. The spectators gasped as he said, "Gentlemen of the Jury, is there one of you who would not be proud to reckon that flaxen-haired little boy yonder among your children? His skin is whiter than the District Attorney's, and his hair not half so curly! And yet, less than six months ago that child was set free in the Probate Court in this city, having been brought, a *slave*, from North Carolina!"[40]

"Slavery," he concluded, "is like a canker, eating out the vitals of our liberties, and . . . the Supreme Court of the United States has become the impregnable fortress and bulwark of slavery: I now say that unless the knife or the cautery be applied to the speedy and entire removal of the diseased part, we shall soon lose the name of freedom, as we have already lost the substance, and be unable longer to avoid confessing that TYRANTS ARE OUR MASTERS."[41]

When his turn came to speak, District Attorney Belden was caustic. To whom had Riddle and Spalding directed their arguments, he asked. "For three days has the crowd been addressed; not the court, not the jury. Are we in a dream? are we in a court of justice? or are we in a political hustings?" Belden called Spalding's identification of the former slave boy the "most disgraceful" scene he had ever witnessed in a court. Judge Willson, he pointed out, had subsequently been on a committee that two months after the judge's condemnation of the Fugitive Slave Law concluded that it was, indeed, constitutional. "What the gentlemen and Saints of Oberlin called Higher Law he [Willson] called Devil's Law," a doctrine that "would make chaos" and "a Hell upon earth." "Do you teach the Bible at Oberlin," Belden derisively asked, "or do you point out the spires of the churches as hell poles?"

Belden concluded his closing argument the next morning, Friday, April 15, saying that it was "perfectly lawful and right for the gentleman from Kentucky to follow the negro to Oberlin with

'Arkansas toothpicks,' bowie knives, and revolvers, if he thought best for the purpose of the capture."[42] As he sat down finally at eleven o'clock, the audience hissed him.

The case was now in Judge Willson's hands. Before he charged the jury, he dismissed the defense motion to quash Bushnell's indictment. The United States Constitution and the Fugitive Slave Law were clear, Willson said. A slaveowner has "a positive and unqualified" right, and his ownership, "like the ownership of any other species of property," implies "the right of seizure and recaption."

Then, turning to the jurors, Willson said the constitutionality of the fugitive law was not a question for them to decide. Slavery, he pointed out, was sanctioned by law in Kentucky. And there was no question either about John's status: "That dark complexion, woolly head, and flat nose, with possession and claim of ownership, do afford *prima facie* evidence of the slavery and ownership charged." The issue was simple: Was the defendant guilty or not guilty of helping a known fugitive slave to escape?

"Much has been eloquently said by learned counsel that would be entitled to great weight and consideration if addressed to the Congress of the United States, or to an ecclesiastical tribunal, where matters of casuistry are discussed and determined," Willson concluded. "It is your duty to take the case and return a verdict according to the evidence."[43]

At Backus's request, the judge clarified some legal technicalities. Then the jury was excused until two o'clock.

✳

When the court reconvened at 2:15, the jurors announced that they had been able to agree upon a verdict. The audience hushed, hopeful that Bushnell would be acquitted. Willson, in clarifying the legal points to the jury, had said that the prosecution had to prove that John was arrested by virtue of the power of attorney, not the federal warrant. The evidence seemed clear to supporters of the Rescuers that few people knew of or were shown the power of attorney. But their optimism was short-lived. The foreman of the jury stood and pronounced the verdict:

"Guilty."[44]

The Rescuers reacted as though they had been struck by a "thunderbolt," an observer noted. Their faces blanched, their movements became nervous, they cast "quick, uneasy glances at one another."[45] And then, no sooner was the verdict announced than

Belden called the name of Charles Langston as the next case. Taken by surprise, Spalding said the defense was not ready to try any other case except that of Henry Peck. That was the proper order and the agreement made between Belden and himself. But the district attorney insisted on taking up Langston's case next. Spalding finally relented and ventured that the defense might be ready to proceed by the time a new jury was selected. It was now Judge Willson's turn to stun the defense counsel. He said the current jurors had been selected for the entire court term and would try all the Rescuer cases.

Backus could not believe his ears. He was "astonished to hear his Honor intimate that this Jury, who have sat through and upon this case—heard all the testimony, and who have now in the presence of the Court rendered a verdict, in which their minds are made up and fixed upon all the important points in this case, are to be held competent to try another case almost exactly similar!"

"Why, it was an unheard of and a most villanous [sic] outrage on the sense of justice of the civilized world, and no one of the defendants would so stultify himself as to attempt a defence before such a jury," Backus declared. "It was a terrible, not to say a monstrous proceeding, the like of which had never been known since courts were first in existence."

Willson saw "no occasion for excitement or intemperate zeal." The jury, he said, "would decide each case upon the evidence offered in that particular case."

The courtroom was in turmoil. Spalding said the district attorney "could call the accused up as fast as he pleased and try them, for neither would they call any witnesses for the defence nor appear by attorney before such a jury."

That was all right with the district attorney. "Very well," Belden said petulantly, "I ask the Court to order these men all in the custody of the marshal."[46]

"I second the motion," Spalding piped up derisively from his chair.[47]

"The District-Attorney is entitled to the order," Willson ruled. "Let the accused be called."[48]

Green, the clerk, read off the names of the defendants, and those who were present rose. Although Ralph Plumb had arranged to have his trial postponed until the November term of the court, he volunteered to join his friends. Willson agreed to Plumb's gesture and to Spalding's subsequent request that the judge cancel the recognizances of all of the Rescuers who were being put into custody. Mathew Johnson officially took all of them into custody.

Willson then adjourned the court until 10:00 A.M. Monday, April 18, when Langston's trial was scheduled to begin. But before the judge retired to his chambers, Belden relented slightly. He recommended that the Rescuers be released from the marshal's custody if they renewed their recognizances by putting up bonds. The judge said he would agree to that if each of the indicted men put up $1,000. With that, Willson left the courtroom, the spectators were ushered out, and the door closed.

Marshal Johnson assembled the twenty Rescuers who were on hand. Bushnell was there, of course; so, too, were his brother-in-law James Fitch, Ralph Plumb, Professor Henry Peck, Oberlin students William Lincoln, Ansel Lyman, Jacob Shipherd, and Richard Winsor, and seven black men—Charles Langston, the Evans brothers, John Scott, Orindatus Wall, David Wilson, and John Wilson. There were also four Rescuers from Wellington in the courtroom at the time: Dr. Eli Boies, Matthew Gillet, Daniel Williams, and Loring Wadsworth—*Mayor* Loring Wadsworth; he had recently been elected. The Rescuers carried with them, in preparation for returning home to Oberlin for the weekend, the carpetbags and valises they had taken to the hotels where they were staying while the trials progressed.

For all his faults, Johnson was not as hostile as Belden was. The marshal offered to let the Rescuers enter their recognizances for their appearance on Monday morning, and said that he, on his own authority and responsibility, would be willing to let them go home that afternoon if they would give their word to return to Cleveland—all, that is, but Simeon Bushnell, who had been convicted and was awaiting sentencing. Bushnell would have to stay in custody.

The Rescuers huddled with their defense counsel in a room off the courtroom. They were convinced that Belden had acted out of "personal malice and a determination to humble them" and that Willson had demonstrated "at least a willingness to have them driven to the wall." They wanted to "enter [a] most emphatic protest against the insult and legal injustice which they had suffered, by remaining in custody of the Marshal until the Court should amend the wrong or the law should relieve them." They also wanted to "share Bushnell's fortunes as long as possible."[49]

The Rescuers chose Henry Peck as their spokesman, a role the Oberlin professor would perform throughout their coming ordeal. When they returned to the courtroom, Peck declared that the Rescuers had resolved that "they would give no bail, enter no recognizance, and make no promises to return to the Court." The matter had become one of pride. The Rescuers were not common criminals. There was no necessity for them to give bail. What would happen next was up to the Marshal. "They were under his orders, and should do, to the letter, what he directed."[50]

Friends of the Rescuers were outside the courtroom door, waiting eagerly to join them for the return trip home. Suddenly, the door opened and two by two the Rescuers, luggage in hand, marched out, Marshal Johnson leading the procession. On his arm was the venerable Matthew Gillet. They marched down the hallway of the second floor of the courthouse, down the stairs to the first floor, and outside into Rockwell Street. It was raining. With their friends escorting them "side by side," the Rescuers walked to the Cuyahoga County Jail. Though the jail was but a few steps away, they were forced to stand outside uncovered except for shawls because Sheriff David L. Wightman was hesitant to take them into custody without written orders from the county commissioners. Marshal Johnson excused himself to draw up a formal request, deputizing Orindatus Wall to watch over his fellow Rescuers until he returned.[51] In the meantime, however, apparently concerned that he was forcing the Rescuers to stand in the rain needlessly, Wightman waved them in. "Gentlemen," the sympathetic sheriff said, "I open my doors to you, not as criminals, but as guests. I cannot regard you as criminals for doing only what I should do myself under similar circumstances."[52]

As the Rescuers filed into the prison, James Fitch turned to one of the friends who had escorted the men from the courthouse. "Get some one to take charge of my Sabbath School for me next Sabbath," Fitch called out. "Four hundred children and youth must be provided for in my absence." Another Rescuer reminded the friend that the church in a neigboring community needed help: "They must not be left destitute."[53]

Eventually, after a lengthy meeting, the commissioners officially consented to accepting the prisoners. By then, the sheriff as well as the jailer, John B. Smith, who was also sympathetic to the Rescuers' cause, had made them as comfortable as possible.

The confinement of the Rescuers would be one of the most unusual in penal history. Smith gave over his own apartment on the top floor of the jail to the Rescuers. That and adjacent rooms were put at their disposal.

The Rescuers' imprisonment began, as might be expected, with the twenty of them gathered in prayer during their very first hour that Friday night. On Saturday, Marshal Johnson made another friendly gesture, offering to let the Rescuers go home for the Sabbath, but again they refused.[54] Instead, braced by their faith and certain that their cause was just, they played host to a throng of friends and sympathizers, including a large group of female parishioners from Cleveland's Plymouth Church, a Congregational church known as the Prospect Street Church. Several of the women made the Rescuers' "'reception room' . . . cheerful and happy with their bright smiles and lively conversation." The *Cleveland Morning Leader* remarked that "President Buchanan hardly holds greater levees." The jail, the *Herald* said, "appeared more like a fashionable place of resort than a prison." Everyone was commenting on Belden's "extraordinary conduct" in ordering the arrest of the Rescuers "in violation of all precedent and in contempt of all decency and propriety."[55]

In high spirits, one of the Rescuers, writing anonymously as "Dungeoner," reported, "Not feeling very guilty, we do feel very happy." The Rescuers, he went on, would remain in jail, "not for the crime of violating the act of 1850, not for the charge or suspicion of so doing, but for declining to intrust our liberty to the keeping of twelve men who had just announced under oath, their fixed opinion of the merits of our case."

"The glass is passing freely around, backed by a huge pitcher," Dungeoner declared. "The contents are as good as the Cleveland Reservoir can furnish, but still a little behind Oberlin wells." The Rescuers, he said, had received newspapers and books and "a steady current of callers," among them "Barristers, Editors, Legislators, Merchants, and Clergymen."

"But, alas!" Dungeoner concluded soberly, "every echo of our laughter rings with the hollow premonition of a sundering Union, a disaffected South, and an excited community."[56]

If District Attorney Belden saw such larger issues involved in the Rescuers' case, he did not express it. Instead, that Saturday, he was gloating over his triumph. He informed Washington of the result in Bushnell's trial, which, he said, had been achieved "notwithstanding the overshadowing influence of the Governor of Ohio, [which] was brought to bear against the prosecution, by his presence and counsel." The verdict was "fair and just," he wrote: "It is a great triumph, considering it was achieved in this region of the country; and, I trust, it will be productive of much good."[57] With his letter, Belden attached a copy of the *Daily National Democrat* of Cleveland, which carried a synopsis of his remarks and Judge Willson's charge to the jury, as well as accounts of the jury's verdict and the imprisonment of the Rescuers. The newspaper opined that the defendants' jailing was either the result of a mistake, or that they had "intentionally misrepresented the action of the District-Attorney and of the Court." Their confinement, it said, "is the result of their own voluntary action; and it is to be hoped that they will fully enjoy the comforts arising from their own resolution." The Rescuers, it added, "will have ample time for that calm and quiet meditation, always so desirable."[58]

The *Plain Dealer* was quick to point out that Bushnell's conviction "will have a very salutary effect upon the furious abolitionists" of Oberlin. It said the jurors "deserved the thanks of every man who loves his country, supports the firm and impartial administration of justice, and wants to see this Union preserved. If we demand of the people of the South the repression of illegal pursuits in the clandestine importation of African negroes, we must be prepared to show that resistance to the statutes of the United States will have no immunity here."[59]

In marked contrast, the *New York Evening Post* published a nine-stanza paean to mark Bushnell's conviction, which read in part:

> Where is the charter freedom gave
> To lands where speeds Ohio's flood,
> Which guarded from the foot of slave
> The soil once wet with patriot blood?
>
> . . . .
>
> Oh, men! roll back this cursed tide;
> Assert the manhood God once gave;
> Stand on free ground its crown and pride;
> Be something more than Slavery's slave![60]

The Rev. James A. Thome was especially angry at Belden's behavior. Thome was one of the Lane Rebels who went to Oberlin to continue his studies. The son of a slaveowner, he was born and reared within ten miles of John Bacon's farm in Kentucky. He left home "to escape from the evils of the slavery" and became an ardent abolitionist; once, in 1839, he was compelled to go into hiding for several months to avoid arrest for helping an old black woman escape from his native state. Thome had known Belden in Canton in 1835, when the district attorney was just beginning his career as a lawyer. At that time, Belden voiced support for the antislavery cause. Thome had gone on to become a professor of rhetoric and belles lettres at Oberlin, a position he held until 1848, and was still one of the editors of the *Oberlin Evangelist*. He was now the pastor of the Congregational church on Detroit Avenue in Cleveland, and he took to his pulpit on Sunday, April 17, to rail against his former protégé.

Hearing Belden deliver his closing argument in Bushnell's trial, Thome found himself praying that God would let the district attorney "foam out his rage, and render himself hateful as the representative of a hateful cause." Indeed, Belden did speak "until the divine restraints were so removed that the Attorney appeared like an incarnate fiend, and shrieked out his malignity with such unearthly tones and outrageous terms, and such accompaniments of horrid grimace and spasmodic violence as constituted a spectacle altogether unique and hardly human."

"There are dastards in this land of heroes, in State and in Church," Thome told his parishioners. "The man who craves the privilege to live in peace is a traitor to his country and his God. The man who congratulates himself that he is free, while the dread of the lower law lays a flattering unction to his soul, he is a slave! The man who thanks God that he may sit under his own vine and fig tree with none to molest or make him afraid, is not worthy of his boasted blessings if he does not mourn at the same time, and take shame and confusion of face, that he cannot invite the weary fugitive to sit by his side beneath his vine and fig tree, and share their fruits and their shade without the fear of the prowling kidnapper or the federal spy. In the name of our Father's God, let us resolve to achieve a larger liberty than we now enjoy."[61]

*

Not far away, across the Cuyahoga River, at 2:30 that Sunday afternoon, Henry Peck conducted perhaps the most unusual Sabbath service ever held in the Western Reserve. A crowd of some six to seven hundred persons gathered inside the large yard of the jail and on the street outside. The windows of the neighboring courthouse were filled with people as well. Others watched from rooftops and sheds. Standing just inside the doorway of the prison, Peck opened the service with a short prayer and then everyone within sight and sound sang the hymn:

> My soul be on thy guard,
>   Ten thousand foes arise;
> The hosts of sin are pressing hard
>   To draw thee from the skies.

After a portion of the Bible was read and another prayer offered, they sang another hymn:

Am I soldier of the cross,
A follower of the Lamb?
And shall I fear to his own cause,
Or blush to speak his name?

Peck then delivered a sermon on the theme that was now close
to the Rescuers' hearts: martyrdom. "Divine will," he said, "is to
be paramount law with us. We must obey God always, and human
law, social and civil, *when we can.*"

Just as "we take the panting fugitive from slavery by the hand,
and help him on his weary way, pointing him to the Northern
Star," he continued, "so we shall presently find that 'the Man of
Sorrows' is also by his side. So let us seek our Lord, going as He
always did, when He was here, where the neediest are."

"Are we persecuted for righteousness' sake," Peck declared,
"and taunted and buffeted by those who are in power—has not He
been in the judgment hall before us, and was not He crowned with
thorns, and did not deriding persecutors mockingly rail at Him as
the King of the Jews?

"And when we have done all and suffered all, let us rejoice to
know that we shall have our reward in the healing which shall
come through us to some wounded spirit, and let us go cheerfully
and joyously on our way, keeping in view Him who has trod the
same weary way before us, assured that as His works followed
Him so our works will follow us, and that the sons of sorrow will
be gladdened by us even when our hands have long mouldered to
dust."[62]

A just cause, noble thoughts, strong words. But how long could
the Rescuers endure being separated from their families behind
walls of stone?

ELEVEN

The Case Against
the Black Schoolteacher

"I am George Harris. A Mr. Harris, of Kentucky, did call me his property. But now I'm a free man, standing on God's free soil; and my wife and my child I claim as mine. Jim and his mother are here. We have arms to defend ourselves, and we mean to do it. . . ."

"O, come! come!" said a short, puffy man, stepping forward, and blowing his nose as he did so. "Young man, this an't no kind of talk at all for you. You see, we're officers of justice. . . ."

"I know very well that you've got the law on your side, and the power," said George, bitterly. "You mean to take my wife to sell in New Orleans, and put my boy like a calf in a trader's pen, and send Jim's old mother to the brute that whipped and abused her before, because he couldn't abuse her son. You want to send Jim and me back to be whipped and tortured, and ground down under the hoofs of them that you call masters; and your law will bear you out in it, . . . We don't own your laws; we don't own your country; we stand here as free, under God's sky, as you are; and, by the great God that made us, we'll fight for our liberty till we die."

Chapter XVI: "Tom's Mistress and Her Opinions"

The days ahead would be filled with a plethora of legal wrangling and odd twists of events, each side jockeying for position as the Rescue attracted increasing national attention.

The usually short-tempered George Belden was now bristling with confidence. The district attorney began making overtures to the Rescuers from Wellington, whom he did not consider "in reality responsible for the Rescue," urging them "to trust themselves to the mercy of the Court." It was the Oberlin Rescuers he was after. "The Oberlinites are the ones the Government wishes to punish," he was quoted as saying. "We shall convict all the Oberlinites."

"It is not so much a violation of the fugitive slave law which is to be punished by the United States as the anti-slavery sentiment," the *Ohio State Journal* remarked. "That is the thing. It is Oberlin, which must be put down. It is freedom of thought which must be crushed out."[1]

The Oberlin Rescuers were confident, too. They did not antici-
pate a long stay in prison. The conflict over the jury, they believed,
would be resolved in their favor once court resumed on Monday
morning, April 18.

Ironically, the twenty Rescuers in the Cuyahoga County Jail
weren't the only ones whose freedom was curtailed. Anderson Jennings and Richard Mitchell were in custody, too; for the past two
weeks, since their arrival in Cleveland, they had been detained in
the County Court House as material witnesses, restricted from
even going out in the street for a walk. Belden was worried about
them on two accounts. For one thing, he believed that, as one trial
tediously followed another and they had to repeat their testimony
over and over again, they might bolt and return home to Kentucky.
For another, he feared that they might be apprehended by Lorain
County law enforcement officers on the kidnapping charges. Writing to Secretary of the Interior Jacob Thompson on Saturday, April
16, Belden said that he intended to keep both Kentuckians in "such
custody, until I shall cease to need their attendance as Witnesses."
He would then "endeavor" to have Jennings and Mitchell returned
to Kentucky "in such manner, as to avoid an arrest by the state
authorities, and thus, if possible prevent all controversy, or litigation, as to them."[2]

Belden was not being paranoid about the possibility of their
being arrested. "Muffled men, standing about in the darkness and
suspicious looking Cabs yawning, to spirit away somebody" were
reported loitering outside the court building.[3]

The district attorney also assured Thompson that he had a plan
to secure Lowe's release from the Lorain County indictment. Once
Lowe completed his testimony, Belden said, he would direct the
deputy marshal to surrender himself in Lorain County and, at the
same time, he, Belden, would take out a writ of habeas corpus
from a federal court that would finally secure Lowe's discharge
"from the unlawful and scandalous attempt of the State authorities to deal with him as a 'kidnapper,' when his only offence is to
be found in the fact that he was engaged in the high duty of executing the laws of the Union." Lowe's assistant, Samuel Davis,
had not appeared in Cleveland as yet, but Belden said he would
"promptly and energetically, in all respects, comply" with Thompson's instructions to assist him, too.[4]

When court resumed on Monday morning, the Rescuers expected that as the first order of business Judge Willson would re-
scind his order that the same jury hear all their cases; that, they
believed, would open the way to their being released again on their

own recognizances without putting up any bail. Before the jury question even came up, however, the Rescuers found to their dismay that the entry in the official daily court journal concerning their incarceration on the past Friday averred that the Rescuers "were taken into custody because they had surrendered themselves in discharge of their recognizances,"[5] that it was *then, and for that reason* that they were ordered into custody.[6] But that wasn't so, they argued. Their attorneys had assured them, "You were *ordered* into custody . . . you *did not surrender* yourselves." Either the government was determined to keep them in custody, or they would have to acknowledge what they had no intention of conceding—"that they had been guilty of folly and indiscretion which well deserved punishment."[7]

The Rescuers asked that the journal be corrected to show that it was Belden who ordered them taken into custody. But Willson refused their request: the journal entry would stand. Believing that the judge was determined to humiliate them, the Rescuers decided that "under such circumstances self-respect forbade their entering into new bonds." They would stay in prison because to do otherwise, they explained in a special statement addressed to citizens of the Western Reserve, "would have encouraged the Prosecution in the belief that they were effectually humbled, and that they had forsaken their cause as being lost."[8]

Writing in the *Oberlin Evangelist*, Henry Cowles compared the Rescuers' predicament to that of Paul and Silas: " 'They have beaten us openly uncondemned, being Romans, and have cast us into prison; and now do they thrust us out privily? Nay verily; but let them come themselves and fetch us out.' So say our friends— We have treated the Court with all honor and truthfulness; let them give us like treatment."[9]

The die was cast. The only recourse the Rescuers now had was to appeal to the Ohio Supreme Court for writs of habeas corpus for their release, and that would lead to another confrontation with the federal government, this one on constitutional grounds and carrying the added threat of a head-to-head encounter between the state and the federal governments. The *Plain Dealer* was certain what the Ohio court would do; it was, after all, made up of what the newspaper derisively called "five Black Republicans," whose views were "diametrically opposed to the opinion of the United States Supreme Court." The newspaper commented, "Great country! Exciting times ahead! Watch and pray!!"[10]

Congressman Joshua R. Giddings also felt certain that the state court would uphold the Rescuers. The "Old War Horse" dined in

prison with the defendants that Monday and then wrote an emotional letter to Ralph Plumb. He said that he had "great confidence" in the state court. The mistake the Rescuers had made, he
went on, was to spare the lives of the slave hunters. Had the Rescuers "executed the slave-catchers promptly," he insisted, "it
would have taught the administration a lesson not soon to be forgotten." Giddings agreed that the Rescuers had been "right" to
refuse giving bail: "They no longer act for themselves in this business, but for justice, for liberty, for the cause of freedom. The eyes
of the nation are upon them." How important were the Rescuers
to the antislavery cause? "Cleveland," Giddings declared, "is now
the Boston of 1775."[11]

From Boston, abolitionist William Lloyd Garrison wrote Professor James Monroe in Oberlin, "What a humiliating spectacle is
presented to the world in the trials now going on at Cleveland of
your humane and Christian citizens." Garrison believed that their
conviction was inevitable. "What a work of moral regeneration yet
remains to be done in Ohio, in Massachusetts, throughout the
North, in opposition to slavery and slave-hunting! But this very
prosecution will give a fresh impetus to our noble cause."[12]

Amazingly, when the jury question arose, it was settled quickly.
Rufus Spalding repeated the defense contention that the Bushnell
jury could not fairly judge any other trial. To do so, he said, "would
be a mere farce." Besides, he added, "it was a Political jury."
George Bliss countered for the prosecution that neither reason was
"sufficient grounds for disqualification." But Albert Riddle recalled his own experience as a public prosecutor when a judge
ordered a new jury for each of three persons who had been sepa-
rately indicted for the same crime.

What convinced Judge Willson to change his mind is not clear.
Once Riddle sat down, however, he said that if the allegation
against Langston was the same as that against Bushnell, "with the
mere substitution of one name for the other," he would disqualify
the Bushnell jurors. Which is exactly what he did, even though
Langston's indictment covered an additional charge. The judge ordered the jurors to vacate the jury box and told Marshal Johnson
to summon new ones for Langston's trial. Franklin Backus remarked to Willson that he hoped the new jury would not entertain
certain "political proclivities."[13]

Despite Backus's comment, the jury that was chosen that afternoon was again weighted in favor of the Democrats, with "nine
Administration men, two Fillmore Whigs, and one Republican,
who had no objections to the Fugitive Slave Law."[14] In that respect,

and in many others, Langston's trial was a repeat of Bushnell's. Many of the twenty-two prosecution witnesses who testified were the same men who had appeared in Bushnell's case. In most respects, the same ground was gone over again, sometimes in more detail, sometimes revealing minor contradictions or confusion over some of the events and the precise time they took place. And like Bushnell, Langston did not testify in his own behalf, but he nonetheless planned to speak out.

There were a few important differences between the two trials. Bushnell was indicted only on the charge of rescuing a fugitive slave. Langston was indicted on that charge and on the charge of failing to heed a federal warrant—for this time Belden had every intention of introducing that document into evidence. There was, in addition, a difference between the two trials of a peculiar nature: Three witnesses for the prosecution in Bushnell's trial testified for the defense in Langston's—Constable Barnabas Meacham, Justice of the Peace Isaac Bennett, and Oberlin student Edward C. Kinney. On the other hand, Rescuer William Sciples of Wellington turned state's evidence and took the stand as a government witness. Moreover, because of several circumstances, not the least of which were the defense efforts to embroil the Ohio Supreme Court in the case, Langston's trial went on for more than three weeks, lasting until the second week in May and covering in all fifteen court days.

There was one other difference as well. Only Henry Peck and Ralph Plumb were allowed in the courtroom with Langston during his trial. With Belden's approval, they were again permitted to sit at the defense table but were escorted to and from the jail by a bailiff. The other seventeen Rescuers, however, had to remain in prison until their own cases were called because they were no longer free on their own recognizances and would not put up bail.

There was no stenographic reporter at Bushnell's trial, which troubled Willson. As a result, he said, there had been no way to prevent the jury from reading the city papers. To forestall their doing so, Willson hired Louis Feeser, a law college reporter, to make an official record of Langston's trial.[15] Newspapermen were shooed away from the reporters' tables near the bench and had to fend for themselves to find seats in the courtroom, but Willson did not stop them from taking notes. The jury was finally empaneled at four o'clock.

The prosecution case hinged on implicating Langston directly, by his words if not his deeds, in the rescue of the slave John. As in Bushnell's trial, however, John Bacon was Belden's first witness;

the Kentucky slaveowner reiterated the testimony he gave in Bushnell's trial. He was followed the next day by Mason County Clerk Robert Cochran. Then Anderson Jennings and Richard Mitchell testified; of the two, only Jennings seemed certain, at first, of what Langston had said and done, but even he equivocated. He initially testified that Langston came "in with the crowd by the door" at the moment of John's rescue from the attic room in Wadsworth's Hotel. But under cross-examination, he qualified that statement and said he "wouldn't swear positively that Langston was there." Then, not realizing that what he was saying would support the defense contention that Langston had not actually instigated the slave's rescue, Jennings recalled that Lowe had earlier asked Langston to assist the captors. "Langston said, 'you might as well give the negro up, as *they* are going to have him any way.'"[16]

Meanwhile, tension in the courtroom was growing. Belden was getting increasingly testy about defense efforts to prolong the proceedings. The defense attorneys, Rescuer John Scott later revealed, were deliberately trying to wear down Willson, arguing "every little technicality for a day at a time."[17] First, when the judge was about to recess the court after Bacon's appearance, Riddle again raised the question of the Rescuers being out for our their own recognizances. Willson had to repeat that they could sign new recognizances and put up bail if they wished to be released, but Riddle, as expected, said they "would do nothing of the kind." Then, with Mitchell on the stand the next day, Belden abruptly halted his questioning. At the defense table, Henry Peck was whispering to Backus. The district attorney was annoyed. He told Willson that unless Peck "desisted from suggesting questions to the opposite counsel," he would order him back to jail. Backus quickly "begged" Belden "to quiet his fears," saying that Peck had not made any suggestions and that even if he had, Belden's "sensitiveness seemed rather out of place."[18]

The next morning, Wednesday, April 20, as Mitchell completed his testimony and stepped down from the witness box, a group of men suddenly rose from the audience and strode quickly toward the front of the court. The leader of the group identified himself as Deputy Sheriff Richard Whitney of Lorain County. With attorney L. C. Thayer of Elyria and several sheriff's assistants at his side, Whitney stepped forward and arrested both Mitchell and Jennings on a warrant issued by the Lorain County Court of Common Pleas on the charge of kidnapping. Federal Marshal Mathew Johnson had apparently foreseen the possibility that this might happen.

He was not in the courtroom, but a deputy of his quickly presented Whitney with the bench warrant that Belden had taken out to prevent just such a seizure. Thayer now advanced to the bench and asked Judge Willson to deliver both Kentuckians into the custody of the sheriff once they were no longer needed as witnesses. Willson said he would take the matter under advisement. Without asking anyone's permission, Whitney and his men then took seats alongside Jennings and Mitchell within the bar circle, and what must have seemed to the spectators like a game of musical chairs began as, incredibly, the trial proceeded.

Chauncey Wack, the next witness, was testifying when Marshal Johnson himself suddenly appeared and removed Jennings and Mitchell from their seats next to Whitney and his assistants. He showed the Kentuckians to seats to the left of the judge's chair, outside the bar circle. Johnson then went over to Whitney and escorted him and the other Lorain County officers to the right of the judge's chair. To Willson's chagrin, however, the matter was far from settled.

At the end of the day, as a legal formality to protect their appearance in court, the judge announced that Johnson had returned the writ by which Jennings and Mitchell were being held. Unless the Kentuckians could provide bail, said the judge, he was "obliged" to commit them. Neither man could furnish bail so Willson ordered them back into Johnson's custody. Whereupon, Thayer renewed his request that the judge order the Kentuckians subject to arrest by Whitney once the trials were over so that the men "might not be spirited away, and thus escape the officers of Lorain County."

Willson was taken aback. What Thayer was suggesting "was an unheard-of proceeding, and a contempt," for which Thayer was liable to arrest. Thayer persisted, saying that there was "no intention of disturbing the Court," but neither Jennings nor Mitchell had been out of the building for two weeks so there had been "no other opportunity for their arrest."[19]

Seemingly mollified by Thayer's explanation, Willson said that the matter would be taken up when all the witnesses had been heard from. With that, Johnson took the two Kentuckians into the judge's chambers—"shoved them in," the *Daily National Democrat* charged, "and, locking the door, held them fast under lock and key." The scene "has scarcely ever had a parallel in reckless impudence," the newspaper said.[20] The incident—an overt effort to assert Ohio's rights over federal jurisdiction—proved, the *Plain*

Dealer declared, that "Oberlin now has taken up and become the champion of the Southern doctrine of 'State Rights.' "[21]

Belden was furious. Although the trial was in progress, he learned that Rufus Spalding was planning to leave Cleveland and go to Columbus to seek writs of habeas corpus for Bushnell and the rest of the imprisoned Rescuers from the Ohio Supreme Court. The district attorney was not about to be outmaneuvered. Belden had informed Spalding that if convicted, the Rescuers would be committed to the notorious state penitentiary in Columbus to serve out their sentences. Bushnell would be the first to be remanded there. His sentencing, it was learned, was already scheduled when Belden received notice of the writ hearing.[22] Frustrated, Belden devised a scheme to keep the young clerk out of state hands should the writ be granted.

About 10:30 in the morning of Good Friday, April 22, as a series of prosecution witnesses were testifying, one of Marshal Johnson's deputies called at the County Jail and said Bushnell was needed in court for a few minutes. The request to bring him to the courthouse was not unusual. Other Rescuers had been summoned in similar fashion by the court or by their own attorneys. And although he was being held in the County Jail, Bushnell was still technically in the custody of Marshal Johnson. The deputy said that Bushnell would be "speedily and safely returned." Bushnell's wife, Elizabeth, happened to be visiting with their infant daughter, Mary, at the time and was told that she could join him.

With the deputy leading the way and accompanied by Sheriff David Wightman, the Bushnells left the prison and walked to the courthouse nearby. Inside and upstairs, as they were passing Johnson's office, the deputy said, "Mr. Bushnell, Marshal Johnson would like to see you barely a moment *before you go up to Court.*" Without any hesitation, Bushnell, his wife on his arm, entered the office while the deputy and Sheriff Wightman continued on to the courtroom. Once inside the marshal's office, Bushnell was invited by Johnson to an adjoining room. The young Oberlin clerk went in to find himself all alone as the door closed behind him and the key turned in the lock. He was now a prisoner of the marshal.

Johnson then walked quickly to the courtroom and caught up with Wightman before the sheriff could sit down. Catching him by his shoulder, Johnson demanded that Wightman turn over to him the *mittimus*—the court order placing Bushnell in Wightman's custody. Wightman said it was not in his pocket. Moreover, the sheriff argued that he had to keep the document on "perpetual file," that it was his only protection against a lawsuit should Bushnell sue him for false detention.

Johnson was now beside himself. He began a rambling, disjointed, contradictory explanation to the sheriff, saying first that the seizure of Bushnell was Belden's idea, then that it was his own idea, and still again that it had been done on the "*advice*" of Belden. The marshal admitted that he was worried by a rumor he had heard that the Ohio Supreme Court had already issued a writ of habeas corpus on Bushnell's behalf. And then Johnson, who was no stranger to duplicity, had the audacity to say that if Bushnell was in his custody, "the writ would be served on him, and he should have the pleasure of obeying it!" He said he "had never once thought of doing otherwise."[23]

Although he went away from his meeting with Wightman empty-handed, Johnson nevertheless refused to return Bushnell into the sheriff's custody at the County Jail. For six days, while the Ohio Supreme Court took up the question of issuing writs of habeas corpus for the Rescuers, the Oberlin clerk was kept in the judge's parlor. Pointing out that now Bushnell as well as Jennings and Mitchell were being held "in close custody" by federal authorities in the Court House, the *Plain Dealer* observed dryly, "Misfortune, indeed, makes strange bed-fellows."[24]

Bushnell's confinement had a bizarre side. His wife and child were permitted to be with him. He was also allowed to receive visitors; in fact, he jokingly complained that he had to be "his own jailer." He had been given the key to his room and admitted visitors himself while a bailiff stood guard outside. As the *Herald* wryly noted, Bushnell could keep out Marshal Johnson, who was not able to enter without the Oberlin clerk's "permission."[25]

Undaunted by being kidnapped, Bushnell wrote to his fellow Rescuers in the jail around the corner: "Well I am now occupying Judge Wilson's [sic] private room—should I be invited to fill his seat on the Bench on Monday I shall meet [sic] out justice to you with a more even hand than has ever been done in this temple." Bushnell called his seizure "something after the manner in which *John* was taken from Oberlin." He was not frightened, he said. The weather outside was dull and cold, and pools of water from a windswept rain Thursday night would freeze over that night,[26] but he had a warm fire,[27] and his accommodations, he told his friends, were "good." He admitted, though, that he "would much rather be" in the county jail with them. However, he had no intention of asking any favors of Marshall Johnson "or any of his *crew*." "They may do their worst & when I am again out I will rescue the first slave I get a chance to rescue. I have sworn eternal enmity to the *fugitive Slave law*, & while God lets me live I mean to defy it, and trample upon it."

Bushnell added that he had "never for one moment regretted the part I took in the Wellington rescue, and I hope none of you will for we did *right*, we did our duty: at least so far as we went. [P]erhaps we did not go far enough—had we given Jennings & his Associates a *coat of tar* before leaving Wellington perhaps they would not now be here." Then, concerned that his letter might fall into the wrong hands, Bushnell added a postscript: "Perhaps you had better burn this, *dead dogs tell no tales*, & burnt letters cannot be read."[28]

Instead of burning Bushnell's letter, his brother-in-law James Fitch enclosed it with a letter he wrote to Professor James Monroe. "We are cheerful and hopeful—yea more we are full of comfort," he said. "We are sure our enemies—the blasphemous enemies of God and humanity—are finding that the farther they go the deeper they sink." Fitch said the Rescuers "had a warm talk with the shuffling & tricky Marshal" and were still convinced that Bushnell's abduction "was wholly illegal as we know it was cowardly and dishonest." The Rescuers, Fitch continued, were "animated" that the "unfair and inhuman proceedings are rousing to the State" and the nation more effectively than a thousand of us could do if *our lives* should be devoted to the work."

Fitch recognized the value of the Rescuers serving as martyrs for the abolitionist cause. "May the God of the poor use us, and these stirring events," he said, "to awaken a sleeping Church and a sleeping State to a knowledge of the fact that the bolts of heaven are hanging over us, and the wrath of heaven is out against us because of our indifference to these miseries of his suffering poor."[29]

Henry Peck also wrote to Monroe. "Belden," he said, "makes no secret of his determination to make us knuckle to him." He quoted the district attorney as saying, "Every man of them shall be tried & punished if a verdict is got." Peck, too, acknowledged the moral role the Rescuers were playing. If the Ohio Supreme Court rejected their motion for a writ of habeas corpus, he said, "we are to have a long & hard job to occupy us. *Well, we are ready*. It will come hard for us to get upon our knees before either Buchanan or Belden. Indeed, I do not believe we can do it [at] all."[30]

Langston's trial, meanwhile, went into recess at Belden's request in the afternoon of the Friday that Bushnell was "kidnapped" so that the district attorney could prepare to fight the motion for the writs of habeas corpus. On the first of a string of springlike days,

Monday, April 25, the Ohio Supreme Court began hearing Spalding's argument for them. The main thrust of the Rescuers' counsel was that "Congress had no more power to enact a law for the arrest and return of a fugitive slave than for the arrest and return of a runaway horse." For his part, Belden had no intention of arguing the constitutionality of the Fugitive Slave Law before the Republican court. The issue in question, he said, was simply whether the state court intended to "allow a writ" in support of "individuals held under a law of the United States?" Because Bushnell was technically in his custody, Marshal Johnson was in Cleveland, too. Speaking for him, attorney Noah H. Swayne also declared that the fugitive slave law was not the issue, though he did not "deny that great wrongs might grow out of it; wrongs which would be insufferable."[31]

The Buchanan administration was closely watching the writ hearing. The likelihood of a head-on clash with Ohio authorities prompted United States Attorney General Jeremiah Black to send Marshal Johnson a three-page letter of instructions about what to do if the state court granted the Rescuers their freedom. Black was especially concerned that Salmon P. Chase would use state troops to enforce the writs and free the Rescuers; two years earlier, the governor had threatened "to protect the state officials in the exercise of their duties" in a fugitive slave case in which a federal marshal's posse was captured.[32] Black told Johnson:

> It is due to the public peace that you and all the other federal officers in Ohio, should be as careful as possible not to give any just cause of offence to the state authorities. But it is necessary that you obey the Court whose officers you are. You will of course see to it that your prisoners are not rescued out of your custody either by the said process of judges who have no jurisdiction or by open and undisguised violence. If you submit to either it will be justly regarded as an acknowledgement that the Constitution and laws of the United States have no longer any practical force within the limits of your district.
>
> The Supreme Court of Ohio may be so far imposed upon as to award a writ of *habeas corpus* for the prisoners in your custody. If this should be done you will respectfully decline to produce the bodies of the prisoners before the state Court or to let them be taken of your own custody. . . .
>
> . . . you are to exert your utmost vigilance, caution, and prudence in avoiding every cause of collision, as long as you can possibly do so without surrendering the legal rights of the government or abandoning your duty as one of its officers. Let your desire to keep the peace be as manifest as you can make it. Any thing except yielding to an unlawful demand is better than a trial of brute force. But the prisoners must not be surrendered.[33]

There was talk, as well, that the Buchanan administration was ordering the *Michigan*, the U.S. Navy's first iron-hulled warship, to steam to Cleveland in case of hostilities with state troops. Spalding thought the vessel might be used as a prison ship to isolate the Rescuers from Cleveland's proabolitionist residents. Another report said that troops from the federal barracks in Newport, Kentucky, across the Ohio River from Cincinnati, were on their way, too. But neither report turned out to be true. The *Michigan*, a side-wheeler armed with a 118-pound cannon, did arrive in Cleveland on May 6, but it was on a routine circuit of Lake Erie and left before dawn five days later to return to its home base at Erie, Pennsylvania. The vessel spent most of June on a cruise to Lakes Huron and Michigan.[34]

On Thursday, April 28, the justices of the Ohio Supreme Court announced that they had unanimously decided that because the Federal District Court had Bushnell's case—that is, his sentencing—still pending before it, and the cases against the other Rescuers were still under its jurisdiction, it could not and would not interfere with the judicial process by issuing any writ of habeas corpus. If the roles were reversed, the jurists declared, if another court were to interfere "with our action and withdraw from our custody a prisoner upon trial before us, and set him at large, we should resist such attempt to the uttermost."[35]

Marshal Johnson immediately wired the White House with the news. "Every thing," he assured the president, "was quiet."[36]

"Oberlitionism in the State is used up," the *Plain Dealer* crowed delightedly. It saw the court decision as a particular blow to the presidential aspirations of the Ohio governor: "Chase is laid on the shelf for the Presidency. This was to be his thunder for the next Presidential campaign."[37]

The administration, however, was still concerned that the defense would make another attempt to persuade the Ohio Supreme Court to issue a writ. Attorney General Black wrote Johnson that the president was directing the marshal "in case any writ of that character is hereafter issued by the state Court, 'to resist at all hazards, and by every means'" any attempt to free the Rescuers.[38]

Before Langston's trial resumed[39] on Monday, May 2, Bliss, who was handling prosecution matters in Cleveland while Belden was away, received a telegram from the district attorney in Columbus advising him to drop the charges against two Rescuers—Jacob Shipherd and Orindatus Wall—because of misnomers in their indictments. Why Belden chose this moment to drop their indictments is unclear. The subject of the misnomers came up on the day of the Rescuers' arraignment in December, nearly five months earlier. Marshal Johnson had notified the court on more than one instance that the mistakes had not been corrected, and Belden himself, when the Rescuers were ordered into prison, had merely shrugged off a reminder about the misnomers with the response, *"Go 'long!"*[40] Belden never offered any explanation for his reversal. After spending eleven days in prison, Shipherd and Wall were released on Monday, April 25.

Shortly afterward, Belden's overtures to the Wellington Rescuers began to pay off. On Thursday, May 5, with the trial of Langston still in process, three of the four Rescuers from Wellington who were in the County Jail—Dr. Eli Boies, Loring Wadsworth, and Daniel Williams—were released on $500 bail after twenty-one days of imprisonment. Their release left only one Wellington Rescuer in the jail: old, stubborn Matthew Gillet.

That same Thursday, Robert L. Cummings finally surrendered himself in Cleveland, and on the next day, May 6, he, John Mandeville, and Henry Niles, together with the newly freed Daniel Williams, entered pleas of *nolle contendere*. Willson ordered each man to pay a fine of $20 plus costs of their prosecution and sentenced each to twenty-four hours in prison. They actually spent the night in the Forest City Hotel. Marshal Johnson even allowed them to roam freely about Cleveland. At the same time, it was reported that "the balance of the Wellington Rescuers have been sent for, and will probably be released in the same way."[41] Although freed from further prosecution, Mandeville protested that he was "not guilty in manner and form" as charged.[42] On the surface, it seemed strange that he issued the protest, but Mandeville was drunk during the Rescue in Wellington so he probably felt justified in believing that he had not participated in the Rescue. He did not, however, complain about being released from further prosecution.

The release of the three Wellington Rescuers from the county jail momentarily caused doubt among the Rescuers still in prison. Should they remain in jail or give bail and gain their freedom, too? "Is it not our duty," asked Ralph Plumb, writing to James Monroe, "to be in a position to demand a speedy trial, and keep the scoundrels at it until they cave in, or if they will not cave in, to keep the thing upon them until the whole thing will stink in the nostrils of all good men?" On the other hand, Plumb said, "Is it not certain if we go out on our own recognizances that the minions of the slave power north south east and west, will feel that we are subdued, cowed, and henceforth slave catching is licensed every where on the Reserve,—nay will not then trials be kept pending for that very purpose?" Plumb said he would appreciate knowing Monroe's opinion or getting the judgment of Professor James Fairchild on the subject. His words revealed, however, that his mind was already made up: "Not one of us court this confinement, our business, our health, our families, all need our freedom, but can we consent to take it under the circumstances in wh[ich] we are placed deliberately by this tyrannical court[?]"[43]

Before the government case against Langston resumed on Monday, May 2, Spalding asked that Willson sentence Bushnell, who was now back in the County Jail, "at the earliest convenience of the Court."[44] Once Bushnell was sentenced, the defense counsel could reapply for a writ of habeas corpus. The judge, however, was in no mood to be rushed. He also assured Spalding that any time Bushnell spent in prison would be taken into account at his sentencing.

Belden, who had spent the weekend with his family in Canton, returned rested and flushed with success now that the state court had turned down the Rescuers. He was confident that several witnesses could implicate Langston directly. One, livery stable owner Norris Wood, had already testified that Langston told him that "we will have him (John) any way."[45]

William Sciples verified Langston's terminology. The turncoat Rescuer quoted Langston as saying, "we will have him at any rate before he shall go South." The self-professed coward, shoemaker N. H. Reynolds, said Langston declared that "we will have him regardless of the law." Deputy Marshal Jacob Lowe recounted how he had shown the federal warrant to Langston and appealed to him to convince the crowd outside the hotel to let him carry it out. Langston had returned and declared that "we will have him any how."[46] His assistant, Deputy Sheriff Samuel Davis, who was the prosecution's last witness, confirmed the statement. The federal warrant itself was introduced in evidence.

The defense began its case on the afternoon of Tuesday, May 3. But after only three of its witnesses had testified, Judge Willson announced that he was ordering an extraordinary recess until Thursday, May 5, because his daughter was being married the next afternoon at his home. The delay annoyed at least one person in the courtroom. Falsely identifying himself as a juror, he wrote an anonymous letter to the Cleveland Morning Leader, complaining, "Would any one but a 'Federal Judge' hired for life-time, adjourn Court at an expense of several hundred dollars (not out of HIS pocket) to attend a wedding; which was made to come off, as it were, in the night, blinds being closed and gas lit in mid-day? Why not have the wedding in the evening and let the Court go on?" The letter writer pointed out that Willson had not wanted to interrupt the Langston trial to sentence Bushnell. "It is an old and true saying," he concluded, "that 'circumstances alter cases.'"[47]

Whoever he was, the letter writer had a valid point about the costs of the trial. The *Daily National Intelligencer* in Washington figured out—though actually underestimated—that if a new jury were allowed for each of the Rescuers' trials, "it will take three hundred and twelve jurors to complete the list, and some five hundred and twenty days to finish the term, at an expense of some twenty thousand dollars to somebody."[48]

Whether in celebration of his daughter's wedding or for some other reason, Willson allowed Jennings and Mitchell to venture out into the streets that Wednesday for the first time. Presumably they went under guard.

When court resumed on Thursday, Spalding offered a motion for the "immediate" sentencing of Bushnell, and once more Willson rejected the request. The judge said it was "evident" that if he did so, the proceedings of the court would again be interrupted. "It would be better," he added, "to conclude this case before passing sentence upon Bushnell."[49]

In all, the defense called up eighteen witnesses. Its aim was to show that Langston urged that legal measures be taken to help John Price. Among them were three Rescuers who were escorted from the County Jail to testify in Langston's behalf. Although he was implicating himself by his testimony, Henry Evans said Langston "was not there" when the door to the attic room in which John was held was opened. The other Rescuers—John Watson and Matthew Gillet—were called to challenge turncoat Rescuer William Sciples's testimony. Rescuer Loring Wadsworth, who had just been released on bail, also testified against Sciples. Both Gillet and Wadsworth, who were neighbors of Sciples in Wellington, said they "would not believe him under oath."[50]

After rebuttal witnesses were called by both sides, testimony was concluded in the early afternoon of Friday, May 6, and closing arguments began. With the usual recess over Sunday, the speeches would take until Tuesday, May 10, to complete. As might be expected, the arguments by both prosecution and defense were substantially the same as in Bushnell's trial with one or two exceptions. Belden, for one, seemed to go out of his way to characterize Langston in strong terms. The defendant, he said, was "very cunning and very hypocritical, very shrewd, but very deceiving." He "was in the crowd not to keep the peace, not to punish kidnappers, but to rescue the negro."[51]

The defense made much of the race question. Seneca O. Griswold, who opened the defense argument this time, questioned whether Langston had received a trial by a jury of his peers. "My client," he declared, "can have no jury of his race or color, or of those who are his peers. Not only is he an alien, but in the view of the law which governs this Court, he is an outcast. He has no equality, no rights, except in being amenable to the penal statutes."[52]

Backus took up the defense argument when court resumed on Monday, May 9. Although he was suffering "under severe indisposition," he droned on for six hours, at one point putting a juror to sleep. Using a diagram to describe Langston's movements in Wellington, Backus attacked, as Griswold had, the testimony of each prosecution witness and questioned the validity of the power of attorney and federal warrant. He, too, raised the issue of race, appealing to the jury that "although an 'African sun may have burned upon him' or upon some of his ancestors, thank God, the defendant has at least one remnant of a right yet left him, and that is the same right to justice in this trial before this Anglo-Saxon jury that any one of their men color would have."[53]

George Bliss concluded the prosecution's arguments on Tuesday morning, May 10, taking the opportunity not only to question Langston's motives but also to strike out at Oberlin College. "It was not a feeling of sympathy for John, that prompted Langston and his associates to rescue him," he said. "No, his purpose, fixed and determined, was to violate and set at defiance one of the laws of the land."

"The students who attend that Oberlin College are taught sedition and treason in connection with science and literature, and they graduate from that institution to go forth and preach opposition and treason," he continued. "The right of a portion of our inhabitants to hold property in slaves may be an unpleasant one to contemplate, and we may regret that such an institution exists, but it is not our sin, and the people of Ohio are not guilty of its commission, and so long as it is recognized as an institution of one portion of the country by the laws of the country, so long must we respect the right of those who hold property in slaves."[54]

Judge Willson charged the jury after lunch. To many, his words were, again, prejudicial. Langston's mere presence in Wellington, he said, made the defendant, according to law, "a party to every act which had before been done by the others, without regard to the time in which he entered into the combination, and, also, a party to every act which may afterwards be done by any of the others, in furtherance of such common design." It did not matter, he added, whether the slave John was freed "by the manual force of the mob" or by "threats and demonstrations of violence. It would be an unlawful rescue as much in the one case as in the other."[55]

Not surprisingly, the jury, after deliberating about half an hour, returned with a verdict of guilty.

TWELVE

"A Common Humanity"

"My sympathies are not for my father's race, but for my mother's. To him I was no more than a fine dog or horse; to my poor heart-broken mother I was a child; and, though I never saw her, after the cruel sale that separated us, till she died, yet I know she always loved me dearly. I know it by my own heart. When I think of all she suffered, of my own early sufferings, of the distresses and struggles of my heroic wife, of my sister, sold in the New Orleans slave-market,—though I hope to have no unchristian sentiments, yet I may be excused for saying, I have no wish to pass for an American, or to identify myself with them.

"It is with the oppressed, enslaved African race that I cast in my lot; and, if I wished anything, I would wish myself two shades darker, rather than one lighter."

Chapter XLIII: "Results"

Simeon Bushnell sat quietly in the prisoners' docket. His wife, Elizabeth, was sitting next to him, holding their infant daughter, Mary. Word had gone out that the young clerk was going to be sentenced, and the courtroom that morning, Wednesday, May 11, was again packed with newspaper reporters and spectators. Bushnell faced a maximum sentence of six months in prison and $1,000 fine.

Willson asked him to stand. Was there any reason why he should not pronounce sentence now? No, Bushnell said. Had he *"any regrets* to express for the offence of which he stood convicted"? No, Bushnell replied again.

"A man of your intelligence," the judge began, "must know, that the enjoyment of a rational liberty ceases the moment the laws are allowed to be broken with impunity."

Willson, everyone immediately realized, was not going to be lenient to the poor clerk. "The good order and well-being of society demand an exemplary penalty in your case," the judge continued. "You have broken the law,—you express no regret for the act done, but are exultant in the wrong."[1]

Bushnell was sentenced to sixty days in prison and ordered to pay a fine of $600, plus prosecution costs. The judge made no mention of whether the sentence took into account the time the Rescuer had already spent in jail—twenty-seven days. Either he forgot or he decided not to honor his promise. The sixty-day term was to start that day.

Even though the sentence was lighter than the maximum, Bushnell was apparently stunned. He did not say a word. Marshal Johnson parted him from his family and led him back to the county jail. At least he would be among his friends there and not at the state penitentiary in Columbus, as Belden once threatened. In fact, it now looked as though he might be free before any of the other Rescuers because Belden was not prepared to begin the next trial.

Spalding asked that the case of John Watson be taken up next, out of order, because one of Watson's principal defense witnesses, Rescuer William Scrimgeour, was "fast wasting away" with consumption and expected to live "but a short time."[2] But Belden objected, offering a number of reasons why the prosecution could not proceed. For one thing, he announced to the surprised courtroom, Sheriff Herman E. Burr of Lorain County had that morning arrested Anderson Jennings, Richard Mitchell, Jacob Lowe, and Samuel Davis on charges of kidnapping. Belden did not explain how that had been possible. He did say that the Buchanan administration had requested that he defend all four men, as a result of which he would now be busy with their case. On top of that, two government witnesses whose testimony "was indispensable," John Bacon and Robert Cochran, had returned to Kentucky without his "consent" after Langston's trial was completed. And besides which, the district attorney added, he understood that the defense was planning to reapply to the Ohio Supreme Court for writs of habeas corpus for Bushnell and Langston, which "would require" his "immediate attention."

Spalding was quick to point out that Belden could, if need be, take out a writ of *habeas corpus ad testificandum* when and if he needed Jennings, Mitchell, Lowe, or Davis. If the prosecution really wanted the case postponed, the defense attorney added, Belden should submit a motion to that effect in writing and have it "sworn to."

Spalding's last remark was too much for the district attorney. His "official character" was "power enough" to ask for a postponement.

"Your official character can add nothing to the statement," sneered Spalding.

"Nor your blackguardism," Belden shot back.

"And your private character still less," said Spalding.

Willson finally was able to break up the spat by asking both men to submit affidavits when the court reconvened after lunch. When it did, Belden offered a seven-part motion for continuance, enumerating his reasons for seeking the delay. The judge studied the motion quickly and said that the district attorney's request complied with court rules. He not only rejected Watson's appeal to be tried immediately but also postponed the cases of all rest of the Rescuers until the next court term—in July, two months away. As a result, the Rescuers were again in limbo, facing a protracted waiting period in the County Jail, unless they put up bail.

Willson's announcement set off another argument over the release of the Rescuers. Riddle tried a new tack, appealing to the judge's sense of decency and fairness: "That this presumption of the law, that these parties must be presumed to be innocent until they are proven to be guilty, is not a mere idle worthless formula." The Rescuers, Riddle insisted, "most assuredly have never coveted imprisonment. There is nothing in such a mode of life to gratify their refined and sensitive tastes, nor have they any morbid relish for self-inflicted martyrdom. But they do value their self-respect; they do prize the dignity of manhood, and they call upon your Honor as a man, as well as a Court, to judicially correct a judicial misapprehension which has subjected them to this gross injustice."

Belden thought Riddle's request "extraordinary." It was the defense attorneys, he insisted, who had urged the Rescuers to surrender themselves into custody.

"That's false, utterly false," said Riddle, interrupting. "That's a lie," Spalding joined in.

"Well, Gentlemen," Belden said sardonically, "I cannot believe you mean to seriously insult me." The Rescuers, he continued, should give bail, that he felt it was his duty "to *demand*" that they do so. "And I do this in no bad spirit," he added, self-righteously. "Much as I have been abused and charged with all manner of unworthy motives, I have not taken any one step which I thought in my own mind would *even look* like unkindness, severity, or unfairness."

Willson settled the dispute. The judge said he still saw no reason to change the journal entry, that his own "recollection accords with it." The Rescuers could be released only if they gave bail—period.[3] Anyway, Willson was tired of the exchange. He adjourned the court until ten o'clock the next morning, Thursday, May 11, when he would sentence Charles Langston.

*

John Mercer Langston offered to speak for his brother, but the Rescuer turned him down. He wanted to address the court himself at the sentencing, and John Mercer had to admit that Charles was a "successful and masterly disputant and orator."[4]

The black schoolteacher now stood before Judge Willson, "respectful but unawed." Had he anything to say? the judge asked.

Langston began by elaborating on the racial injustices all blacks, whether free or slave, faced in the United States. He spoke eloquently, with, as the reporter for the *Leader* observed, "force, clearness, earnestness, rhetoric, logic and truth."[5] The address, his brother John Mercer later said, was "perhaps the most remarkable speech that has been delivered before a court by a prisoner since Paul pleaded his own cause before Agrippa."[6]

"I know the courts of this country, that the laws of this country, that the governmental machinery of this country, are so constituted as to oppress and outrage colored men, men of my complexion," Charles Langston declared. "I cannot, then, of course, expect, judging from the past history of the country, any mercy from the laws, from the constitution, or from the courts of the country."[7]

Langston recalled going to Oberlin in September of 1858 and how the community was so "filled with alarming rumors" about "slave-catchers, kidnappers, negro-stealers" that mothers "dare not send their children to school, for fear they would be caught up and carried off by the way. Some of these people had become free by long and patient toil at night, after working the long, long day for cruel masters, and thus at length getting money enough to buy their liberty. Others had become free by means of the good-will of their masters. And there were others who had become free—to their everlasting honor I say it—by the exercise of their own God-given powers;—by escaping from the plantations of their masters, eluding the blood-thirsty patrols and sentinels so thickly scattered all along their path, outrunning bloodhounds and horses, swimming rivers and fording swamps, and reaching at last, through incredible difficulties, what they, in their delusion, supposed to be free soil."

Langston said he identified with John Price "by color, by race, by manhood, by sympathies, such as God has implanted in us all," that he "felt it my duty to go and do what I could toward liberating him."

"I had been taught by my Revolutionary father—and I say this with all due respect to him—and by his honored associates, that

the fundamental doctrine of this government was that *all* men
have a right to life and liberty, and coming from the Old Domin-
ion, I brought into Ohio these sentiments, deeply impressed upon
my heart."

Langston said he had acted in Wellington to verify the validity
of the federal warrant. "I supposed it to be my duty as a citizen of
Ohio," he continued, then caught himself because no black person
was a citizen, "excuse me for saying that, sir—as an *outlaw of the
United States*, to do what I could to secure at least this form of
Justice to my brother whose liberty was in peril." He had never
said that *"we* will have him any how."

"The law under which I am arraigned is an unjust one, one made
to crush the colored man, and one that outrages every feeling of
Humanity, as well as every rule of Right. I have nothing to do with
its constitutionality; and about it I care a great deal less." Langston
said he "had always believed" that "the provisions of this odious
statute would never be enforced within the bounds of this State."

There was another reason, besides the fact that it was an unjust
law, why he should not be sentenced: "I have not had a trial before
a jury of my peers." The Constitution, he said, "guarantees—not
merely to its citizens—but *to all persons* a trial before an *impartial
jury. I have had no such trial."*

"The colored man is oppressed by certain universal and deeply
fixed *prejudices*," said Langston. "And the prejudices which white
people have against colored men, grow out of this fact: that we
have, as a people, *consented* for two hundred years to be *slaves* of
the whites. We have been scourged, crushed, and cruelly oppressed, and have submitted to it all tamely, meekly, peaceably; I
mean as a people, and with rare individual exceptions; and to-day
you see us thus, meekly submitting to the penalties of an infamous
law. Now the Americans have this feeling, and it is an honorable
one, that they will respect those who will rebel at oppression, but
despise those who tamely submit to outrage and wrong; and while
our people as a people submit, they will as a people be despised.
Why, they will hardly meet on terms of equality with us in whis-
key shop, in a car, at a table, or even at the altar of God." As a
result, he insisted, the jury, the judge, the prosecutor, even his
own defense counsel were "prejudiced" against him.

Langston said that he had gone to Wellington "knowing that
colored men have no rights in the United States which white men
are bound to respect; that the courts had so decided; that Congress
had so enacted; that the people had so decreed.

"There is not a spot in this wide country, not even by the altars of God, nor in the shadow of the shafts that tell the imperishable fame and glory of the heroes of the Revolution; no, nor in the old Philadelphia Hall, where any colored man may dare to ask a mercy of a white man. Let me stand in that Hall, and tell a United States Marshal that my father was a Revolutionary soldier; that he served under Lafayette, and fought through the whole war; and that he always told me that he fought for *my* freedom as much as for his own; and he would sneer at me, and clutch me with his bloody fingers, and say he had a *right* to make me a slave! And when I appeal to Congress, they say he has a right to make me a slave; when I appeal to the people, they say he has a right to make me a slave, and when I appeal to your Honor, *your Honor* says he has a right to make me a slave; and if any man, white or black, seeks an investigation of that claim, they make themselves amenable to the pains and penalties of the Fugitive Slave Act, for" he said, raising his voice, "BLACK MEN HAVE NO RIGHTS WHICH WHITE MEN ARE BOUND TO RESPECT."

Langston paused as the spectators in the courtroom burst into applause.

It was a delusion, he began again, to say that there was no danger that free blacks could be seized and carried off as slaves. "Sir, *four* of the eight persons who were first carried back under the act of 1850, were afterwards proved to be *free men*." And recently, he noted, a letter had been found on a counterfeiter from a "Southern gentleman" who wrote:

"'Go among the niggers; find out their marks and scars, make good descriptions and send to me, and I'll find masters for 'em.'"

"If ever again a man is seized near me, and is about to be carried Southward as a slave, before any legal investigation has been had, I shall hold it to be my duty, as I held it that day, to secure for him, if possible, a legal inquiry into the character of the claim by which he is held. And I go farther; I say that if it is adjudged illegal to procure even such an investigation, then we are thrown back upon those last defences of our rights, which cannot be taken from us, and which God gave us that we need not be slaves. I ask your Honor, while I say this, to place yourself in my situation, and you will say with me, that if your brother, if your friend, if your wife, if your child, has been seized by men who claimed them as fugitives, and the law of the land forbade you to ask any investigation, and precluded the possibility of any legal protector or redress;— then you will say with me, that you would not only demand the protection of the law, but you would call in your neighbors and your friends, and would ask them to say with you, that these your friends *could not* be taken into slavery."

As for himself, "when I come to be claimed by some perjured wretch as his slave, I shall never be taken into slavery. And as in that trying hour I would have others do to me, as I would call upon my friends to help me; as I would call upon your Honor, to help me; as I would call upon you"—he said, turning to Belden—"to help me; and upon you"—turning to Bliss—"and upon you"— turning to his own defense counsel—"*so help me* God! I stand here to say that I will do all I can, for any man thus seized and held, though the inevitable penalty of six months imprisonment and one thousand dollars fine for each offence hangs over me!

"We have a common humanity. You would do so; your manhood would require it; and no matter what the laws might be, you would honor yourself for doing it; your friends would honor you for doing it; your children to all generations would honor you for doing it; and every good and honest man would say, you had done *right!*"

The applause that rang out now was loud and prolonged, despite the efforts of both the judge and Marshal Johnson to quiet the spectators. Willson ordered the marshal to clear the courtroom if the outburst was repeated.

In spite of his prejudices, the judge had been moved by Langston's words, "so affected," a reporter for the *Independent Democrat* of Elyria remarked, that "he could scarcely proceed to pass sentence upon him."[8] Willson said that he was fully aware of Langston's "advice to others to pursue a legal course." The judge said that he was not inclined to question the jury's integrity, but he saw "mitigating circumstances" that precluded his sentencing Langston to "the extreme penalty of the law."

"This Court does not make laws; that belongs to another tribunal," the judge declared. "We sit here under the obligations of an oath to execute them, and whether they be bad or whether they be good, it is not for us to say. We appreciate fully your condition, and while it excites the cordial sympathies of our better natures, still the law must be vindicated."[9]

Willson sentenced Langston to serve twenty days in prison and ordered him to pay a fine of $100, plus prosecution costs. Both the sentence and fine were much lighter than Bushnell's. As with Bushnell, the time Langston had already spent in jail—twenty-eight days now—was not taken into account. John Mercer Langston wondered how the government was going to collect the fines from either man. "They are said to be destitute of lands, and all manner of personal property," he commented. "It is reported that they are very poor. Then blessed be nothing."[10]

The question now was what the remaining Rescuers in the County Jail could do to get themselves out of prison before the next term of the court in July.

THIRTEEN

"Wightman's Castle"

"Wait!" said Casey. "Haven't I waited?—waited till my head is dizzy and my heart sick? What has he made me suffer? What has he made hundreds of poor creatures suffer? Isn't he wringing the life-blood out of you? . . ."

"No, no, no!" said Tom, holding her small hands, which were clenched with spasmodic violence. . . . "The dear, blessed Lord never shed no blood but his own, and that he poured out for us when we was enemies. Lord, help us to follow his steps, and love our enemies."

"Love!" said Casey, with a fierce glare; "love such enemies! It isn't in flesh and blood."

"No, Misse, it isn't," said Tom, looking up; "but He gives it to us, and that's the victory. When we can love and pray over all, and through all, the battle's past, and the victory's come,—glory be to God!" . . .

And this, O Africa! latest called of nations,—called to the crown of thorns, the scourge, the bloody sweat, the cross of agony,—this is to be thy victory; by this shalt thou reign with Christ when his kingdom shall come on earth.

Chapter xxxviii: "The Victory"

"Horse thief, 1; counterfeiting 1; murder 1; drunkenness 1; assault and battery 1; grand larceny 7, petit larceny 8; burglary 3; and believing in the higher law 20."

That is the way one of the Rescuers—presumably Ralph Plumb, who had lived in Ashtabula County—anonymously described to the *Ashtabula Sentinel* the roster of inmates at the Cuyahoga County Jail. He and his fellow Rescuers, he said, "find ourselves incapable of realizing the fact that we are *criminals*, while we do most fully comprehend the fact that we are imprisoned."[1]

In the beginning, they were full of spirit, certain of the course they were taking. Their determination shows in a photograph that was taken shortly after their imprisonment on April 15. In the picture, taken by Cleveland photographer J. M. Green, the twenty Rescuers are standing in the prison yard, which is cluttered with wooden planks that have been laid across the rough earth. They are dressed in their Sunday best, all except Orindatus Wall holding

This well-known photograph of the Rescuers by Cleveland "daguerrean" J. M. Green, was widely circulated. In New York, *Frank Leslie's Illustrated Newspaper*, for one, ran a line cut of it on its front page. The photograph was taken in the courtyard of the Cuyahoga County Jail in Cleveland sometime between April 15, 1859, when the Rescuers were first imprisoned, and April 22, when Simeon Bushnell was "kidnapped" for six days by federal court officers. From left to right are Jacob F. Shipherd, Orindatus S. B. Wall, Loring Wadsworth, David Watson, Wilson Bruce Evans, Eli Boies, Ralph Plumb, Henry Evans, Bushnell, John H. Scott, Matthew Gillet, Charles Langston, Ansel W. Lyman, James Bartlett, William E. Lincoln, Richard Winsor, John Watson, James M. Fitch, Henry E. Peck, and Daniel Williams. Courtesy of Oberlin College Archives

their hats in their hands. Wall is wearing his, a top hat. Old Matthew Gillet, standing behind Charles Langston, looks as fit as anyone, though federal authorities were worried about his health. The Rescuers do not look disheartened. Instead, they seem resolute.

The photograph itself was cause enough for good spirits. It was widely disseminated. In New York City, a line cut of it appeared on the front page of *Frank Leslie's Illustrated Newspaper*.[2] Charles Langston's address to the court was also receiving extensive cir-

The sympathetic sheriff, David L. Wightman. Courtesy of Western Reserve Historical Society, Cleveland

culation in the North and abroad; the Ohio State Anti-Slavery Society reprinted it in pamphlet form,[3] and the British *Anti-Slavery Reporter* published extracts.[4] Rallies were being held throughout the Western Reserve in support of the Rescuers and for repeal of the Fugitive Slave Law. The biggest of all, however, was yet to

The friendly jailer, John B. Smith, and his wife. Courtesy of Oberlin College Archives

come; on the same day that Langston was sentenced, the call went out for a major demonstration to be held in Cleveland at 11:00 A.M. on Tuesday, May 24. The militant tone of the rally was established when, on the eve of Langston's sentencing, the Phi Delta Society at Oberlin College debated whether "it would be wise" to release the Rescuers "by force provided they are not protected by our state courts."[5]

If the lines of direct confrontation with the Buchanan administration were not totally clear before, they were now: it was the U.S. government versus Oberlin. Within a matter of weeks, the cases of almost all the Wellington Rescuers had been disposed of, and those that remained were effectively separated from the cases of the Oberlin defendants. One of the Wellingtonians, stubborn old Matthew Gillet, was almost literally thrown out of the prison.

On the same day that Langston was sentenced, pleas of *nolo contendere* were entered for three Wellington Rescuers, one of whom, Loring Wadsworth, had been released from jail a week earlier. The others were Matthew DeWolf and Abner Loveland. The three men had been advised by a friend to say that their connection with the rescue of John Price "was entirely incidental," that they had desisted from encouraging Constable Meacham to serve the kidnapping warrant on John's captors after they learned that John was being held legally.[6] The *Cleveland Morning Leader* attributed the change of heart of the three Wellington Rescuers, all of whom were fifty-eight years old or older, to fear that the fines and costs they faced "would leave them in their old age homeless and penniless."[7] As with the four other Wellington Rescuers who had changed their pleas, each was fined $20 plus prosecution costs and sentenced to spend twenty-four hours in prison but actually had the run of the city.[8] Just as Mandeville had complained when his plea was changed, Loveland, too, protested. Even though he was now pleading *nolo contendere,* he insisted in a special statement to the *Herald,* "I am not guilty of violating any law."[9]

As for the others from Wellington, Dr. Eli Boies was free on $500 bail; Sciples, who had testified for the prosecution in the Langston trial, was still technically indicted but was free without bail; Walter Soules had never appeared again in court once he was arraigned; and Lewis Hines had never been arraigned.

The latest round of changes in plea had left Matthew Gillet as the only Wellington Rescuer who still felt duty-bound to share the fate of the Oberlin Rescuers. Gillet—whom a prison visitor described as a "remarkable patriarch," who "has seen the snows of seventy-four winters"[10]—refused to budge. "I used to think Oberlin was a pretty bad kind of a place, but I've changed my mind about it now," he explained. Anyway, he confided to defense attorney Rufus Spalding, if he changed his plea, his "sons at home would shut the door against him."[11]

In an attempt to persuade him to change his mind, if not his plea, federal officials mustered every inducement possible. They took Gillet aside in the courtroom after Langston's sentencing on May 12 and offered to release him on his personal recognizance. He would not have to change his plea or put up bail. But he refused.

"I was ordered to jail when you had my recognizance inviolately observed," the old white-haired farmer said, "*I never give you another.*"

"Will you give us your *word* to return when we send for you?" he was asked.

"Never, gentlemen," replied Gillet. "You have treated me like cowards, insulting my honor when it was pledged. I shall not allow you an opportunity to repeat the outrage."

The federal officials were getting exasperated. *"Will you go home if you are turned out of jail?"*

"If the choice were to sleep in the streets or go home," Gillet answered laughingly, "I think I should *go home!"*

"And come back when *your counsel* advise it?"

"I shall likely to follow the advice of my counsel so long as I employ them."

"Well, then," Gillet was told, *"go!"*

Gillet asked to be taken back to the jail. He wanted to get his clothes and *"to bid my friends good-by."*[12]

Marshal Johnson escorted him to the prison and then drove him home, a trip that amused Gillet very much: "''Taint often I get a ride in a carriage." While they were riding, Johnson candidly explained, "You see we want to get rid of you Wellington folks," but "don't say nothing 'bout it," he cautioned Gillet.

"O no," the farmer answered, "I ain't going to say nothing about it."

"And then," Johnson added, "we will drive those Oberlin fellows *to the wall."*

Gillet thought to himself, "then you'll have *something to drive,* that's all!"[13]

✳

The prison, a severe-looking edifice, consisted of two abutting stone sections, one slightly higher than the other, but each three stories high. Small, narrow, and barred arched windows ringed the top floor of the main section. Below them were a lesser number of tall, slender arched windows. The roofs of both buildings were crenelated, with medieval-like watch towers at the corner of the main building—hence its nickname: Wightman's Castle.

The Oberlin Rescuers tried to make themselves at home. They were given free run of the third floor of the prison, and no restrictions were placed on the number of visitors they received. The family quarters that jailer John B. Smith turned over to them included a "commodious" twelve-by-eighteen-foot sitting room whose doors were kept "wide open"[14] and two sizable bedrooms. They also had at their disposal three cells about the same size as the bedrooms, twelve by ten feet. Although an "old friend" of Ralph Plumb's who visited the jail found the Rescuers "scattered" through "gloomy halls and hateful cells,"[15] the lodgings, one of the Res-

"Wightman's castle," the crenelated Cuyahoga County Jail, where the Rescuers were held for nearly three months. Courtesy of Western Reserve Historical Society, Cleveland

cuers professed, were "kept as neat as they can be" and the food "is good and served with neatness which challenges our constant gratitude."[16] Those who could afford the expense were permitted to send out to restaurants for meals.[17] Both Sheriff Wightman and jailer Smith, the Rescuer said, were treating them with "fraternal kindness." The sheriff's daughter Lucy and Smith's wife and his sister-in-law Eliza Morrill were performing household chores for the Oberlin men.

There were, of course, inconveniences: vermin and rats, for one thing—"occasion for quicksilver and mouse traps." Moreover, there was a tendency for "bad air" to gather quickly if one of the cells was occupied by more than two persons.[18] William Lincoln, who had once conquered a bout of consumption, complained of "the closeness, dampness, & very poor drainage of the prison." However, he said, "we are all surprised at the vigor & physical strength of the whole of us."[19] The most troubling aspect was the "lunatics." Wightman was responsible for the care of mental patients until arrangements could be made for them in either an asylum or an infirmary. Some of them were violent. Once, shortly after the Rescuers were imprisoned, Smith was attacked and struck on the head by one of the mental patients wielding a huge lump of coal. "Fortunately," the *Morning Leader* reported, Smith "was so near to him that he did not receive the full force of the blow, otherwise it must have killed him."[20] The mental patients were kept in cells on the same floor as the Rescuers, separated only by a thin partition. One Rescuer complained that they bayed at "the moon (early and late) with howlings and ravings which do not promote the sleep of those who are near."[21]

Boredom was never a problem. The students—William Lincoln, Ansel Lyman, and Richard Winsor—had been brought books to keep up with their studies, though, in truth, they all fell behind. James Bartlett—"late of Royce's extensive Manufactury, Oberlin"—set up a cobbler's shop in "cell No. 3, up stairs, Cuyahoga County Jail, where he will be happy to meet his patrons." John Scott began making hogskin saddles and harnesses under a shed in the prison yard ("N.B. Dog Collars of all sizes made to order"), and the Evans brothers ("late of Oberlin, O.") were "one door west" and offering to manufacture beds, though "Government officials need not apply." At the same time, Ralph Plumb kept busy writing "declarations," and Henry Peck wrote sermons.[22]

The Rescuers were undaunted, their "consciences clear" and, one of them boasted, their "spirits sustained by various consolations we wait greater trials."[23] Each morning and evening they joined together in prayer. On Sundays, they held two Sabbath services. Peck usually preached on Sundays, and on Easter Sunday, April 24, he held a Bible class. John Scott recalled that one day before Jacob Shipherd was released from prison, the Rescuers broke into laughter when the Oberlin student offered the prayer: "Oh, Lord, take the slave-holders and grind them to powder and spread their dust over Lake Erie."[24]

The Rescuers exercised daily in the jail yard and on the prison roof. The view from the roof did "not command a very extended landscape, but which, owing to want of drainage in the neighborhood, does enjoy only five less smells than Coleridge found in

Cologne."[25] The roof became a special place of meditation for Peck, who took to strolling on it every day at sunset.

The Rescuers never lacked company. Literally thousands of people—"not less than four thousand," one Rescuer estimated[26]—came to the jail to see them. The visitors' support and encouragement were important for the Rescuers' morale. The "stream of living souls," said Richard Winsor, included "old man and maiden, mother and son, patriot and statesman." They "sat in our midst in that upper room, and tears rolled down the cheeks of many a sire as we related the story of the day. From the far West, from the distant North, from Canada, from the East, and even from the South, came thousands to hear and to see for themselves, to sympathize and to become strong in their purposes, more fervent than ever, more resolute to rise and stand against the great curse of American civilization."[27]

Professor James Monroe made it a habit to visit two or three times each week. He now regretted that he had not taken part in the Rescue and been "arrested with his friends." His ten-year-old daughter Emma, who often accompanied him, brought books, nuts, and candy for the Rescuers. She was allowed into the cells to chat with them. Father and daughter also ate with the Rescuers in a common dining room. "They were a cheerful set of prisoners," she remembered.[28] The Rev. James Thome came often from his church in Cleveland. Jane Fitch sent her husband, James, a message: "Flinch not an inch!"[29] One of Plumb's daughters wrote him: "Father, it is a great boon to be the lever, or even the stone upon which that lever rests, which is to lift a nation and a whole people up into purer atmosphere where freedom can live and bless."[30]

A special friend was Cleveland realtor Henry R. Smith, who took upon himself the not small chore of mailing the letters the Rescuers sent to their families and supporters; in all, they wrote nearly two thousand of them.[31] Smith himself wrote the philanthropist Gerrit Smith, who had taken part in the Jerry Rescue in Syracuse in 1851, to appeal for "some Material Aid for these good men and true." Some of the students, he noted, did not have "one dollar in the world": "Can you do something for us, it will be truly acceptable."[32]

Perhaps the two most unusual visitors were John Brown and his assistant John Kagi. Brown was no stranger to Oberlin. His father, Owen, had been a trustee of the college and solicitor of funds during its first decade, and Brown himself had once surveyed for the school and considered settling on some land across the Ohio

River in Virginia that Gerrit Smith had given to it. Although federal authorities were searching for him, Brown spent some two weeks in Cleveland, arriving just as Bushnell's trial was about to start. He audaciously auctioned off some mules and horses he had stolen during a raid in Missouri in which he liberated eleven slaves and also held a public lecture for which he charged twenty-five cents admission to help defray the cost of the raid. Because the city was already in such a highly charged state over the Rescue case, federal authorities, including Marshal Mathew Johnson, ignored posters calling for Brown's arrest. Brown actually attended Bushnell's trial in the County Court House and then paid a call on the Rescuers at the jail. He made an effort to disguise his appearance, however, apparently tucking his long beard into his collar or vest for the visit to the prison.

Brown tried to get William Lincoln to join him in a plan to raid the federal arsenal at Harpers Ferry, Virginia, but Lincoln told him frankly that "you have made a great mistake, as a military man." Lincoln suggested that Brown not "fight on the hills & among the railroads & also good roads: you are much, very much inferior in numbers, & in ammunition, food, &c hence shd. fight not on the hills but in the swamps: then you could retreat before superior forces."

"If it cost the U.S. $1,000,000 today to slay one Seminole Indian," Lincoln continued, "it ought to cost her $2,000,000 to kill one of your men, fighting in the same swamp. There you could find places, here & there for saving food, & by boats we could get ammunition from the West Indies."

"Young man," Brown replied, "had you been with us 6 mos. ago you wd. have altered all our plans & our war plans wd. have been placed in your hands." It was now too late, he said, to change the scheme.

"How many are there of you?" Lincoln asked. Brown answered twenty-two. "Brother Brown 22 are enough for death; I shall reserve myself for better & wiser plans."

"God bless you, young man," Brown said as he hid his beard again, preparing to leave. "God bless you, Good Bye."[33]

Kagi tried to recruit Lincoln, too. He slept overnight in the same cell with him, trying by flattery to induce him to join Brown and his men. "You are the calmest man in danger, of all the men I have ever known," Kagi said, but Lincoln still was not convinced.[34]

The only sour note, and a minor one at that, was sounded by one of Oberlin's original faculty members, irascible James Dascomb, professor of biology, botany, and physiology. Ione Munger and some classmates went to him one day and asked if they could visit the Rescuers "to express our sympathy and approval." But Dascomb, "a hard-headed old man," replied in his "very nasal twang" that " 'I think you better save your money and give it to the missionaries.' "[35]

✳

If the Rescuers were even aware of Dascomb's remark, they made no mention of it. Their thoughts were now on the upcoming rally in Cleveland on Tuesday, May 24. The day had assumed increasing significance because the Ohio Supreme Court had co-incidentally scheduled its hearing on a writ of habeas corpus for Bushnell and Langston for the next day. The prospect that the rally would be held on the eve of the hearing revived talk among the more militant backers of the Rescuers of taking the law into their own hands to release the Rescuers. A protest demonstration in Jefferson resolved that if the state court "shall refuse relief the necessity for action by the people will become obvious and *no prison shall hold them.*"[36] At that same rally, Congressman Joshua R. Giddings persuaded nearly one hundred Ohioans to sign up on the spot when he urged the revival of the Sons of Liberty, which had been organized before the American Revolution to resist British tax policies and was responsible for the Boston Tea Party.[37] "A gentleman from Portage county the other day told me," Giddings said, "there were two thousand men ready to march, or do any thing else to relieve the prisoners at Cleveland."[37] Ralph Plumb's anonymous "old friend" wrote the *Portage County Democrat* of Ravenna, "We must no longer submit to the despotism of the Federal government. Our wrongs we must right if we can through the Ballot Box, and if this fail us, through the Cartridge Box."[38] The newspaper opined that the larger issue was the "conclusion, that the peaceful influence of the ballot box will never restore our Government to the principles of freedom, justice and equity on which it was founded." It foresaw the time "in the not distant future, of a revolution *not bloodless.*" Once people realize that "the ballot box has failed as a remedy, another remedy will be sure to be applied. What that remedy will be, time will develop. A forcible writer has said, 'Revolution is the Genius of the World.' "[39] The *Oberlin Students' Monthly* was preparing to come out with an article titled "The Union" that questioned whether the separation of the North and South would inevitably or necessarily result in civil war. Should civil war be "waged in defence of the lowly and defenceless, when it is a contest for liberties ruthlessly plundered, for law and order disregarded and trampled down; for national honor and probity forgotten and disregarded, then baptized in a love for humanity, instead of a nation's dread, it becomes her safeguard—her brightest star of hope and promise."[40]

The editorials, resolutions, and political pronouncements worried Attorney General Jeremiah Black. Both Bushnell and Langston were going to appear in person for the hearing in Columbus, despite federal objections. Sheriff David Wightman had received an official summons that commanded him to have the Rescuers in the supreme court in Columbus at ten o'clock on the morning of May 25. He told George Belden and Marshal Johnson that he had to comply. Johnson decided that he had better go to Columbus, too. The *Plain Dealer* predicted that if Bushnell and Johnson were freed, the marshal would immediately rearrest them, thus forcing the "long-dreaded collision of authority."[41]

Apparently skeptical that federal officials in the state capital could handle the situation, Black quickly dashed off letters to the federal marshal and district attorney headquartered in Cincinnati. In the letter to the marshal, he enclosed a copy of the instructions he had sent to Johnson in Cleveland together with the order: "I repeat here that the body of the prisoner[s] must under no circumstances be surrendered. The State Court have no authority to meddle with this business." Black told the marshal, "In case of attack upon you by State Officers, you must defend yourself and maintain the rights of the United States against all lawless aggressions." Black's letter to the district attorney was in the same vein.[42]

In the background, unspoken, was the fact that the federal government had a well-equipped standing army, most of whose officers were Southerners under the command of a Southerner, Secretary of War John B. Floyd of Virginia. A few people even wondered whether Southern Democrats might not relish an outbreak that would result in federal intervention and the opportunity to establish their power firmly and avoid secession.[45]

FOURTEEN

The Rally and the Ruling

"I forgive ye, with all my heart!" said Tom, faintly.
"O, Tom! do tell us who is Jesus anyhow?" said Sambo . . .
The word roused the failing, fainting spirit. He poured forth a few
energetic sentences on that wondrous One,—his life, his death, his
everlasting presence, and power to save.
They wept,—both the two savage men.
"Why didn't I never hear this before?" said Sambo; "but I do
believe!—I can't help it! Lord Jesus, have mercy on us!"
"Poor critturs!" said Tom, "I'd be willing to bar all I have, if it'll
only bring ye to Christ! O, Lord! give me these two more souls, I
pray!"

Chapter XL: "The Martyr"

They started to arrive early in the morning of the twenty-fourth,
hundreds of men and women disembarking and making their way
to the Public Square. The several railroad lines serving Cleveland
put on extra coach cars to handle the swell of people coming. By
prior arrangement, all the companies were selling half-price tickets
to and from the rally. Every seat was taken in the thirteen cars
that made up the train from Oberlin. The same was true for trains
arriving from Elyria, Columbus, Cincinnati, Toledo, and Pittsburgh. The Lake Shore Railroad alone brought in sixteen carloads
of rallygoers. No less than thirty-five hundred persons, black and
white, hurried through the passenger depot on Front Street.[1]

The delegations from Lorain, Ashtabula, and Lake counties were
accompanied by brass bands, and once outside the depot they
formed in line and marched to the Public Square. The contingents
proudly carried banners that harked back to the days of America's
struggle for independence. Their banners snapped in the stiff
breeze.

Sons of Liberty.
1765.
Down with the Stamp Act!
1859.
Down with the Fugitive Act!

Here is the Government,
Let Tyrants Beware.

As the procession turned off Water Street toward the public square, a huge American flag bearing a Liberty cap was unfurled. On it was the legend:

SONS OF LIBERTY
We Welcome You!

Matthew Gillet headed the Oberlin delegation, which marched two abreast behind the Oberlin Brass Band. As the band came in sight of the square, it struck up the "Marseillaise." The wind whipped the American flag that the aged Rescuer bore aloft. On it was written the simple inscription, "1776."

The scene, the ever-hostile *Plain Dealer* said, was a "carnival"; the crowd was "considerably swelled by townspeople, who go to see an elephant through a love for the animal, or curiosity, or whatever else it may be." The newspaper took a particularly nasty tone regarding the "acres" of black men and women who showed up: "We never saw so many Negroes in Cleveland before. The Public Square was so dark with them at one time this forenoon, that they were almost forced to light candles for the Orators to speak by."[2]

If anything, the number of people who traveled to Cleveland served notice on the administration in Washington that enforcement of the Fugitive Slave Law in northern Ohio was a dead issue. At the same time, the demonstration pointed up dramatically the division among supporters of the Rescuers and abolitionists in general over the use of violence. Ralph Plumb, for one, believed that all the Rescuers had to do was give the "word" and "not one stone would have been left upon another" at the prison.[3] Most of the Rescuers and others of calmer mind, however, were afraid that such violence would backfire and hurt their cause.

There were two men in particular who feared that an outbreak of violence would damage the antislavery movement and were determined to do anything they could to prevent it: Rush R. Sloane and Henry D. Cooke. Both were in their early thirties and from Sandusky. Sloane, an Erie County judge, was himself a "victim" of the Fugitive Slave Law. In 1852, he helped a group of runaway black men, women, and children escape from a hearing in Sandusky brought by their slave master. He was tried, convicted, and fined $3,000 plus prosecution costs, most of which was raised by a popular subscription. Cooke was the editor of the *Sandusky Gazette* and prominent in the local Republican party. Sloane and

Cooke journeyed to Columbus early that morning in the belief that "only one man in Ohio could prevent a resort to arms on the day of the mass meeting." That man was Governor Salmon P. Chase, but he "had refused to come to Cleveland, for objections satisfactory to himself and difficult to answer."[4] Sloane and Cooke hoped to convince Chase to change his mind.

In a body, the demonstrators walked to the county jail and surrounded it. Fearing the worst, Sheriff Wightman closed off the yard. But he permitted the Rescuers to stand in it, and they and the demonstrators just outside the gate called out to one another and shook hands over the rough wooden fence. Cries rose out for Charles Langston to speak. The black man mounted the fence to a chorus of cheers. Raising his voice so that the demonstrators could hear, Langston reacted to their belligerence with incendiary words of his own:

"We are taught that this is the land of the free; yet we are imprisoned for breaking the bonds of the oppressor, giving liberty to the captive, and letting the down-trodden and the oppressed go free. Shall we submit to this outrage on our rights?"

"No!" the crowd shouted back.

"Are you here to-day to obey the Fugitive Slave Law?"

"No!"

"Are you here to sustain the dicta of the Dred Scott decision?"

"No!"

"Are you here to support the decision of the United States Court of the Northern District of Ohio?"

"No!" the crowd roared thunderously.[6]

The mood was ugly and could easily have turned dangerous. But other Rescuers who followed Langston urged caution, echoing the sentiments of a recent declaration from Oberlin College. The faculty and resident trustees of the college had joined in the declaration, which, though critical of the federal government, cautioned against a violent response. "Our citizens," the faculty and trustees noted, "are sometimes counselled to resort to their own strength for protection, and to take the law into their own hands. But we see no hope in this direction. Unless help should yet come from the State courts, we see no escape from the persecution so vigorously unscrupulously commenced."[7]

Henry Peck now mounted the fence to speak. He was accepted by one and all as the chief spokesman for the Rescuers. As another Rescuer held a parasol over his head to shield him from the sun, Peck spoke in a carefully measured way. His words, intended to distract the demonstrators from doing anything rash, were calming. "Irksome and painful as our present life is," he said, "it is not so trying as was the life we led when we were anticipating the assault which terminated in the arrest and rescue of John Price." It cheered the Rescuers, Peck went on, to know that what they had done "is doing something" toward preventing another runaway slave from being seized on the Western Reserve. "Let us charge you to fear no bonds, and to be terrified by no penalties when the law forbids you to give succor to the fugitive," he said.[8]

Ralph Plumb said he would be content if "our noble State now utter her sovereign voice through an undivided judiciary in favor of State rights, and the protection of the liberty of the citizen from persecutions of the slave power, through a federal judiciary."[9]

"Upon what times are we fallen," said James Fitch, "when our little children must call after us, as they stand weeping upon the threshold of our dwellings, and say as mine did, 'Come back, Pa, as soon as you can get out of jail.' . . . No, Gentlemen, we have not violated law. Ours is not the status of felons."[10]

Amid cheers, the Rescuers retired, and the crowd, placated for the time being, turned back to the Public Square for the formal round of speeches. The bandstand in the park was filled with musicians from several of the visiting bands. Not far away a large platform had been erected on the north side of the square, within sight and earshot of the county jail, so the Rescuers could hear every word that was spoken from their third-floor rooms. The list of speakers was impressive, among them Congressmen Joshua R. Giddings and Edward Wade, brother of Ohio Senator Benjamin F. Wade; former Congressmen D. K. Cartter, Columbus Delano, and Joseph Root; state legislators Peter Hitchcock and O. P. Brown; Judge Daniel Rose Tilden of Cuyahoga County; and Oberlin's own John Mercer Langston. Langston was the only person from Oberlin on the speakers' platform. He was also the only black man, and his presence symbolized the emerging strength of the radical wing of the Republican party.

There were letters of support to read from, among others, Kentucky abolitionist Cassius Marcellus Clay and Cincinnati businessman William Dennison, Jr., who was a Republican candidate for governor. Before the first oration, Clay's letter, an inflammatory call to action, was read to the crowd. The protesters, whose anger had been allayed by the tone set by Henry Peck, grew excited once again. "I say, *are you ready to fight?*" Clay demanded. "Not to fight the poor Judge at Cleveland—not to fight the marshal—not to fight the miserable packed Jury—not to fight the tools of the Despots—but the Despots themselves!" Clay warned the Re-

publicans not to select a standard-bearer who was a "submission-
ist." Don't, he said, "put up a 'compromiser!' Don't look out for
a 'conservative!' They'll all betray you, as they have done!" Clay
said that he wanted "no cornstalk general, but a real general. I
want a man whose banners bear no uncertain sign."

"When the slave-holders say if you elect a Republican President,
we will dissolve the Union, I don't want any one to put off the
evil day which would follow such events by saying, 'let it slide!'
but some one who would stand by the tomb of Andrew Jackson,
and become infused to such an extent with the spirit of that old
patriot and hero—that he would be ready to cry out in the fulness
of inspiration: 'By the Eternal—the Union shall be preserved!' I
would have no man to be precipitate—bandy no hard words—be
by no means 'fussy'—but standing upon the great rocks of *State
Sovereignty* and *National Supremacy*, I would defy the canting
traitors to Liberty, Law, Civilization, and Humanity! That's what
I mean by asking you, are you *ready to fight!*"

If, however, they were not ready to fight, Clay concluded, "I'll
have none of your conventions—no more farcical campaigns; no
more humbugs; no more Fourth of July orations—no more Declarations of Independence—no more platitudes—no more glittering
generalities—no more rights of man—no more liberty, equality,
and fraternity! In obscure places—in silence and humility, I will
crush out the aspirations of earlier and better days—and attempt
the dutiful but hard task of forgetting that I was *born free.*"[11]

Giddings was even more radical. He was ready to settle the issue
there and then. The Ohio congressman urged that the demonstrators apply that same day for a writ to release the Rescuers. If Judge
Tilden, who was on the speakers' platform with him, refused to
issue one, "I would never speak to him again or give him my hand.
If he failed, I would go to another, and another, until death came
close to my eyelids."

"I want all in this crowd who are ready to tamely and timidly
submit to tyranny to speak out," continued Giddings. Not one
person spoke up.

"Now let all those who are ready and resolved to resist when
all other means fail—when your rights are trampled into the
dust—when the yoke is fixed upon your necks—and when the heel
of oppression crushes your very life out—all those who are thus
ready to resist the enforcement of this infamous Fugitive Slave
Law—speak out."

The crowd's response was deafening.

"I would have this voice sound in the mouth of the cannon,"

Giddings declared, "and I would have it resound over every hill, through every vale, by every winding stream and rushing river. I would have it go roaring in every free mountain wind which rocks your forests, until all the world shall hear."[12]

If ever the protesters were on the verge of taking matters into their own hands, it was now. Then, as they roared with eagerness, a surprise speaker stepped to the podium. It was Governor Salmon P. Chase. A new wave of cheers rang out across the Public Square. Sloane and Cook had succeeded in convincing Chase to attend the rally. The Ohio governor no doubt found himself caught in a dilemma. He had come slowly to support the abolitionist cause during his early years in practice as a lawyer in Cincinnati, but now he made no bones about the importance of helping escaped slaves and his belief that the Fugitive Slave Law was unconstitutional. However, he had great respect for federal authority—and he wanted to be his party's candidate for president.

The governor looked the orator—"tall, broadshouldered, and proudly erect, his features strong and regular and his forehead broad, high and clear"—but in truth he was an awkward speaker, his voice was "somewhat thick," and he had a lisp. What distinguished him was the clarity and strength with which he usually presented his argument.[13] This time, however, the governor—the one person in Ohio who had the authority to call out the state militia—had a dual and contradictory purpose in mind. He began by playing the role that Sloane and Cooke had urged him to take, that of appeaser. "Citizens of Cleveland! law-abiding citizens of Cleveland!" he called out, silencing the crowd.[14]

"A few hours ago," Chase said, he had been sitting in his office in Columbus, not expecting to attend, but he "felt it his duty to come." But he was not about to advise the crowd, he said, "to do any thing which they hereafter might have occasion to regret." He "had not come to counsel any violence."

The governor described the Fugitive Slave Law as "a symbol of the supremacy of the Slave States and the subjugation of the Free," but he believed the answer to it was at the voting place. "We exist under a State Government and a Federal Government, and if the Government does wrong, turn it out." The solution—"the great remedy," he said—"is in the people themselves, at the ballot box. Elect men with backbone who will stand up for their rights, no matter what forces are arrayed against them. See to it, too, what President you elect again."

On the other hand, Chase declared, if the Ohio Supreme Court issued a writ to release any Rescuer, "as long as Ohio was a Sov-

ereign State, that process *should be executed.*" The governor, who
had been criticized for not doing more to aid Margaret Garner
when she escaped with her family across the frozen Ohio River in
January 1856, insisted that, although he "did not counsel revolutionary measures," nevertheless "when his time came and his duty
was plain," he "would meet it as a man."[15]

Chase's words, threatening as they might sound, were less militant than the crowd wished to hear and put a final damper on the
demonstrators. The governor, it was agreed, had at least put the
federal government on notice that he intended, should the Ohio
Supreme Court issue a writ, to back it up with force if necessary.
However, the officials of the American Anti-Slavery Society felt
the rallygoers failed to seize a unique opportunity. If, as Giddings
had suggested, a writ had been immediately sought, "the men
might have been set free." After all, the governor was "at hand to
sanction it" and "a *posse* of ten thousand eager volunteers at call"
as well as a sheriff "much more than willing to obey the writ."
The Rescuers, the society contended, "might have been set free in
the presence of the rejoicing multitude, and such a moral victory
won, moreover, as would have made the minions of the Slave-
power shrink from any attempt to rearrest them, or would have
ensured the right another triumph, had the contest been renewed.
That would have been a day's work to go home from with honest
exultation." The society blamed Chase for his "countervailing influence" in holding back "the enthusiasm of the crowd."[16]

The rally broke up soon after a number of declarations and resolutions were unanimously endorsed. One denounced the United
States Supreme Court for its "pliant subserviency" to "party politics." Another decried the federal government for assuming "un-
delegated powers" and enacting laws that "are unauthoritative,
void, and of no force, and being void, can derive no validity from
mere judicial interpretation." As might be expected, still another
resolution labeled the Fugitive Slave Law unconstitutional, and
yet another denounced the Federal District Court that had convicted Bushnell and Langston. A "Fund for Liberty" was established to help pay for the Rescuers' defense, any surplus to go for
"the advancement of *Republicanism and Liberty.*"[17]

All eyes were now on Columbus.

*

The importance that Ohio attached to the hearing before the
State Supreme Court on the writ of habeas corpus for Bushnell and
Langston was plain to see as the five justices filed into the court-

room in Columbus. Both Chase and United States Senator George E. Pugh were seated in the audience. No less than Ohio's attorney general, Christopher P. Wolcott, was going to present the chief case for the Rescuers. He and Albert Gallatin Riddle were going to rely, ironically, on arguments for states' rights that were usually the province of Southern extremists.

The appeal for the writ was opened by Riddle. No crime had been committed, the Rescuers' counsel began, because Congress had no power under the Constitution to enact a law such as the Fugitive Slave Law. The Ohio Supreme Court, he said, was the "exclusive court of the last resort" on the question of state sovereignty. Turning to the issue of slavery, Riddle noted that the institution was "not national, but local" and that it thus did not "naturally fall within the sphere" of the national government. Foreshadowing the adoption of the Fourteenth Amendment in 1868, he said that the Fugitive Slave Law violated the Fifth Amendment's guarantee that no person could *be deprived of life, liberty, or property, without due process of law.*"[18]

Riddle's argument took the entire morning session that Wednesday, May 25. Wolcott's was even lengthier; he spoke almost the entire afternoon session and all of the morning session the next day, going over in great detail the origins of the Constitution, its intent, and the rights accorded by it to the states. He began by describing the writ of habeas corpus as "universally called the great bulwark of freedom." Every state, he declared, has the right to "inquire into the validity of any authority imposing restraint upon its citizens," and "Ohio, thank God, is still a sovereign State, and has therefore never yielded this right, as she never could yield it, and still preserve her sovereignty, to the Federal, or any other government." Every state, he emphasized, "has the complete, exclusive, unlimited, and undeniable jurisdiction and power over all persons and things within its limits to the same supreme extent which has ever pertained to any nation in any age."[19]

Wolcott went on to enumerate principles of common law, one of which, he said, "is older than the Constitution,—older than the Declaration of Independence,—older than Magna Charta,—older even than the common law itself,—wherever the right of man to his liberty is the subject of question, every doubt is to be resolved in favor of liberty." Once John Price crossed the Ohio River, he said, "he became invested with the characteristics which the Constitution of this State and the Federal Constitution impressed upon him, with these and none other, since these alone bear sway on the soil of Ohio." Moreover, he persisted, "Congress has no more power to provide the caption [sic] of fugitives from service within the States, than the Parliament of Great Britain, or a 'Pow Wow' of the Camanche Indians.''[20]

Wolcott attacked the United States Supreme Court, charging that five of its nine justices "are themselves slaveholders, and therefore, directly and personally interested in all these questions." But "it is absolutely of no importance," he declared, "what any Court has said or ruled" about the prosecution afforded everyone under the United States Constitution. "If they have decided contrary, their decisions, of course, are erroneous, and they beat in vain against its steadfast base.''[21]

There was one issue, Wolcott concluded, that no one had dared mention as yet: what would happen if the Ohio Supreme Court granted the writ and precipitated "a collision between the State and the Federal Government. WHAT THEN? Are we children; are we old women, that we shall be frightened from duty by this menace? Are the court, coerced by these threats, to pronounce a decision which shall stultify their judgments and blast their consciences? Has it come to this, that the Federal authorities . . . are to trample your judgments under foot in your very presence? And are you, therefore, to remand these applicants to an unlawful imprisonment? If these be the only alternatives—if collision can be avoided only by striking down every safeguard with which the Constitution has hedged about the liberty of the citizen, LET COLLISION COME—come now. Let the question be settled while I live. I don't want to leave the alternative of collision or of the absolute despotism of the Federal Government as a legacy to my children. . . . PEACE—that I would preserve at almost any cost—but not that peace which is only the quiet of the grave.''[22]

Neither George Belden nor Noah H. Swayne, who was again representing Marshal Johnson, chose to make an oral argument in response. Instead, they submitted a written brief that, in eight points supported by numerous citations, upheld the constitutionality of the federal government's authority and jurisdiction to put Bushnell and Langston on trial.

*

The five justices retired to deliberate over the weekend. If as the *Plain Dealer* suspected, they followed their political suasion—all were Republicans—the outcome was clear. But none of them was taking his position lightly. Chief Justice Joseph R. Swan, in particular, realized that their decision would be the most significant one of his tenure on the court. An eminent authority on the law and one of the most respected jurists Ohio would ever produce, Swan wrestled with his conscience that Saturday and Sunday. He personally was against slavery, was a founder of the state Republican party, and had at one time been a vice-president of the abolitionist Kansas Emigrant Aid Society.

The five justices returned to the courtroom with their decision at 3:24 P.M. Monday, May 30. By a vote of three to two, they rejected the Rescuers' petition. Swan wrote the majority opinion, stating that Article IV, Section 2, of the Constitution guaranteed the right of a slaveowner to reclaim his property and that alone made a citizen who interfered with that reclamation guilty. Congress, Swan said, had the constitutional right to enact a fugitive slave law, and punishing violators was no "vital blow" to state sovereignty.[23] Then Swan added a personal note. The decision, he confided, had been a particularly difficult one for him:

> As a citizen I would not deliberately violate the Constitution or the law by interference with fugitives from service; but if a weary, frightened slave should appeal to me to protect him from his pursuers, it is possible that I might momentarily forget my allegiance to the law and Constitution, and give him covert from those who were upon his track. . . . and if I did it, and were prosecuted, condemned and imprisoned, and brought by my counsel before this tribunal on a *habeas corpus,* and were there permitted to pronounce judgment in my own case, I trust I should have the moral courage to say before God and my country, as I am now compelled to say, and, under my solemn oath as a judge, bound to sustain the supremacy of the Constitution and the law, *the prisoner must be remanded.*[24]

*

"Whatever may be the conflicting popular opinions" about the court's decision, the *New York Tribune* opined, "the people of Ohio will doubtless regard it as the deliberate judgment of the highest tribunal of the State, and will respect it accordingly."[25]

The *New-York Commercial Advertiser* said it was "glad to see that the supremacy of a law that is unpopular can be maintained in any part of the Union."[26]

Professor James Fairchild believed that if the court had decided for the Rescuers, "This would have placed Ohio in conflict with the general government in defence of State rights, and if the party of freedom throughout the North had rallied, as seemed probable, the war might have come in 1859 instead of 1861, with a secession of the Northern instead of the Southern States."[27]

A crisis may have been averted, but the issues that caused it were still very much alive. The *Cleveland Morning Leader* said that the "struggle between Freedom and Slavery, Liberty and Despotism is but begun. The past is full of encouragement, the Future of promise, for 'Revolutions never go backward.' "[28]

"Well, then let the Revolution go on," the *Plain Dealer* retorted. "There is a Revolution going on in Italy, another threatened in Hungary. . . . There is also a Revolution going on in Mexico, another in Central America, and one prayed for in Cuba. It is a pity that Black Republicans and Red Republicans in this freest of all countries cannot revolt if they choose to do so."[29]

The *Norwalk Reflector* was convinced that the "nigger driving democracy" would "exult" over the court's decision "as they would at the enforcement of any other law that has for its object the crushing out of democracy."[30]

As if in answer to that Ohio newspaper, the *Maysville Tri-Weekly Eagle* was satisfied, if not exultant: "This is doing pretty well for a set of Black Republican Judges, in a Black Republican State." The Kentucky newspaper said that "the people here thus far have had the most substantial evidences that a dignified tribunal like the Supreme Court of Ohio—presided over as it is by learned jurists who know and respect the law, will not stultify itself and disgrace their high position by refusing to properly and honestly administer any law of country—however odious it may be."[31]

✳

The Rescuers were devastated. Within hours of the court's decision, they received a telegram in prison with the news. "I suffered more on that dreadful night than I did when my dear firstborn died in my arms," Henry Peck said. "We had for days and weeks looked forward to this decision with most agonizing expectation."

The "sorrowful group" of Rescuers gathered that evening in prison for their customary evening worship service. As usual, Peck conducted it. He opened the Bible that he had brought with him into the prison. By chance, it fell open to page 476, Psalm 37:

"Fret not thyself because of evil doers."

The Oberlin professor could not believe his eyes. He thought he had opened the Bible "*accidentally*, but as I soon knew *providentially*." As he read the first verse, "it seemed as if the words were written purposely for us." Peck paused momentarily. He reread

This photograph of the Oberlin martyrs was taken between May 13, 1859, after the last of the Wellington Rescuers was released, and June 1, when Charles Langston completed his sentence. All in the photograph, aside from the sheriff and jailer, are from Oberlin. Standing from left to right are Sheriff David L. Wightman, jailer John B. Smith (note the keys dangling from his little finger), Richard Winsor, Simeon Bushnell, David Watson, William E. Lincoln, Charles Langston, Wilson Bruce Evans, John H. Scott, Ansel W. Lyman, Henry E. Peck, and James M. Fitch. Seated are Ralph Plumb, James Bartlett, John Watson, and Henry Evans. Jacob B. Shipherd and Orindatus S. B. Wall had been released on April 25 because of misnomers in their indictments. Courtesy of Oberlin College Archives

the first line: "Fret not thyself because of evil doers." To Peck, "every syllable of the sentence went like a plummet to the bottom of our hearts." He read another verse, which "seemed better than the first. It was received with breathless silence from all." The Rescuers took heart. "It seemed," Peck said in wonder, "as if the whole Psalm had been *written for our special use at that particular time*":

"Commit thy way unto the Lord; trust also in him; and he shall
bring *it* to pass. . . ."

"For yet a little while, and the wicked *shall* not *be*. . . .

"The steps of a *good* man are ordered by the Lord: and he de-
lighteth in his way.

"Though he fall, he shall not be utterly cast down."[32]

✳

The Rescuers posed for a second photograph sometime after May
13, when the last of the Wellington Rescuers, Matthew Gillet, was
released, and before June 1. There are fourteen Rescuers in the
picture. They are posed again in the prison yard. This time, four
of them are seated. At the left are Sheriff David Wightman and
jailer John Smith, who is dangling a ring of prison keys from his
little finger. The Rescuers are dressed, it seems, in the same
clothes they wore when the first photograph was taken several
weeks earlier. This time, however, the expression on their faces
seems to be one of resignation. If so, it is understandable. By June
1, they had experienced both elation at the widespread support for
the moral stand they had come to symbolize and the depression
that comes from defeat. As Ralph Plumb put it, "Sometimes all
were cheerful and sometimes sad as our plans for baffling the slave
power seemed to succeed or fail."[33]

FIFTEEN

"I Was in Prison, and Ye Came unto Me"

George and his wife stood arm in arm, as the boat neared the small town of Amherstburg, in Canada. His breath grew thick and short; a mist gathered before his eyes; he silently pressed the little hand that lay trembling on his arm. . . . The little company were landed on the shore. They stood still till the boat had cleared; and then, with tears and embracings, the husband and wife, with their wondering child in their arms, knelt down and lifted up their hearts to God! . . .

Who can speak the blessedness of that first day of freedom? Is not the sense of liberty a higher and a finer one than any of the five? To move, speak, and breathe,—go out and come in unwatched, and free from danger! . . . And yet, these two had not one acre of ground,— not a roof that they could call their own. They had nothing more than the birds of the air, or the flowers of the field,—yet they could not sleep for joy. "O, ye who take freedom from man, with what words shall ye answer it to God?"

Chapter XXXVII: "Liberty"

Roeliff Brinkerhoff rushed from Columbus to Cleveland upon hearing the Ohio Supreme Court's ruling. It was imperative that he speak to Henry Peck. Brinkerhoff was worried that the Republican party in Ohio would split as a result of the court's decision. Its state convention was scheduled to open in Columbus in two days, and delegates from the Western Reserve, who had supported Chief Justice Swan's election to the court five years earlier, now wanted to dump him as a candidate for a second term. On the other hand, conservative Republicans in the southern half of the state saw nothing wrong in Swan's position, and even Brinkerhoff's kinsman, Justice Jacob Brinkerhoff, who wrote one of the minority opinions in support of Bushnell and Langston, did not think that Swan should be struck from the party slate. Afraid that the controversy had become so "excited" that it "threatened the disruption of the party," Roeliff Brinkerhoff wanted to sound out Republican politicians in the Western Reserve about Swan's renomination. He also wanted to dispel the idea that was now making the rounds that "the more violent" among the "large preponderance of Republicans redhot against Judge Swan" wanted Peck and several other Rescuers to put up bail and go to the convention themselves—"which, of course, would add fuel to the fire."[1]

Brinkerhoff, who was only thirty years old, was a lawyer by profession, but he owned and was the editor of the *Mansfield Herald* and immersed himself in politics. He served as Jacob Brinkerhoff's personal manager and considered Salmon P. Chase his "political godfather."[2] As soon as he heard the court's decision, he took the next train to Cleveland. After meeting with party leaders the following day, he went to the County Jail, "the storm center of the existing disturbance." Brinkerhoff knew Peck "very well" and was cordially received by the Oberlin professor. The prison, he saw, "was crowded with politicians, coming and going, some advising one thing and some another." The Oberlin professor was in a quandary as to what to do.

Taking Brinkerhoff aside, Peck explained his "perplexities." The Rescuers had now been in prison forty-seven days and, although their faith was strong, the outlook appeared bleak. Should they put up bail and return to their families? Should he, Peck, and perhaps some of the others attend the state convention? Or should they hold firm in their resolve and remain in prison? Every visitor, whether personal friend or friendly politician, had a different opinion. Peck said that he thought he could trust Brinkerhoff's judgment because the young publisher was from a part of the state "outside of the local excitement." What would he recommend?

Brinkerhoff told Peck that he knew "perfectly well" what the Rescuers should do, but he was unwilling to offer advice unless Peck would agree to follow it, "not otherwise." Peck realized that he had to decide "one way or the other." Brinkerhoff's "judgment," he believed, was "less likely to be biased" than the opinions "of those about me." Peck agreed to abide by Brinkerhoff's recommendation without having any idea what it would be.

Brinkerhoff's advice was clear-cut and unequivocal: "As a conspicuous protest to the iniquities of the fugitive slave law," the Rescuers should remain in prison. That way they would serve as a constant and continuing symbol of good against the evils embodied in the act. The Rescuers could do more for the antislavery movement by remaining where they were. Brinkerhoff promised that he and others would "take care of the convention."

Peck kept his side of the bargain. Despite the temptation to put up bail, he convinced the rest of the Rescuers to hold fast and stay in jail. Their martyrdom was an important political asset.

Political ally Roeliff Brinkerhoff, in later life. Courtesy of New York Public Library

The next morning, on the eve of the convention, Brinkerhoff left for Columbus. At every stop, other delegates boarded the train. They were from the Western Reserve and were almost to a man opposed to Swan's renomination. But the farther south the train went, the more delegates who favored his renomination got on. As it rolled along, "the battle began in earnest. Before evening, it was evident that Judge Swan must go, but it was equally evident that the Swan men would bolt the convention unless some compromise could be brought about."

Once in Columbus, Brinkerhoff was able to get himself selected as Richland County's representative on the twenty-one-member Resolutions Committee, chiefly because of his relationship to Justice Brinkerhoff, whose position others thought he shared. Soon afterward, he received a request from Salmon P. Chase to come to the State House. There, Chase took him into his private room. The governor had several proposals for the Resolutions Committee to consider. As Brinkerhoff read them, he realized that Chase's platform would make harmony at the convention impossible. He personally agreed with them, he told Chase, but if they were adopted, he said, "a bolt is inevitable" and "the state will be lost." Chase, however, wanted to "proclaim the truth and go down with our flag flying." He had found it impossible to "harmonize conflicting opinions." If the minority wanted to bolt the Ohio Republican party, the governor declared, "let them take the responsibility for defeat upon themselves."

Brinkerhoff thought otherwise. "An army fighting a common enemy," he reasoned, "ought to find some plan of joint action and not turn their guns on each other." Defeat in Ohio, he said, "meant danger to the cause all over the country, and probably the loss of the presidential election next year."

It was a terrible moment for Chase, Brinkerhoff later recalled, "the loss of all hope for his nomination for President." The governor paused for a moment, looking at Brinkerhoff but deep in thought, then said, "I don't want you to consider any personal interest I may have in this matter. If I know myself, and I think I do, I would not jeopardize for an instant any principle involved in this contest to promote in the slightest my personal ambitions."

The young publisher had no intention of asking Chase to abandon any principle. "Let us see if something cannot be done." With that, Brinkerhoff sat down at Chase's table and drafted a resolution:

> *Resolved*, That proclaiming our determination rigidly to respect the constitutional obligations imposed upon the states by the federal

compact, we maintain the union of the states, the rights of the states and the liberties of the people; and in order to attain these important ends, we demand the repeal of the fugitive slave act of 1850, as subversive of both the rights of the states, and the liberties of the people, and as contrary to the plainest dictates of humanity and justice, and as abhorrent to the moral sense of the civilized world.

Intentionally, the resolution did not say that the Fugitive Slave Law was unconstitutional—a sop to the Swan faction—but clearly depicted it, Brinkerhoff explained, as "an outrage, which ought to please the anti-Swan men, and did not stultify anybody." Chase said he "could accept" the resolution but he doubted that the Resolutions Committee would. "Let me try," said Brinkerhoff.

Brinkerhoff went about his task very cleverly. He suggested to the committee that any discussion of the act be postponed until all other resolutions had been worked on. And as the other resolutions came up for discussion, Brinkerhoff made himself helpful, clarifying the ideas of other members, helping "every one I could to succeed in his specialty," until by the time the committee got around to considering the Fugitive Slave Law, he had "quite a number of delegates under some obligations to me for friendly votes." Still, Brinkerhoff bided his time. A long and bitter argument broke out, while at the same time calls came from the convention floor to finish work on the platform so that the delegates could vote. Finally, feeling that his "time had come," Brinkerhoff asked to speak.

Looking around the table, Brinkerhoff reminded the other committee members that "in the great contest for the restriction of slavery" they were all "friends and not enemies," that they should find some common ground "upon which we could unite our forces." In general, he continued, he could agree with party members from northern Ohio that the law was unconstitutional, but he could also understand how those from southern Ohio could think otherwise. Brinkerhoff pointed out that the committee's own chairman, Thomas Corwin, had been secretary of the treasury under Millard Fillmore in 1850 and had assented to the fugitive law. "We certainly could not ask him now to declare it unconstitutional," said Brinkerhoff, "but I could ask him to assent to the evil effects of that law and to ask for its repeal." With that, Brinkerhoff presented his resolution. The conservative Corwin nevertheless objected to it, but with the support of other delegates, including Professor James Monroe of Oberlin, who was also a committee member, Brinkerhoff's resolution was reported out to the convention. The Republican delegates, Brinkerhoff boasted, approved it "with substantial unanimity." It became the "famous" third resolution in the party's platform. In addition, Chief Justice Joseph Swan was not renominated. The radical wing of Ohio's Republican party had won.

*

Over the objections of both George Belden and Marshal Mathew Johnson, Langston was released from the county jail after completing his sentence on June 1. In all, he had been in prison forty-eight days. Both federal officers wanted him and Bushnell to serve six additional days, to cover what they called the two men's "constructive escape from jail"—the time they had been absent from prison to attend the writ hearing in Columbus. Sheriff Wightman would have none of it. He said that he had been advised by "his counsel" that he could be sued for false imprisonment if he did so.[3]

Belden, however, would not let it rest at that. At the same time that the sheriff discharged Langston, Belden had him served notice that he had sixty days to pay his fine—$100—and $872.20 in court costs. Interest had been charged from the day of his sentencing, May 12. In addition, the federal marshal in Cincinnati was told to attach property Langston owned with his brother John Mercer in Columbus. The marshal had Jacob Lowe inspect the land there. Lowe reported back that he could find "No goods or Chattles" on it so on June 6 the marshal had a lien placed on Charles's half of the parcel.[4]

Langston's departure left thirteen Rescuers still in the County Jail—James Bartlett, Simeon Bushnell, Henry and Wilson Bruce Evans, James Fitch, William Lincoln, Ansel Lyman, Henry Peck, Ralph Plumb, John Scott, David Watson, John Watson, and Richard Winsor. The month of June passed slowly, day following day, week following week in monotonous fashion. The weather turned cool one week, warm and muggy the next.

It was evident now that the Rescuers would be confined for months; no new legal moves were in the offing in the federal court. They tried to keep busy. Those who had set up shop in the prison yard or their cells busied themselves with turning out harnesses, shoes, and cabinetwork. Late in the month, James Fitch and Simeon Bushnell came up with the idea of starting their own newspaper to provide an opportunity for the Rescuers to keep their cause alive before the public. The two men—both printers by trade—were able to scrounge up the tools and gear needed to set type. They got Oberlin printers Shackland & Harmon to lend them a font of small pica. They used a policeman's club as a mallet to make proofs and shackles to pound the type down in place. A fellow Rescuer supplied them with "side-sticks," "quoins," and a "relget" made from a whitewood board. Another sawed up a fence board to make a "rack." Fitch and Bushnell themselves hewed a piece of stave to make a shooting stick and used a "door-stone" for a composing table. They planned to publish their newspaper— *The Rescuer*—on alternate Mondays. Henry Peck and Ralph Plumb were serving as writers and editors; a slew of stories were planned for the first issue—articles about the Fugitive Slave Law, the Rescue, the reason for their imprisonment, what their life in prison was like. John Scott was handling circulation; he volunteered to hawk the periodical for three cents a copy to visitors in the prison yard. All they lacked, Fitch and Bushnell grumbled, was a font of italics for emphatics: "Many were needed."[5]

Whenever their spirits sagged, the Rescuers were bolstered by the continued encouragement of their supporters and by the assurance that their remaining in prison was having its intended effect. One man from Michigan, Peck said, told him of a "perfect *revival* of anti-slavery zeal in that state in consequence of our troubles." Fitch believed the Rescuers "have not suffered in vain," that the "weak back of our Republican Party in Ohio has been strengthened."[6]

The Rescuers would certainly have been cheered if they had had any inkling of the devious machinations that their friends in Lorain County were employing to put pressure on John Price's captors.

✳

The Kidnappers, as they were now being called—Anderson Jennings, Richard Mitchell, Jacob Lowe, and Samuel Davis—spent eight days in the Lorain County Jail following their arrest at the conclusion of Langston's trial on May 11. They were released on $800 bail each on May 19, pending their trial on kidnapping charges. Malachi Warren, the onetime Alabama planter who lived in Oberlin, and Wellington innkeeper Oliver Wadsworth were among the county's Democrats who put up the bond money. The four men were scheduled to go on trial at the next session of the Lorain County Court of Common Pleas on Wednesday, July 6. Just as the citizens of Oberlin had rushed to the support of the Rescuers, the citizens of Mason County, Kentucky, were now being rallied for the defense of Jennings and Mitchell. "Every Slave-holder in the county, and in fact every *citizen* of the county," the *Tri-Weekly Maysville Eagle* noted, "is interrested [sic] in the defence of these men." The newspaper pointed out that there was no danger of their being convicted "on the charge that is hatched up against them, yet it will subject them to very great inconvenience, loss of time, and doubtless heavy expense." Everyone in the county, it added, "should take an interest sufficient at least, to share a portion of the expense."[7]

Jennings, incidentally, was trying to capitalize on the publicity he was receiving over the Rescue case. At one and the same time that June, he announced himself both a convert to the Democratic party and a party candidate in an upcoming election to the Kentucky legislature. His candidacy, however, was not greeted with enthusiasm by his friends and neighbors. The *Tri-Weekly Maysville Eagle* said it thought it "decidedly in bad taste, for a man to change his politics, and become a candidate for office on the same day." All the other candidates were "just as staunch pro-slavery men as he is" and would do just "as much" as Jennings had "to reclaim their slaves, should any of them escape to the State of Ohio," the newspaper said, adding: "We shall suggest to the other candidates that to get even with Mr. Jennings they ought to start out after some runaway and get themselves made Martyrs of."[8]

Belden planned to block the Kidnappers' trial altogether. He and Marshal Johnson went to Washington to confer with officials of the Buchanan administration. It was decided to curtail the extensive support the Rescuers were attracting by bringing their cases to a speedy conclusion. A court term of ninety days was to start on July 16, during which the trials of the remaining twelve Oberlin Rescuers would be held. In addition, Belden got writs of habeas corpus, signed by United States Supreme Court Justice John McLean, to free the Kidnappers from Lorain County's jurisdiction. The writs would permit the Kidnappers to testify at the Rescuers' trials and, Belden apparently believed, would also take the four men completely out of Lorain County's jurisdiction. First, however, the writs had to be properly served. This required the Kidnappers technically to surrender their bail and return to the custody of the Lorain County sheriff. Anxious to make his move before the Kidnappers' trial got under way, Belden promised the four men that if they gave themselves up to Lorain County authorities, he would see to it that they were immediately freed on the federal writs of habeas corpus.

The Kentuckians, meanwhile, were taking matters into their

own hands. Acting independently of Belden, Jennings and Mitchell unexpectedly came north ten days before their July 6 trial date. But they did not stop in Ohio. In company with John Bacon, they went into Canada. The Kentuckians had a madcap scheme: to find John Price and promise him his freedom if he returned to Ohio and testified that he was really Bacon's slave both at their kidnapping trial in Elyria and before the federal court in Cleveland. Where precisely the three men went to search for John is not known. But considering the thousands of black men who had fled the United States and now lived in numerous black enclaves in Canada and that many of them had changed their names once in Canada, their task must have seemed difficult if not impossible. In any event, they did not find John. Their only choice now was to go along with Belden's plan.

Meanwhile, Roswell G. Horr, the clerk of the Court of Common Pleas, who had helped plan the grand jury action against the Kidnappers, got wind of the writs that Belden had obtained for their release.[9] He called in the Lorain County sheriff, Herman E. Burr, to discuss "what was best done in such an emergency." Burr's answer was simple: he would make himself scarce by leaving Elyria on business "in the remote part of the county!"

Belden and Marshal Johnson, together with the Kidnappers, arrived in Elyria in the blustery early morning of Saturday, July 2, to surrender the four Kidnappers—and then serve the writs. And sure enough, they found that the sheriff had just "happened" to have left the old red-brick courthouse. Johnson sent a postal clerk after Burr with a message summoning him back. The clerk caught up with Burr in Amherst. The sheriff sent back word that if Johnson wanted to see him he had better come to Amherst because he expected to be detained there "rather late."

Johnson decided not to go after Burr. Instead, he and the others waited for the sheriff to return to Elyria. About seven o'clock, shortly before sunset that evening, the Kentuckians spotted Burr returning. Jennings confronted him on the street. The sheriff said he first had to put away his horse and attend to some other business.[10] Jennings and Mitchell rushed to tell Belden and Johnson that Burr was back. Together with Lowe and Davis, they went to the courthouse with the idea of surrendering the Kidnappers into Burr's custody and then gaining their release by serving the writs on Probate Judge Charles H. Doolittle. But now Burr could not be found. Belden and Johnson searched through Elyria for him, finally giving up at eleven o'clock and taking rooms for everyone in a local hotel.

The next morning, Sunday, July 3, the district attorney and the marshal located both Burr and Doolittle. Johnson tried to take over the sheriff's office in the courthouse for his own use, which raised Burr's hackles. He took an instant dislike to the way the marshal was "apt to *order* folks" around, and even the way Johnson announced "with, O how much importance, 'I am the United States Marshall [sic].'"[11] The sheriff informed Johnson that he did not keep his office open on the Sabbath and told him to get out of it.[12] As for Judge Doolittle, who was not known as a pious man, he was "for the first time in a dog's age, 'fixed up'" in his best suit and on his way to church.[13] The judge said that he didn't open his office on Sundays either. Johnson asked the judge whether he would be in his office the next morning, Monday, July 4. Doolittle said he would. Johnson and Belden conferred furtively, then announced that they were going to leave Elyria for Cleveland immediately and not return until after the Fourth of July. However, the marshal and the district attorney had a trick up their sleeves. Instead of leaving Elyria, they went back to their hotel and holed up in their rooms. They planned to outwit both Burr and Doolittle, but they were seen in the evening, perhaps when they and the Kidnappers dined. According to Horr, it became obvious that the federal officers were playing a "double game," that their talk about going to Cleveland "was a mere ruse gotten up solely to throw the officers of our county off their guard."

Judge Doolittle, meanwhile, had walked home and told his wife, Elizabeth, about what had happened. Like her husband, she was an abolitionist. She suggested that he immediately inform Burr, Horr, and Prosecuting Attorney W. W. Boynton of Belden's intentions. The judge did, and that night, while Johnson and Belden huddled in the hotel and planned their surprise, the four county officials met and decided on a simple countertactic.[14]

Belden did not sleep much that night. He was at the judge's home, ringing the front doorbell, at sunrise, about 4:30, the next morning, July 4. Mrs. Doolittle answered the call. No, she said, the judge was not at home; he had left two hours ago. "I had an appointment with the Judge," Belden whined. "True," she said, but the judge had been told that Belden would not be back until Tuesday and so had gone off to visit some "long *neglected* friends." She didn't amplify, but Doolittle had risen at three in the morning and left by carriage for Oberlin. Belden left empty-handed but not defeated.

The district attorney, the marshal, and the Kidnappers returned to the courthouse the next morning, Tuesday, July 5, hoping to

Rescuer ally Roswell G. Horr. Courtesy of Spirit of '76 Museum, Wellington

find the judge or the sheriff. Again, neither Doolittle nor Burr was to be found. The judge had returned home the night before, but learning that Belden was still in town, turned right around and went back to Oberlin. Belden and Johnson tried the sheriff's home,

Foe of the Kidnappers W. W. Boynton, son of Lewis D. Boynton, in later life. Courtesy of New York Public Library

but Burr was absent and his wife refused to put the Kidnappers behind bars without the proper papers to commit them.[15] Completely stymied at last, Belden and Johnson left the writs with her and returned to Cleveland to figure out what to do next.

By now, the four Kidnappers were up in arms at Belden's inability to gain their freedom. Their trial was about to start the next day. The Kentuckians had already wired home for help, and that evening one of Maysville's most prominent attorneys, former Democratic Congressman Richard Henry Stanton, arrived by train and went into immediate consultation with them. Stanton had stopped off briefly in Cleveland to try to find out from Albert Gallatin Riddle what the Rescuers' defense counsel planned. Riddle answered frankly that he wanted "to force the United States to abandon further prosecution of the 'rescuers,' and to liberate those already convicted."

"Don't you know," Stanton said, "that John was a slave, and that his pursuers had a right, under the United States laws, to take him by any means they chose?"

"I know all that," Riddle replied, "but don't *you* know that although John was a slave, you can't identify the man you captured as John the slave? He is beyond your reach now, and you have not a witness in the world by whom you can prove that he was a slave. Your gang, instead of executing their warrant like men, kidnaped the boy as thieves; and as kidnapers they shall be tried, convicted, and sent to the penitentiary, unless these men are liberated."[16]

Stanton recounted to the Kentuckians what Riddle had said and advised them that it might be better to reach some terms with the Rescuers. Meanwhile, D. K. Cartter, whom W. W. Boynton had invited to assist him in prosecuting the Kidnappers, arrived in Elyria. Cartter, a former Republican congressman, knew Stanton from Washington; their terms had overlapped in the early 1850s. Meeting Stanton, Cartter discovered that the Kentuckians "were in great terror at the prospect of 'facing the music.'" The "scapegraces were so scart," Cartter, who stuttered, said, "you could ha' was-a-a-ashed your ha-a-ands in the sweat o' their faces!"[17]

Taking advantage of the Kentuckians' fears, Cartter worked out a deal with Stanton. The only problem was whether Belden would agree to it. Returning to Cleveland that day, Tuesday, July 5, they quickly drew up and sent three letters of petition to the district attorney. The approach was clearly intended to mollify Belden and to take the responsibility of what might look like capitulation off his shoulders. One of them, signed by Jennings, Mitchell, Lowe, and Davis, said the "undersigned" believed the prosecution so far in the Rescue cases was "a sufficient vindication of the law." The four men said they had "made every reasonable exertion to surrender ourselves to the authorities of Lorain county" but had been "defeated." They pointed out their "personal inconvenience and sacrifice" in pursuing the matter further, especially because Jennings and Mitchell were "residents of another State." They said that Lorain County officials were willing to dismiss the kidnapping charges against them if Belden, with the consent of the federal court, would enter pleas of *nolle prosequi* in the Rescuers' cases— in other words, a quid pro quo.

The second letter, signed by Bacon, Stanton, and Robert Cochran, the Mason County clerk, who had come north to testify for the Kentuckians, urged Belden to accept the arrangement that had been worked out. The Constitution and the Fugitive Slave Law, they wrote, "have had a just and righteous vindication in the conviction of a portion of the rescuers. . . . As Kentuckians, this is all we could ask at your hands." They thanked Belden and his assistant, George Bliss, "for the fidelity, firmness and patriotism which have characterized your conduct, in these unpleasant prosecutions."

In the third letter, Stanton and Cartter wrote that neither the district attorney nor any other federal officer "had any agency whatever, either directly or indirectly, in originating or perfecting the settlement agreed upon." The two former congressmen said, "Whatever responsibility is attached to the agreement or settlement belongs to Messrs. Jennings, &c., and to us as the friends and Attorneys of the parties, and to none others."[18]

✳

Although Elyria was little more than twenty-five miles from Cleveland, the Rescuers were totally unaware of the efforts being made on their behalf. On Saturday, July 2, when Belden, Johnson, and the Kidnappers first arrived there, more than four hundred young boys and girls comprising the entire Oberlin Sunday school, the largest in northern Ohio, traveled by train to Cleveland to pay a call on the school's superintendent, James Fitch. The bookstore proprietor was deeply loved by his pupils, and he returned their affection. He prepared the lessons for his "little folks" a year in advance, and when Sundays came, as one of his daughters recalled, "There was a certain exalted happiness in his face which we never saw at other times."[19] On one day alone while in prison, Fitch received sixty letters from his pupils. One of them was from a young black girl born in South Carolina who wrote that she "never knew what freedom was" until she came to Oberlin: "I was not allowed to go to school nor Sabbath School. They made us say some questions after them, such as 'Servants be obedient to your masters,' and the like."[20] Emma Monroe won a brass-bound purple velvet-covered Bible as first prize in a school contest—with her father's help—for coming up with "the best passages of Scripture to prove that our dear James Fitch had done right."[21]

Led by a band, the Sunday school pupils marched "like little angels" from the train station up Superior Street to the county jail. Each class bore a banner, and at the head of the procession was the largest of all:

1833   1859
Oberlin Sunday School,
J. M. Fitch, Superintendent.
"Stand up for Jesus."
"Them that Honor Me I will Honor."
"Feed my Lambs."[22]

The children thronged the prison, jamming the hallways and the rooms in which the Rescuers lived. Some were frightened when they saw fierce thieves and robbers watching them through the barred windows. Later, from their own barred windows on the top floor of the jail, the Rescuers watched the youngsters frolicking at a picnic the school held in the Public Square. Despite the heat and dust that day in Cleveland, the children then walked to the Plymouth Church Sunday school for special exercises that included singing "There is a happy land" and a series of short speeches by, among others, "Father" John Keep of Oberlin. Keep called on all the children to rise and "give their testimony against slavery." As one, the youngsters stood.

Afterward, the group returned to the prison yard, where Fitch addressed them. He had always, he reminded the youngsters, instructed them in morals and religion and had "often especially warned" them "to be careful" in their habits and "to avoid the disgrace of *being sent to jail*":

"But what do I now see! What great evil has overtaken you! What great crime have you now committed! Here I behold you *all in jail!*"

"You must have noticed, my children," Fitch continued, "that two classes of people have in all ages been made the inmates of prisons. Wicked people, who harm the world, and the good and holy, who are so far in advance of their age that the wicked world misunderstands them. . . . To which class do your Superintendent and his companions belong? . . .

"On what times are we fallen when such men are considered felons,—fit tenants of a jail; but their persecutors, who, perhaps, have defrauded the halter of its due, go free as if they were the good!

"Yet thus has it always been. . . . We are compelled to endure painful imprisonment, but we have done no wrong. We appeal to God above and all the holy, that to feed the hungry, to clothe the naked, and to securely hide and safely convey away a poor and helpless brother, who is panting in his haste to escape from the hands of robbers, is to do right, and only right."

Fitch then read "a sweet hymn":

> God made all his creatures free:
> Life itself is Liberty;
> God ordained no other bands
> Than united hearts and hands.
>
> . . . .
>
> But a better day shall be,
> Life again be Liberty,
> And the wide world's only bands
> Love-knit hearts and love-knit hands.
>
> So shall envy, slavery cease,
> All God's children dwell in peace
> And the new-born earth record,
> Love, and love alone, is Lord.[23]

On Monday, July 4, when Belden showed up at dawn at judge Doolittle's home to find that the judge had skipped town, John Scott began selling in the prison yard the first issue of *The Rescuer*, which had just been published. Five thousand copies of the four-page newspaper were printed. Among its numerous articles were two obituaries. One was for abolitionist editor Gamaliel S. Bailey, whose *National Era* first published in serial form Harriet Beecher Stowe's *Uncle Tom's Cabin*. The other was headlined "Painful Death":

> Died in the cells of the Jail in this city, early this morning, Ohio State Rights aged just Eighty three years. The deceased was one of a numerous family, all born July 4th, 1776. Their father's name was American Independence.

The Rescuer also contained a few advertisements, one of them from the two publishers touting Fitch's bookstore in Oberlin:

> PRINTERS AND BOOKSELLERS!
> FITCH & BUSHNELL.
> Are not in partnership and never were; but as they agree so perfectly as to what should be done with fugitives and fugitive slave laws, they are sure they can still do business together. . . .
> Bibles and Testaments will be sold to Administration Democrats

strictly at cost; and to Lower Law men generally at very low rates. Hoping to check the progress of barbarism *as well as of slave catchers*, they have filled their shelves with many good books, which are real "Helpers." Hallam's Middle Ages is highly recommended as a valuable aid in settling the dispute as to whether Democratic America has yet advanced in civilization, beyond the Medieval Period.[24]

The next day, Tuesday, July 5, while the settlement petitions to Belden were being crafted, William Lincoln, who was in one of his despondent moods, wrote Gerrit Smith: "Our hopes are not high; we expect to be condemned & to be removed to other prisons to serve out our sentences." Lincoln said the Rescuers believed that "as to the prosecution for kidnapping at Elyria, we have but little hope since the Supreme Court has failed us." However, although discouraged, he continued, "They may kill us; but hinder God's truth from ongoing, they never will nor can." Yet Lincoln said he was "thinking carefully" whether it might be "wisest" to change his plea. "I am praying & thinking over it: the Republicans say no; but I think their foundation idea wrong." Despite his insistence that he was a pacifist, the Oberlin student had resorted to violence in the past—to save the Catholic priest on the steamboat to Maysville and during the rescue of John Price. He now said he was "loth [sic] to act independently" in changing his plea, but violence—war—he implied, might be the only answer:

> I am striving to get into the presence of God's truth, that being imbued with that I may act aright: for all along these trials the conviction has been deepening that not Republicanism, nor any Compromise must save this country, but the acting out of the Deliverance of God's Truth. If this last position come into action of course the struggle will be longer, & the end aimed at more deferred, than under Republicanism; but when gained it will have so disciplined, & excited the moral powers of the nation, that all other reforms will either be gained or be of easy attainment.[25]

Except for opening his mind to Smith, Lincoln kept his thoughts to himself. Ralph Plumb would later say that "never for a moment did one of us waver in our purpose not to give bail."[26]

The next day, Wednesday, July 6, began as usual for the Rescuers. It was a pleasant summer morning. The mail was delivered, and with the numerous letters was a check for $100 from a Quaker in Philadelphia. Several visitors came by to see them. One of them was a wealthy Cleveland man with a donation "which exceeded all but one of the many gifts" the Rescuers had received. Among the students visiting that day was Agnes Ferguson Smith, who was in the fourth year of the Young Ladies' Course at Oberlin. She had with her a little red embossed leather autograph book that was already becoming filled with the signatures of classmates. She was there in the early afternoon when Sheriff David Wightman brought the news that a settlement had been worked out. Faced with the certain prospect of being convicted for kidnapping if they were tried, Jennings and Mitchell were fed up with the way they had been treated by the federal government. They had made it clear to Belden that "he had betrayed them, had induced them to give themselves up," but "now that it had failed, there was nothing but the penitentiary in prospect."[27] Realizing that he could no longer count on the Kentuckians, Belden had accepted defeat and acceded to the agreement. But Judge Hiram Willson didn't like the settlement at all. He wanted to press the cases against the Rescuers but was finally convinced by Belden of the futility of doing so. Moved by "only a fellow-feeling" for the Kentuckians, Willson relented.[28]

The settlement was far from concluded, however. The Rescuers wanted no part of the agreement. Lorain County authorities tried to convince them that it was the best step to take.[29] But the Rescuers hesitated. They would agree only if a stipulation was added that the Kidnappers "promise never again to hunt fugitives in Northern Ohio."[30] Assured that the Kentuckians would abide by such a promise—Jennings and Mitchell had no wish to return to the Western Reserve whatsoever—the Rescuers finally acceded.

As preparations were made for their departure—the papers for their release had to be drawn up, and they had to pack their clothing, books, and tools—Agnes Smith circulated her autograph book.

"It is with a Moistening eye that I set myself about penning these lines," Peck, who was one of her teachers, wrote. Their classroom days together, he said, "entices me back to scenes in wh. I have had pleasant & profitable converse with the class to wh. you belong. . . . More than one beneficial result from it have I experienced since I came to this gloomy abode."

Ralph Plumb made a minor mistake: "This 'day' is the last 'day' of Eighty four days spent in prison for the want of the light of 'Day.'" July 6 was actually the eighty-third day of the Rescuers' imprisonment.

Some of the other Rescuers penned religious thoughts. "If ever you are called to suffering or imprisonment for *Christ* or *humanity's sake*," Richard Winsor wrote, "May the *scriptures*, and *He* of whom they speak, be thy support and comfort."

David Watson inscribed a page: "Let not the Oppressor triumph."

"Let thy motto ever be to do right," wrote Ansel Lyman.

Henry Evans added, "O give thanks unto the Lord for he is gracious because his mercy endureth for ever."[31]

Sheriff David Wightman and their *"honest Postmaster,"*[32] Cleveland realtor Henry R. Smith, signed the autograph book, too. So did the one Rescuer who was not going home, Simeon Bushnell. Spiteful to the end, Belden refused to agree to his release. Bushnell had to remain in prison until the balance of his sentence—five more days—was served. " 'Break every bond and let the oppressed go free,' " the young clerk wrote, quoting Isaiah 58:6.[33]

As they prepared to leave the County Jail, the "Oberlin Rescue Company," as Plumb dubbed them, drew up and unanimously adopted a series of resolutions expressing, among other things, their gratitude to their supporters and their determination to "hereafter, as we have heretofore, help the panting fugitive to escape from those who would enslave him."[34]

News of the settlement had spread rapidly. The parlor of the jail was filled with friends and wives as the Rescuers came downstairs from their quarters. Plumb had several packages in his hands—silver napkin rings, forks, and spoons for Sheriff Wightman, Jailer John Smith, "good Samaratin" Henry R. Smith,[35] and their attorneys, Spalding, Riddle, Backus, and Griswold. Each was engraved with the recipient's initials and the legend "From Rescuers; Matthew 25.36," a reminder of the biblical passage "Naked, and ye clothed me: I was sick, and ye visited me: I was in prison, and ye came unto me."[36] Plumb handed the gifts to the men's wives with the request that they place "the gift before their husbands, at meals, three times a day while they lived, that they might at such times, when surrounded by their families and those dear to them, when noble and generous feelings were sure to come, look upon the memento, and remember the exciting scenes through which they had just passed."[37]

As they were about to leave the prison, Henry Peck pointed out that the Rescuers had spent their first hour there almost three months earlier in prayer. He suggested that "it would consonant with their feelings to spend the last moments in thanksgiving" as well.[38]

The Rescuers left the prison about five o'clock. Outside hundreds of people had gathered to escort them to the railroad station. A few blocks away, along the lakefront, a hundred cannons fired a salute. The Rescuers and their supporters marched down Superior and Water streets. In the lead was a band playing "Hail Columbia," "Hail to the Chief," and "Yankee Doodle." At the depot,

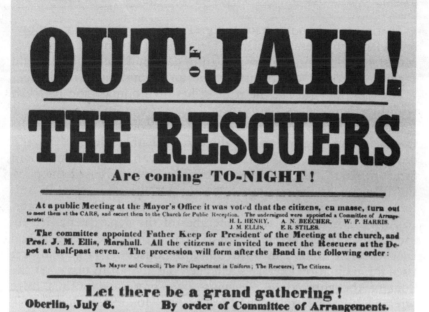

OUT of JAIL!

THE RESCUERS

Are coming TO-NIGHT !

At a public Meeting at the Mayor's Office it was voted that the citizens, en masse, turn out to meet them at the CARS, and escort them to the Church for Public Reception. The undersigned were appointed a Committee of Arrangements:

H. L. HENRY,   A. N. BEECHER,   W. P. HARRIS.
J. M. ELLIS,   E. R. STILES.

The committee appointed Father Keep for President of the Meeting at the church, and Prof. J. M. Ellis, Marshall. All the citizens are invited to meet the Rescuers at the Depot at half-past seven. The procession will form after the Band in the following order:

The Mayor and Council; The Fire Department in Uniform; The Rescuers; The Citizens.

Let there be a grand gathering !

Oberlin, July 6.   **By order of Committee of Arrangements.**

Victory celebration, the poster alerting Oberlin residents to the meeting held in honor of the released Rescuers. Courtesy of Oberlin College Archives

there was a parting speech and three "stentorian cheers," and, as their train pulled away, the band played "Home, Sweet Home."

At Grafton, Jane Fitch, Esther Peck, Marrilla Plumb, and John Watson's wife, Margaret, boarded the train for the last twenty minutes of the journey to Oberlin. The entire town was out to greet them when it pulled into Oberlin just at sunset.[39] Mayor A. N. Beecher had hastily organized a committee to arrange their reception and to distribute a poster throughout the community alerting the citizens to their return. Every resident, every student, every professor saw the message or heard the news. As the train braked, James Fitch looked down from it at the assembled crowd. It seemed to him like a "sea of heads," and everyone was cheering and shouting. As the Rescuers alighted, "the heavens rang again with the united and prolonged huzzas of nearly *three thousand* persons." John Scott was elated: "We left our loved home ere the snows of early spring had melted, and we returned not till the gardens were filled with flowers, and the fields clothed with green-ness."[40]

There was only one person whom Fitch saw who was not glow-ing with happiness: Oberlin's Democratic postmaster, Edward Munson. He "stood motionless, grim, dark and dreary, like a bald eagle on a rock, or a stork on a seashore." Fitch thought to himself, "Poor tool, let him eat the fruit of his own doings, and be *filled* with his own devices."[41]

Professor James Monroe delivered a welcoming speech by the trackside and then all of Oberlin, with "Father" John Keep and old Matthew Gillet of Wellington in the van, marched up Main Street to First Church, banners flying, the Oberlin Brass Band play-ing. The town's fire companies lined the route; they were in uni-form, holding their hats in their hands, a special tribute, perhaps, to Ansel Lyman, who was a member of the department. He re-membered flowers being strewn in their path as the Rescuers and their escort thronged into the meeting house.[42] A large platform used for graduation exercises had been hastily put in place. At the door of the church the Rescuers were presented with a huge wreath—"like a barrel hoop, it was so big," John Scott thought[10]—and as they walked up the aisle to the rostrum, each was handed a bouquet of flowers. Sheriff Wightman and jailer John Smith, who had journeyed with them from Cleveland, were shown seats on the stand with the Rescuers as the church choir of 125 singers "poured forth" with song.

The celebration began precisely at eight o'clock with an opening prayer by Keep, and everyone who was there that night remem-bered it all their lives. "Never shall I forget the occasion," Oberlin student Ione Munger wrote. "The audience remained until mid-night with no thought of *rules* on the part of the students, and gave them such an ovation as was never known before."[44] There were speeches galore—by Rescuers Ralph Plumb, Henry Peck, James Fitch, John Watson, William Lincoln, John Scott, Henry Evans, Ansel Lyman, and Richard Winsor. Roswell Horr and Her-man Burr described the events in Elyria that had led up to the settlement. Sheriff Wightman and Matthew Gillet spoke, too. Also George G. Washburn, editor and publisher of the *Lorain Indepen-dent Democrat* of Elyria, and Henry R. Smith. More prayers were said, more hymns sung. A resolution was unanimously adopted to express the community's "greatly increased abhorrence of the Fu-gitive Slave Act" and to reaffirm its citizens' "determination that no fugitive slave shall ever be taken from Oberlin either with or without a warrant, if we have power to prevent it."[45]

Then the choir rose for the "Marseillaise." It was sung "as never before," James Monroe's young daughter Emma remembered. "No mortal would ever hear it again as it was heard that night."[46]

*

"This has put an end to nigger-catching in Northern Ohio," the *Cleveland Herald* joyously proclaimed.[47]

"Never," the *Cleveland Morning Leader* said, "were a set of men worse used than have been Jennings, Bacon and Mitchell ... by the Government officials who sought to make a good thing out of it for themselves and for Democracy."[48]

The *Ashtabula Telegraph* quoted the *Springfield* (Massachusetts) *Republican* as declaring, "The persecution of Christian men for showing kindness to runaway negroes is a losing operation socially and politically."[49]

The *Cleveland Plain Dealer* was forced to admit that "the Government has been beaten at last ... and Oberlin, with its rebellious Higher Law creed is triumphant."[50]

"As goes Oberlin," it conceded, "so goes the United States in 1860. (!)"[51]

SIXTEEN

Aftermath

The rest of our story is soon told.
Chapter XLIII: "Results"

Like so many other Northerners, Abraham Lincoln had no taste for slavery but was not an abolitionist. A steamboat trip he took from Louisville to St. Louis in 1841 left an indelible impression in his mind. On board, "shackled together with irons," were ten or twelve slaves. "That sight was a continual torment to me," he recalled in a letter he wrote in 1855 to the friend who had accompanied him, "and I see something like it every time I touch the Ohio, or any other slave-border."[1]

As sick at heart and as "miserable" as the sight of the shackled blacks "continually" made him feel, Lincoln nonetheless did not believe in granting black people any civil rights beyond protection of their life and property. Like many other whites, his solution was colonization abroad. Lincoln was, to be sure, against the extension of slavery: "If we cannot give freedom to every creature, let us do nothing that imposes slavery upon any other creature."[2] However, at the very time in 1858 when the seizure and rescue of John Price took place, he was campaigning in Illinois against Stephen A. Douglas for election to the United States Senate and telling a political rally, "I am not, nor ever have been in favor of bringing about in any way the social and political equality of the white and black races." He was not in favor, Lincoln said as his audience applauded, "of making voters or jurors of negroes, nor of qualifying them to hold office, nor to intermarry with white people." All he asked "for the Negro," he said at another time, "is that if you do not like him, let him alone. If God gave him but little, that little let him enjoy."[3]

It is ironic that Lincoln did not condone the struggle against the Fugitive Slave Law, for it contributed to his political success. He believed that Americans should obey the fugitive law because it was an act of Congress and therefore constitutional. He wrote three anxious letters after the Ohio Republican party came out for its repeal. Two of them were to Salmon P. Chase. They were identical in their plea, Lincoln warning in each that the Ohio plank could destroy the national party. "This is already damaging us here," he wrote in the first letter from Springfield, Illinois, on June 9. "I have no doubt that if that plank be even *introduced* into the next Republican National convention, it will explode it. . . . I assure you the cause of Republicanism is hopeless in Illinois, if it be in any way made responsible for that plank."[4]

Lincoln's third letter on the subject, written on July 28, was addressed to Samuel Galloway, an attorney in Columbus, Ohio: "Two things done by the Ohio Republican convention—the repudiation of Judge Swan, and the 'plank' for a repeal of the Fugitive Slave Law—I very much regretted. These two things are of a piece; and they are viewed by many good men, sincerely opposed to slavery, as a struggle against, and in disregard of, the constitution itself. And it is the very thing that will greatly endanger our cause, if it be not be [sic] kept out of our national convention."[5]

Yet Roeliff Brinkerhoff thought otherwise. In the October 1859 state elections, Salmon P. Chase's successor as the Republican gubernatorial candidate won by a margin that exceeded Chase's in 1857 by nearly twenty-four thousand votes, and Republicans regained control not only of both houses of the Ohio legislature but of every state office as well. Nearly three out of every four voters went to the polls, the highest turnout in the state's history. Among those who won election in the Western Reserve, together with Oberlin's own James Monroe, who was reelected to the state legislature, were a future Civil War general and Ohio governor—Jacob D. Cox (Oberlin College, Class of 1851)—and a future president—James A. Garfield. The legislature then chose Chase as United States senator. Brinkerhoff believed not only that the entire Republican ticket in Ohio was "triumphantly elected" that fall because of the party's advocacy of repeal of the Fugitive Slave Law but that the repercussions of that triumph could be felt throughout the North as well. Thirteen months later, an estimated 90 percent of Ohio's voters turned out for the presidential election, giving Abraham Lincoln more than twenty thousand votes more than all the other candidates combined. Two out of every three voters in the Western Reserve voted for him.[6] "Our victory in Ohio, in 1859," Brinkerhoff declared, "made a national victory possible in 1860, and its culminating result was the election of Abraham Lincoln as President."[7]

It is ironic that, although the Rescuers played an instrumental part in those victories, neither they nor their fellow abolitionists in Oberlin were enthusiastic about Lincoln. His score with regard to "humanity toward the oppressed," they thought, was "too low. It did him no honor."[8] Although nearly eight out of ten of Oberlin's voters chose Lincoln, they supported him in 1860 only because he was the lesser of two evils. A month before his inauguration in 1861, as the sectional crisis deepened, a mass meeting adopted resolutions to protest *against any concession to Slavery or to the demands made by its abettors in any form whatever*, and especially against making such concessions at the behest of traitors in arms against the Union."[9]

❋

Simeon Bushnell was freed from prison on Monday, July 11. Of all of the Rescuers who were imprisoned, he spent the most time in the Cuyahoga County Jail, a total of eighty-eight days. Oberlin turned out to welcome him home in almost a duplicate version of the earlier festivities. Like a conquering hero, Bushnell left the prison for the train station in a carriage with Sheriff Wightman's family late that morning. A band led the way, while several carriages decorated with banners and flags followed and a group of black men escorted the entourage. This time, Oberlin had more time to prepare a reception, and as Bushnell stepped from the train, the guns of a state artillery unit fired a one-hundred-shot salute that boomed across the small community. The trustees of Russia Township had met earlier in the day to designate Bushnell as town clerk, a position to which he was elected on the eve of his trial in April. It was a hot, dusty day and in the middle of harvesting season, but the entire town turned out to greet the clerk, many of them waving banners they had made for the occasion. Bushnell was escorted to First Church, where the speeches, songs, and prayers went on for nearly five hours. Those who spoke included Joshua Giddings, D. K. Cartter, and defense attorneys Rufus Spalding and Albert Gallatin Riddle.

Professor James Fairchild had more presents for the Rescuers' friends—a set of spoons for the wife of jailer John Smith, a dress and book for both her sister Eliza Morrill and the sheriff's daughter Lucy, and gold-headed ebony canes for Sheriff Wightman and Cleveland realtor Henry R. Smith. The canes were inscribed "from the citizens of Oberlin."[10]

John Mercer Langston apologized for his brother Charles's absence but wanted to say a few words himself, to thank "his noble friends who had gone up to Cuyahoga county jail." He wanted to thank them "in his character as a negro—as a white man—as one in whom the blood of both races joined—as a *man*—and as an American citizen."[11] He hoped, Langston added, waxing poetic, that "God had not scooped out the Mississippi Valley as the grave of Liberty, erecting the stony tablet of the Rocky Mountains to commemorate its burial, while Niagara chanted its funeral requiem."[12]

One of Oberlin's harshest critics, Joseph W. Gray, founder and editor of the *Cleveland Plain Dealer*, was touched by the ceremonies. Just a week earlier, *The Rescuer*, in what had turned out to be its first and only edition, had castigated him, describing his editorials as "profane belchings" and saying that Judas Iscariot was "his great prototype."[13]

Gray went to Oberlin to cover Bushnell's welcome home. He was recognized at once and, ill feelings pushed aside, offered a seat among the other reporters on the platform in First Church. He was obviously touched by the ceremony and the speeches. Gray was observed wiping tears from his eyes when the choir and congregation unexpectedly joined in the chorus as Oberlin student Lois M. Church sang the "Marseillaise."[14] Afterward, he was invited to join a special victory dinner at Henry Peck's home. The next day, the *Plain Dealer* carried Gray's favorable article about the celebration under the headline "OBERLIN AT A DASH!" He said he returned to Cleveland from the celebration "satisfied that we did not know half as much about Oberlin as we did before we went there."[15]

✳

Some months later, John Mercer Langston received a visit in his office from a young stranger who gave his name as John Thomas. Langston was busy at the time and suggested that Thomas return later. The man came back about noon and asked to accompany Langston on his walk home for dinner. As they strolled down East College Street, the man stopped abruptly and put his hand on Langston's shoulder. He identified himself as Rescuer Ralph Plumb's friend and onetime neighbor in Ashtabula County, John Brown, Jr.: "I have called to see you upon matters strictly secret and confidential. Young Brown explained that his father "proposed to strike at an early day, a blow which shall shake and destroy American slavery itself." But he needed "men of nerve and courage." Langston invited Brown to join him for dinner and afterward they talked in the parlor.[16]

Oberlin's black community must have seemed an ideal source

of manpower to young Brown. Black men there acted as though they were not "afraid of the white man," William Watson once observed: "There is a sort of you-touch-me-if-you-dare about them."[17] But Langston believed the raid, an attack on the federal arsenal at Harpers Ferry, Virginia, "would discover such audacity on the part of its promoters and supporters, as to drive the very class—the enslaved—away rather than draw them in needed numbers to it, and thus defeat the ostensible and real object had in view."[18]

His brother, Rescuer Charles Langston, was also leery about joining the expedition. He pleaded poor health, but young Brown didn't believe him. In a cryptic letter to John Kagi, Brown said that Langston "was discouraged about the mining business" because there were not enough men to carry it out successfully. "Physical weakness is his fault," Brown believed.[19]

John Brown, Jr., was able to recruit only two black men from Oberlin for his father's scheme—though they were, John Mercer declared, "two of the bravest negroes that this country has produced."[20] One was Lewis Sheridan Leary, who participated in the Rescue but had not been indicted. Leary was the descendant of an Irishman, Jeremiah O'Leary, who had fought in the Revolution under General Nathanael Greene and later married a woman of mixed Indian and black blood. Leary had heard Brown's father lecture in Cleveland the previous March. "Men must suffer for a good cause," the young man later told a meeting of the Oberlin Anti-Slavery Society.[21] Leary, who was related by marriage to Rescuer John A. Copeland, Jr., convinced Copeland to enroll in the scheme. Copeland, who disappeared after being indicted and was never arrested or arraigned, joined, he said, "to assist in giving that freedom to at least a few of my poor and enslaved brethren who have been most foully and unjustly deprived of their liberty."[22] Rescuer Ralph Plumb and his brother Samuel donated $15 to the two young men to help pay their way to Chambersburg, Pennsylvania, where Brown's "army" initially assembled.

A third black man from Oberlin took part in the plans, a newcomer to Oberlin, Shields Green, a runaway slave from South Carolina. Green, whose real name was Esau Brown, had escaped to Canada but later moved to Rochester, New York, and became Frederick Douglass's servant. A self-confident, well-built man who called himself "Emperor Green,"[23] he was with Douglass that August when John Brown met with the abolitionist leader and tried to get him to join in the raid. Douglass turned Brown down, but Green, to Douglass's surprise, decided to join him: "I b'leve I'll go wid de ole man," he said.[24]

The three Oberlin blacks were among the eighteen men who marched with John Brown into Harpers Ferry on the night of Sunday, October 16, 1859. The small band severed telegraph wires to the east and the west and captured three main targets—the armory, the arsenal, and a rifle works. By noon the village was in a state of siege when federal troops under Robert E. Lee arrived from Washington. Copeland and Leary were in the rifle works with John Kagi when it was assaulted. Kagi, who had covered the Rescuer trials for the *New York Tribune*, was killed as he fled from the back of the structure and tried to cross the Shenandoah River. Leary was mortally wounded and suffered a great deal until he died the next day. Copeland, who was wounded and captured, was almost lynched, but a local minister interceded and saved him. Green was captured with John Brown in an engine house.

The bodies of Leary, Kagi, and a third man were buried in shallow graves on the riverbank where dogs soon rooted them out and partly destroyed them before some medical students stole the bodies for dissection. Eventually, their remains and those of five others killed in the raid were wrapped in blankets and shawls and buried in two large boxes at the water's edge. In 1899, their decomposed bodies were exhumed, placed in a single coffin, and reinterred in North Elba, New York, the site of John Brown's farm.

Brown, Copeland, Green, and two others who had been captured were charged with treason, tried, convicted, and sentenced to be hanged. In a strange coincidence, two days before his trial, Copeland was questioned by two federal marshals, one of whom was Mathew Johnson of Cleveland. Johnson unsuccessfully tried to implicate Rescuers Ralph Plumb and Charles Langston in the Harpers Ferry raid; he trumped up a confession in Copeland's name that involved them. While awaiting execution, Copeland himself wrote a number of letters to his family and friends in Oberlin, believing, as Brown did, that history would vindicate him.

Brown was hanged on December 2, 1859, in Charlestown. Copeland and Green were scheduled to hang two weeks later, on December 16. "If I could be the means of destroying Slavery," Copeland's mother said at a vigil that morning, "I would willingly give up all my menfolks."[25] As he was about to leave his cell to go to the gallows, Copeland himself declared, "If I am dying for Freedom, I could not die for a better cause—*I had rather die than be a Slave!*"[26]

According to one report, Green "died very easy, his neck being broken by the fall," but Copeland "seemed to suffer very much," his body writhing "in violent contortions for several minutes."[27]

Their bodies were buried in plain poplar coffins in a nearby field, but within the next hour students from the Winchester Medical College dug them up and took them for dissection.

Even before his execution, Copeland's parents had asked permission to recover his body. The governor of Virginia finally agreed to their request but with the proviso that the body be recovered by a white person. By state law, free blacks were not allowed into Virginia. The Copelands prevailed upon Professor James Monroe to make the trip to Winchester.

The furor over John Brown's raid and the terror it caused had not subsided, and Oberlin was accused of involvement in its planning. "Oberlin is located in the very heart of what may be called 'John Brown's tract,'" the *Pennsylvanian* of Philadelphia charged: "Here is where younger Browns obtain their conscientiousness in ultraisms, taught from their cradle up, so that while they rob slaveholders of their property, or commit murder for the cause of freedom, they imagine that they are doing God service."[28] The *National Democrat* of Cleveland chided the white citizens of Oberlin for getting "innocent blacks" to participate in the raid because they were "too cowardly themselves to run the risk." "The blood of the poor ignorant blacks, Leary and Copeland," it said, "will forever stain the character of the whites of Oberlin and other places in Ohio!"[29]

Most abolitionists were dismayed by John Brown's attack; Gerrit Smith, who donated money to him, suffered a nervous breakdown and went into an asylum. Many felt the need to refute the insinuations that Oberlin citizens were active partners in the raid. The *Oberlin Evangelist* warned that even if "the day of hope in moral influence for the abolition of slavery is past already ... it is a satisfaction to us to be conscious of not having unwisely precipitated its setting sun. If a mad infatuation has fallen upon southern minds, and they will not hear the demands of justice, nor the admonitions of kindness, let the responsibility rest where it belongs."[30] Although he spoke at a commemoration for Brown in Cleveland on the day of his execution, Charles Langston issued a "card of denial," stating that he had not taken any part in the raid. However, he added: "But what shall I deny? I cannot deny that I feel the very deepest sympathy with the immortal John Brown in his heroic and daring efforts to free the slaves."[31]

Under the circumstances, Monroe was leery of identifying himself as being from Oberlin so he registered at the hotel in Winchester, Virginia, as "James Monroe, Russia." Alerted to his arrival, students had broken into the dissecting rooms the night before and removed Copeland's body so when Monroe visited the school all he found was Green's body, stretched out on a table, his eyes open and "staring wildly upward."[32] The students refused to return Copeland's body, and their teachers were fearful of a showdown. "Sah," the leader of students said, "this nigger that you are trying to get don't belong the Faculty. He isn't theirs to give away. They had no right to promise him to you. He belongs to us students, sah. Me and my chums nearly had to fight to get him. I stood over the grave with a revolver in my hands while my chums dug him up."[33] A member of the faculty implored Monroe to forget his mission because "the whole country about us would soon be in a state of excitement."[34] Monroe had to return to Oberlin empty-handed.

The day after Monroe's arrival home, Christmas Day, there was a funeral service in First Church for both Copeland and Green, and the following year a monument to them and Lewis Sheridan Leary—"heroic associates of the immortal John Brown"—was erected in a corner of Westwood Cemetery. It was resurrected from that obscure site and rededicated in 1972 in a small park on East Vine Street (once Mill Street), on property where Rescuer John Scott once lived and across the street from the home of Rescuer Wilson Bruce Evans.

✳

One other Rescuer did not live to see the Civil War. On August 20, 1860, William Douglas Scrimgeour died of consumption. He was thirty-one years old. Despite his illness, which prevented him from participating in the Cleveland trials, Scrimgeour had been able to graduate with the class of 1859 the previous year and was a junior in the seminary at the time of his death. As untiring as always, he also tutored in the Preparatory Department. His obituary in the *Oberlin Evangelist* described him as intellectually "one of the most extraordinary young men we have ever seen. His thirst for knowledge seemed to be unbounded. . . . But he was more than a mere accumulator and repository of knowledge. He had a passion for teaching."[35] Scrimgeour was buried in Westwood Cemetery.

Nearly sixteen months later—eight months after the outbreak of the Civil War—another Rescuer was buried nearby: Simeon Bushnell. The thirty-two-year-old clerk also died of consumption. He collapsed in the vestibule of the College Chapel after attending Sabbath services on the unusually warm Sunday of December 8,

1861. Coughing violently, he ruptured a blood vessel and died within minutes.

Bushnell's last year of life was especially grim. The federal government was dunning him to recover the fine and court costs that he owed. By mid-November of 1860, with interest accrued since his sentencing eighteen months earlier, the sum ran to $1,391.56. Marshal Johnson visited Oberlin to enforce a notice of payment in January 1861, while Elizabeth Bushnell was in the last weeks of her pregnancy with the Bushnells' second daughter, Jane. The marshal found nothing that the poor family possessed that he could put a lien on.[36] Then, six months and ten days after her birth, Jane died. The grieving Bushnell followed her to the grave four months later and was buried next to her. The inscription on their joint monument, from 1 Corinthians 15:57, reads: "Christ hath given us the victory."

*

Four other Rescuers, three of them from Wellington, died during the Civil War: Loring Wadsworth on November 3, 1862, at the age of sixty-two; Dr. Eli Boies on July 6, 1863, at the age of sixty-three; "Father" Matthew Gillet on September 5, 1863, at the age of seventy-seven; and John Watson's son William on July 1, 1864, at about twenty-five years of age. Matthew DeWolf of Wellington died shortly after the war ended, on July 10, 1865, at the age of seventy-three. Nothing is known about any of the other Wellington Rescuers except for "the last to go," Abner Loveland, who died March 2, 1879, at the age of eighty-two.[37]

As the national crisis deepened and the war approached, most Oberlin citizens remained unstintingly committed to, and bellicose about, the abolitionist movement. James Buchanan issued a call for a national day of prayer and fasting on Friday, January 4, 1861. The president asked that every American go to his house of worship and repent for both individual and national sins, in particular for the "false pride of opinion which would impel us to persevere in wrong for the sake of consistency, rather than yield to a just submission." Buchanan, the *Oberlin Evangelist* countered, failed to cite the most serious national faults—that the "most grinding oppression" of slavery continued to exist, that the government was "prostituted" to its support, and that compromises "involving the sacrifice of right and justice" were repeatedly made to extend slavery.[38]

When the Civil War did break out, Oberlin—the college and the town—responded with patriotic enthusiasm. Soon after the firing on Fort Sumter in April 1861, when Abraham Lincoln, now President, called for volunteers, the faculty immediately repealed an injunction against students belonging to military companies and within three days several hundred men had enlisted and $10,000 was subscribed to support the volunteers and their families. In all, during the war, more than 750 Oberlin students and alumni served in several Ohio units, six of them becoming generals. Because many others went home to enlist in their own local outfits, a complete total of Oberlin men who participated in the war was never compiled, and the precise number who died during the war is not known. A Soldiers' Monument by Plumb Creek contains the names of ninety-six men identified as having fallen in action. The school's policy of admitting young women undoubtedly helped it to survive because by 1863 enrollment was down by more than 50 percent.

The first unit assembled—known as the Monroe Rifles—became Company C of the Seventh Regiment, Ohio Volunteer Infantry (OVI), the only company in the regiment never to report a deserter. At the same time that Company C was formed, five hundred women from the school and the community formed a Florence Nightingale Association to make woolen socks and underclothing for the volunteers. Company C first saw action on August 25, 1861, when it was caught by surprise by Confederate forces at Kesler's Cross Lanes, in western Virginia, and forced to retreat. Thirty-four of the men were captured. Company C subsequently fought at Winchester and at Cedar Mountain the following year and at Antietam in 1862 before being mustered out after three years in the field. Of the 150 men connected with Company C, 23 fell in battle, 3 died of disease—2 of them in Southern prisons— and 20 were discharged because of wounds.

Another unit, made up chiefly of farmers in the Oberlin area and known as the Lorain Guards, became Company H of the Forty-first Regiment, OVI, and fought at Shiloh, Chickamauga, Chattanooga, Resaca, and the siege of Atlanta. When Confederate Kirby Smith threatened Cincinnati in 1862, a ragtag group of eighty poorly armed Oberlin young men—mostly college and preparatory students without uniforms and called the Squirrel Hunters— rushed to that city's defense but were sent back home after a few days. Ten Oberlin boys served in the Second Ohio Cavalry, which chased rebel marauders William Clark Quantrill and John Hunt Morgan and served in the Wilderness campaign, under George Armstrong Custer in Virginia, and at the Battle of Five Forks. In

1864, eighty-six students and residents formed Company K of the 150th Regiment, OVI, which guarded the route into Washington when Jubal Early threatened the nation's capital.

In addition, twenty-one men from Oberlin joined the first black regiment raised by a Northern state, the famous Fifty-fourth Massachusetts, and for a time both its regimental flags were carried by Oberlin blacks. John Mercer Langston, who campaigned aggressively to allow black men to serve in the army, was the recruiting officer for the Fifty-fourth in the West and later for its sister black regiment, the Fifty-fifth Massachusetts, as well. The Fifty-fourth spearheaded the unsuccessful assault on Fort Wagner, South Carolina, in July 1863, suffering 25 percent casualties. Langston also organized Ohio's first black regiment in 1863. To do so, he had to overcome the resentment of many black men over numerous restrictions and inequality in pay for black troops. His pitch to his black compatriots was simple: "Of all the people in the land, we can less afford to miss playing a part in the mighty struggle going on between the powers represented by Abraham Lincoln and Jefferson Davis."[39] As with other Union units, white officers commanded the Ohio regiment. Giles Shurtleff, an Oberlin theological student who had served with Company C, became the unit's colonel, and James L. Patton, who participated in the rescue of John Price, its chaplain. The regiment, the 127th OVI, was later renamed the Fifth United States Colored Troops (USCT) and fought around the Crater during the siege of Petersburg and at New Market Heights.

In all, six of the Oberlin Rescuers are known to have served in the war. Richard Winsor, a private in Company C, was wounded at the Battle of Winchester on March 23, 1862, and subsequently discharged. (In the same battle, another Oberlin student, Edward G. Sackett, who was at William Lincoln's side during the rescue of John Price, was fatally wounded and died six days later.) Ralph Plumb was with a quartermaster corps, serving as a captain on the staff of James A. Garfield. Orindatus S. B. Wall was active with his brother-in-law John Mercer Langston in recruiting black troops after racial barriers against black men serving in the army were dropped. After helping to recruit a second Ohio black regiment, the Twenty-seventh USCT, Wall was commissioned a captain, the first regularly commissioned black captain in the army, early in 1865. Wall left Oberlin to serve in the war with a sword presented to him by Henry Peck in a ceremony in the College Chapel. Light-skinned Wilson Bruce Evans was able to enlist at the age of forty in September 1864 in the all-white 178th Regiment, OVI, spending most of his time on detached service to a post commissary in Tennessee. John Scott tried to enlist at the outbreak of the war but was at first rejected because he was black. Long after the restriction against black troops was lifted, he finally joined the Fifth Ohio Cavalry in January 1865, when he was about thirty years old, but he fell ill eight months later in Morehead City, North Carolina, and was discharged that December. Jeremiah Fox joined the Fifth United States Colored Heavy Artillery in February 1865 and spent his year in service at Vicksburg.

*

Though he did not serve in the war, Henry Peck was perhaps Oberlin's most tireless war supporter, heading recruitment drives and spending many months visiting students at their encampments. He inadvertently got into an acrimonious dispute with Lorain County residents when he championed having a company of young Oberlin men, many of them students, separated from a sister unit of Elyria men when they were called up for duty in May 1864. Elyrians were annoyed that Peck wanted to have the Oberlin men assigned to a "city regiment" rather than a "country regiment," and they felt that he believed the Elyrian recruits were not fit company for them. Peck explained that he wanted the Oberlin men to "escape the physical and moral dangers which always infest camps." He wired Cleveland urging that the Oberlin unit be separated. The Elyria company subsequently became part of a state militia unit and suffered heavy losses. The Oberlin unit eventually became Company K of the 150th OVI, which served around Washington, and lost only one man in action against Jubal Early.[40]

During the war, Peck took over the *Lorain County News,* and at its conclusion, he resigned from the college to serve as United States minister to Haiti. He died of yellow fever in Port au Prince on June 9, 1867, shortly before his forty-sixth birthday. His body was brought back to Oberlin for burial in Westwood Cemetery.

*

Though he denied any connection with John Brown's raid, Charles Langston still found inspiration in it. He was unable to attend a commemoration for Brown held in Boston in December 1860, but he wrote a militant letter to be read at the tribute. "Various plans," he noted, "have been proposed for the abolition of American Slavery, no *one* of which can, in my opinion, prove effectual":

Let Republicans by their *votes* stop the extension of Slavery. Let radical Abolitionists make the Constitution of the United States purely Anti-Slavery. Let Garrisonians proclaim "No Union with Slavery," and the immediate dissolution of the American Union. Let Christians pray and preach for the overthrow of slavery. Let colored men by their words and actions demonstrate the equality of the races. But above all, let the friends of physical revolution continue to plot insurrection. Let the benevolent give money to *arm* the slave; and united with, and aided by their friends, let them *wage war to the knife*. . . . Tyrants and slaveholders have no right to live—they ought not to breathe God's air, nor enjoy His sunlight.[41]

Two months before the war broke out, the federal government was still dunning Langston to pay the fine and court costs that he owed. By January 5, 1861, the total had risen to $993.10, and George Belden ordered the sale of Langston's half of the parcel of land in Columbus that he owned with his brother John Mercer. Deputy Marshal Jacob Lowe had the property assessed that month; it was valued at $1,200. The land was advertised for auction for four weeks in a Cincinnati weekly, but not one bid was received.[42] There is no record of what happened after that; presumably, the change of administrations in Washington caused the government to stop pursuing the matter further, or perhaps the war was the distracting factor.

Thus the federal government never collected the fines and court costs levied as a result of the trials of Bushnell and Langston. Moreover, the entire episode cost the government thousands of dollars. Belden's assistant counsel, George Bliss, put in a bill for $1,200, which Attorney General Jeremiah Black disputed. A fee of $800 was finally agreed upon, but Bliss had trouble collecting even that sum and was still writing Washington in the summer of 1859 asking for it. Louis Feeser, the court stenographer at Langston's trial, experienced the same trouble. He was owed $150, and on July 14, Feeser, whose wife was sick, pleaded, "Ten weeks or more have elapsed without receiving any pay. None. I live on very heavy expenses here & I am poor in the bargain." Noah H. Swayne, who represented Marshal Mathew Johnson, was still trying on December 23, 1859, to collect $1,000 "for professional services in the Supreme Court of the State of Ohio," and as late as June of the next year, Johnson himself was still asking for $651.37 for "Extraordinary Expenses" connected with the trials.[43]

Langston tried to enlist when the Civil War broke out, but, like other blacks, was rejected. Later, when the Fifty-fourth Massachusetts was formed, he helped his brother John Mercer recruit black men, then went to the Leavenworth area of Kansas in 1862 to teach liberated slaves and work for the enfranchisement of blacks. He ultimately returned to resume his recruiting efforts in Ohio and in other states in the Midwest. He was back in Kansas, in Topeka, in 1865 with his brother John Mercer, lobbying for equality for black people. In 1869, Charles married Lewis Sheridan Leary's widow, the former Mary Simpson Patterson. He was about fifty years old at the time and she twenty-eight. A native of Fayetteville, North Carolina, Mary was enrolled in the Preparatory Department of Oberlin College during the 1857–58 academic year. In 1858, she married Leary, and at the time of his death in John Brown's raid on Harpers Ferry, she was pregnant with their daughter, Louise. Louise later attended the Preparatory Department at Oberlin. Mary Langston subsequently raised her daughter Louise's son, the noted poet and playwright Langston Hughes. Charles and Mary Langston settled on a farm near Lawrence, Kansas, in the 1870s. He subsequently opened a grocery store in Lawrence and tried to go into politics, "looking," Langston Hughes wrote in his autobiography, "for a bigger freedom than the Emancipation Proclamation had provided." But Charles was an indifferent farmer and grocer and "didn't much care about making money. When he died, none of the family had any money."[44] Langston passed away in 1890, aged about seventy. Mary was too proud to beg or borrow from anyone or to work as a domestic. To support herself, she rented out rooms to college students. She lived until 1913.

In contrast, Charles's brother John Mercer Langston enjoyed enormous success. At the start of the war, he was engaged not only in campaigning for the recruitment of black men but also in pressing Abraham Lincoln to emancipate by proclamation all the slaves in the South. Toward the war's end, he was instrumental in the founding of the National Equal Rights League, of which he served as first president, and campaigned extensively for the enfranchisement of blacks. By then, he was talked about by blacks with the same reverence they felt toward Frederick Douglass; both men were "the Aurura Borealis of our people."[45]

Langston was in Washington, pursuing his application for a commission as a colonel in the army, when Robert E. Lee surrendered at Appomattox. From 1865 to 1867, he was a member of the Oberlin Council and for two years after that served on its Board of Education. (A public school on North main Street now bears his name.) He subsequently was appointed inspector-general of the Freedmen's Bureau, then became a professor of law at Howard University, dean from 1869 to 1876, and acting president in 1872.

He became United States minister-resident in Haiti in 1877 and remained in the diplomatic service until 1885. In 1890, while living in Virginia, he served in Congress, the first and only black representative ever elected in the state. He died in 1897, a month before his sixty-eighth birthday.

One of the law students at Howard University when John Mercer was there was his brother-in-law Rescuer Orindatus Wall. Shortly after the war ended, Wall moved to Washington to be employment agent for the Freedmen's Bureau. While there, he attended Howard University Law School and was in its first graduating class in June 1872. He practiced in Washington and was arguing a case in court in 1890 when he was suddenly stricken with paralysis. "Broken in body and shattered in intellect, most of the time helpless, with his reason gone," Wall lingered on until April 1891, when he died at the age of sixty-seven.[46]

Like John Mercer Langston, Rescuer Ralph Plumb served in Congress. Hired by a syndicate of coal-mining investors, Plumb migrated to Illinois in 1866, founding and laying out the town of Streator. He was the community's first mayor and served two terms in Congress between 1885 and 1889, when he retired. In 1895, when he was seventy-nine years old, he was described as having "the habits and appearance of a man not over sixty-five."[47] He died in Streator on April 8, 1903, aged eighty-seven.

Not long after Plumb left Oberlin, James Fitch died. Fitch had moved his bookstore across Main Street, from East College Street to West College Street, in 1859. (On its site is now the Co-Op Book Store.) He continued to operate it until 1867, when he became seriously ill with what was described as consumption, though the disease affected not his lungs but his bowels. For nine months, the fifty-one-year-old Fitch was tortured by "Large internal tumors and ulcerations," which finally caused his death "by suffocation." Oberlin's Sunday school superintendent died at noon on a Sabbath, gasping "his last breath just as the churches were singing the Doxologies."[48]

The Evans brothers suffered a setback during the war when their shop, the college's old Walton Hall, which they had moved to Mill Street, was destroyed by fire in 1864. By then, Henry Evans was partly disabled because of an injury suffered in 1861, when a heavy iron wrench fell on a planer he was operating. The wrench crushed the bones in his nose and upper face and may have left him blind in one eye. He died in 1886, when about seventy years old, after another accident. His wife, Henrietta, moved to Harpers Ferry, the site of the death of her brother, Lewis Sheridan Leary, dying there herself in 1908. Four of Henry and Henrietta Evans's daughters and one son attended Oberlin, one of them graduating from the college.

Henry's younger brother, Wilson Bruce, served one year in the army during the Civil War. It was never discovered that he was not a Caucasian. By 1890, when sixty-six years old, he was described by neighbors as "somewhat broken down."[49] He applied for and was granted a government pension because of the rheumatism he suffered in his back and hips. His wife, Sarah, who was almost totally blind, died in May 1898. Two of their daughters were Oberlin graduates. Wilson Bruce was with one of them, on a trip to Cincinnati four months after his wife's death, when he died at the age of seventy-four on September 16, 1898—three days after the fortieth anniversary of the rescue of John Price.

After being discharged from the cavalry in 1865, John Scott ran a business west of Oberlin in Kipton and then in 1887 moved to Chattanooga to avoid Ohio's severe winters. He returned to Oberlin seven years later because he did not like the way black persons were treated in Tennessee or business prospects in the South. He reopened a business in Oberlin, selling used furniture, and also worked as an undertaker. A fervent temperance man, he was incensed when an Elyria beer company sent a wagon to Oberlin to sell its product and was especially troubled that black residents were being pointed at as the wagon's best patrons. He remained a religious man, once giving his grandson his violin but with the stipulation that he would take it back if the boy played it at dances. The grandson, Clarence Cameron White, later a noted composer and violinist, violated his promise after Scott's death to earn college tuition, but, he said, "in order to ease my conscience, despite my boss' protest, I refused to play first violin."[50] Four of Scott's daughters attended Oberlin, two of them graduating. Scott lived to be about eighty-five years old, dying in 1912.

Rescuer Ansel Lyman left the Preparatory Department in 1859 and taught school in southern Ohio for a while and then ran a livery stable in Oberlin. He married in 1860 and moved to his wife's hometown, Philadelphia, the next year. He became a merchant, then was inspector of customs in Philadelphia for eighteen years and later attendance officer for the city's public school system. In 1908, in response to a college questionnaire, he described himself as retired but said that in summers he ran a "large Temperance Hotel" in Ocean Grove, New Jersey, a religious seaside resort.[51]

Rescuer Jacob R. Shipherd earned two Oberlin degrees, an A.B.

in 1862 and an A.M. in 1865. He subsequently preached in Chicago, did Freedmen's Bureau aid work in Chicago and Washington, and was head of the western department of the American Missionary Society in 1868. He later changed careers and became a banker, working both in Chicago and New York City. He died on Staten Island, New York, on May 7, 1905, a month before his sixty-ninth birthday.

Of all the Rescuers who served in the clergy, Richard Winsor, who personally led John Price from the attic room where he was being held captive, was evidently the most successful. After being wounded in the war and discharged, Winsor temporarily served as a clerk in the Provost Marshal's Department for the Northern District of Ohio. He returned to classes in 1863, graduating from the college in 1867 and from the Theological Department in 1870. He was ordained and married on the same day that September and the following month sailed for India to work as a missionary among the Marahti people of Stara. The Winsors resided for the next thirty-five years in Sirus, the Poona District. Winsor, who received the decoration of Kaiser-i-Hind from the Indian government for his distinguished service, died of heart disease there on March 3, 1905, at the age of sixty-nine.

In 1861, Rescuer Jeremiah Fox married the Irishwoman with whom he lived. Two of the children that were later born to them were deaf mutes and were injured while walking along railroad tracks during a snowstorm in 1888. One of them died two years later in another train accident. By 1890, when about sixty years old, Fox was blind in his right eye, had only partial vision in his other eye, and suffered from rheumatism, hernia, and hemorrhoids. He died penniless in 1909, aged about seventy-nine.

Rescuer John Watson continued his activities on behalf of black people after the war, presiding at one time at a state convention of black men in Columbus. He replaced John Mercer Langston on the Oberlin school board when Langston moved to Washington. Watson died in October 1872, when about fifty-four years old.

Rescuer David Watson left Oberlin. He was reported working as a druggist in Detroit in 1909, when he would have been about seventy-three years old.[52]

Apparently the oldest surviving Rescuer was William E. Lincoln. Because the abolition of slavery was not a motivating factor in the Union's political program, the temperamental Lincoln purposely avoided serving in the Civil War. The reason, he acknowledged, had alienated him from his friends. "Oberlin," he wrote Gerrit Smith at the outbreak of the war in 1861, "does not sympathize with me in these ideas, but holds me rather as a crazy loon." For one thing, Lincoln believed that actions such as John Brown's raid were needed. "Would an armed diversion a la Garabaldi be of use?" he asked. "Surely now we could recruit to [sic] one or 2 thousand for such a diversion," he said. Lincoln said that he regarded "this war as God's judgment upon the North; for its cruel indifference to the groans & chains of the slave. I regard it as God's greater judgment upon the south for their unutterable oppression." He, of course, hoped that the North would win, "but I have no hope for the slave immediate." Lincoln wondered whether there was some way to get Abraham Lincoln "to decree the abolition of slavery" in the country. "I am ready to fight at any time in this way," he declared. "To fight for the Union wh. will rivet the chains of the bondman tighter, I never will nor can."[53]

Lincoln spent most of the war in Kentucky, working with John Fee among the black people there, because he believed that the slaves "would have to be raised to gain their freedom."[54] One day in 1863, while back in Ohio, by chance he encountered one of the Kidnappers—Deputy Sheriff Samuel Davis, the man who had arrested him while he was teaching youngsters in Dublin, outside of Columbus. They met on a road near Dublin. Davis was distraught. His brother had been killed "by rebels." "You God men saw; we were blind," Davis said. "God has poured out his fury as you said."[55]

Lincoln's idiosyncrasies—his impetuosity, for one—seemed to accentuate as time passed. He never did graduate from Oberlin College. Breaking a longstanding school rule that forbade undergraduates from marrying, he was refused a diploma when, at the age of thirty-three, he wed an alumna of the class of 1862, Frances L. Marshall, on March 10, 1865. After taking his bride home to London, and then to Paris, Lincoln returned to the United States and was graduated from the Hartford, Connecticut, Theological Seminary in 1866 and ordained as a Congregationalist minister in Hope, Ohio. Both Lincolns hoped to be medical missionaries to China and spent three years at a Cleveland homeopathic medical school, graduating with M.D. degrees. But because they had to care for her mother, the couple was unable to go to China and settled in Painesville. They had ten children, six of whom died in childhood, three of them within two weeks of one another during a diphtheria epidemic. Two of their sons, John and James, founded the highly successful Lincoln Electric and Reliance Electric companies of Cleveland.

By an odd coincidence, William Lincoln's marriage made him a distant relation of John G. W. Cowles, another Oberlin student who participated in the rescue of John Price.[56] Cowles graduated from the seminary in August 1859 and, when war broke out, served for a while as chaplain of the Fifty-fifth Regiment, OVI. John Copeland's father, then fifty-two years old, signed on as his cook. Later, during the war, Cowles became pastor of a Congregational church in Mansfield, Ohio, but he abandoned the pulpit in 1871 because of poor health. He subsequently became associate editor of the *Cleveland Leader* and later, among other business affiliations, a personal agent of John D. Rockefeller, purchasing the land that Rockefeller later presented to Cleveland as a park. He became a trustee of Oberlin College in 1874, serving until his death in 1914 at the age of seventy-eight.

William Lincoln's career was much less successful. His ministries were marred by clashes with his congregations, and he moved from parishes in the Western Reserve to others in Michigan and Illinois. He was, it was said, "a feckless clergyman, always getting into bitter arguments with parishioners and being let out after a year or two of a pastorage."[57] Nearly two years after the death of his wife, Lincoln died in Painesville on May 6, 1920, at the age of ninety—the last of the Rescuers.

*

As for some of those who helped the Rescuers:

James Fairchild, in whose home John Price was hidden, succeeded Charles Grandison Finney as president of Oberlin College in 1866. He continued in that post until 1889 and died in 1902. His brother Edward left Oberlin in 1869 to become president of Berea College in Kentucky, where he died in 1889.

James Monroe became a state senator in 1860, served as United States consul at Rio de Janeiro, Brazil, from 1863 to 1870, and was then elected to five consecutive terms in the United States House of Representatives. He returned to teach at Oberlin in 1883 and died in his home there in 1898. His daughter Emma, who accompanied him so frequently on visits to the Rescuers in prison, graduated from Oberlin in 1869, married a classmate who became a Congregational minister, and spent the next forty-five years with him in various pastorates in Ohio, New York, Connecticut, Colorado, and South Dakota. She lived until the age of ninety, dying in 1939.

Following his chaplaincy with the Fifth USCT during the war, James L. Patton became a preacher in Ohio and for twenty-four years until his death at the age of sixty-three in 1890 was pastor of the First Congregational Church in Greenville, Michigan.

As critics charged, several of the attorneys who defended the Rescuers did reap political benefits as a result. Seneca O. Griswold, who also defended John Brown at his trial, was elected to the Ohio House of Representatives in 1862. Albert Gallatin Riddle was elected to Congress in 1860, was chief counsel in the prosecution of John H. Surratt, who was charged with conspiracy in the assassination of Abraham Lincoln in 1865, and was for twelve years following 1877 law officer of the District of Columbia. Rufus P. Spalding followed Riddle into Congress from the same district in 1862, serving four terms.

Salmon P. Chase was an unsuccessful nominee for the presidency in 1860. In an ironic twist, he approved Lincoln's suspension of the writ of habeas corpus during the war after being appointed secretary of the treasury in 1861. Lincoln named Chase as chief justice of the United States Supreme Court in 1864.

Roeliff Brinkerhoff served with a quartermaster corps during the Civil War, leaving after five years with the rank of brigadier general. He remained active in politics and was especially interested in tariff reforms. In 1873 he established the Mansfield Savings Bank and subsequently involved himself in charities and penal reform, as well as archaeology.

Brinkerhoff's kinsman Jacob Brinkerhoff became chief justice of the Ohio Supreme Court when Joseph R. Swan left the post. Swan was criticized so severely for his vote against granting Bushnell and Langston a writ of habeas corpus that he declined an appointment to a vacancy on the court when a judge died in 1862. There was talk of his being appointed to the United States Supreme Court in 1862, but Lincoln chose Noah H. Swayne—Marshal Mathew Johnson's counsel—instead, even though Swayne had no judicial experience.

W. W. Boynton was elected to the Ohio House in 1865 and tried unsuccessfully to have the word *white* eliminated from the state constitution. He later served as a justice on the Ohio Supreme Court.

✳

There is little to tell about the Kidnappers or the Democrats in Oberlin who betrayed the Rescuers. Anderson Jennings was soundly defeated in his bid for election to the Kentucky legislature on August 1, 1859. He ran last among four candidates in Mason County, winning only 671 of the nearly 4,300 votes cast.[58]

Sometime between 1870 and 1880, John Bacon's first wife, Jacova, apparently died and he remarried. The census of 1880 gives his wife's name as Catherine. Perhaps Jacova had died in childbirth because a son aged ten is listed in that census. His name is given as Langston Bacon. At first glance, one is tempted to believe that the onetime slaveowner was paying tribute to one or the other of the Langston brothers, but Langston was an old family name passed down by the Bacons.

Despite the part he played in betraying the Rescuers, eccentric Chauncey Wack was never disavowed by his Oberlin neighbors. In fact, in a fluke campaign in 1870, which outraged so many temperance voters that they declined to vote, he was elected to the Town Council. Until that year and the adoption of the Fifteenth Amendment, he challenged black men who tried to vote. As a council member, Wack cast negative votes against an ordinance to regulate a billiard hall that had sprung up in town and against paying the city marshal a salary. He also argued against the annual commemoration of the Oberlin-Wellington Rescue, pointing out that the Rescue had been in violation of the law. He was not reelected. A daughter married one of his hotel boarders, Stephen W. Dorsey, who later became a United States senator from Arkansas and was subsequently involved in a number of financial scandals.

Malachi Warren's relationship with his former slave resulted in 1860 in a jury finding them guilty of cohabitation in a state of fornication. The former Alabama planter was sentenced to serve a day in the county jail and pay a fine of $100 plus court costs. He apparently then moved to a 320-odd-acre farm west of Oberlin. His mistreatment of his wife and children—he whipped her—prompted his son James to have him arrested on April 24, 1861, for abusing the family. The arrest occurred just after the formation of Oberlin's Monroe Rifles, and their presence prevented a mob of angry citizens from trying to lynch Warren. James had even slung a rope over a lamppost himself. Warren agreed to execute a trust deed on his property that favored the family, to donate $100 to Union volunteers, and to leave town. He returned to Alabama, dying there the following year, at the age of seventy. The will he left behind set off a complicated legal battle that lasted for more than thirty years.

Anson P. Dayton made the mistake of returning one Friday night to Oberlin about mid-February 1860. Word of his arrival spread rapidly through town, and the next day a committee of citizens visited him and informed him that his "presence was not desirable." Dayton was given one hour to leave town. He was gone within ten minutes. Five black men—including Rescuer John Scott and John A. Copeland, Jr.'s brother Henry—decided to make certain that he would not return. Because it had snowed, they were able to follow his tracks and by mid-afternoon caught up with Dayton about six miles out of town. The frightened deputy marshal scaled a rail fence and tried to run away, but the blacks cut him off and surrounded him. Dayton asked for "quarter," which the men said they would grant if he resigned as deputy and never visited Oberlin again. Moreover, they wanted Dayton to make a written confession right there and then of his complicity in betraying the Rescuers. Dayton denied any involvement but said he knew who had betrayed the Rescuers. He wrote "with great apparent sincerity" on some stationery that was handed to him:

> This may certify that I have resigned as Deputy U.S. Marshal,—that I will never go to Oberlin again. That I furnished no names to be prosecuted in the Oberlin Rescue Cases, nor the names of witnesses in said cases. I was informed by Mr. Munson, that he and Chancy [sic] Wack, and Bela Farr, furnished the names of parties and of witnesses in those cases. . . . Boynton informed me on the day of the arrest and rescue of "John" at Wellington that he expected "Shake" was going to make $10 in trying to get John
>
> The above is the truth in the above matter, as I believe and know, so help me God.[59]

*

One winter evening in 1896, a writer named Lida Rose McCabe stepped off the train in Oberlin. She was working on an article about the Oberlin-Wellington Rescue for *Godey's Magazine*.[60] She visited first with James Fairchild, who was then retired as president of Oberlin College. "I was probably the most culpable man in the Oberlin-Wellington rescue," he said, "but somehow I was above suspicion and escaped indictment." Fairchild's neighbor James Monroe dropped by and added his recollections to the story. There were only two Rescuers alive then in Oberlin, he told her: John Scott and Wilson Bruce Evans.

McCabe found the two men together. With them was Evans's wife—Sheridan Lewis Leary's sister Sarah—who was "stone blind" by then: "a yellow woman; large, imposing, almost tragic in her mien."

Evans, she said, was a "singularly modest, winning old man," who did not display "the slightest betrayal of colored blood in the refined features of his beautiful face," though his children were "as black as the native African." Visitors liked to take his photograph because of his close resemblance to poet Walt Whitman.

On the other hand, there was "no mistaking John Scott's African ancestry," McCabe observed. She found Scott "proud of the penalty he endured for his prowess in the rescue" of John Price.

"What has become of John?" McCabe asked. No one knew. McCabe persisted, asking the same question repeatedly. Though John Price, after all, had been the cause of all the commotion, "the hapless fugitive," the writer observed, was considered "but a cat's-paw to pull the chestnut out of the fire." The reply she got from Evans and Scott was always the same no matter how many times she asked:

"Never heard of since."

Epilogue

"My mother used to tell me of a millennium that was coming,
when Christ should reign, and all should be free and happy. And
she taught me, when I was a boy, to pray, 'Thy kingdom come.'
Sometimes I think all this sighing, and groaning, and stirring among
the dry bones tells what she used to tell me was coming. But who
may abide the day of his appearing?"

Chapter XIX: "Miss Ophelia's Experiences and Opinions"

Oberlin was scarred by the Reconstruction era that followed the Civil War. Attitudes it once disdained began first to surface, then to predominate. Both the college and the community increasingly mirrored the rest of the nation in attitude toward and treatment of black persons.

Oberlin, to be sure, had never been perfect. Instances of racial prejudice—though rare—did occur at the school during its formative years. And black residents were evidently put off by, among other things, Charles Grandison Finney's once saying that slavery was a "dispensation of providence."[1] But such strains were minor and did not mar the overall sense of community unity. After the war, however, Oberlin—once a leader in the movement for black rights—became a follower. It turned conservative in the wake of attitudes in the United States as a whole. The black middle class dwindled, and black residents played less and less of a role in the town's social and political life, especially after John Mercer Langston sold his home in 1871 and left.

Part of the change of heart among the town's white citizens was a result of the enormous influx of former slaves freed by the war, which caused Ohio's black population to grow by more than 70 percent between 1860 and 1870.[2] Those who were settled in Oberlin by the Freedmen's Bureau stirred hostility. The community's attitude was best expressed by a backhanded aspersion made by Edward Fairchild in 1867. He was at once patronizing toward the new wave of black residents and, although Oberlin had not attracted European immigrants, hostile toward aliens:

"Many of them, having recently come from slavery, retain, in a great measure, the ignorance and peculiar habits of that institution. A more intelligent, cultivated population would be desirable; but if asked to exchange them for an equal number of foreigners, of which we have none, we should beg to be excused."[3]

In time, the community's attitudes seeped into college life. A professor in 1882 objected when a black student planned to room with a white student. In the next year, white students in the women's dormitory refused to eat with blacks, though the seating of black women at a separate, segregated table set up such a storm of protest by both black and white alumni that it was abandoned. Giles Shurtleff, who had commanded black troops during the war, was so concerned at the way black students were being treated in 1884 that he publicly scolded the student body.

By the turn of the century, when discrimination was taken for granted throughout the North, blacks in Ohio could not join most labor unions, often were excluded from restaurants, hotels, and theaters, had to take the most low-paying, menial jobs, and could find housing only in the least desirable sections of most towns. Not surprisingly, Oberlin followed suit. Black students felt moved to have their own receptions and parties, and in 1910 they formed their own literary society because only one of the 254 members of the school's current literary groups was black. Oberlin's president then, Henry Churchill King, excused white students, pointing out that their attitude "is merely representative of the attitude of the whole north toward the question."[4] To a great extent, this was true. Oberlin athletic teams with black members had difficulty getting accommodations when they traveled to play other schools. No black men served in an Oberlin unit during World War I because the War Department informed the college that they could not be housed in the same barracks as whites; those who wished to volunteer were encouraged instead to go to Howard or Wilberforce universities. Even alumni events were affected: Fund-raisers found it difficult to find hotels that would permit blacks to attend banquets. There was a dual standard with regard to practice teaching in Oberlin High School; in 1934, a white student with a B average in his or her major could practice teach, but a black student who was not a music conservatory major had to have an A average. Black dance bands from outside the community were banned in 1938.

Nevertheless, the inspiration represented by men such as the Langstons, James Bartlett, Simeon Bushnell, Henry and Wilson

Bruce Evans, James Fitch, Henry Peck, the Plumb brothers, John Scott, John Watson—by college students such as William Lincoln, Ansel Lyman, Jacob Shipherd, and Richard Winsor—by all the Oberlin Rescuers, by the college's first president, Asa Mahan, by James Monroe, by John Keep—that inspiration lingered and eventually resurfaced. During World War II, a senior class elected a Japanese-American student as its president. And because white barbers would not cut a black's hair, members of the faculty, as well as some college students, joined townspeople in integrating the barbering business by becoming shareholders in a new shop and bringing a black barber to town.

Even before the nation's attitudes began to change with the advent of the civil rights movement in the 1960s, Oberlin shrugged off its complacency and took a leading role in promoting black rights. As early as the 1930s, black residents picketed a local chain to employ a black clerk, and an ad hoc committee formed in 1935 was finally successful in urging the school board to hire black teachers. An interracial group began monthly meetings in the 1940s. Later in that decade the college hired its first black faculty member, and black residents were working in the municipal offices.

In the early 1970s, the college initiated a black studies program that has evolved into a regular academic department, becoming an important presence on campus. It also began an Upward Bound Program, one of the nation's first, to recruit more black students from inner-city schools, providing supportive services for them. Today, about 8 percent of the student population is black.

The town of Oberlin had the first fair housing law in the state, one of the first, in fact, in the country. In 1989 its police chief was black, so, too, were two City Council members as well as a member of the Board of Education. The high school contained an equal number of black and white youths.

The community is still by no means perfect. The black middle class has never fully revived; the one black resident who was a store owner retired recently.

The rescue of John Price, accomplished primarily by black residents and white students, remains the major event in the community's history, a source of continuing pride and an influence in the way Oberlin confronts the present and the future. Moral indignation against oppression—sensitivity to an individual's right to follow his or her own conscience—the spirit that prompted the spontaneous reaction to John Price's seizure—lives on. Today, the

264 THE TOWN THAT STARTED THE CIVIL WAR

Oberlin Overground Railroad Coalition aids refugees en route to Canada from Guatemala, El Salvador, and Nicaragua.

And now, after more than 130 years, a radical community that swung conservative, then inched toward liberalism, is once again considered by many of its neighbors in surrounding communities as "too radical."

Notes
Bibliography
Index

Notes

"One thing more," said George, as he stopped the congratulations of the throng; "you all remember our good old Uncle Tom?"

George here gave a short narration of the scene of his death, and of his loving farewell to all on the place, and added,—

"It was on his grave, my friends, that I resolved, before God, that I would never own another slave, while it was possible to free him; that nobody, through me, should ever run the risk of being parted from home and friends, and dying on a lonely plantation, as he died. So, when you rejoice in your freedom, think that you owe it to that good old soul, and pay it back in kindness to his wife and children. Think of your freedom, every time you see UNCLE TOM'S CABIN.

Chapter XLIV: "The Liberator"

Several caveats are in order. There was no court reporter at the first of the two trials, Bushnell's, and though there was one at the second trial, Langston's, no copy of that transcript survives. Like other writers and historians before me, I have therefore had to rely on newspaper accounts or on Jacob R. Shipherd's *History of the Oberlin-Wellington Rescue*, which was published within days of the release from prison of the last of the Rescuers in 1859 and which includes most of the testimony of both trials, though not verbatim in many instances. Shipherd wrote what he called the "digest of the testimony in Mr. Bushnell's case," but he relied heavily on newspaper accounts for major sections of both trials. Shipherd singles out J. H. Kagi for his "kind offices." Kagi, who was reporting for the *New York Tribune*, was a close ally of John Brown as well as a recruiter and fund-raiser for him and subsequently a member of the raiding party at Harpers Ferry. He was scarcely an uninterested observer, but then none of the newspaper correspondents was completely objective.

Shipherd purposely did nothing to correct the various misspellings that were included in the indictments and/or reported in the newspapers of the time—not even those of his own name. Discrepancies also occur on other records dealing with individuals involved in the Rescue, both in the spelling of names and other data. A glaring example is the indictment of the Rescuers, which says the Rescue took place on the "first day of October" 1858 rather than the actual date—which is irrefutable—September 13. How that mistake occurred befuddles me. That it was never corrected seems peculiar.

I occasionally found that the age provided by an individual to the census taker in 1850 varied by more than one year from the age given by that same individual to the census taker in 1860 (when, incidentally, Chauncey Wack was the census taker in Oberlin). Also typical is the experience I encountered with regard to one Rescuer. The indictment gives his last name as *Scrimeger* and sometimes in court papers he is listed as *Scrimmager*; the list of editors in the *Oberlin Students' Monthly* and an obituary in the *Oberlin Evangelist* as well as the 1858–59 annual school catalog give his name as *Scrimgeour*; however, some school records, including the 1937 alumni catalog, say Scrimegeour. I have chosen to use the spelling given in the magazine, the obituary, and the 1858–59 catalog. (The 1937 catalog also incorrectly gives Scrimgeour's middle name as Douglass.) The last name of Eli Boies is sometimes spelled phonetically—Boyce. Matthew DeWolf's name is sometimes given as Mathew De Wolfe, Matthew Gillet's as Mathew Gillette, Loring Wadsworth's first name as *Loren*, and William Sciples's last name as *Siples*. Similar mistakes sometimes occur with regard to other participants or eyewitnesses; for example, Edward C. Kinney is give as E. S. Kinney in Shipherd's book. For both Rescuers and other individuals, I have usually used the spelling given in a federal census, though the censuses were by no means infallible. In the 1850 one, for example, the name of John Copeland's mother is given as Deborah; her name actually was Delilah and is given correctly in the 1860 census. Also in the 1860 census, Ansel Lyman's first name is given as Anselon, although the 1858–59 school catalog gives it as Anson. Other official documents can also be misleading. James Bartlett, Jr.'s, first name appears as John in the list of *nolo prosequi* filed on July 12, 1859 (National Archives, Record Group 21, Records of U.S. District Courts, 1803–). That same document lists Orindatus S. B. Wall, although the cases against him and Jacob Shipherd had already been dropped because of misnomers. In trying to reconcile all the differences as well as provide descriptive matter, I have relied whenever possible on a variety of sources in addition to the federal census and school records—biographical sketches, obituaries in newspapers or magazines, municipal directories, and the like, all of which are listed in the Bibliography.

The testimony that appears in Shipherd's book, when taken witness by witness, is often confused and sometimes contradictory, especially for the sequence of events that occurred on September 13. It almost seems as though everyone who participated or witnessed the Rescue had a different sense of time. Only two time periods can be distinguished with any certainty—the hour from noon to one o'clock, which was the dinner hour at Oberlin and in the community, and 5:13 P.M., which was when the anxiously awaited train from Cleveland was due to arrive in Wellington. I have tried to make sense of the jumble of testimony, to provide a coherent and cohesive account of what transpired that September afternoon. If any mistakes, misinterpretations, or misrepresentations have resulted, they are my responsibility.

*

The following abbreviations are used on second reference to citations in the notes:

Annals	*Annals of Cleveland—1818–1935.* Vol. 42, 1859. Cleveland: WPA Project 9395, Cleveland, 1936.
Cochran	William C. Cochran, *The Western Reserve and the Fugitive Slave Law: A Prelude to the Civil War.* Publication No. 101, Collections. Cleveland: Western Reserve Historical Society, 1920.
Fletcher	Robert Samuel Fletcher, *A History of Oberlin College: From Its Foundation through the Civil War.* 2 vols. Oberlin: Oberlin College, 1943.
NA, RG 21	National Archives, Record Group 21, Records of U.S. District Courts, 1803–.
NA, RG 24	National Archives, Record Group 24, Bureau of Naval Personnel, Logs, 1801–1946.
NA, RG 29	National Archives, Record Group 29, Census Books.
NA, RG 60	National Archives, Record Group 60, Attorney General Records, 1818–1918.
OCA	Oberlin College Archives.
OCLSC	Oberlin College Library, Special Collections.
Shipherd	Jacob R. Shipherd, *History of the Oberlin-Wellington Rescue,* 1859. Reprint. New York: Da Capo Press, 1972.
WRHS	Western Reserve Historical Society.

EPIGRAPHS

1. David Ross Locke, *The Struggles (Social, Financial and Political) of Petroleum V. Nasby* (Boston: I. N. Richardson & Co., 1873), 45.
2. Harriet Beecher Stowe, *Uncle Tom's Cabin; or, Life Among the Lowly* (Boston: Houghton, Osgood and Company, 1878). Subsequent quotations preceding each chapter are from this edition.

CHAPTER ONE

1. J. Winston Coleman, *Slavery Times in Kentucky* (Chapel Hill: Univ. of North Carolina Press, 1940), 235.

2. Charles L. Blockson, *The Underground Railroad* (New York: Prentice-Hall, 1987), 83.

3. Richard F. Odell, "The Early Antislavery Movement in Ohio" (Ph.D. diss., Univ. of Michigan, 1948), 238.

4. Coleman, *Slavery Times*, 205, 165.

5. National Archives, Record Group 29, Census of 1860, Slave Schedule, shows 3,542 slaves living in Mason County.

6. Details about John P. G. Bacon and his family are culled from census records; the photocopy of the endpapers of the family Bible, published in 1818, on file at the Mason County Museum in Maysville, Kentucky; and the following records held in the Mason County Clerk's Office in Maysville: Marriage Records, 1849–50, pp. 23, 36; Order Book O, 1845–51, p. 83; Will Book N, pp. 438–39; and Will Book Y, pp. 141–44. John and Jacova Bacon's children were Mollie, who was one year old, and Kearny, who was four. The Bacon home was near the current site of an electric power station on the Ohio River just east of Dover.

7. Jacob R. Shipherd, *History of the Oberlin-Wellington Rescue* (1859; reprint, New York: Da Capo Press, 1972), 16–17.

8. References to John's deformity are made by Riddle and Wood, ibid., 52 and 105.

9. The power of attorney that Bacon and Loyd later took out describes John, Dinah, and Frank (ibid., 16). For the variations in John's description, see notes below relating to testimony at the trials.

10. *Oberlin Tribune*, July 5, 1901. The details of their escape are in a Letter to the Editor from J. N. Beabout. He says four slaves escaped—John, Frank, Dinah, and a woman called "Joe," who was John's girl friend. However, nothing was ever said about a fourth escaped slave in any other account at the trials or by the Kentucky slaveowners themselves.

11. William E. Lincoln, "Wellington Rescue," in William Pendleton Palmer Collection, WRHS. According to an Addendum by Henry Holcomb and dated Painesville, Ohio, September 6, 1915, Lincoln's reminiscence about the Rescue was apparently written in 1915. It was written on the pages of three 1905 pollbooks and is unpaginated. Lincoln also included in his reminiscence the story of his adventures in Kentucky as well as other experiences. Unless otherwise noted, all quotes that follow are from this reminiscence. Lincoln was the author of other material relating to the Rescue—recollections and letters to the editor—which are cited when employed in later chapters. Interestingly, he often chose in them to repeat certain events—his conversion to abolitionism after reading *Uncle Tom's Cabin* and various details about his participation in the Oberlin-Wellington Rescue, in particular his kneeling to pray for guidance and his leadership in the endeavor. It is almost as though nothing else in his long life meant anything to him. I have sometimes combined quotations from these sources to provide a more cohesive and dramatic narrative. When I do so, I cite all the sources that are employed. In addition to those sources, Lincoln wrote a lengthy letter to the president of Berea College (Berea, Kentucky), William G. Frost, in which he iterated his admiration of John G. Fee and included other incidents he experienced while preaching

and teaching in Kentucky. In it, he takes credit for helping to found Berea College. He also repeats in this letter the incident involving the Catholic priest aboard the steamboat bound for Maysville and the shooting attempt on his own life (William E. Lincoln to Bro. [William G.] Frost, October 18, 1909, William E. Lincoln Papers, Founders and Founding Collection, Berea College Archives).

12. Richard D. Sears, *The Day of Small Things: Abolitionism in the Midst of Slavery, Berea, Kentucky, 1854–1864* (Lanham, Md.: Univ. Press of America, 1986), 185.

13. *Village Item*, May 20, 1852.

14. Sears, *Day of Small Things*, 184.

15. Robert Samuel Fletcher, *A History of Oberlin College: From Its Foundation through the Civil War*, 2 vols. (Oberlin: Oberlin College, 1943), 263.

CHAPTER TWO

1. Nat Brandt and John Sexton, *How Free Are We? What the Constitution Says We Can and Cannot Do* (New York: M. Evans, 1986), 277. The 1842 case cited in the following paragraph was *Prigg* v. Pennsylvania.

2. *Fugitive Slave Bill* (Boston: N.p., 1854), 4.

3. Wilbur H. Siebert, *The Underground Railroad from Slavery to Freedom* (New York: Macmillan, 1898), 192.

4. Robin W. Winks, *Canada and the United States: The Civil War Years* (Baltimore: Johns Hopkins Press, 1960), 8.

5. Stanley W. Campbell, *The Slave Catchers: Enforcement of the Fugitive Slave Law, 1850–1860* (Chapel Hill: Univ. of North Carolina Press, 1968), 6.

6. John Hope Franklin, *From Slavery to Freedom: A History of Negro Americans*, 4th ed. (New York: Knopf, 1974), 203.

7. Siebert, *Underground Railroad*, 351.

8. Leon Alilunas, "Fugitive Slave Cases in Ohio prior to 1850," *Ohio State Archaeological and Historical Quarterly* 46 (1940): 168.

9. William C. Cochran, *The Western Reserve and the Fugitive Slave Law: A Prelude to the Civil War*, Publication 101, Collections (Cleveland: Western Reserve Historical Society, 1920), 166n, 168.

10. Blockson, *Underground Railroad*, 31.

11. *U.S. Reports: Cases Adjudged in the Supreme Court of the United States*, vols. 57–67 inclusive (Howard 16–24, Black 1–2) (Cleveland: Baldwin Law Book Company, 1926), *Ableman* v. *Booth* and *U.S.* v. *Booth*, 21 Howard 525.

12. Blockson, *Underground Railroad*, 272–73. The teenager quoted was Charlotte Forten.

13. Ralph A. Keller, "Northern Protestant Churches and the Fugitive Slave Law of 1850" (Ph.D. diss., Univ. of Wisconsin, 1969), 320.

14. Leon F. Litwack, *North of Slavery* (Chicago: Univ. of Chicago Press, 1961), 251.

15. Siebert, *Underground Railroad*, 333.

16. Anti-Slavery Tracts, n.d., n.p., p. 37, Schomburg Center for Research in Black Culture, New York. Margaret Garner's story was the apparent inspiration for Toni Morrison's *Beloved*, a Pulitzer Prize winner in 1988.

17. Keller, "Northern Protestant Churches," 336 ("Notes"). The author says the "best estimates" are that 200 to 250 cases occurred.

18. *Bits of Mason County Heritage* (N.p.: Limestone Chapter of Daughters of the American Revolution, n.d.), 32.

19. Blockson, *Underground Railroad*, 203.

20. Harriet Beecher Stowe, *Uncle Tom's Cabin; or, Life Among the Lowly*, Intro. by Raymond Weaver (New York: Random House Modern Library Edition, 1938), xviii.

CHAPTER THREE

1. Fletcher, 566.

2. Ibid., 249.

3. Robert S. Fletcher, "The Wellington Rescue," *Oberlin Alumni Magazine* 54 (November 1958): 6.

4. Sears, *Day of Small Things*, 153.

5. William E. Lincoln to Philip D. Sherman, March 1918, Secretary's Office, 1833–1970, Oberlin College Archives (OCA).

6. J. H. Fairchild, "Baccalaureate Sermon: Providential Aspects of the Oberlin Enterprise," in *The Oberlin Jubilee, 1833–1883*, ed. W. G. Ballantine (Oberlin: E. J. Goodrich, 1883), 95.

7. J. H. Fairchild, *Oberlin: Its Origin, Progress and Results* (Oberlin: R. Butler, 1871), 4–5.

8. Harriot K. Hunt, *Glances and Glimpses; or Fifty Years Social, Including Twenty Years Professional Life* (1856, reprint, Boston: Source Book Press, 1970), 352.

9. Fletcher, 127.

10. 1909 General Catalogue, Oberlin College, int. 38, College General (Catalogues), 1833–1987, OCA.

11. Fletcher, 615.

12. J. G. W. Cowles, "rhetorical embellishment," paper delivered at commencement, 1900, at presentation of a portrait of his father, the Rev. Henry Cowles, pp. 1–3, Robert S. Fletcher Papers, 1833–1958, OCA.

13. A. L. Shumway and C. DeW. Brower, *Oberliniana* (1883; reprint, Galion, Ohio: Fisher Printing, 1983), 20.

14. E. H. Fairchild, *Historical Sketch of Oberlin College* (Springfield, Ill.: Republic Printing Company, 1868), 17.

15. William E. Lincoln to Philip D. Sherman, March 1918, Secretary's Office, OCA.

16. Fletcher, 154.

17. Ibid., 158.

18. Harriet Beecher Stowe, *Uncle Tom's Cabin; or, Life Among the Lowly* (Boston: Houghton, Osgood and Company, 1878), lvix.

19. Fletcher, 171.

20. Bertram Wyatt-Brown, *Lewis Tappan and the Evangelical War against Slavery* (Cleveland: Press of Case Western Reserve Univ., 1969), 177.

21. Fletcher, 175–76.

22. 1909 General Catalogue, Oberlin College, int. 38, College General (Catalogues), OCA.

23. Fairchild, *Historical Sketch*, 6.

24. Clayton S. Ellsworth, "Oberlin and the Anti-Slavery Movement Up to the Civil War" (Ph.D. diss., Cornell Univ., 1930), 26.

25. Fletcher, 523, 536.

26. Ellen Lawson and Marlene Merrill, "The Antebellum 'Talented Thousandth': Black College Students at Oberlin before the Civil War," *Journal of Negro Education* 52 (Spring 1983): 142–43, 145, 148.

27. Fletcher, 524.

28. Litwack, *North of Slavery*, 141.

29. Fletcher, 526.

30. Benjamin Quarles, *Black Abolitionists* (New York: Oxford Univ. Press, 1969), 114, 112. The clergyman was John M. Brown, a former Oberlin student.

31. Sherlock Bristol, *The Pioneer Preacher* (London: Walter G. Wheeler, 1898), 97.

32. William E. Lincoln to Philip D. Sherman, March 1918, Secretary's Office, OCA. Despite her aversion to so much praying, Arabella Phillips led an exemplary life. A lifelong advocate of temperance, she graduated from Oberlin in 1862 and taught school in Indiana until 1868, when she became principal of the Colored High School of Hannibal, Missouri. She was there for eight years. She lived in Onondaga, Michigan, from 1879 to 1892, working occasionally as a teacher. She died at the home of a sister in Missouri in 1915, when in her eighties.

33. Clyde A. Holbrook, "A Great Preacher, Charles G. Finney, 1792–1875," in *The History of First Church in Oberlin, Ohio* (Weekly Calendar, First Congregational Church, 1984), 22.

34. Ellsworth Carlson, "The Oberlin Church, its Wider Affiliations," in *History of First Church*, 29. The Huron Presbytery refused to license two of Oberlin's first students, James and Edward Fairchild, and would not even grant them an examination.

35. Ibid., 69–70.

36. *Oberlin Evangelist*, December 7, 1859.

37. Ellsworth, "Oberlin and the Anti-Slavery Movement," 86.

38. Siebert, *Underground Railroad*, map.

39. A. R. Webber, *Early History of Elyria and Her People* (Elyria, Ohio: N.p., 1930), 140.

40. Wilbur G. Burroughs, "Oberlin's Part in the Slavery Conflict," *Ohio Archaeological and Historical Quarterly* 20 (April–July 1911): 289.

41. Geil's Map of Oberlin, 1857, *Land Ownership Maps* (Washington, D.C.: Library of Congress, 1967; microfiche).

42. *Williams' Medina, Elyria and Oberlin City Guide, and Business Mirror*, vol. 1, 1859–60 (N.p.: C. S. Williams, 1859), 108–9.

43. *Annual Catalogue of the Officers and Students of Oberlin College, for the College Year 1858–59* (Oberlin: Evangelist Office, 1858), 38, College General (Catalogues), OCA.

44. Fletcher, 259.

45. J. H. Fairchild, *The Underground Railroad*, Tract 87, vol. 4 (Cleveland: Western Reserve Historical Society, 1895), 97.

46. Fairchild, *Historical Sketch*, 11.

47. *Louisville Daily Courier*, April 18, 1859.

48. Charles Farrar, *The Complete Works of Artemus Ward* (New York: G. W. Dillingham Co., 1898), 51–53.

49. Fairchild, *Historical Sketch*, 9.

50. *Liberator*, March 2, 1849.
51. Cochran, 119.
52. NA, RG 29, Census of 1860.
53. William E. Bigglestone, *They Stopped in Oberlin: Black Residents and Visitors of the Nineteenth Century* (Scottsdale, Ariz.: Innovation Group, 1981), xiii–xiv.
54. NA, RG 29, Census of 1860. Based on the author's count. Other sources disagree slightly. Bigglestone (*They Stopped in Oberlin*, xiv), for example, comes up with a combined figure of white and black residents of 2,115, one more person than I found. The *Lorain County News* of April 11, 1860, reported several months before the federal census was taken that Oberlin's population was 2,132 "exclusive of students," but the newspaper did not indicate the identity of the "census taker" it quoted.
55. Bigglestone, *They Stopped in Oberlin*, xv.
56. John Mercer Langston, *From the Virginia Plantation to the National Capitol* (Hartford, Conn.: American Publishing Company, 1894), 101.
57. Journal of Fannie White (transcribed copy), entry of September 20, 1960, p. 134, Oberlin File, Writings by, OCA.
58. Delavan L. Leonard, *The Story of Oberlin* (Boston: Pilgrim Press, 1898), 381.
59. Hunt, *Glances and Glimpses*, 352.
60. Fletcher, 391.
61. Ibid., 583. See Chapter 8, note 69, for Dayton's and Munson's connections with the church.
62. Richard Morris, ed., *Encyclopedia of American History* (New York: Harper & Row, 1961), 713.
63. [Wendell Phillips Garrison], *William Lloyd Garrison: The Story of His Life Told by His Children*, 4 vols. (New York: Century Co., 1885–89), 2: 202.
64. William Cheek and Aimee Lee Cheek, *John Mercer Langston and the Fight for Black Freedom, 1829–1865* (Urbana: Univ. of Illinois Press, 1989), 326.

CHAPTER FOUR

1. Fairchild, *Oberlin*, 27.
2. Lorain County, Russia Township, Trustee Records, 1855–87, OCA. John Price is mentioned on page 81 of the records, as well as on pages 76, 77, and 87 of the Orders on Township Fund, 1857 [sic], and on page 89 of Orders on Treasurer, 1858. The name of the farmer with whom John was staying was James Armstrong. Armstrong, who was paid $1.25 a week to shelter him, received in all $13.75 for "keeping John Price" for a total of eleven weeks between May 7 and August 27, 1858, though the weeks were evidently not always consecutive. Earlier, John had stayed with another Oberlin resident, George Logan, who was paid $3 for boarding and keeping John for two weeks, starting March 27, 1858.
3. Shipherd, 106.
4. Cochran, 122–25. Unless otherwise noted, all the incidents involving Cochran are from this source.
5. Record of conversation between William E. Bigglestone and Mary

Rudd Cochran, Monroe, Ohio, November 8, 1972, Subject File, Underground Railroad, OCA.

6. Shipherd, 32.

7. Ibid., 77.

8. NA, RG 29, Census of 1850, Slave Schedule.

9. Shipherd, 20.

10. Ibid., 19. Jennings addressed the letter to a Mr. Reynolds for forwarding to Bacon. Reynolds was apparently a neighbor of Bacon's. Jennings never explained why he did not address the letter directly to Bacon.

11. Dayton did not want to assist Langston in tracking down and capturing John Price. Dayton was working with a Kentuckian named McMillen, who already claimed to have a warrant for John's capture, but how he acquired it is unclear; Jennings believed that McMillen had falsified it "for his own use" (ibid., 101). McMillen participated in the attempt to seize the Wagoner family in early September and then disappears from the story of John Price.

12. Bigglestone, *They Stopped in Oberlin*, 215.

13. Shipherd, 101.

14. NA, RG 29, Census of 1850, Slave Schedule.

15. Shipherd, 29.

16. *Maysville City Directory* (St. Louis, Mo.: H. N. McEvoy, 1860), 27, 38.

17. Shipherd, 16, 99. The name of Cochran's deputy was William H. Richardson.

18. Ibid., 28.

19. Ibid., 102.

20. Writing many years later, Cochran says (p. 121) that the attempt to seize the Wagoners occurred about mid-August, but Mitchell (Shipherd, 29) says it occurred two days before his arrival in Oberlin.

21. Shipherd, 175.

22. H. G. Blake to Professors James Monroe and Henry Peck, September 6, 1858, James Monroe Papers, 1841–98, OCA. Blake, writing from Medina, said: "Gents, here are five Slaves from the House of Bondage, which I need not say to you that you will see to them—they can tell their own story." Ordinarily, such messages were not that frank; the word *Slaves* would not have been employed.

23. *Oberlin News*, October 13, 1909.

24. Shipherd, 99.

25. Ibid., 101, 116–17, 119–20.

26. Ibid., 35, 100–101. At Bushnell's trial, Jennings said he spoke to Boynton first, before approaching Shakespeare (ibid., 19). He reversed himself at Langston's trial. The latter testimony is quoted here.

27. Ibid., 100.

28. Ibid., 106.

CHAPTER FIVE

1. Robert B. Thomas, *The Old Farmer's Almanac, 1858* (Boston: Hickling, Swan & Brewer, 1857), 22; Journal of Fannie White, p. 112, OCA. White's journal is frequently the source of weather conditions mentioned in the narrative.

2. Fairchild, *Underground Railroad*, 112.

3. Shipherd, 22.
4. Ibid., 118.
5. Ibid., 29.
6. Ibid., 151, 35. The road is now called Oberlin Road.
7. Ibid., 116. Lowe testified, "This was about 12 o'clock, at noon."
8. Details of John's capture are taken from a synthesis of the trial testimony, ibid.: Shakespeare Boynton, 35; Samuel Davis, 120; Richard
Mitchell, 29 and 103; and Lowe, 118.
9. The Cleveland-Oberlin Road, later Route 10, renumbered 10/511 in
August 1988.
10. The road now encompasses a portion of Route 20; the remainder is
Hallauer Road.
11. Shipherd, 20.
12. The Oberlin-Wellington Road is now Route 20. The cemetery still
exists.
13. Shipherd, 42, 22.
14. A. W. Lyman letter, undated, stamped upon receipt at Oberlin College, April 14, 1908, Alumni Records (Formers/Graduates), 1833–1960,
OCA. In writing this brief account of the Rescue, Lyman wrote in the
third person: "On the way they were met by Mr. Lyman and a companion,
to whom the boy pleaded for help."
15. Shipherd, 22.
16. Cleveland Plain Dealer, August 25, 1953.
17. Shipherd, 118, 29.
18. Ibid., 22.
19. A. W. Lyman, letter undated, stamped April 14, 1908, OCA, was
signed "Anse Lyman."

CHAPTER SIX

1. Shipherd, 33. The store Wack went into was run by William E. Kellogg.
2. A. W. Lyman, letter undated, stamped April 14, 1908, OCA.
3. Shipherd, 24.
4. Cleveland Plain Dealer, April 9, 1859.
5. Shipherd, 22.
6. Portage County Democrat, May 11, 1859.
7. Oberlin News, March 3, 1899. The recollection in the newspaper is
under her married name, Mrs. A. A. F. Johnston. She had graduated in
1856 and served as principal of the Black Oak Grove Seminary in Mossy
Creek, Tennessee, for three years. Returning to Ohio in 1859, she married
James M. Johnston, who died three years later. She became principal of
the Women's Department at Oberlin College in 1870, a position she held
until 1900, by which time the title had been changed to dean and she had
been appointed professor of medieval history as well.
8. New York Daily Tribune, September 18, 1858. The anonymous letter
writer identified himself only as "R."
9. Shipherd, 126.
10. Shipherd, 23. Halbert (ibid.) says he hung about for three hours, but
on page 109 he says he reached Wellington at 3:00 P.M., which would not
have been possible had he tarried in Oberlin for three hours. His distorted

idea of time is typical of the misconceptions of many participants and witnesses.

11. *Oberlin News*, October 13, 1909. Some of the details of John Scott's account in this newspaper interview, nearly fifty years after the Rescue, are in error. Fabrel's (he meant Favel's) livery stable did not exist at that time. In addition, the noted black writer Charles W. Chesnutt—whose last name was misspelled in the newspaper—was born June 20, 1858, so he was less than three months old at the time of the Rescue. Scott undoubtedly meant Chesnutt's father, Andrew Jackson Chesnutt.

12. Journal of Fannie White, OCA. According to Fannie White, Ryder died suddenly of epilepsy at 11:00 P.M., June 29, 1858 (p. 109). Mary Tripp, in an interview for the *Lorain Journal* printed on December 11, 1939, said there were two horses hitched to the buggy, but both Winsor and Scott, who were in it, say there was one horse.

13. Richard Winsor, "How John Price Was Rescued," in *The Oberlin Jubilee, 1833–1883*, ed. W. G. Ballantine (Oberlin: E. J. Goodrich, 1883), 252.

14. Ibid., 251, 254.

15. Ibid., 254, 251.

16. Lida Rose McCabe, "The Oberlin-Wellington Rescue," *Godey's Magazine* 133 (October 1896): 376. McCabe misidentified Wilson Bruce Evans, calling him Henry Evans. Henry Evans had died in 1886.

17. Artemas Halbert (Shipherd, 23) identifies a number of participants, including a "Lairie." There is no record of a Lairie in Oberlin at that time. Because John Scott explicitly cites Leary as bringing him the news of John's capture, and because so many other misspellings occur in the oral testimony, I have assumed that "Lairie" was phonetic for "Leary." In view of his later participation in the Harpers Ferry raid, it seems reasonable to assume that he would have taken part in the Rescue if he had the opportunity.

18. Winsor, "How John Price Was Rescued," 254, refers to Bushnell as "Sim."

19. The recounting of Lincoln's joining in the Rescue is based on four sources: William E. Lincoln's "Wellington Rescue," Palmer Collection, WRHS; *Oberlin News* articles of September 15, 1909, and July 26, 1916; and Sears, *Day of Small Things*, 189–90.

20. Henry Viets.

21. Ione T. Hanna (née Munger), "A Chapter of Reminiscences," 37–38, Oberlin File, Writings by, OCA.

22. Shipherd, 123.

23. Hanna, "Chapter of Reminiscences," 39, Oberlin file, OCA. She does not identify Patton by name but refers to "a man from my class, a large, stalwart fellow, who knew the U.S. marshal." It is clear that she meant Patton because, she continues, he "went to them and told them that he would guarantee their safety provided they would leave the negro and betake themselves home again." The actual number of students who participated in the Rescue and their names is unknown. No record was ever compiled. Moreover, apparently many students did not identify themselves as participants because of fear of incrimination. Abdiel Campbell Parsons (Class of 1863), for one, did not acknowledge his participation until responding to an alumni questionnaire in 1908.

24. G. Frederick Wright, "The Oberlin I First Knew and Oberlin To-day," *Oberlin Alumni Magazine* 17 (April 1921): 150.

25. Albert T. Swing, *James Harris Fairchild or Sixty-Eight Years with a Christian College* (New York: Fleming H. Revell, 1907), 377. During the Civil War, Nettleton served with the Second Ohio Cavalry, the first cavalry unit raised in the northern part of the state, about which George Armstrong Custer said, "In my entire division, numbering twelve regiments from different states, I have none in which I repose greater confidence than the 2nd Ohio" (Fletcher, 868). During the Appomattox campaign in 1865, Nettleton commanded his regiment on the last charge at Five Forks and was breveted a brigadier general for bravery.

26. Ernst L. Henes, *Historic Wellington Then and Now* (Wellington, Ohio: Southern Lorain County Historical Society, 1984), 32.

27. The recounting of this episode is based on Lincoln's "Wellington Rescue," Palmer Collection, WRHS, and the *Oberlin News* article of September 15, 1909.

28. *New York Daily Tribune*, September 18, 1858.

CHAPTER SEVEN

1. Shipherd, 118.
2. Ibid., 29.
3. *Owl*, June 6, 1896.
4. *New York Daily Tribune*, September 18, 1858.
5. Ibid.
6. *Lorain Journal*, December 11, 1939. The interview with Mary Tripp —identifying her by her married name, Mary Tripp Terry—cannot be totally trusted. She says, for example, that two horses, not one, were hitched to the buggy that took John away.
7. *Oberlin News*, March 3, 1899.
8. The description that follows is based on several sources, but especially Shipherd's book. When necessary, quotations are documented, but much of the action is a synthesis of the testimony of participants and witnesses given at the trials.
9. *New York Daily Tribune*, September 18, 1858.
10. Shipherd, 26.
11. Ibid., 120.
12. Details of Wheeler's interview with John Price are based on Wheeler's testimony, Shipherd, 26, and that of Richard Mitchell, ibid., 28.
13. Ibid., 118.
14. Ibid., 20.
15. Ibid., 26.
16. *Owl*, June 6, 1896.
17. Shipherd, 105, 28. The first to question John was, oddly enough, Democrat Norris Wood, whom John had worked for in August.
18. *Owl*, June 6, 1896.
19. Shipherd, 105.
20. *Owl*, June 6, 1896. The two men Griffin encountered in the Public Square were J. L. Magraugh, who wrote the account published in the *Owl*, and Councilman Walter F. Herrick. It was Magraugh who got the youngster to fetch a ladder. Magraugh was certain that there were a thousand

people jammed into the Public Square during the Rescue, but his estimate
seems exaggerated.

21. Shipherd, 123.
22. Ibid., 31.
23. Ibid., 25.
24. Cheek and Cheek, *John Mercer Langston*, 112.
25. Shipherd, 37.
26. *New York Daily Tribune*, September 18, 1858.
27. Shipherd, 34.
28. Ibid., 119.
29. Ibid., 39. Despite the dark, Howk recognized John Mandeville and
David Wadsworth, brother of innkeeper Oliver Wadsworth.
30. Ibid., 272.
31. Lincoln, "Wellington Rescue," Palmer Collection, WRHS.
32. Shipherd, 38.
33. Ibid., 102.
34. Ibid., 39.
35. Ibid., 124. Patton refers to Griffin as a "stranger."
36. Ibid., 119.
37. Ibid., 33, 104, 34.
38. Ibid., 176.
39. Ibid., 119.
40. Blacksmith R. E. Thayer's experience (Shipherd, 115) illustrates
how jumpy people were. He sent a messenger to query Constable Meacham about a personal matter. The youngster started up a ladder to the
second-floor balcony in order to get into the hotel. Apparently concerned
that he might get hurt, Thayer pulled the youth back. A black man saw
his action and evidently misunderstood his intention. The black man
"snapped" his gun at Thayer, who grabbed the black's head. Others rushed
to the black man's defense, and the next thing Thayer knew, he was being
carried off on their shoulders.
41. Ibid., 123.
42. Lincoln, "Wellington Rescue," Palmer Collection, WRHS.
43. *Oberlin News*, July 26, 1919.
44. Shipherd, 27.
45. Unless otherwise noted, the incident relating to Lincoln and his
men's storming of the hotel and details of what occurred once they were
inside are from Lincoln, "Wellington Rescue," Palmer Collection, WRHS,
and accounts he wrote for the *Oberlin News* issues of September 15, 1909,
and July 26, 1916.
46. According to Lincoln, his shout was heard by Charles H. Penfield,
professor of Latin language and literature.
47. Lincoln, "Wellington Rescue," Palmer Collection, WRHS. In the
July 26, 1916, article in the *Oberlin News*, however, Lincoln said "45
shots to my 11."
48. *Oberlin News*, October 13, 1909.
49. Shipherd, 25.
50. Ibid., 116.
51. *Oberlin News*, October 13, 1909.
52. Shipherd, 126.
53. Ibid., 124.

54. Winsor, "How John Price Was Rescued," 253, says Lincoln told him in 1883 that he still retained the note.

55. *Oberlin News*, October 13, 1909.

56. Winsor, "How John Price Was Rescued," 253–54.

57. Shipherd, 32 and 121. Kinney testified at both trials. The student who accompanied Kinney on the way to Wellington was John Lang.

58. Ibid., 104.

59. *New York Daily Tribune*, September 18, 1858.

60. Langston, *From the Virginia Plantation*, 184–85.

61. *New York Sun*, May 7, 1895. The decision where to hide John was so secret that Bushnell's sister Jane Fitch did not know that John was taken to Fairchild's home.

62. Fairchild, *Underground Railroad*, 113–14.

63. Emma Monroe Fitch, "The Wellington Rescue Case in 1858," Frances Hosford Papers, 1925–35, OCA. Fitch was the stepdaughter of Charles Grandison Finney's daughter Julia Finney Monroe.

64. NA, RG, Census of 1860.

65. McCabe, "Oberlin-Wellington Rescue," 375.

66. Swing, *James Harris Fairchild*, 190.

67. McCabe, "Oberlin-Wellington Rescue," 375.

68. Unspecified daughter of Fairchild to William Cochran, Subject File, Underground Railroad, OCA.

69. Fairchild, *Underground Railroad*, 113.

70. Langston, *From the Virginia Plantation*, 185.

71. *Cleveland Plain Dealer*, September 14–16, 1858.

72. *Oberlin News*, October 13, 1909.

73. In his testimony, Oberlin resident Philip Kelly says (Shipherd, 106) Charles Langston spoke after John Mercer, but William B. Worden, an Oberlin carpenter, says (ibid.) John Mercer spoke last and Shipherd spoke first.

74. *New York Daily Tribune*, September 18, 1858. Gaston (Shipherd, 107) identifies Shipherd as leading the "groans."

75. Shipherd, 107.

76. *New York Daily Tribune*, September 18, 1858.

CHAPTER EIGHT

1. *Lorain County Eagle*, September 15, 1858.

2. Shipherd, 30.

3. *New York Daily Tribune*, September 18, 1858.

4. Shipherd, 241.

5. Cochran, 121.

6. Shipherd, 241–42.

7. Lorain County, Russia Township, Justices Court Civil Dockets, 1836–1906, vol. 5, December 1856 to vol. 7, January 1869, OCA. Beecher's partner was Myron Bronson. All of the suits against Dayton were decided in favor of the plaintiffs by Justice of the Peace Daniel Bushnell.

8. Shipherd, 241.

9. Cochran, 133, quoting *Cleveland Plain Dealer*, September 24, 1858.

10. *Portage County Democrat*, May 11, 1859.

11. Cochran, 134.

12. Shipherd, 14–15.

13. *Cleveland Morning Leader,* December 12, 1858.

14. Denton J. Snider, *The American Ten Years' War* (St. Louis: Sigma Publishing Co., 1906), 244 and 257.

15. *Portage County Democrat,* May 11, 1859.

16. Siebert, *Underground Railroad,* 425. Siebert's list is also the source for other Rescuers identified as being known members of the Underground Railroad.

17. Richard J. Hinton, *John Brown and His Men* (1894; reprint; New York: Arno Press and the New York Times, 1968), 505.

18. Benjamin Quarles, *Allies for Freedom: Blacks and John Brown* (New York: Oxford Univ. Press, 1974), 34.

19. Bigglestone, *They Stopped in Oberlin,* 52.

20. Langston, *From the Virginia Plantation,* 193.

21. *Portage County Democrat,* May 11, 1859.

22. Robert Ewell Greene, *The Leary-Evans, Ohio's Free People of Color* (Washington, D.C.: Keitt Printing Co., 1979), 24.

23. Leary's middle name sometimes appears as Sherrard.

24. Mill Street was subsequently renamed Vine Street. The house, at 33 Vine Street, is now on the National Register of Historic Buildings.

25. *Oberlin News,* October 13, 1909.

26. Charles W. Torrey, "James Mason Fitch," *Congregational Quarterly,* whole no. 38, vol. 10 (April 1868): 149.

27. *Portage County Democrat,* May 11, 1859.

28. Torrey, "James Mason Fitch," 148.

29. *New York Sun,* April 7, 1895.

30. Bigglestone, *They Stopped in Oberlin,* 74.

31. *Portage County Democrat,* May 11, 1859, gives Charles Langston's age as thirty-eight, but his brother John Mercer Langston indicates that Charles Langston was born in 1817.

32. *Portage County Democrat,* May 11, 1859.

33. Langston, *From the Virginia Plantation,* 21-22.

34. *Portage County Democrat,* May 11, 1859.

35. Fletcher, 691.

36. *Portage County Democrat,* May 11, 1859.

37. James Monroe, *Oberlin Thursday Lectures: Addresses and Essays* (Oberlin: Edward J. Goodrich, 1897), 100.

38. "A Biographical Sketch of Ralph Plumb," *The Biographical Dictionary and Portrait Gallery of Representative Men of the United States,* Illinois volume (Chicago: Lewis Publishing Company, 1896), in Edward B. Plumb Papers, OCA.

39. McCabe, "Oberlin-Wellington Rescue," 376.

40. *Portage County Democrat,* May 11, 1859.

41. McCabe, "Oberlin-Wellington Rescue," 376.

42. Note in letter from A. Atwater re: his sister, Mrs. Geo. W. Neely, June 1, 1900, to Howard H. Russell, Student Files and Roll Books, OCA. The note reads: "Mr. Scrimegeour [sic], a man of fine intellect and great industry, who died a year or two after graduated, was associated with her (Mary Atwater '59) and others as editors (of the Oberlin Monthly)."

43. *Oberlin Evangelist,* August 19, 1860.

44. Note by Cha[rle]s A. Kellogg, June 1941, Alumni Records (Formers/Graduates), OCA. Kellogg identified himself as the stepson of Scrimgeour's classmate John Vetter.

45. Shipherd entered Oberlin College the same year he was ordained, 1857.

46. Docket of Oberlin Town Records, OCA. Wall was one of twenty-one marshals appointed for one month's service by Mayor David Brokaw on January 28, 1858, "for the safety and good morals of the people of this village. It requires more marshalls [sic] to protect us from great evils." Wilson Bruce Evans was appointed at the same time. No further reason is given for this unusual round of appointments, and local newspapers provide no hint as to what may have prompted it.

47. *Portage County Democrat*, May 11, 1859.

48. Docket of Oberlin Town Records, OCA. David Watson pleaded guilty to the charge.

49. Bigglestone, *They Stopped in Oberlin*, 222.

50. *Portage County Democrat*, May 11, 1859.

51. Docket of Oberlin Town Records, OCA. Interestingly, in the same ledger that records the charges against William Watson and David Watson is an entry, dated June 24, 1861, in which C. H. Baldwin complains that on June 11 John Mercer Langston assaulted him "with great violence, strike and push him." Langston, who pleaded guilty, was fined $5 plus $2.15 in court costs.

52. *Portage County Democrat*, May 11, 1859.

53. NA, RG 29, Census of 1860, lists Niles as a resident of Wellington.

54. *Commemorative Biographical Record of the Counties of Huron and Lorain, Ohio*, 2 vols. (Chicago: J. H. Beers & Co., 1894), 887, incorrectly gives his birth date as May 16, 1821, which would have made him thirty-seven years old at the time of the Rescue.

55. Shipherd, 115. When on May 2, 1859, the federal district attorney, George W. Belden, sought a warrant for Samuel Davis to appear in court, he said he needed Davis to testify in the cases of eleven Rescuers—Matthew DeWolf, the Evans brothers, Langston, Lincoln, Lyman, Mandeville, Scott, Wadsworth, John Watson, and Winsor (National Archives, Chicago Branch, Record Group 21, Records of U.S. District Courts, 1803–, Application for warrant for Witness, *U.S.* v. *Charles Langston & others*). But Belden did not mention Sciples at all, though Davis was in the attic room when Sciples was there and could have testified against him as well—if Belden intended to prosecute him. Sciples appeared as one of Belden's prosecution witnesses against Langston that same day.

56. *Cleveland Morning Leader*, December 10, 1858.

57. *Rescuer*, Cuyahoga County Jail, July 4, 1859, OCA.

58. Shipherd, 4.

59. *Cleveland Morning Leader*, December 10, 1858.

60. Shipherd, 4.

61. Ibid.

62. Siebert, *Underground Railroad*, 282. Spalding, however, said every lawyer connected with the "Bar of Cuyahoga" with "possibly a few exceptions" were "ready and eager" to defend the Rescuers (Shipherd, 279).

63. *Portage County Democrat*, May 11, 1859.

64. Shipherd, 5. The presiding judge at the arraignment was never identified.

65. *Cleveland Morning Leader*, December 10, 1858.

66. Cheek and Cheek, *John Mercer Langston*, 330.

67. *Louisville Daily Courier*, December 11, 1858.

68. Cheek and Cheek, *John Mercer Langston,* 356. There is a mysteri-
ous letter to Gerrit Smith, dated January 10, 1859, Bloomington, Kansas,
in *Black Abolitionist Papers: 1830–1865* (N.p.: Microfilming Corporation
of America, 1981), purportedly written by John A. Copeland, Jr. It is signed
"J. Copeland," and though "Bro. Fox" [Rescuer Jeremiah Fox?] is mentioned, the writer refers to the "death of my father" and goes into detail
about some money owed to Smith. Unless it is written in code, the letter
could not have been written by John A. Copeland, Jr. His father did not
die until 1894.

Besides the seven indicted Rescuers who were never apprehended, William Watson, who had appeared with his father for the arraignment, never
showed up in court again. Neither did Lewis Hines of Wellington. The
senior Bartlett, who had been served with a warrant, was in Cleveland on
December 7 but for some reason did not appear at the arraignment. He
was, however, included in the group that Spalding represented at that
session and did return to Cleveland for the trials.

69. Dayton's home on Pleasant Street was between Lorain and College.
According to the Vestry Minutes and Parish Register of Christ Episcopal
Church for the period April 18, 1855–January 7, 1887 (microfilm), OCA,
Dayton's decision to leave Oberlin apparently prompted church elders to
appoint on December 13, 1858, a committee made up of Edward F. Munson and Marshal T. Gaston—to "correspond with or wait on Mr. Dayton"
regarding the financial records of the church's building committee, which
Dayton headed. The church (*sans* parsonage) was then still in the process
of being built and was not consecrated until May 11, 1859. Earlier that
year, on March 20, 1858, B. L. Pierce, an Oberlin mason who appeared at
the Bushnell trial as a prosecution witness (Shipherd, 42–43), submitted
a disputed bill for plastering that came to $459.35. Dayton, with Munson
and Gaston, was among the original thirty members of the church who
signed the parish's constitution on May 18, 1855; he was named a junior
warden on that same day and on May 30 was elected as the parish association's first secretary. He was reelected a junior warden on Easter morning 1856, clerk on May 10, 1856, and named a trustee, along with Munson
and Gaston, on November 23, 1857. His name disappears from church
records after Munson and Gaston were asked in mid-December 1858 to
contact him about the building committee's records.

70. *Cleveland Morning Leader,* December 14, 1858, also quoting the
Plain Dealer.

CHAPTER NINE

1. *Oberlin Students' Monthly,* February 1859.
2. *Daily Cleveland Herald,* January 15, 1859.
3. Ibid.
4. *Oberlin Evangelist,* January 19, 1859.
5. Shipherd, 6. Those of the Rescuers present for the banquet, in addition to the husbands of the nine wives mentioned, were Simeon Bushnell, Wilson Bruce Evans, Ansel Lyman, William Scrimgeour, and Jacob
Shipherd of Oberlin; Eli Boies, Matthew DeWolf, Matthew Gillet, Lewis
Hines, Abner Loveland, John Mandeville, William Sciples, Walter Soule,
Loring Wadsworth, and Daniel Williams of Wellington; Henry Niles of
Pittsfield; and Chauncey Goodyear of Penfield.

Only one Rescuer from the Wellington contingent did not appear at the banquet: Robert L. Cummings. Ten Oberlin Rescuers were absent. Charles Langston did not attend, nor, as might be expected, did the three fugitive slaves. Also absent were Copeland, young Bartlett, Franklin Lewis, and John Watson's son William. Oberlin students William Lincoln and Richard Winsor were still away on school vacation.

6. Unless otherwise noted, the account of the Felon's Feast that follows is from Shipherd, 5–11.

7. Cheek and Cheek, *John Mercer Langston*, 327–28.

8. Shipherd, 11.

9. Unless otherwise noted, the account of Lincoln's arrest is taken from his "Wellington Rescue," Palmer Collection, WRHS.

10. *Liberator*, January 28, 1859.

11. Shipherd, 11.

12. *Annals of Cleveland—1818–1935*, vol. 42, 1859 (Cleveland: WPA Project 9395, Cleveland, 1936), 407, quoting *Cleveland Morning Leader*, May 4, 1859.

13. Shipherd, 12. "Capias" is Latin for "You are to arrest."

14. Ibid.

15. *Liberator*, January 28, 1859.

16. Henry R. Smith to Gerrit Smith, April 19, 1859 (photostat), Robert S. Fletcher Papers, OCA.

17. Cochran, 137–38.

18. Sears, *Day of Small Things*, 184. Henry Peck had urged Lincoln to go to Kentucky to help Fee (ibid., 185).

19. *Liberator*, January 28, 1859.

20. *Oberlin Students' Monthly*, December 1859.

21. *Anti-Slavery Reporter* (London: British and Foreign Anti-Slavery Society, n.s., 7, April 1, 1859), 93–94.

22. Fund Book, James Monroe Papers, OCA.

23. Samuel S. Cox to Jacob Thompson, March 29, 1859, National Archives, Record Group 60, Attorney General Records, 1818–1918. Enclosed with the letter is a true copy of the Lorain County Grand Jury's kidnapping indictment that was made by Jacob Lowe. The indictment is dated February 15, 1859. It contained a misnomer, giving Mitchell's first name as Rufus instead of Richard, which was not corrected for several months but did not hinder Lorain County authorities from trying to arrest the kidnappers.

24. *Cleveland Morning Leader*, July 7, 1859.

25. The description of Jeremiah S. Black is based on Elbert B. Smith, *The Presidency of James Buchanan* (Lawrence: Univ. Press of Kansas, 1975), 19, and *Dictionary of American Biography*, 20 vols. (New York: Charles Scribner's Sons, 1928–36), 1:311.

26. John Bassett Moore, ed., *Works of James Buchanan*, 12 vols. (1908–11; reprint; New York: Antiquarian Press, 1960), 10:345.

27. Jeremiah S. Black to George Belden, March 10, 1859, NA, RG 60, M699, Roll 3.

28. Struck jurors list, March 8, 1859, *U.S. v. Simeon Bushnell*, NA, RG 21.

29. Warren Guthrie, "The Oberlin-Wellington Rescue Case, 1859," in J. Jeffrey Auer, ed., *Antislavery and Disunion, 1858–1861* (New York:

Harper & Row, 1963), 91. The deputy marshal who served on the jury was Charles N. Allen of Cadiz.

30. Application of district attorney for warrant for witnesses, March 29, 1859, *U.S.* v. *Simeon Bushnell*, NA, RG 21.

31. Warrant for witnesses, April 4, 1859, ibid. In an odd mistake, Dayton noted that Jennings and Mitchell were served the warrant "at the Rail-Road Station of Orange, on the C.C. and C. Rail-Road in the County of Delaware in the Northern District of Ohio." Orange is in Cuyahoga County, but Delaware County is north of Columbus in central Ohio.

32. Jacob S. Cox to Jacob Thompson, March 29, 1859, Thompson to George Belden, April 5, 1859, NA, RG 60.

33. Journal of Fannie White, p. 118, OCA.

CHAPTER TEN

1. Mathew Johnson to Jacob Thompson, February 19, 1859, NA, RG 60. The courthouse stood on the north side of Rockwell Street, between Seneca and Ontario streets. An office building now occupies the site.

2. Apparently, some prosecution witnesses were not well prepared. For example, Chauncey Irish, a Wellington blacksmith, was called by the prosecution as a witness but testified that he did not know Bushnell and could not identify him even though he had been in the Public Square. He "supposed," he said, that Bushnell "was a colored man" (Shipherd, 30). Similarly, an Oberlin blacksmith and livery stable owner, Richard K. Whitney, testified that he did not have any idea "when John was brought back to Oberlin, or when taken away, or how, or any thing about it" (Shipherd, 34). Perhaps because Bushnell and King were so busy, they did not have the time or opportunity to examine all their witnesses in advance. Or perhaps a witness such as Irish or Whitney decided not to be candid. The case of James Bailey is especially interesting. He was the husband of Fannie White, whose journal is a source of information about the weather and other local details. The couple was married August 7, 1849, in South Reading, Massachusetts, in a joint ceremony with his brother Samuel. Bailey was a shoe manufacturer and operated a store with W. H. Cheesman on South Main that sold saddles, harnesses, and trunks. According to Fannie White (Journal, p. 121, OCA), Bailey went to Cleveland the day of the Rescue, apparently on business, and did not return until the next day. Yet in November he was summoned to appear before the federal grand jury (ibid., 114), and on April 5, 1859 (ibid., 119), his wife noted that he had returned to Cleveland "as witness in the Slave Rescue case"—a prosecution witness. But Bailey never testified, nor is there any indication what he might have testified to, inasmuch as he was away from Oberlin during the entire day of the Rescue. Moreover, he presumably was a supporter of the Rescuers because he went to Cleveland on May 24 to attend the mass rally there ("the Convention," as Fannie White calls it, p. 121).

An amazing number of subpoenas were issued for individuals who did not testify. Thirty-three persons were issued subpoenas to appear as either prosecution or defense witnesses in Bushnell's trial. Nine of them—including Chapin S. Fay, who was beaten up inside Wadsworth's Hotel—were never served the summonses. The others were served but did not testify, although several of them were paid $1.50 a day and a five cents a mile travel allowance for going to Cleveland (NA, RG 21, *U.S.* v. *Simeon Bushnell*). In Langston's trial, only six persons were served subpoenas but did not testify (NA, RG 21, *U.S.* v. *Charles Langston*).

Those who testified for the prosecution but are not mentioned in this chapter or in the paragraph preceding the one above were Wellington Justice of the Peace Isaac Bennett, Oberlin shoemaker George Dewey, E. P. Dodge of Cleveland, Oberlin cabinetmaker Harvey Dodge, John S. Dodge of Oberlin, Oberlin carpenter Marshal T. Gaston, Oberlin laborer Bela Farr, Oberlin merchant William E. Kellogg, Wellington Constable Barnabas Meacham, Oberlin mason B. L. Pierce, Wellington innkeeper Oliver S. Wadsworth, and Oberlin carpenter William B. Worden. E. P. Dodge and John S. Dodge, who identified themselves as childhood friends of Seth Bartholomew, were apparently sons of Harvey Dodge.

Those who testified for the defense but are not mentioned in this chapter were Wellington attorney Joseph H. Dickson, Wellington Justice of the Peace William Howk, and Dr. Homer Johnson of Oberlin.

3. *Daily Cleveland Herald*, April 5, 1859.

4. Hinton, *John Brown*, 453.

5. George Belden to Jacob Thompson, April 16, 1859, NA, RG 60

6. *Cleveland Plain Dealer*, April 25, 1859.

7. Shipherd, 82.

8. Warren Guthrie, "The Oberlin-Wellington Rescue Case, 1859," in J. Jeffrey Auer, ed., *Antislavery and Disunion, 1858–1861* (New York: Harper & Row, 1963), 92.

9. Shipherd, 14. The start of the trial was held up briefly when Belden asked Judge Willson for a writ of habeas corpus *ad Testificandum*, which he said he would need to get Jacob Lowe out of the Lorain County Jail. However, before Willson could respond, Lowe suddenly appeared in the courtroom, free on bail from the jail in Elyria, from which he had rushed to Cleveland for the trial. Even so, he did not testify.

10. Charles T. Marks also chose to ignore the judge's order (ibid., 32).

11. *Daily Cleveland Herald*, April 6, 1859.

12. Shipherd, 17.

13. Ibid., 16.

14. Ibid., 18. Jennings undoubtedly meant John Watson, who was in the attic room at the hotel at one point.

15. Ibid., 21.

16. Ibid., 21–22.

17. Ibid., 26.

18. Ibid., 28–29.

19. Ibid., 30.

20. Ibid., 32.

21. Ibid., 33. Under questioning by Belden, Wack said he heard "*only a little* testimony." He said he had been informed that witnesses "must keep out of the Court Room, but didn't know it was an order of the Court." Anyway, he continued, he was not present when the order was given—which Ansel Lyman immediately rose to say was untrue.

22. Ibid., 35.

23. *Daily Cleveland Herald*, April 9, 1859.

24. Shipherd, 35.

25. Ibid., 35–36.

26. Ibid.

27. Ibid., 36. According to a footnote, ibid., 37, Bartholomew was "indicted by the Grand Jury of Cuyahoga county, for *perjury*." However, there is no record whether he ever was put on trial.

28. Ibid., 37.

29. *Cleveland Plain Dealer*, April 18, 1859.

30. Shipherd, 40.

31. Ibid., 41.

32. Ibid.

33. Ibid., 42. The *Cleveland Plain Dealer* of April 12, 1859, opined that Wall's testimony was challenged because he was in court and heard the testimony of other defense witnesses.

34. Shipherd, 43.

35. Ibid., 43–45.

36. Ibid., 45–46.

37. Ibid., 56.

38. Ibid.

39. Ibid., 62.

40. Ibid., 68–70.

41. Ibid., 81.

42. Ibid., 82–83.

43. Ibid., 86–87.

44. Ibid., 88.

45. *Daily National Democrat*, April 16, 1859, NA, RG 60. The newspaper, a Democrat rival of the *Plain Dealer*, was enclosed with George Belden's letter to Jacob Thompson dated April 16, 1859.

46. Shipherd, 88–89.

47. Ibid., 184.

48. Ibid., 181.

49. Ibid.

50. Ibid., 89, 181.

51. *Daily Cleveland Herald*, April 20, 1859.

52. *Oberlin Evangelist*, April 27, 1859.

53. Ibid. The friend was Henry Cowles.

54. *Cleveland Plain Dealer*, April 18, 1859.

55. Shipherd, 92, 90.

56. Ibid., 93.

57. George Belden to Jacob Thompson, April 16, 1859, NA, RG 60.

58. *Daily National Democrat*, April 16, 1859, NA, RG 60. The newspaper was enclosed in the letter from Belden to Thompson, April 16, 1859.

59. *Cleveland Plain Dealer*, April 20, 1859.

60. *Cleveland Morning Leader*, May 2, 1859.

61. *Oberlin Evangelist*, May 11, 1859.

62. Shipherd, 91–92.

CHAPTER ELEVEN

1. The "mercy" quote is from Shipherd, 180. The "Oberlinites" quote is from Cochran, 156–57, and the remark from the *Ohio State Journal* (May 9, 1859), is from Cochran, 157n.

2. George Belden to Jacob Thompson, April 16, 1859, NA, RG 60.

3. *Cleveland Plain Dealer*, April 28, 1859.

4. George Belden to Jacob Thompson, April 16, 1859, NA, RG 60.

5. Shipherd, 182.

6. *Oberlin Evangelist*, May 25, 1859.

7. Shipherd, 184.

8. Ibid., 182.

9. *Oberlin Evangelist*, May 25, 1859.

10. *Cleveland Plain Dealer*, April 18, 1859.

11. Ibid., May 5, 1859.

12. William Lloyd Garrison to James Monroe, April 22, 1859, Monroe Papers, OCA.

13. Shipherd, 95–96.

14. Ibid., 97.

15. Unfortunately, Feeser's court transcript has been lost.

16. Shipherd, 102.

17. *Oberlin News*, October 13, 1909.

18. Shipherd, 99, 102–3.

19. Ibid., 105. It was Whitney, incidentally, who had arrested Lowe the day before the trials began in April.

20. As quoted in the *Daily National Intelligencer*, April 29, 1859.

21. *Cleveland Plain Dealer*, April 21, 1859.

22. James M. Fitch to James Monroe, April 22, 1859, Monroe Papers, OCA.

23. Shipherd, 108. The name of Johnson's deputy was Seth A. Abbey.

24. *Cleveland Plain Dealer*, April 22, 1859.

25. *Cleveland Herald*, April 25, 1859.

26. Journal of Fannie White, pp. 119–20, OCA.

27. *Cleveland Morning Leader*, April 25, 1859.

28. Except as otherwise noted, Bushnell's comments are from his letter to "*My dear friends in the Jail*," April 23, 1859, Monroe Papers, OCA.

29. James M. Fitch to James Monroe, April 23, 1859, Monroe Papers, OCA.

30. Henry E. Peck to James Monroe, undated, Monroe Papers, OCA.

31. Shipherd, 110–11.

32. Siebert, *Underground Railroad*, 335.

33. Jeremiah S. Black to Mathew Johnson, April 26, 1859, NA, RG 60.

34. Rough Log of U.S. Steamer Michigan April 30, 1859–January 4, 1861, NA, RG 24, Bureau of Naval Personnel, Logs, 1801–1946. The ship's captain, Commander Joseph Lanman, makes no mention of anything connected with the Rescuers or the trials. The vessel was back in Erie on July 1, celebrated the Fourth of July there with a salute of twenty-one guns, and was still in Erie on July 6, when the Rescuers were freed. The ship did not return to Cleveland until July 22. Although many believe that the *Merrimac* and the *Monitor* of Civil War fame were the first iron-hulled warships, the *Michigan* was fabricated in 1842 and commissioned by the navy in 1844.

35. Shipherd, 113.

36. Ibid., 182.

37. *Cleveland Plain Dealer*, April 29, 1859.

38. *Frank Leslie's Illustrated Newspaper*, May 21, 1859.

39. Affidavit of Defense, April 20, 1859, *U.S.* v. *Charles Langston*, NA, RG 21. Before the trial resumed, Langston appealed to the court to un-

derwrite the costs of summoning witnesses in his defense, saying that he did not have enough money for subpoenaing them. He said he needed them to prove that he had "advised all to pursue a legal course." Willson complied.

Witnesses for the prosecution who testified but are not mentioned in this chapter were George Barber of Wellington, Wadsworth's Hotel employee James Bonney, Acting U.S. Commissioner for the Southern District of Ohio Sterne Chittenden of Columbus, Oberlin tailor George W. Ells, Oberlin carpenter Marshal T. Gaston, Oberlin housepainter Artemas Halbert, Philip Kelly of Oberlin, Ansel W. Lyman's brother Edmund S. Lyman, innkeeper's son Charles Wadsworth, and Oberlin carpenter William B. Worden. Defense witnesses who are not mentioned in this chapter were Wellington Justice of the Peace Isaac Bennett, Cleveland lawyer William Bryce, Oberlin student John G. W. Cowles, Wellington attorney Joseph Dickson, Oberlin carpenter Clark Elliott, Wellington Justice of the Peace William Howk, Oberlin merchant Isaac M. Johnson, Oberlin student Edward C. Kinney (misidentified as E. S. Kinney), Wellington Constable Barnabas Meacham, Nelson Sexton of LaGrange (now spelled Lagrange), and J. L. Wadsworth of Wellington.

40. Shipherd, 114.
41. *Cleveland Plain Dealer*, May 5, 1859.
42. Shipherd, 126.
43. Ralph Plumb to James Monroe, April 30, 1859, Monroe Papers, OCA.
44. Shipherd, 114.
45. Ibid., 106.
46. Ibid., 115 17.
47. *Annals*, 408, quoting *Cleveland Morning Leader*, May 6, 1859.
48. *Daily National Intelligencer*, May 6, 1859.
49. Shipherd, 121.
50. Ibid., 126–27.
51. Ibid., 128.
52. Ibid., 129.
53. Ibid., 140, 158, 157.
54. Ibid., 165.
55. Ibid., 169.

CHAPTER TWELVE

1. Shipherd, 170.
2. Ibid., 172.
3. Ibid., 170–75.
4. Langston, *From the Virginia Plantation*, 22.
5. Cochran, 152n, quoting *Cleveland Morning Leader*, May 13, 1859.
6. Cheek and Cheek, *John Mercer Langston*, 332.
7. The following paragraphs, quoting Charles Langston, are from Shipherd, 175–78.
8. Cochran, 152n, quoting *Independent Democrat*, May 18, 1859.
9. Shipherd, 178.
10. John Mercer Langston, "The Oberlin Wellington Rescue," *Anglo-African Magazine* 1 (July 1859): 215.

CHAPTER THIRTEEN

1. *Cleveland Herald*, April 30, 1859, quoting the *Ashtabula Sentinel*, no date given.

2. *Frank Leslie's Illustrated Newspaper*, May 7, 1859.

3. *Black Abolitionist Papers*. The title page of the speech, which was published at the printing plant of E. Cowles & Co. of Cleveland, reads: "Should Colored Men Be Subject to the Pains and Penalties of the Fugitive Slave Law? / Speech of C. H. Langston before the U.S. District Court for the Northern Dis. of Ohio. / May 12, 1859. / Delivered when about to be sentenced for Rescuing a Man from Slavery."

4. *Anti-Slavery Reporter* (London: British and Foreign Anti-Slavery Society, n.s. 8, February 1, 1860), 31–32.

5. Fletcher, 409.

6. Shipherd, 178. DeWolf, Loveland, and Wadsworth were advised to capitulate by former Congressman Sherlock J. Andrews.

7. Ibid., 180.

8. *Annals*, 411, quoting the *Cleveland Morning Leader*, May 13, 1859.

9. Shipherd, 180.

10. *Portage County Democrat*, May 11, 1859.

11. Shipherd, 274, 277.

12. Ibid., 184.

13. Ibid., 274.

14. *Cleveland Plain Dealer*, April 29, 1859.

15. *Portage County Democrat*, May 11, 1859.

16. *Rescuer*, July 4, 1859.

17. *New York Sun*, April 7, 1895.

18. *Rescuer*, July 4, 1859.

19. William E. Lincoln to Gerrit Smith, July 5, 1859 (photostat), Fletcher Papers, OCA.

20. *Cleveland Morning Leader*, April 26, 1859.

21. *Rescuer*, July 4, 1859.

22. Ibid.

23. Ibid.

24. *Oberlin News*, October 13, 1909.

25. *Rescuer*, July 4, 1859.

26. Ibid.

27. Winsor, "How John Price Was Rescued," 255.

28. Fitch, "Wellington Rescue Case in 1858," Hosford Papers, OCA.

29. *Oberlin Evangelist*, July 13, 1859.

30. Shipherd, 278.

31. Ibid., 275.

32. Henry Smith to Gerrit Smith, April 19, 1859 (photostat), Fletcher Papers, OCA.

33. Lincoln, "Wellington Rescue," Palmer Collection, WRHS.

34. Ibid.

35. Hanna, "Chapter of Reminiscences," 42, Oberlin File, OCA.

36. Cochran, 177.

37. Shipherd, 247, 245.

38. *Cleveland Plain Dealer*, May 11, 1859.

39. Cochran, 178–79.

40. *Oberlin Students' Monthly*, June 1859. The article was written by sophomore George W. Phinney.

41. Cochran, 189n, quoting *Cleveland Plain Dealer*, May 30, 1859.

42. Jeremiah S. Black to Lewis W. Sifford, May 21, 1859, and Black to Stanley Matthews, May 21, 1859, NA, RG 60.

43. Cochran, 213.

CHAPTER FOURTEEN

1. Shipherd, 247.

2. *Cleveland Plain Dealer*, May 24, 1859.

3. Ralph Plumb, "Jail-Bird Experience," *Jubilee Notes* (n.p.: N.p., June 1883): 36.

4. Rush R. Sloane, "The Underground Railroad of the Firelands," *Magazine of Western History* 8 (May–October 1888): 52.

5. *Cleveland Plain Dealer*, May 24, 1859.

6. Shipherd, 257.

7. *Oberlin Evangelist*, May 25, 1859.

8. Shipherd, 258.

9. Ibid.

10. Ibid., 258–59.

11. Ibid., 250–51.

12. Ibid., 252–53.

13. Frederick J. Blue, *Salmon P. Chase: A Life in Politics* (Kent, Ohio: Kent State Univ. Press, 1987), 102.

14. Albert Bushnell Hart, *Salmon Portland Chase* (Boston: Houghton Mifflin, 1899), 169.

15. Shipherd, 254–55.

16. *Annual Report of the American Anti-Slavery Society . . . for the Year Ending May 1, 1860* (New York: American Anti-Slavery Society, 1861), 73.

17. Shipherd, 253–54.

18. Ibid., 187–88, 192.

19. Ibid., 198, 202.

20. Ibid., 202, 213, 204.

21. Ibid., 218, 209.

22. Ibid., 225.

23. Ibid., 226. Judge Josiah Scott orally assented to Swan's opinion. Judge William V. Peck wrote a concurring opinion. The two judges who voted for granting the writs were Jacob Brinkerhoff and Milton Sutliff, both of whom wrote dissenting opinions.

24. *Biographical Cyclopaedia and Portrait Gallery with an Historical Sketch of the State of Ohio*, 3 vols. (Cincinnati: Western Biographical Publishing, 1883–95): 1:123.

25. *New York Daily Tribune*, June 2, 1859.

26. *New-York Commercial Advertiser*, May 31, 1859.

27. James H. Fairchild, *Oberlin: The Colony and the College, 1833–1883* (Oberlin: E. J. Goodrich, 1883), 128.

28. *Annals*, 416, quoting *Cleveland Morning Leader*, May 31, 1859.

29. Cochran, 192n, quoting *Cleveland Plain Dealer*, May 31, 1859.

30. Cochran, 191n, quoting *Norwalk Reflector*, June 7, 1859.

31. *Tri-Weekly Maysville Eagle*, June 2, 1859.

32. Shipherd, 261. The Bible Peck used is now in the Oberlin College Library, Department of Special Collections.

33. Plumb, "Jail-Bird Experience," 36.

CHAPTER FIFTEEN

1. Roeliff Brinkerhoff, *Recollections of a Lifetime* (Cincinnati: Robert Clarke Company, 1900), 109–17. The scenes in the prison, with Salmon P. Chase, and at the Republican convention in Columbus are taken in their entirety from these pages, unless otherwise noted.

2. Ibid., 107.

3. Shipherd, 231.

4. Execution No. 11, Case No. 71, June 1, 1859, *U.S.* v. *Charles Langston*, NA, RG 21. The federal marshal was Lewis W. Sifford. Among the prosecution witnesses whose daily fee and travel expenses Langston was charged with paying was Rescuer William Sciples (spelled *Siples*), who had turned state's evidence.

5. *Rescuer*, July 4, 1859.

6. Cheek and Cheek, *John Mercer Langston*, 337, 339.

7. *Tri-Weekly Maysville Eagle*, May 19, 1859.

8. Ibid., June 21, 1859.

9. Shipherd, 271. Except as noted, the incidents in Elyria are taken from this source.

10. *Cleveland Morning Leader*, July 6, 1859.

11. Shipherd, 274.

12. *Cleveland Morning Leader*, July 6, 1859.

13. *Lorain County Eagle*, July 6, 1859.

14. Webber, *Early History of Elyria*, 166–67.

15. Ibid., 168.

16. *Biographical Cyclopaedia of the State of Ohio*, 3: 818.

17. Shipherd, 271.

18. *Liberator*, July 22, 1859.

19. Torrey, "James Mason Fitch," 147.

20. *Rescuer*, July 4, 1859.

21. Fitch, "Wellington Rescue Case in 1858," Hosford Papers, OCA.

22. Shipherd, 259.

23. Ibid., 260.

24. *Rescuer*, July 4, 1859.

25. William E. Lincoln to Gerrit Smith, July 5, 1859 (photostat), Fletcher Papers, OCA.

26. Plumb, "Jail-Bird Experience," 36.

27. Shipherd, 269, 263.

28. *Oberlin Evangelist*, July 13, 1859.

29. A. W. Lyman, letter, undated, stamped April 14, 1908, OCA.

30. Plumb, "Jail-Bird Experience," misnumbered 35, should be 37.

31. All of the quotes are from Agnes Smith, Autograph book, OCLSC.

32. Shipherd, 275.

33. Agnes Smith, Autograph book, OCLSC.

34. Shipherd, 264–65.

35. Ibid., 278.

36. Bible, 778, OCLSC.

37. Shipherd, 264.

38. Ibid.
39. According to the *Oberlin Evangelist*, July 13, 1859, the train arrived in Oberlin at 7:40. Sunset that day, according to Robert B. Thomas, *The Old Farmer's Almanac, 1859* (Boston: Hickling, Swan & Brewer, 1858), was at 7:39.
40. Shipherd, 265, 272.
41. Ibid., 265.
42. A. W. Lyman, letter, undated, stamped April 14, 1908, OCA.
43. *Oberlin News*, October 13, 1909.
44. Hanna, "Chapter of Reminiscences," 41, Oberlin File, OCA.
45. Shipherd, 275.
46. Fitch, "Wellington Rescue Case in 1858," Hosford Papers, OCA.
47. Cochran, 201n, quoting the *Daily Cleveland Herald*, July 6, 1859.
48. Cochran, 201n, quoting the *Cleveland Morning Leader*, July 7, 1859.
49. Cochran, 201n, quoting the *Ashtabula Telegraph*, July 9, 1859, which was quoting the *Springfield Republican*, July 7, 1859.
50. Cochran, 200n, quoting the *Cleveland Plain Dealer*, July 6, 1859.
51. *Cleveland Plain Dealer*, July 6, 1859.

CHAPTER SIXTEEN

1. Abraham Lincoln to Joshua Speed, August 24, 1855, in Roy P. Basler, ed., *The Collected Works of Abraham Lincoln, 1824–1865*, 8 vols. (New Brunswick, N.J.: Rutgers Univ. Press, 1953), 1:320.
2. *Created Equal? The Complete Lincoln-Douglas Debates of 1858* (Chicago: Univ. of Chicago Press, 1958), xxvii.
3. Litwack, *North of Slavery*, 276–77.
4. Abraham Lincoln to Salmon P. Chase, June 9, 1859, in Basler, ed., *Collected Works*, 3: 384.
5. Abraham Lincoln to Samuel Galloway, July 28, 1859, ibid., 394.
6. Cheek and Cheek, *John Mercer Langston*, 339, 372.
7. Brinkerhoff, *Recollections*, 117.
8. Cheek and Cheek, *John Mercer Langston*, 370.
9. Fletcher, 844.
10. Shipherd, 279.
11. Ibid.
12. *Cleveland Plain Dealer*, July 12, 1859.
13. *Rescuer*, July 4, 1859.
14. Shumway and Brower, Oberliniana, 43.
15. *Cleveland Plain Dealer*, July 12, 1859.
16. Langston, *From the Virginia Plantation*, 191.
17. Quarles, *Allies for Freedom*, 72.
18. Langston, *From the Virginia Plantation*, 196.
19. Quarles, *Allies for Freedom*, 75.
20. Langston, *From the Virginia Plantation*, 193.
21. Quarles, *Allies for Freedom*, 87.
22. Quarles, *Black Abolitionists*, 239–40.
23. Otto J. Scott, *The Secret Six: John Brown and the Abolitionist Movement* (New York: Times Books, 1979), 279.
24. Quarles, *Allies for Freedom*, 78.
25. Cheek and Cheek, *John Mercer Langston*, 356.

26. *Annual Report of the American Anti-Slavery Society . . . for the Year Ending May 1, 1861* (New York: American Anti-Slavery Society, 1861), 135.

27. Richard A. Folk, "Black Man's Burden in Ohio" (Ph.D. diss., Univ. of Toledo, 1972), 350.

28. Quoted in *Oberlin Evangelist*, December 7, 1859; also quoted in Fletcher, 299.

29. Cheek and Cheek, *John Mercer Langston*, 359.

30. Wilbur H. Phillips, *Oberlin Colony: The Story of a Century* (Oberlin: Oberlin Printing Company, 1933), 94.

31. Charles Langston to *Cleveland Plain Dealer*, November 18, 1859. *Black Abolitionist Papers* contain reprint of *Weekly Anglo-African*, December 3, 1859.

32. Monroe, *Oberlin Thursday Lectures*, 175.

33. Robert S. Fletcher, "John Brown and Oberlin," *Oberlin Alumni Magazine* 28 (February 1932): 140.

34. Monroe, *Oberlin Thursday Lectures*, 172.

35. *Oberlin Evangelist*, August 29, 1860.

36. Execution Order No. 28, Case No. 74, January 12, 1861, and attachments, *U.S.* v. *Simeon Bushnell*, NA, RG 21. Bushnell had until January 13, 1861, to pay what he owed. Johnson went by the Bushnell home on January 8, 1861, and noted that he had found "No Goods or Chattels."

37. *History of Lorain County, Ohio* (Philadelphia: Williams Brothers, 1879), 359. In his *Historic Wellington Then and Now*, Ernst L. Henes says that DeWolf and Loveland served in the Civil War (p. 32). In discussing the Oberlin-Wellington Rescue in a talk I gave on the 130th anniversary of the Rescue on September 13, 1988, at the Oberlin College Archives, I pointed out a number of discrepancies in accounts of the events and used as an illustration Henes's statement regarding DeWolf and Loveland, both of whom were in their sixties when war broke out and obviously could not have fought in it. Shortly afterward I received a note from Henes's widow, who had been in the audience. She had typed and proofread her husband's manuscript and instead of "served in" her husband had actually written "survived the war." "My mistake," Mrs. Henes said.

38. Keller, "Northern Protestant Churches," 355.

39. Folk, "Black Man's Burden," 391.

40. *Elyria Chronicle Telegram*, December 14, 1962.

41. Langston's statement, dated November 28, 1860, was published in the *Weekly Anglo-American*, April 6, 1861, in *Black Abolitionist Papers*.

42. Execution No. 33, Case No. 71, January 5, 1861, and attachments, *U.S.* v. *Charles Langston*, NA, RG 21.

43. George Bliss to Jacob Thompson, July 12, 1859, Louis Feeser to Thompson, July 14, 1859, Noah H. Swayne to Jeremiah S. Black, December 23, 1859, and Mathew Johnson to Jacob Thompson, June 2, 1860, all in NA, RG 60.

44. Langston Hughes, *The Big Sea* (New York: Hill and Wang, 1984), 13.

45. Cheek and Cheek, *John Mercer Langston*, 435.

46. Langston, *From the Virginia Plantation*, 306.

47. "A Biographical Sketch of Ralph Plumb," in *Biographical Dictionary and Portrait Gallery of Representative Men of the United States*, in Plumb Papers, OCA.

48. Torrey, "James Mason Fitch," 148, 152.

49. Bigglestone, *They Stopped in Oberlin*, 71.

50. Ibid., 184.

51. A. W. Lyman, letter, undated, stamped April 14, 1908, OCA.

52. *Oberlin News*, October 13, 1909.

53. William E. Lincoln to Gerrit Smith, April 20, 1859 (photostat), Fletcher Papers, OCA.

54. William E. Lincoln, response to letter from Philip D. Sherman to Mrs. William E. Lincoln, dated March 7, 1918, written on the back of Sherman's letter, Secretary's Office, 1833–1970, OCA.

55. Lincoln, "Wellington Rescue," Palmer Collection, WRHS.

56. According to an "Addendum" written by Henry Holcomb at the end of William Lincoln's "Wellington Rescue," Palmer Collection, WRHS, and dated September 6, 1915, Lincoln was the son-in-law of Cowles's sister Roxanna Cowles Marshall.

57. John W. Love to Secretary [Donald Love], Oberlin College, September 13, 1956, Alumni Records (Formers/Graduates), 1833–1960, William E. Lincoln, OCA.

58. *Tri-Weekly Maysville Eagle*, August 4, 1859.

59. *Cleveland Morning Leader*, February 21, 1860.

60. McCabe, "Oberlin-Wellington Rescue," 361–76. As previously noted, McCabe misidentified Wilson Bruce Evans as his brother Henry, who had died ten years earlier.

EPILOGUE

1. Cheek and Cheek, *John Mercer Langston*, 288.

2. James Rodabaugh, "The Negro in Ohio," *Journal of Negro History* 31 (January 1946): 22.

3. Fairchild, *Historical Sketch*, 25.

4. W. E. Bigglestone, "Oberlin College and the Negro Student, 1865–1940," *Journal of Negro History* 56 (July 1971): 204.

Bibliography

*For many years of her life, the author avoided all reading upon or
allusion to the subject of slavery, considering it as too painful to be
inquired into, and one which advancing light and civilization would
certainly live down. But, since the legislative act of 1850, when she
heard, with perfect surprise and consternation, Christian and humane people actually recommending the remanding escaped fugitives into slavery, as a duty binding on good citizens,—when she
heard, on all hands, from kind, compassionate, and estimable people, in the free states of the North, deliberations and discussions as
to what Christian duty could be on this head,—she could only think,
These men and Christians cannot know what slavery is; if they did,
such a question could never be open for discussion. And from this
arose a desire to exhibit it in a living dramatic reality. She has en-
deavored to show it fairly, in its best and its worst phases. In its
best aspect, she has, perhaps, been successful; but, oh! who shall
say what yet remains untold in that valley and shadow of death,
that lies the other side!*

Chapter XLV: "Concluding Remarks"

ARCHIVES AND MANUSCRIPT SOURCES

Berea College Archives, Berea, Kentucky
    William E. Lincoln Papers, Founders and Founding Collection
Cleveland Public Library, Cleveland, Ohio
    Map Division
Library of Congress, Washington, D.C.
    Papers of Jeremiah S. Black, 1813–1904
Lorain County Engineers Office, Elyria, Ohio
    Tax Maps
Mason County Clerk's Office, Maysville, Kentucky
    Marriage Records, Order Books, Will Books
Mason County Museum, Maysville, Kentucky
    Bacon Family Bible (photocopy, partial)
National Archives, Chicago Branch
    Record Group 21, Records of U.S. District Courts, 1803–
National Archives, Washington, D.C.
    Record Group 24, Bureau of Naval Personnel, Logs, 1801–1946
    Record Group 29, U.S. Census Books
    Record Group 60, Attorney General Records, 1818–1918
New York Public Library

Map Collection
Oberlin College Archives
  Institutional Holdings:
    Alumni & Development Records (former Faculty, Staff & Trustees),
      1834–1988
    Alumni Records (Formers/Graduates), 1833–1960
    College General (Catalogues), 1833–1989
    College General, Class Files
    Map Collection, 1833–1980
    Oberlin File, Writings by
    Secretary's Office, 1833–1970
    Student Files and Roll Books, 1833–1986
    Student Life Records, Organizations: Literary, 1839–1950
  Non-Institutional Holdings (Manuscript Collections):
    Christ Episcopal Church: Vestry Minutes, 1855–87, and Parish
      Register, 1857–96 (microfilm)
    Betsey Mix Cowles Papers, 1835–68
    Henry Cowles Papers, 1824–81
    James H. Fairchild Papers, 1835–86
    First and Second Congregational Churches
    Robert S. Fletcher Papers, 1833–1958
    Frances Hosford Papers, 1925–35
    Lawson-Merrill Papers, 1978–83
    Lorain County, Russia Township, Justices Court Civil Dockets,
      1836–1906
    Lorain County, Russia Township, Trustee Records, 1855–87
    Fred H. (Tip) Maddock Papers, 1894–1935
    James Monroe Papers, 1841–98
    Oberlin Town Records, 1859–1988
    Edward B. Plumb Papers, 1854–1910
    The Rescuer, Cuyahoga County Jail, July 4, 1859
    Subject File, Underground Railroad
    G. F. Wright Papers, 1850–1921
Oberlin College Library, Special Collections
  Autograph book of Agnes Smith
  Bible. New York: American Bible Society, 1854. Inscribed: "From the
    Private Library of Henry E. Peck (Prof. Oberlin College)."
  Circular: To the Friends of Freedom. Dated June 16, 1859, Oberlin,
    Lorain Co., Ohio
Schomburg Center for Research in Black Culture, New York
  Anti-Slavery Tracts
Spirit of '76 Museum, Wellington, Ohio
Western Reserve Historical Society Library, Cleveland, Ohio
  William Pendleton Palmer Collection

ADDRESSES, PAMPHLETS, TRACTS, ETC.
Boynton, W. W. "Western Reserve, and Early History of Lorain County,"
  address delivered July 4, 1876.
Fairchild, E. H. *Historical Sketch of Oberlin College.* Springfield, Ill.: Republic Printing Company, 1868.

Fairchild, J. H. *Oberlin: Its Origin, Progress and Results.* Oberlin: Shankland and Harmon, 1860; Oberlin: R. Butler, 1871.
———. *The Underground Railroad.* Tract 87, vol. 4. Cleveland: Western Reserve Historical Society, 1895.
The History of First Church in Oberlin, Ohio. Weekly calendar, First Congregational Church, 1984.
Jubilee Notes. N.p.: N.p., June 1883.
McDougall, Marion G. *Fugitive Slaves (1619–1865).* Fay House Monographs No. 3. Boston: Ginn & Company, 1891.
Memorial of the Hon. James Monroe, A.M., LL.D., 1821–1898. Oberlin: Oberlin College, 1898.
Sperry, Earl E. *The Jerry Rescue, Oct. 1, 1851.* Syracuse: Onondaga County Historical Association, 1924.
Summit County Looks Back, 1840–1940. Souvenir program. Akron, Ohio: N.p., n.d.

PRINTED DOCUMENTS

Annals of Cleveland—1818–1935. Vol. 42, 1859. Cleveland: WPA Project 9395, Cleveland, 1936.
Annual Report of the American Anti-Slavery Society . . . for the Year Ending May 1, 1860. New York: American Anti-Slavery Society, 1861.
Annual Report of the American Anti-Slavery Society . . . for the Year Ending May 1, 1861. New York: American Anti-Slavery Society, 1861.
Anti-Slavery Reporter. London: British and Foreign Anti-Slavery Society, n.s., 4 (April 1, 1859) vol—n, and 5 (February 1, 1860) 31–32.
Atlas of Lorain County, Ohio. Philadelphia: Titus, Simmons & Titus, 1874.
Biographical Annals of Ohio, 1902–1903. N.p.: 75th General Assembly, 1904.
Bits of Mason County Heritage. N.p.: Limestone Chapter of Daughters of the American Revolution, n.d.
Black Abolitionist Papers: 1830–1865. N.p.: Microfilming Corporation of America, 1981.
Boyd's Cleveland City Directory, 1857. New York: William H. Boyd, 1857.
Browne, Charles Farrar. *The Complete Works of Artemus Ward.* New York: G. W. Dillingham Co., 1898.
Cemetery Inscriptions of Lorain County, Ohio. Elyria, Ohio: Lorain County Historical Society, 1980.
Charter and Ordinances of the Town of Oberlin. Oberlin: V. A. Shankland, 1861.
Chas. R. Camp's Directory of Oberlin, 1873. Oberlin: Lorain County News Print, 1873.
Directory of the City of Cleveland, 1859–1860. N.p.: J. H. Williston & Co., 1859.
Fugitive Slave Bill. Boston: N.p., 1854.
George W. Hawes' Ohio State Gazeteer and Business Directory, for 1859 and 1860. Cincinnati: George W. Hawes, 1859.
Highway Map of Lorain County, Ohio. Chester, Vt.: National Survey, 1986.

Land Ownership Maps. Washington, D.C.: Library of Congress, 1967 (microfiche).

Maysville City Directory. St. Louis, Mo.: H. N. McEvoy, 1860.

Moore, John Bassett, ed. *Works of James Buchanan.* 12 vols. 1908–11. Reprint. New York: Antiquarian Press, 1960.

Oberlin City Guide, pp. 93–109, in *C. S. Williams' Medina, Elyria & Oberlin City Directory, City Guide, and Business Mirror.* N.p.: C. S. Williams, 1859.

Official Opinions of the Attorneys General of the United States. Vol. 9. Washington, D.C.: W. H. & O. H. Morrison, 1866.

Reports of Cases Argued and Determined in the Supreme Court of Ohio. N.s., 10, compiled by Leander J. Critchfield. Columbus: Follett, Foster and Company, 1860.

U.S. Reports: Cases Adjudged in the Supreme Court of the United States. Vols. 57–67 inclusive (Howard 16–24, Black 1–2). Cleveland: Baldwin Law Book Company, 1926.

Williams' Columbus Directory, City Guide, and Business Mirror. Vol. 2, 1858–59. Columbus: J. H. Riley & Co., 1858.

Williams' Medina, Elyria and Oberlin City Guide, and Business Mirror. Vol. 1, 1859–60. N.p.: C. S. Williams, 1859.

NEWSPAPERS AND PERIODICALS

The following newspapers and periodicals were used extensively, chiefly to reproduce the events surrounding September 13, 1858, and the trials that began April 5, 1859, but as otherwise noted in notes: *Cincinnati Daily Gazette, Cleveland Morning Leader, Cleveland Plain Dealer, Daily Cleveland Herald, Daily National Intelligencer* (Washington, D.C.), *Elyria Chronicle Telegram, Frank Leslie's Illustrated Newspaper* (New York), *Independent Democrat* (Elyria), *Liberator* (Boston), *Lorain County Eagle* (Elyria), *Lorain County News* (Oberlin), *Lorain Journal* (Lorain), *Louisville* (Ky.) *Daily Courier, New-York Commercial Advertiser, New York Daily Tribune, New York Sun, New-York Times, New York Weekly Tribune, Oberlin Evangelist, Oberlin News, Oberlin Students' Monthly, Oberlin Tribune, Owl* (Oberlin), *Painesville Telegraph, Portage County Democrat* (Ravenna), *Tri-Weekly Maysville* (Ky.) *Eagle, Village Item* (Oberlin).

BOOKS

Appletons' Cyclopaedia of American Biography. 6 vols. New York: D. Appleton and Company, 1886–99.

Auer, J. Jeffrey, ed. *Antislavery and Disunion, 1858–1861.* New York: Harper & Row, 1963.

Banta, R. E. *The Ohio.* New York: Rinehart & Company, 1949.

Barnard, John. *From Evangelicalism to Progressivism at Oberlin College, 1866–1917.* [Columbus]: Ohio State Univ. Press, 1969.

Basler, Roy P., ed. *The Collected Works of Abraham Lincoln, 1824–1865.* 8 vols. New Brunswick, N.J.: Rutgers Univ. Press, 1953.

Bigglestone, William E. *Oberlin from War to Jubilee, 1866–1883.* Oberlin: Grady Publishing Co., 1983.

———. *They Stopped in Oberlin: Black Residents and Visitors of the Nineteenth Century.* Scottsdale, Ariz.: Innovation Group, 1981.

Biographical Cyclopaedia and Portrait Gallery of Distinguished Men, with an Historical Sketch, of the State of Ohio. 3 vols. Cincinnati: John C. Yorston & Company, 1879.

Biographical Cyclopaedia and Portrait Gallery with an Historical Sketch of the State of Ohio. 3 vols. Cincinnati: Western Biographical Publishing, 1883–95.

Biographical Directory of the American Congress, 1774–1961. Washington, D.C.: U.S. Government Printing Office, 1961.

Biographical Encyclopaedia of Ohio of the Nineteenth Century. 3 vols. Cincinnati: Galaxy Publishing Company, 1876.

Blockson, Charles L. *The Underground Railroad.* New York: Prentice-Hall, 1987.

Blodgett, Geoffrey. *Oberlin Architecture, College and Town: A Guide to Its Social History.* Oberlin: Oberlin College, 1985.

Blue, Frederick J. *Salmon P. Chase: A Life in Politics.* Kent, Ohio: Kent State Univ. Press, 1987.

Brandt, Nat, and John Sexton. *How Free Are We! What the Constitution Says We Can and Cannot Do.* New York: M. Evans, 1986.

Brinkerhoff, Roeliff. *Recollections of a Lifetime.* Cincinnati: Robert Clarke Company, 1900.

Bristol, Sherlock. *The Pioneer Preacher.* London: Walter G. Wheeler, 1898.

Campbell, Stanley W. *The Slave Catchers: Enforcement of the Fugitive Slave Law, 1850–1860.* Chapel Hill: Univ. of North Carolina Press, 1968.

Cheek, William, and Aimee Lee Cheek. *John Mercer Langston and the Fight for Black Freedom, 1829–1865.* Urbana. Univ. of Illinois Press, 1989.

Clift, G. Glenn. *History of Maysville and Mason County.* Vol. 1. Lexington, Ky.: Transylvania Printing Company, 1936.

Cochran, William C. *The Western Reserve and the Fugitive Slave Law: A Prelude to the Civil War.* Publication No. 101, Collections. Cleveland: Western Reserve Historical Society, 1920.

Coleman, J. Winston. *Slavery Times in Kentucky.* Chapel Hill: Univ. of North Carolina Press, 1940.

Commemorative Biographical Record of the Counties of Huron and Lorain, Ohio. 2 vols. Chicago: J. H. Beers & Co., 1894.

Concise Dictionary of American Biography. 2d ed. New York: Charles Scribner's Sons, 1977.

Cover, Robert M. *Justice Accused: Antislavery and the Judicial Process.* New Haven: Yale Univ. Press, 1975.

Created Equal? The Complete Lincoln-Douglas Debates of 1858. Chicago: Univ. of Chicago Press, 1958.

Davenport, F. Garvin. *Ante-Bellum Kentucky: A Social History, 1800–1860.* Oxford, Ohio: Mississippi Valley Press, 1943.

Dictionary of American Biography. 20 vols. New York: Charles Scribner's Sons, 1928–36.

Dictionary of American Naval Fighting Ships. 8 vols. Washington, D.C.: U.S. Government Printing Office, 1959–81.

Duff, William A. *History of North Central Ohio.* 3 vols. Topeka: Historical Publishing Company, 1931.

Encyclopedia of Cleveland History. Bloomington: Indiana Univ. Press, 1987.

302   BIBLIOGRAPHY

Fairchild, James H. *Oberlin: The Colony and the College, 1833–1883.* Oberlin: E. J. Goodrich, 1883.

Farrar, Charles. *The Complete Works of Artemus Ward.* New York: G. W. Dillingham Co., 1898.

Fee, John G. *Autobiography of John G. Fee.* Chicago: National Christian Association, 1891.

Fletcher, Robert Samuel. *A History of Oberlin College: From Its Foundation through the Civil War.* 2 vols. Oberlin: Oberlin College, 1943.

Franklin, John Hope. *From Slavery to Freedom: A History of Negro Americans.* 4th ed. New York: Knopf, 1974.

Gara, Larry. *The Legend of the Underground Railroad.* Lexington: Univ. of Kentucky Press, 1961.

[Garrison, Wendell Phillips]. *William Lloyd Garrison: The Story of His Life Told by His Children.* 4 vols. New York: Century Co., 1885–89.

Greene, Robert Ewell. *The Leary-Evans, Ohio's Free People of Color.* Washington, D.C.: Keitt Printing Co., 1979.

Hart, Albert Bushnell. *Salmon Portland Chase.* Boston: Houghton Mifflin, 1899.

Henes, Ernst L. *Historic Wellington Then and Now.* Wellington, Ohio: Southern Lorain County Historical Society, 1984.

Herringshaw's National Library of American Biography. 5 vols. Chicago: American Publishers' Association, 1909–14.

Hinton, Richard J. *John Brown and His Men.* 1894. Reprint. New York: Arno Press and the New York Times, 1968.

Historical Collections of Ohio. Vol. 2. Cincinnati: State of Ohio, 1907.

History of Cuyahoga County, Ohio. Cleveland: D. W. Ensign & Co., 1879.

History of Lorain County, Ohio. Philadelphia: Williams Brothers, 1879.

Hughes, Langston. *The Big Sea.* New York: Hill and Wang, 1984.

Hunt, Harriot K. *Glances and Glimpses; or Fifty Years Social, Including Twenty Years Professional Life.* 1856. Reprint. Boston: Source Book Press, 1970.

Kennedy, James H. *The Bench and Bar of Cleveland.* Cleveland: Cleveland Printing and Publishing Company, 1889.

Kentucky's Black Heritage. Frankfort, Ky.: Kentucky Commission on Human Rights, 1971.

Kouwenhoven, John A. *Columbia Historical Portrait of New York.* Garden City, N.Y.: Doubleday, 1953.

Langston, John Mercer. *From the Virginia Plantation to the National Capitol.* Hartford, Conn.: American Publishing Company, 1894.

Leonard, Delavan L. *The Story of Oberlin.* Boston: Pilgrim Press, 1898.

Lewis, Walker. *Without Fear or Favor: A Biography of Chief Justice Roger Brooke Taney.* Boston: Houghton Mifflin, 1965.

Litwack, Leon F. *North of Slavery.* Chicago: Univ. of Chicago Press, 1961.

Locke, David Ross. *The Struggles (Social, Financial and Political) of Petroleum V. Nasby.* Boston: I. N. Richardson & Co., 1873.

Lossing, B. J. *Pictorial Description of Ohio.* New York: Ensign & Thayer, 1850.

Military History of Ohio. Toledo: H. H. Hardesty, 1887.

Monroe, James. *Oberlin Thursday Lectures: Addresses and Essays.* Oberlin: Edward J. Goodrich, 1897.

Morris, Richard, ed. *Encyclopedia of American History.* New York: Harper & Row, 1961.

Official Roster of the Soldiers of the State of Ohio in the War of the Rebellion, 1861–1866. Compiled by the Roster Commission. 12 vols. Cincinnati: Ohio Valley Press, and Akron: Werner Company, 1886–93.

Ohio: A Four-Volume Reference Library. 4 vols. Chicago: Lewis Publishing Company, 1937.

Orth, Samuel P. *History of Cleveland, Ohio.* Cleveland: S. J. Clarke, 1910.

Overman, William D. *Ohio Town Names.* Akron: Atlantic Press, 1959.

Phillips, Wilbur H. *Oberlin Colony: The Story of a Century.* Oberlin: Oberlin Printing Company, 1933.

Quarles, Benjamin. *Allies for Freedom: Blacks and John Brown.* New York: Oxford Univ. Press, 1974.

———. *Black Abolitionists.* New York: Oxford Univ. Press, 1969.

———, ed. *Blacks on John Brown.* Urbana: Univ. of Illinois Press, 1972.

Ragan, O. G. *History of Lewis County (Ky.).* Cincinnati: Jennings and Graham, n.d.

Render, Sylvia Lyons. *Charles W. Chesnutt.* Boston: Twayne Publishers, G. K. Hall & Co., 1980.

Rhodes, James Ford. *History of the United States from the Compromise of 1850.* Vol. 2. New York: Harper & Brothers, 1893.

Riddle, Albert G. *Recollections of War Times.* New York: G. P. Putnam's Sons, 1895.

Roseboom, Eugene H., and Francis P. Weisenburger. *A History of Ohio.* Columbus: Ohio State Archaeological and Historical Society, 1961.

Ryan, Daniel J. *A History of Ohio.* Columbus: A. H. Smythe, 1888.

Sandburg, Carl. *Abraham Lincoln: The Prairie Years.* 2 vols. New York: Harcourt Brace & Company, 1926.

Scott, Otto J. *The Secret Six: John Brown and the Abolitionist Movement.* New York: Times Books, 1979.

Sears, Richard D. *The Day of Small Things: Abolitionism in the Midst of Slavery, Berea, Kentucky, 1854–1864.* Lanham, Md.: Univ. Press of America, 1986.

Shipherd, Jacob R. *History of the Oberlin-Wellington Rescue.* 1859. Reprint. New York: Da Capo Press, 1972.

Shumway, A. L., and C. DeW. Brower. *Oberliniana.* 1883. Reprint. Galion, Ohio: Fisher Printing, 1983.

Siebert, Wilbur H. *The Underground Railroad from Slavery to Freedom.* New York: Macmillan, 1898.

Smith, Elbert B. *The Presidency of James Buchanan.* Lawrence: Univ. Press of Kansas, 1975.

Snider, Denton J. *The American Ten Years' War.* St. Louis: Sigma Publishing Co., 1906.

Standard History of Lorain County, Ohio. 3 vols. Chicago: Lewis Publishing, 1916.

Stowe, Harriet Beecher. *Uncle Tom's Cabin; or, Life Among the Lowly.* Boston: Houghton, Osgood and Company, 1878.

———. *Uncle Tom's Cabin; or, Life Among the Lowly.* New York: Random House Modern Library, 1938.

Swing, Albert T. *James Harris Fairchild or Sixty-Eight Years with a Christian College.* New York: Fleming H. Revell Company, 1907.

Taylor, John M. *Garfield of Ohio: The Available Man.* New York: Norton, 1970.

Taylor, Wm. A. *Ohio in Congress, from 1803 to 1901*. Columbus: XX Century Publishing Co., 1900.

Thomas, Robert B. *The Old Farmer's Almanac, 1858*. Boston: Hickling, Swan & Brewer, 1857.

———. *The Old Farmer's Almanac, 1859*. Boston: Hickling, Swan & Brewer, 1858.

Tibbitts, George W. *A Brief Sketch of the Cleveland Grays*. Cleveland: A. S. Gilman Printing Company, n.d. [1903].

Tyler, Alice Felt. *Freedom's Ferment*. New York: Harper & Row, 1944.

Upton, Harriet T. *History of the Western Reserve*. 2 vols. Chicago: Lewis Publishing Company, 1910.

Vexler, Robert I., and William F. Swindler, eds. *Chronology and Documentary Handbook of the State of Kentucky*. Dobbs Ferry, N.Y.: Oceana Publications, 1978.

Villard, Oswald Garrison. *John Brown, 1800–1859: A Biography Fifty Years After*. Boston: Houghton Mifflin, 1911.

Webber, A. R. *Early History of Elyria and Her People*. Elyria, Ohio: N.p., 1930.

Weisberger, Bernard A. *They Gathered at the River: The Story of the Great Revivalists and Their Impact upon Religion in America*. Boston: Little, Brown, 1958.

Winks, Robin W. *Canada and the United States: The Civil War Years*. Baltimore: Johns Hopkins Press, 1960.

Wright, G. Frederick. *Representative Citizens of Ohio*. Cleveland: Memorial Publishing Company, 1915.

Wyatt-Brown, Bertram. *Lewis Tappan and the Evangelical War against Slavery*. Cleveland: Press of Case Western Reserve Univ., 1969.

ARTICLES

Alilunas, Leo. "Fugitive Slave Cases in Ohio prior to 1850." *Ohio State Archaeological and Historical Quarterly* 46 (1940): 161–84.

Bigglestone, W. E. "Oberlin College and the Negro Student, 1865–1940." *Journal of Negro History* 56 (July 1971): 198–219.

Blodgett, Geoffrey. "Myth and Reality in Oberlin History." *Oberlin Alumni Magazine* 68 (May–June 1972): 5–10.

Burroughs, Wilbur G. "Oberlin's Part in the Slavery Conflict." *Ohio Archaeological and Historical Quarterly* 20 (April–July 1911): 269–334.

Cheek, William F. "John Mercer Langston: Black Protest Leader and Abolitionist." *Civil War History* 16 (June 1970): 101–20.

Day, Robert H. "The Oberlin-Wellington Rescue Case: The Supremacy of the Law." *Advocate*, January 5, 1929, pp. 7–8, 14, 16.

Fairchild, J. H. "Baccalaureate Sermon: Providential Aspects of the Oberlin Enterprise." In *The Oberlin Jubilee, 1833–1883*, ed. W. G. Ballantine. Oberlin: E. J. Goodrich, 1883.

Fletcher, Robert S. "John Brown and Oberlin." *Oberlin Alumni Magazine* 28 (February 1932): 135–41.

———. "The Wellington Rescue." *Oberlin Alumni Magazine* 54 (November 1958): 6–8, 23.

Galbreath, C. B. "John Henry Kagi—Biographical Sketch." *Ohio Archaeological and Historical Society Publications* 34 (1925): 263–91.

Gara, Larry. "The Underground Railroad: Legend and Reality." *Timeline*, August–September 1988, pp. 18–30.

———. "The Underground Railroad: A Re-evaluation." *Ohio Historical Quarterly* 69 (July 1960): 218–30.

Guthrie, Warren. "The Oberlin-Wellington Rescue Case, 1859." In J. Jeffrey Auer, ed., *Antislavery and Disunion, 1858–1861*, pp. 85–97. New York: Harper & Row, 1963.

Hanmer-Croughton, Amy. "Anti-Slavery Days in Rochester." *Rochester Historical Society, Publication Fund Series* 14 (1936): 113–55.

Johnston, Adelia A. F. "Recollections of Early Oberlin People." *Oberlin Alumni Magazine* 6 (November 1909): 51–63.

Langston, John Mercer. "The Oberlin Wellington Rescue." *Anglo-African Magazine* 1 (July 1859): 209–16.

Lawson, Ellen. "Observations on an Antebellum Interracial 'Utopia.'" *Observer*, March 4, 1982: 4–3.

Lawson, Ellen, and Marlene Merrill. "The Antebellum 'Talented Thousandth': Black College Students at Oberlin before the Civil War." *Journal of Negro Education* 52 (Spring 1983): 142–55.

McCabe, Lida Rose. "The Oberlin-Wellington Rescue." *Godey's Magazine* 133 (October 1896): 361–76.

"Necrology, Class of 1832." *Hamilton Literary Monthly* 12 (June 1877): 37–39.

Peterson, Ira. "The Oberlin-Wellington Case." *Midwest Journal* 7 (Spring 1955): 80–93.

Rodabaugh, James H. "The Negro in Ohio." *Journal of Negro History* 31 (January 1946): 9–29.

Sloane, Rush R. "The Underground Railroad of the Firelands." *Magazine of Western History* 8 (May–October 1888): 32–57.

Stewart, G. T. "The Ohio Fugitive Slave Law." *Firelands Pioneer*, n.s. 5 (July 1888): 60–82.

Suttler, Boyd B. "John Brown and the Oberlin Lands." *West Virginia History* 12 (April 1951): 183–99.

Torrey, Charles W. "James Mason Fitch." *Congregational Quarterly*, whole no. 38, vol. 10 (April 1868): 140–54.

Wilson, Charles Jay. "The Negro in Early Ohio." *Ohio Archaeological and Historical Publications* 39 (1930): 717–68.

Winsor, Richard. "How John Price Was Rescued." In *The Oberlin Jubilee, 1833–1883*, W. G. Ballantine, ed. Oberlin: E. J. Goodrich, 1883.

Wright, G. Frederick. "The Oberlin I First Knew and Oberlin Today." *Oberlin Alumni Magazine* 17 (April 1921): 148–51.

DOCTORAL DISSERTATIONS

Ellsworth, Clayton S. "Oberlin and the Anti-Slavery Movement Up to the Civil War." Cornell Univ., 1930.

Fletcher, Juanita D. "Against the Consensus: Oberlin College and the Education of American Negroes, 1835–1865." American Univ., 1974 (on microfilm).

Folk, Richard A. "Black Man's Burden in Ohio." Univ. of Toledo, 1972.

Huff, Carolyn Barbara. "The Politics of Idealism: The Political Abolitionists of Ohio in Congress, 1840–1866." Univ. of North Carolina at Chapel Hill, 1969 (on microfilm).

Keller, Ralph A. "Northern Protestant Churches and the Fugitive Slave Law of 1850." Univ. of Wisconsin, 1969.
Middleton, Stephen. "Ohio and the Antislavery Activities of Attorney Salmon Portland Chase, 1830–1849." Miami Univ., Oxford, Ohio, 1987.
Odell, Richard F. "The Early Antislavery Movement in Ohio." Univ. of Michigan, 1948 (on microfilm).
Pendleton, Lawson A. "James Buchanan's Attitude toward Slavery." Univ. of North Carolina at Chapel Hill, 1964 (on microfilm).

MASTER'S THESIS

Fairchild, Mildred. "The Negro in Oberlin." Oberlin College, 1925.

Index